HISTORICAL AND CURRENT PERSPECTIVES ON STRESS AND HEALTH

RESEARCH IN OCCUPATIONAL STRESS AND WELL BEING

Series Editors: Pamela L. Perrewé and Daniel C. Ganster

Volume 1:   Exploring Theoretical Mechanisms and Perspectives

RESEARCH IN OCCUPATIONAL STRESS AND WELL BEING
VOLUME 2

HISTORICAL AND CURRENT PERSPECTIVES ON STRESS AND HEALTH

EDITED BY

PAMELA L. PERREWÉ

Florida State University

DANIEL C. GANSTER

University of Arkansas

2002

JAI
An Imprint of Elsevier Science

Amsterdam – Boston – London – New York – Oxford – Paris
San Diego – San Francisco – Singapore – Sydney – Tokyo

ELSEVIER SCIENCE Ltd
The Boulevard, Langford Lane
Kidlington, Oxford OX5 1GB, UK

First edition 2002

Library of Congress Cataloging in Publication Data
A catalog record from the Library of Congress has been applied for.

British Library Cataloguing in Publication Data
A catalogue record from the British Library has been applied for.

ISBN: 0-7623-0970-9

♾The paper used in this publication meets the requirements of ANSI/NISO Z39.48-1992 (Permanence of Paper).
Printed in The Netherlands.

CONTENTS

OVERVIEW

We are pleased to bring you Volume 2 of the annual series titled *Research in Occupational Stress and Well Being*. The objective of this series is to promote theory and research in the ever-growing area of occupational stress, health and well being. We try to accomplish this by bringing together and showcasing the work of the best scholars in occupational stress and well being. As with Volume 1, we provide a multidisciplinary and international perspective that gives a thorough and critical assessment of issues in occupational stress and well being. The theme for this volume, *Historical and Current Perspectives on Stress and Health* focuses on two main concerns: historical as well as current perspectives on occupational stress research and an emphasis on the healthy individual and organization.

In our lead chapter, Larry Murphy presents an overview of job stress research at the National Institute for Occupational Safety and Health (NIOSH) from its inception in 1972 through current and proposed research in 2002. During this 30-year period, NIOSH has funded a wide range of job stress projects and activities. Murphy reviews the large-scale intramural research projects carried out by NIOSH researchers as well the significant extramural projects they sponsored. This chapter provides an invaluable history of NIOSH job stress research that should serve as a must read chapter for anyone interested in the field. Finally, Murphy offers suggestions for future research that include a request for more research examining the theoretical and empirical connections between job stress and health.

The next several chapters address the relationship among job stress and occupational health factors. Robert Vandenberg, Kyoung-Ok Park, David DeJoy, Mark Wilson, and Shannon Griffin-Blake examine the Healthy Work Organizational Model. Vandenberg and colleagues provide an insightful conceptual model as well as preliminary results supporting their Healthy Work Organization Model. They argue that stakeholder interest (e.g. the individual worker, medicine and health, organizational decision makers, labor unions) is not just in occupational stress per se. Rather, Vandenberg and his colleagues delineate the various elements that combine to create a healthy work organization, including issues related to health promotion, safety, and risk management.

Lois Tetrick examines health and well being and argues that health is more than merely the absence of illness. Her conceptualization of health allows for an integration of stress research with positive psychology to address occupational health (not simply ill health). Specifically, Tetrick links individual and organizational health to the literatures on pay structure and organizational learning.

The next chapter addresses health and well being by considering the crossover of job stress and strain between job incumbents and their partners. Mina Westman examines the research on crossover and models of job stress and the work-family interface. She develops a comprehensive framework and describes the specific mechanisms underlying the crossover process.

Julian Barling, Michelle Inness, and Daniel Gallagher propose that our models of job stress and employee well being are no longer applicable to the majority of workers today. They argue that alternative work arrangements (not the assumed standard Monday through Friday work schedule) are more prevalent in today's workforce, and they question the use of the current job stress theories that guide our research.

Few would argue that examining occupational stress from a multilevel perspective is not important. Paul Bliese, Steve Jex, and Ronald Halverson examine the increasingly popular data analytic technique, multilevel modeling, and provide specific examples as to how this technique has been used to analyze occupational stress data. Bliese and colleagues argue that multilevel analysis can enhance the theory and methodology of occupational stress research.

Johannes Siegrist provides an interesting discussion of his effort-reward imbalance model. Siegrist introduces a specific approach to examining the adverse health effects of an unfavorable psychosocial work environment. The model of effort-reward imbalance assumes that personal self-regulation, which is important for health and well being, is largely dependent upon successful social examples. Siegrist argues this new theory-based approach can enrich and reshape our thinking about preventing stress at work.

Finally Helge Hoel, Cary Cooper, and Dieter Zapf examine an interesting phenomenon – the relationship between bullying and job stress. Drawing upon the empirical evidence available, individual and organizational antecedents and outcomes of bullying are described. The recent research that has emerged within less than a decade provides sufficient evidence to suggest that bullying is an important psychosocial hazard in the workplace with negative implications for both individuals and organizations.

We believe the readings in Volume 2 represent exciting and forward-thinking approaches to occupational well being. We look forward to bringing you new perspectives and developments in occupational stress and well being in future volumes of this series.

Pamela L. Perrewé
Daniel C. Ganster
Series Editors

JOB STRESS RESEARCH AT NIOSH: 1972–2002

Lawrence R. Murphy

ABSTRACT

This chapter presents an overview of job stress research at the National Institute for Occupational Safety and Health (NIOSH) from its inception in 1972 through current and proposed research in 2002. During this 30-year period, NIOSH funded a wide range of job stress projects and a detailed account of each is not possible in a single chapter. In some cases, the research will be discussed in great depth, especially if the work was unique to NIOSH (e.g. mass psychogenic illness) or was large in magnitude (e.g. Job Demands and Worker Health study). In many other cases, however, the research will be mentioned briefly and citations provided. Since many of the early reports referenced in this chapter are long out of print, the chapter makes liberal use of "Text Boxes" that contain sections of narrative text from NIOSH reports. The inclusion of such narrative text will provide the reader with a more authentic 'feel' for the research than would a summary statement.

The chapter does not include NIOSH research in the areas of ergonomics, musculoskeletal disorders, or indoor air pollution, although psychosocial factors and job stress were elements of many studies in these areas.

Historical and Current Perspectives on Stress and Health, Volume 2, pages 1–55.
Copyright © 2002 by Elsevier Science Ltd.
All rights of reproduction in any form reserved.
ISBN: 0-7623-0970-9

1

FORMATION OF NIOSH

The National Institute for Occupational Safety and Health (NIOSH) is the principal Federal agency responsible for research and recommendations for the prevention of work-related disease and injury. NIOSH was established by Public Law 91–596 (Occupational Safety and Health Act of 1970) and was charged with assuring, in so far as possible, safe and healthful working conditions for America's workers (Key, 1971). That behavioral and motivational factors were important was acknowledged in certain provisions of the Act. For example, Sections 20(a)(1) and 20(a)(4) explicitly directed NIOSH to include psychological, behavioral and motivational factors in researching problems of worker safety and health, and in developing remedial approaches for offsetting such problems. Section 20(a)(7), in referencing the need to undertake industry-wide studies of certain worker groups, authorized the evaluation of job conditions to assess the potential for illness, disease, or loss of functional capacity. Job conditions were broadly interpreted to include those of a psychological nature, consisting of undue task demands, work conditions, or work regimens which, apart from or combined with exposures to physical and chemical hazards, may degrade worker physical or mental health (Cohen & Margolis, 1973). Public Law 91–596 also created the Occupational Safety and Health Administration (OSHA) and they were charged with setting, promulgating, and enforcing industrial safety and health standards. OSHA uses research conducted by NIOSH to develop new workplace safety and health standards.

Structurally, NIOSH is part of the Centers for Disease Control and Prevention (CDC) within the Department of Health and Human Services (DHHS), and has research facilities in Cincinnati, OH, Morgantown, WV, Pittsburgh, PN, and Spokane, WA. The placement of NIOSH within DHHS, instead of in the Department of Labor with OSHA, was done to separate NIOSH from the regulation and enforcement process and allow the Institute to conduct research and develop recommendations independently of those activities. NIOSH research addresses all issues related to safety and health at work, and topic areas include toxicology, physical agents (noise, vibration, etc.), respiratory disease, safety, and hazard evaluation. Other prominent activities include health and hazard surveillance, training, respirator certification, and technical assistance. Job stress research activities are located primarily in Cincinnati, Ohio in the Work Organizational and Stress Research Section, Organizational Science and Human Factors Branch, Division of Applied Research and Technology, although researchers at other Institute locations often collaborate.

At its inception, the NIOSH job stress research group was small, consisting of four full-time, Ph.D. level researchers. By the late 1980s and early 1990s, the size of the stress section had grown to seven researchers and has remained at about that level ever since. NIOSH has supplemented the research staff by funding postdoctoral positions that are filled through the National Research Council Associateship program.

The primary impetus for NIOSH job stress studies has always been ideas submitted by bench level researchers. Even today, new research ideas submitted by NIOSH researchers remain the fundamental source for NIOSH job stress studies. A second mechanism that drives NIOSH job stress research is requests from workers, unions, and/or organizations for technical assistance (*http://www.cdc.gov/niosh/request.html*). While most NIOSH technical assistance requests over the years have concerned exposure to physical or chemical agents, a handful of requests dealt with job stress issues, and these became more frequent over the next 10 years as job stress became a more widely recognized workplace health and safety topic. For instance, NIOSH studies of mass psychogenic illness were generated from technical assistance requests, as were studies of machine-pacing, postal workers, video display terminal (VDT) operators and organizational downsizing. For this reason, most of the job stress research conducted by NIOSH has a distinct applied, as opposed to basic, research flavor.

More recently, NIOSH job stress research benefited from funding initiatives that targeted certain health conditions or industry sectors (e.g. HIV/AIDS, agriculture, and construction) and also from the commencement of the National Occupational Research Agenda (NORA) in 1996. NORA includes Organization of Work as one of 21 safety and health priority areas having a national focus, and highlights organizational factors as potential contributors to stress-related illnesses or injuries.

The NIOSH research program operates on a project-based system, wherein bench-level researchers submit ideas for new research and these are evaluated at the Section, Branch, Division, and Institute levels for approval. Projects typically run 3–5 years and often involve collaborations among intramural and extramural researchers. NIOSH can establish cooperative arrangements with other agencies and organizations to perform research that would be difficult to perform independently. Finally, NIOSH has a competitive, extramural grant program that is administered independently from the internal research program.

Table 1 presents a list of the major NIOSH activities in the area of job stress from 1972 to 2002. The list shows major project work and related activities, and provides reference citations for each listing. Glancing through the table gives the reader a sense of the nature and scope of NIOSH research over the past 30 years.

Table 1. List of Major NIOSH Job Stress Studies and Activities: 1972–2002.

Year	Activity	Citation
1970	NIOSH created by OSHAct	Public Law 91-596 (1970)
1972	Job stress items added to the 1972–1973 Quality of Employment Survey	Margolis, Kroes and Quinn (1974).
1972	Police officers and administrators	Kroes and Hurrell (1975); Hurrell, Pate and Kliesmet (1984)
1972	1st Cornell conference on stress	McLean (1974)
1972	Job demands and worker health	Caplan, Cobb, French, Harrison and Pinneau (1975)
1973	Coal miners	Althouse and Hurrell (1977)
1974	State of Tennessee health records study	Colligan, Smith and Hurrell (1977)
1974	Shift work and health	Tasto, Colligan, Skjei and Polly (1978); Smith, M.J., Colligan, Frockt and Tasto (1979).
1974	Longitudinal study of coronary heart disease	Chadwick, Chesney, Black, Rosenman, and Sevelius (1979)
1974	Mass psychogenic illness	Colligan and Murphy (1979); Murphy and Colligan (1979); Colligan, Pennebaker and Murphy (1982)
1975	Job termination	Cobb and Kasl (1977)
1977	Postal workers	Smith, Hurrell and Murphy (1981); Hurrell (1985)
1977	1st NIOSH/UCLA conference held	National Institute for Occupational Safety and Health (1978)
1977	2nd Cornell conference	McLean, Black and Colligan (1978)
1978	Video display terminal operators	Smith, Cohen, Stammerjohn and Happ (1981)
1978	2nd NIOSH/UCLA conference	National Institute for Occupational Safety and Health (1980)
1979	Machine-pacing and stress	Murphy and Hurrell (1980); Salvendy and Smith (1981); Stammerjohn and Wilkes (1981); Wilkes, Stammerjohn and Lalich (1981)
1980	Demand/control model of strain	Karasek, Schwartz and Theorell (1982); Karasek, Theorell, Schwartz, Schnall, Pieper and Michela (1988)
1980	Office worker stress	Cohen (1984)
1980	Stress management training	Murphy (1983, 1984a, b, 1988, 1996)
1982	Follow-up studies on VDT operators	Sauter, Gottlieb, Jones, Dodson and Rohrer (1983); Sauter and Swanson (1996)
1984	Stress measurement methods	Hurrell and McLaney (1988)

Table 1.   Continued.

Year	Activity	Citation
1985	Fatigue effects of work schedules	Rosa and Colligan (1988); Rosa, Colligan and Lewis (1989); Rosa (1991); Rosa and Colligan (1997); Rosa, Bonnet and Cole (1998); Rosa and Bonnet (1993); Schroeder, Rosa and Witt (1998)
1986	National strategy for prevention of work-related psychological disorders	National Institute for Occupational Safety and Health (1988); Sauter, Murphy and Hurrell (1990)
1987	Workshop on control and health	Sauter, Hurrell and Cooper (1989)
1989	Healthy work organizations	Sauter, Lim and Murphy (1996); Lim and Murphy (1997); Murphy and Lim (1997); Murphy and Cooper (2000)
1990	1st APA/NIOSH conference	Keita and Sauter (1992); Quick, Murphy and Hurrell (1992)
1991	Occupational HIV/AIDS	Gershon, Murphy, Felknor, Vesley and DeJoy (1995); DeJoy, Murphy and Gershon (1995)
1992	Stress in agricultural work	Kidd, Scharf and Veazie (1996); Scharf, Kidd, Cole, Bean, Chapman, Donham and Baker (1998)
1992	2nd APA/NIOSH conference	Keita and Hurrell (1994); Murphy, Hurrell, Sauter and Keita (1995); Sauter and Murphy (1995)
1992	Harassment and violence at work	Cole, Grubb, Sauter, Swanson and Lawless (1997)
1993	Letter of Agreement between NIOSH and Corning Inc.	Monroy, Jonas, Mathey and Murphy (1998)
1995	3rd APA/NIOSH conference	Gowing, Quick and Kraft (1998)
1995	Organizational downsizing, restructuring, and health	Murphy and Pepper (2002)
1996	National Occupational Research Agenda (NORA)	National Institute for Occupational Safety and Health (1996)
1996	Analysis of National Medical Expenditure Care Survey (NMES)	Grosch and Murphy (1998)
1997	Stress in construction work	Grubb and Swanson (1999); Goldenhar, Swanson, Hurrell, Ruder and Deddens (1998)
1998	4th APA/NIOSH conference	Galinsky, Swanson, Sauter, Hurrell and Schleifer (2000)
1998	Organizational interventions to reduce stress in IRS call centers	
2000	Health of aging workers	
2000	Quality of work life module for the 2002 General Social Survey	
2001	Depression, coronary heart disease and work	
2002	National Organizations Survey 2002	
2003	5th APA/NIOSH conference	

1970s: INITIAL JOB STRESS ACTIVITIES

One of the early tasks facing NIOSH's stress research program was character-izing the job stress concept. Job stress implied so many events and processes that it was a nebulous construct difficult to study in a scientific manner (Margolis & Kroes, 1974). As a first step, NIOSH set up a relationship with the Center for Occupational Mental Health, Cornell University Medical College. The collaboration was a natural one since the goal of the COMH, namely, a healthier relationship between employee and employer, fit nicely with the NIOSH mission. Moreover, the COMH had prior experience in the field of job stress, through their sponsorship of symposia (McLean, 1967, 1970) and publication of the quarterly journal *Occupational Mental Health*, which carried abstracts of relevant literature, original articles and commentary as well as news of activ-ities in the field.

As part of the collaboration, NIOSH co-sponsored an Occupational Mental Health Conference in 1972 in White Plains, New York. The purpose of this endeavor was to bring together representatives of various disciplines to present their points of view so that the current thinking on the subject of job stress could be discerned (McLean, 1974). As a result of this seminal conference, a paradigm of job stress was adopted which would guide future NIOSH research. This paradigm defined job stress as the condition in which some factor, or combination of factors, at work interacts with the worker to disrupt psycho-logical or physiological homeostasis (Margolis & Kroes, 1974).

The concept of factors interacting with the worker in this paradigm was deemed significant. Indeed, a broad and diverse literature was known to exist dealing with individual differences in physical and psychological state that can alter human response in a variety of situations. What was not completely clear was how much of this information was relevant to occupational situations. Thus, a literature review (Sleight & Cook, 1975) was undertaken that focused on: (a) questions of hypersusceptibility or predisposition of certain workers to job related illnesses and injuries; (b) selection criteria for placing workers in stressful or hazardous jobs; (c) needs for standards or guidelines to protect worker groups with special physical or psychological characteristics; and (d) research needs. The results of the review were significant in that they high-lighted first, the paucity of empirical data linking job conditions, individual characteristics and health consequences and secondly, problems with existing research methodologies. These early endeavors provided NIOSH with a para-digm of job stress and information as to the kinds of methodologies that would be needed to examine it.

The 1972–1973 Quality of Employment Survey

The earliest NIOSH job stress study involved a cross-sectional interview survey. In an effort to add to the small body of literature linking psychological job factors to ill health, a number of questions were added by NIOSH to the triennial interview survey of workers conducted in 1972–1973 by the U.S. Department of Labor (Quinn & Shepard, 1974). The Quality of Employment Survey's general purpose was to sample representative workers' reactions to their jobs. The questions added by NIOSH examined six potential sources of stress at work and ten different mental and physical health problems in workers (Margolis, Kroes & Quinn, 1974). Sources of stress included role ambiguity, underutilization, overload, resource inadequacy, insecurity and non-participation. Indicators of strain included overall physical health, escapist drinking, depressed mood, loss of self-esteem, life and job satisfaction, motivation to work, frequency of suggestions to employer, intent to leave, and absenteeism.

Analyses of this data revealed that overall physical health was related to job stress, the latter operationally defined as a simple composite of six specific job stressors. These relationships were evident in spite of the fact that physical health status is clearly a function of many variables other than psychological job conditions (e.g. diet, exercise, genetic composition, exposure to illness, including toxic agents, and non-job related psychological factors). All six stressors in the survey, considered individually, played a role in worker physical and mental health. Although statistically significant, the degree of correlation was quite low in most instances ($r < 0.20$). One stressor, non-participation, was of special significance and correlated highest with the eight measures of strain. Moreover, responses to the job stressors and strain questions varied considerably across occupations but not always in a predictable fashion. For instance, professional and technical workers had the highest levels of job satisfaction but also the highest levels of depressed mood. Machine operators had the lowest scores for job satisfaction and perceived health. Laborers had the second worst job satisfaction scores but their perceived health was good and mental health scores were high. In general, white-collar workers showed much greater job satisfaction than blue-collar workers but had lower perceived health and more depressed mood.

Of special interest were worker ratings of importance. When asked to rate the importance of 25 aspects of work, the following list emerged in order of importance: interesting work, enough help and equipment to get the job done, enough information to get the job done, enough authority to get the job done, good pay, opportunity to develop special abilities, job security, and seeing the results of one's work.

Job Demands and Worker Health Study

The most ambitious undertaking was a study of job stress and strain among 2,000 workers in 23 occupations. This *Job Demands and Worker Health Study* (Caplan et al., 1975) also included a sub-sample of 390 workers who were subjected to clinical-biological tests to ascertain any physical bases for apparent stress states. Figure 1 shows the theoretical model that guided the study design and analysis. The model distinguishes between the objective and subjective environment, the former being independent of worker perceptions, and allows for moderator variables (the person and social support). In the model, the objective environment influences worker responses (affective, physiological, behavioral) and health-illness *directly* (the arching lines at the top of the figure) and *indirectly*, via the subjective environment. How the worker responds to the subjective work environment is conditioned or moderated by three sets of factors: the person, social support, and the degree of person-environment fit.

Text box 1 shows the main findings from the study as they appeared in the original NIOSH technical report (Caplan et al., 1975). The results showed clear occupational differences in stress and strain. For instance, low utilization of skills and abilities, lack of participation, low work complexity, and role ambiguity were major stressors for assembly line workers, fork-lift drivers, and machine operators, but were not stressors for professionals such as university professors, physicians, and white collar supervisors. Machine-paced workers had the highest scores for boredom and dissatisfaction with workload and had the highest scores for measures of strain. There were no significant relationships between physiological measures of strain (blood pressure and serum uric acid) and job stressors, although these analyses were limited to only a few occupations (administrators, scientists, air traffic controllers, electronic technicians, and supervisors). Personality variables were not directly related to measures of psychological (anxiety, depression), physiological (somatic complaints), or behavioral (smoking, caffeine consumption) strains.

The importance of the *Job Demands and Worker Health* study was four-fold. First, it produced data on levels of job stress and strain across multiple occupations and in so doing, helped NIOSH identify occupations and job stressors in need of additional study. Second, it set forth a model of stress and strain (Person-Environment fit) that NIOSH and others would utilize in many later studies. The P-E fit model suggested that the discrepancy between what a worker desires on a job (P) and what a worker has in a job (E) was the best predictor of strain. Third, the methods and findings from this study served to drive many future NIOSH studies of job stress. Indeed, it is impossible to

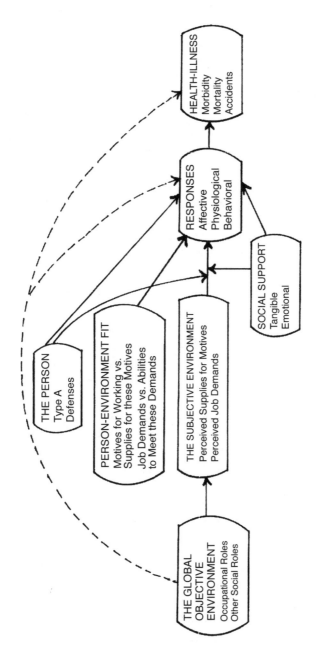

Fig. 1. Theoretical Model from Job Demands and Worker Health (1975) Study.

Text Box 1.   Main findings as presented in the *Job Demands and Worker Health* (1975) study.

Occupational Differences

(1) The occupations in this study differ considerably in age and length of service.

(2) University professors in administrative posts and family physicians score highest on a measure of the coronary-prone personality; tool and die makers are somewhat high on this measure.

(3) The number of hours worked per week is highest for family physicians and administrative professors (over 55 hours per week), followed by professors, blue collar supervisors, scientists, and police. At the low end, air traffic controllers (whose hours are regulated for reasons of safety), average 38 to 39 hours per week.

(4) The most unwanted overtime is put in by the administrative professors, blue collar supervisors, physicians, tool and die makers, and white collar supervisors.

(5) A measure of quantitative workload shows high scores for family physicians, administrative professors and train dispatchers.

(6) The greatest variation in workload occurs for air traffic controllers and train dispatchers; the least variation is found-in assemblers, especially on machine-paced lines.

(7) A demand for high concentration on the job is typical for air traffic controllers, train dispatchers, and family physicians; the lowest concentration is required on the machine-paced assembly line.

(8) Several job stresses (low utilization of one's abilities, low participation, low complexity of the work, poor person-environment fit on job complexity, poor fit on responsibility for persons, and poor fit in role ambiguity) tend to have similar levels in any given job. Occupations that are high on these stresses include assembly line workers, fork lift drivers, and machine tenders. The occupations that are low on these stresses are professors, family physicians, and other professions.

(9) The men in high stress jobs in 8 above also suffer from low social support, whereas the men in low stress jobs report high support from their supervisors and others at work.

(10) The occupations where the workers report both the most boredom and the greatest dissatisfaction with the workload are the assemblers and the relief men on the machine-paced assembly line. Our small sample of machine tenders is also high on these strains. The most satisfied with their jobs are university professors, family physicians, white-collar supervisors, police, and air traffic controllers at small sites.

(11) The results for anxiety, depression and irritation present a picture similar to the above results for job dissatisfactions. These psychological strains are highest among the machine tenders and the assemblers and relief men on the machine paced assembly line. The least such affective strain is found among physicians and continuous flow workers.

(12) Somatic complaints were most frequent in assemblers and relief men on machine-paced assembly lines. Such complaints were least common among university professors, family physicians, and scientists.

(13) Scientists had the lowest blood pressure of the seven occupations measured.

(14) The assemblers and relief workers on the machine-paced assembly lines have the highest stress and strain of any of the 23 occupations (see 6, 7, 8, 9, 10, 11, and 12 above).

(15) Air traffic controllers at large sites have been shown previously to have more psychosomatic disease than those at small sites. The findings of this study suggest that the former may have more disease because they have more job ambiguity, more conflicting demands in their work, and less social support from others at work.

Source:

Caplan, R. D., Cobb, S., French, J. R. P., Jr., Van Harrison, R., & Pinneau, S.R. (1975). *Job Demands and Worker Health*. DHEW (NIOSH) Publication No. 75-160. Washington, D.C.: U.S. Government Printing Office.

overstate the influence of the Job Demands study on later NIOSH research. For instance, the finding that machine-paced workers had the highest levels of job stress and strain led to a series of NIOSH-funded studies on the health consequences of machine-pacing (Multiple Position Letter Sorting Machine (MPLSM) operators, poultry inspection workers, and lab studies of pacing). Fourth, the measures of stress and strain in the Job Demands study would be utilized in countless other NIOSH studies, and some scales continue to be used today (e.g. quantitative workload, social support, role ambiguity, conflict, worker control, and somatic complaints).

Work in America (1973) Report

Shortly after the OSHAct was signed into law, a task force was established on December 29, 1971 by the U.S. Department of Health, Education and Welfare (DHEW) to examine ". . . health, education, and welfare problems from the perspective of one of our fundamental social institutions – work" (Work in America, 1973). The work was performed under contract with the W. E. Upjohn Institute for Employment Research and involved: (1) a review of the published literature; (2) preparation of 50 background papers by experts in business, academia, labor unions, and government; and (3) interviews with a large number of blue- and white-collar workers. The background papers and interviews provided the evidence upon which the report was based, and were published in a separate document (O'Toole, 1974)

The report confirmed the centrality of work to life, its contribution to identity and self-esteem, and its value in providing meaning and order to life. While offering no simple solutions to the problems highlighted in the report, the summary of the report indicated that ". . . in the institution of work, we believe we have found a point where considerable leverage could be exerted to improve the quality of life" (Work in America, 1973, p. xv).

Some of the conclusions reached by the task force were:

(1) Many workers, at all levels, feel locked-in to unchallenging jobs, with low mobility and few opportunities to grow in their jobs.
(2) Job satisfaction appears to be the best predictor of longevity, better than known medical or genetic factors
(3) Work redesign holds great promise for decreasing mental and physical health costs, increase productivity, and improve the quality of work life for many Americans while for the first time, giving voice to many workers in important decision-making processes (Work in America, 1973).

NIOSH FIVE-YEAR RESEARCH PLAN

The first long-term plan for NIOSH job stress research was developed in 1974 and spanned a five-year period. The plan, shown in Text Box 2, contained five general research topics and multiple studies within each topic.

Of special interest are two research ideas that were never implemented: a national study of job stress and health among 10–20,000 workers and studies of primary stress prevention techniques. The former was not implemented due to the high cost of conducting such a large national study. The latter studies of stress prevention and reduction were never initiated due to the difficulty in

---

Text Box 2. NIOSH 5-year plan for job stress research.

(A) JOB DEMANDS AND WORKER HEALTH

(1) Correlation of stress factors in 20 job types and evident psychological and physiological strain indications.

(2) Examination of morbidity data on all major occupations within one state (Tennessee) to uncover frequency of stress-related disorders characteristic of different jobs.

(3) National questionnaire survey of 10,000–20,000 U.S. workers to ascertain evidence of physical and emotional problems arising from job stress factors.

(4) Interview survey to determine mental health consequences of job stress in workers in Cincinnati establishments.

(B) JOB STRESS IN SPECIFIC OCCUPATIONS

(1) Determine psychological job stressors particular to police officers and associated mental health consequences.

(2) Determine psychological job stressors and associated mental health consequences in coal miners.

(3) Survey job stress factors evident in 2–4 of the highest ranked occupations in terms of the frequency of stress-related disorders (as identified in A-1 above).

(C) SELECT FACTORS IN JOB STRESS

(1) Study of job stress in the etiology of coronary heart disease.

(2) Shift work as a job stress factor, its consequences to physical and emotional health, and recommended guidelines for optimum shift routines re: worker adjustment.

(3) Study of a job stress factor (to be selected) for its health impact.

(D) DEVELOP AND TEST TECHNIQUES AND WORK PRACTICES FOR ALLEVIATING JOB STRESS OR ENHANCING WORKER ADJUSTMENT TO IT

(1) Evaluate stress reduction measures for police officers and formulate program packages for use.

(2) Define stress reduction measures in 2–4 high stress occupations and formulate program packages for use.

Text Box 2. Continued.

(E) EFFECTIVENESS OF SELECT APPROACHES TO STRESS-ALLEVIATION IN INDUSTRY

(1) Implications of job enrichment techniques for stress reduction
(2) Implications of the role of social support in reducing job stress.
(3) Utility of "troubled employee" programs for reducing job stress.
(4) Participatory management as a stress reduction activity.

Source: Abstracted from NIOSH internal memo: December 19, 1974.

---

securing access to organizations to implement job and organizational change programs. Aside from these two areas, the remainder of the five-year plan was implemented, as described below.

Implementing the Research Plan

One of the first elements of the 5-year plan that was implemented was an evaluation of mental health admission records to identify high stress jobs. The aim of the study was to equip health professionals with an empirical basis for identifying and selecting specific occupations for more in-depth research into the relationship between job stress and worker health. The data for this study were collected from the records of 22 of the 27 mental health centers operated by the State of Tennessee. The records of all first admissions to the 22 participating mental health centers from January 1972 through June 1974 constituted the sampling frame. The selection of cases for inclusion in the study was based on the following criteria: (1) the individual must have been a resident of Tennessee, in the primary working age group of 18–64; and (2) s/he must have been employed in one of the state's major occupations (1,000 or more workers) within two years prior to admission. Data were recorded for a total of 8,450 cases.

The results indicated a disproportionate incidence of mental health disorders among workers in health care professions; these professions comprised seven of the top-ranked occupations. Clouding the interpretation of this data was the high proportion of females in health care professions. Women in general, and health care workers in particular, are more likely to report mental health disorders relative to the general population and this factor, not excess job stress, could partially explain the obtained results (Colligan, Smith & Hurrell, 1977). While mental health admissions provide only a crude index of distress, and the direction of the causal arrow between occupation and admission rate is certainly tenuous, later studies supported the conclusion of excess mental health problems and stress-related disorders among health care workers (e.g. Hoiberg, 1982).

Police Officers

Another element of the 5-year plan involved studies of two high stress occupations: police work and coal mining. NIOSH's first in-house job stress study was a semi-structured interview of 100 police officers in the City of Cincinnati (Kroes, Margolis & Hurrell, 1974). The 45-minute semi-structured interview contained information about the officer's background (e.g. age, work assignment) and perceptions of job stress. Interviews were carried out with officers from all three work shifts. A similar interview (Kroes, Hurrell & Margolis, 1974) was used to elicit job stress information from 30 police administrators.

The results revealed a large number of psychological job stressors perceived by police officers, especially role conflict and role ambiguity, both in the organization and with respect to community and societal expectations. The extent to which these problems generalized to other police departments, however, was unknown. This information, along with insights gained in a NIOSH sponsored symposium of stress in policing (Kroes & Hurrell, 1976), was used to develop a large cross-sectional survey study of stress and health in police work (Hurrell, Pate & Kliesmet, 1982). In this study, conducted in collaboration with the Police Foundation and the International Union of Police Officers, patrol officers in 28 police departments representing various geographic locations received self-report type questionnaires for rating job stressors and consequent health problems. The questionnaire contained a number of the scales developed by Caplan et al. (1975) as well as items aimed at job stressors that appeared to be unique to police officers. In all, more than 2,200 officers were surveyed. Those features receiving the higher stress ratings related primarily to organizational and management practices, notably lack of participation in job decisions, frustration with court leniency, and too much repetitiousness in work routines. Job future insecurity and role conflict showed the most significant associations with negative health and emotional states. It was concluded that stress among police officers involves needs for greater clarification of job roles and expectations, and the development of strategies for better coping with conflicts that relate to professional and familial responsibilities.

Coal Miners

A second high stress occupation examined by NIOSH was coal mining (Althouse & Hurrell, 1977). This study examined the impact of psychological stress and strain among working coal miners in order to determine whether features of those mines characteristically exhibiting higher rates of accidents affect the health perceptions of their employees. It was designed to compare responses between workers in mines with exceptionally high accident rates to those working in mines with low accident rates. It was reasoned that systematic differences between miners working in high or low accident environments could be examined to develop information that might be applied to the promotion of worker well-being and positive health among underground miners.

Based on accident statistics for every underground coal-mine operating in the United States, candidate mines were selected from the upper and lower extremes of the continuum. Once a sample population of candidate mines had been generated, mines were selected on a matched-pair basis from nine different states. Each pair was matched as closely as possible on: (1) geographic location; (2) number of employed miners; (3) annual production figures; (4) seam height; (5) unionization; (6) "captive" vs. commercial operations; and (7) conventional vs. continuous methods of extraction. A total of 15 matched pairs were selected. At each mine site, questionnaires containing indicies of stress and strain similar to those used by Caplan et al. (1975) were distributed to volunteer study participants. In all, some 486 miners and mine foremen participated in the study.

No difference in stress level and associated strain was found between the miners drawn from the high and low accident mines and miners reported no greater prevalence of stressful conditions than blue collar workers in Caplan et al. (1975) sample. Contrasted with these blue-collar workers, however, miners reported significantly more psychological distress including symptoms of anxiety, depression, irritation and somatic problems. Job discontent was the best predictor of psychological distress experienced by miners. Indeed, dissatisfaction with work, rather than actual characteristics of work, was most directly consequential for the psychological distress of the miner (Althouse & Hurrell, 1977).

Studies of Specific Job Stressors

While the initial NIOSH job stress studies targeted high stress occupations, the focus quickly changed to examination of job stressors and health outcomes. The logic for this shift in focus was straightforward: with limited funds, NIOSH got a 'bigger bang for the buck' by focusing on job stressors instead of individual occupations. Two job stressors that were selected for initial study were shiftwork and machine-pacing.

Shiftwork

Using both a cross-sectional survey and a health records examination, NIOSH collaborated with the Stanford Research Institute to examine the health effects of shiftwork (Tasto & Colligan, 1978). In this study, a questionnaire designed to elicit information concerning the incidence and prevalence of physical complaints and illness histories, eating patterns, sleep patterns, medication usage, life style and domestic patterns, and psychological profiles was distributed to 3,500 shift workers, composed of nurses and food processors, dividing the distribution equally among day, afternoon, right, and rotating shift categories. Data for a sample of about 1,200 nurses and a similar number of food processors were also collected by reviewing health and accident files.

Findings from the study confirmed European studies in that rotating shift workers, who not only work at unconventional hours but who move from shift to shift, reported more sleep disturbances, gastrointestinal complaints, chest pains; fatigue, nervousness, alcohol consumption, and use of stimulants. Examination of employee records indicated that rotating shift workers took more sick leave and far more serious reasons than fixed shift workers and had a higher accident rate (Tasto et al., 1978). Shift work appeared to pose a distinct health hazard for rotating shift workers. An adaptation index was also developed in conjunction with the analyses of questionnaire results and suggested among other things, that shift workers adapt best if they are satisfied with their shift schedule and satisfied with the type of work they are doing.

Machine-pacing
A second job stressor that attracted the attention of NIOSH was machine-paced work. Machine-paced work, almost from inception, has been a source of worker complaints. Such a work process can enhance productivity, but there is reason to suspect that it may have adverse effects on worker physical and mental health. Indeed, machine-paced assemblers in the Job Demands and Worker Health study (Caplan et al., 1975) reported more stress and strain than the 22 other occupations studied. At the request of the U.S. Department of Agriculture, NIOSH conducted a study of job stress in a nationally representative sample of self- and machine-paced poultry inspectors. The task of the inspector required high vigilance, and it consisted of the post-mortem inspection of poultry carcasses moving at a machine-paced rate of 15 to 23 carcasses per minute. Workers in 121 of the 240 poultry plants in the continental USA were surveyed with a questionnaire that contained elements of the Caplan et al. (1975) instrument. Results confirmed findings from the earlier *Job Demands* study in that machine-paced worker inspectors having most time in the inspection task reported higher levels of workload, underutilization of abilities, job dissatisfaction, and more health complaints than did those who spent only part of their day in this work (Wilkes, Stammerjohn & Lalich, 1981; Stammerjohn & Wilkes, 1981).

In order to identify the potential sources and consequences of stress in machine-paced work in a different kind of job, NIOSH conducted a large scale cross sectional survey of Multiple Position Letter Sorting Machine (MPLSM) operators in the U.S. postal service. The job of MPLSM operator was chosen for study because with over 29,000 operators, it represented one of the largest work groups in the United States engaged in machine-paced work. The task of the MPLSM operators, like that of the poultry inspector in the study cited above, involves high vigilance but unlike the poultry inspection task, the MPLSM task is highly cognitive in nature requiring rapid encoding, manipulation and decoding of visually presented information. Questionnaires were mailed to a nationally representative sample of 6,000 MPLSM operators and to 6,000 non-paced workers who performed the same task. The questionnaire included a number of core scales derived from the work of Caplan et al. (1975), a variety of items aimed at tapping the more cognitive kinds of demands encountered in machine-paced mail sorting, measures of non-work related stressors, social support and the Type A behavior pattern. The results indicated that the MPLSM operators reported higher levels of job demands, particularly in relation to high workload, work pressure, and concentration and memory demands and decreased job satisfaction. They also reported greater levels of health complaints, indicating visual arm/wrist/hand, and neck strains and mood distur-bances including depression and anxiety (Smith, Hurrell & Murphy, 1981; Hurrell, 1985).

Studies of Stress Outcomes

Having funded studies of high stress occupations and then studies of high-risk job stressors, the next step was to address specific health outcomes in more detail. Two distinct outcomes were selected for initial study: coronary heart disease (CHD) and mass psychogenic illness (MPI).

Coronary Heart Disease

The first study was done by the Stanford Research Institute International who conducted a longitudinal study of job stressors and CHD risk factors (additional NIOSH funded studies on this topic are described in a later section). The subjects in the study were a sample of male, salaried employees of Lockheed Missiles and Space Company (LMSC), a large aerospace corporation in Sunnyvale, California. The principal subjects of the study ($n = 397$) were the focal subjects. As an initial step in the survey plan, data were also obtained relative to the working environment from associates of focal subjects, including up to five persons named by each focal subject as being part of his close working group. The average Work Environment Scale (WES) scores from the close associates of each focal subject became part of the data file.

Among the focal subjects there were three experimental groups and one comparison group. The comparison group was drawn from a cross-section of salaried employees from Lockheed. The three experimental groups were drawn from among specially chosen categories of lower-level managers and supervisors in: (a) New Business project leaders; (b) Finance and Accounting managers; and (c) Product Assurance managers. A reduced set of focal subjects, 220 or about half the original number, was then selected to participate in the repeat examinations. Because five additional examinations were to be carried out on each of these subjects, it was felt that the smaller number of subjects would be sufficient to allow the detection of significant effects. The selection process was random, but weighted to bring all study groups to approximately the same size.

The total employee population was approximately 19,000, of which 15,700 or 83% were males. Of the males, about 11,500 or 74% were salaried. Of the salaried males, about 1,250 were lower-level managers and supervisors, and approximately 400 of these were in the target categories. The 253 subjects in the experimental groups constitute approximately 60% of the target population for the specialized samples. By ethnic origins the sample was 84% white, 6% Hispanic, 6% Asian-American, and 4% black. A broad range of data was collected from each participant, including demographics, job title, Work Environment Scale, Family Environment Scale, Type A behavior, other personality scales, workload, job satisfaction, life stress, psychological distress, blood pressure, physiological variables from blood and urine samples (lipids, catecholamines), CHD status, other medical history, and full set of weekly workload reports.

The results of the study did not support the concept of job stress and behavior as an extraordinary component of CHD risk, i.e. as a component much larger than conventional CHD risk factors. The data were consistent with the concept of job stress and behavior, in combination, as ordinary components of CHD risk, having effects that are comparable to the classic factors. For instance, there were a fairly large number of low-grade, but seemingly consistent, relationships between psychosocial variables defining job stress and behavior and physiological measurements known or believed to relate to CHD risk. Previously reported relationships between certain psychosocial variables (principally anxiety, neuroticism, and depression) and self-reports of CHD status, such as angina, were replicated in the study. However, the variables that had the strongest relationship to self-reported CHD status did not have the strongest relationships to physiological variables, again indicating the existence of multiple mechanisms and paths.

Mass Psychogenic Illness

In July 1974, a team of psychologists from NIOSH was asked to aid in the investigation of an illness outbreak in a garment manufacturing plant in the southwest. This unusual request for psychological evaluation came about after preliminary measurement of chemical agents in the workplace had failed to detect any significant levels of known toxicants. Within a period of a week, approximately 100 women in a plant population of 340 workers (325 women, 15 men) had expressed or displayed symptoms of nausea, dizziness, fainting, and burning sensations in the eyes and throat. A majority of the affected workers reported smelling a peculiar odor or gas in the work environment, which they felt produced their illness. Extensive environmental sampling by industrial hygienists and medical examinations, however, failed to identify the presence of any toxicants capable of producing the observed symptoms. It was felt that the illness might have involved psychogenic components (e.g. stress or anxiety).

The immediacy of the situation did not allow for the development of a systematic research protocol by NIOSH psychologists. Nevertheless, it was felt that sufficient information could be obtained through observation of the work environment and interviews with affected and non-affected workers to permit generalizations to other reported cases of this nature. However, a post-investigation literature review was extremely disappointing and revealed only two published cases of apparent mass psychogenic illness in American work settings (Stahl & Lebedun, 1974; Kerckhoff & Back, 1968). In these two case studies, as was also true of the NIOSH investigation, the spontaneity of the phenomenon and the absence of a guiding theoretical framework hampered the collection of systematic and comparable data. Consequently, understanding of contagious psychogenic illness was more impressionistic than empirical and limited by the scarcity of existing data.

It was apparent that a critical need existed for systematic research into the etiology and methods for remediation of mass psychogenic disturbance in industry. Therefore, in 1976, NIOSH initiated a programmatic effort to develop, field test, and refine a research protocol for investigating cases of this nature. This approach involved combining individual interviews with questionnaire data collected from a random sample of affected and non-affected workers at each worksite. In addition to sociodemographic (e.g. age, sex, level of education, marital and parental status, etc.) and epidemiological information (date and time of illness, symptomatology, location of workplace at time of onset), the questionnaire contained items designed to measure perceived job stress along a variety of dimensions (e.g. unwanted overtime, quantitative work overload, role ambiguity, lack of social support, boredom, etc.). Life stress experienced outside the job situation was measured via the Holmes-Rahe Social Readjustment Scale. Sociometric (e.g. friendship choices at work, most frequent interpersonal contacts, etc.) and personality/psychodiagnostic (e.g. Eysenck Personality Inventory, MMPI Hysteria, Hypochondriasis and Depression Scales) measures were also included.

Since the original investigation, NIOSH investigated eight outbreaks of mass psychogenic illness (MPI) in shoe factories, a warehouse, an aluminum lawn furniture assembly plant, a fish packing plant, and electronics assembly plants using the standard survey protocol described above. The eight incidents shared some important features that are noteworthy (Colligan, Pennebaker & Murphy, 1982). First, affected workers were predominately female (89%) although women were disproportionately represented in each of the workplace populations also. Second, the symptomatology across cases was remarkably similar. Headache was the most frequent symptom and lightheadedness, dizziness, sleepiness, and weakness were all in the top five most frequent symptoms in 75% of the studies. Third, in all cases, the onset of symptoms and their subsequent contagion was preceded by a triggering event (e.g. strange odor) that was viewed as causally related to the malady. Fourth, the work settings in which MPI occurred tended to involve boring, repetitive, rigidly-paced jobs with little opportunity for advancement. Moreover, in many cases, workers reported high work pressure, poor labor/management relations, and physical discomfort at work. Physical discomfort at work, which included worker ratings of noise levels, temperature, air quality, and lighting levels, consistently correlated highly with affected status. The finding that personality characteristics could not be conclusively linked with affected status suggested that MPI outbreaks involve normal individuals in stressful work environments (Colligan & Murphy, 1979).

While the data base on MPI outbreaks continued to grow (e.g. Boxer, Singal & Hartle, 1984), much remained unknown about this phenomenon and the appropriate remedial interventions. The spontaneous nature of the illness, which dictates a *post facto* investigation, severely limits the range of usable methodologies. Extent company records are usually of too poor quality and/or insufficiently detailed to pinpoint causes of the illness outbreaks. Aggregate analyses of MPI data, in which the organization, not the individual, becomes the unit of analysis (exemplified by Schmitt & Fitzgerald, 1982), may be the most fruitful course to pursue for increasing understanding of this phenomenon.

1977 Conference on Work and Stress
In 1977, NIOSH again co-sponsored a conference with the Center for Occupational Mental Health that was held in White Plains, New York in 1977 (McLean, Colligan & Black, 1978). The conference included presentations from 23 speakers that covered a broad range of topics including sources of occupational stress, prevention and remediation programs, and legislative efforts to

manage job stress. Indeed, the assemblage of speakers and the enduring relevance of the topics were so significant at this early stage of job stress research that the table of contents from the meeting is shown in Text Box 3.

At this conference, House and Wells presented early research suggesting that social support buffers the effects of job stress on some health conditions (neurosis and ulcers) more so than others (e.g. angina pectoris). Arthur Shostak highlighted job insecurity and job loss as major blue-collar stressors in the 1970s, and suggested that a revolution in managerial thinking was needed to bring about needed job redesign. Tores Theorell presented early evidence of a link between job stressors and myocardial infarction, citing workload and increased responsibility as major risk factors. Jerome Rosow pointed to significant changes in worker attitudes toward work, and noted that the quality of working life should be viewed broadly to encompass the organization of work, hierarchical structures, relationships with coworkers, organizational climate, participation in decision making, and opportunities for development and advancement. Bertil Gardell provided details of a legislative/regulatory approach to reducing psychosocial stressors at work in Scandinavian countries, and described the co-determination Act passed in 1977 and the work environment Act in 1978. The former gave trade unions the right to influence decisions at all levels in the organization, while the latter specified that working method be adapted to the worker, both a physiological and psychological point of view. Finally, Lennart Levi made clear that while it is common in discussions of job design to hear that the worker is adaptable, he/she is also deformable and working conditions should be redesigned so that they do not 'deform' the worker in terms of subjective well-being, behavior, and physiology.

It is important to remember that job stress was not a mainstream health and safety issue in the 1970s, nor was it a much-discussed topic in industrial/organizational psychology. Presentations of job stress studies at national scientific or trade group meetings were typically met with skepticism. Fundamental questions about its' legitimacy as a workplace issue and the quality of the underlying science (i.e. worker perceptions) were common, even routine. One major objection in the 1970s (and well into the 1980s) was that stress was not a work environment issue, but rather a worker problem, and hence solutions would require individual worker attention. The analogy to counseling for alcoholism was often made. It was not until a good deal more research was completed before these types of objections would become less common.

1980s: GROWTH AND EXPANSION

The 1980s saw an expansion in the scope of inquiry of NIOSH job stress research, as reflected by new research on job demands/worker decision latitude,

Source: McLean, Black, G., & Colligan, M. (Eds). *Reducing Occupational Stress*. DHHS
(NIOSH) Publication No. 78-140, Washington, D.C.: U.S. Government Printing Office.

stress management, video display terminal and office worker stress, and stress measurement methods. Moreover, NIOSH formally recognized psychological disorders as one of the top ten leading causes of work-related disease in its National Strategy for the Prevention of Work-related Disease (Millar, 1984; National Institute for Occupational Safety and Health, 1988). However, this expansion occurred in the absence of any budget increases; more projects were initiated but they were small relative to the size of projects in 1970s.

Demand/Control Model of Strain

NIOSH provided funding to test a new hypothesis that job strain (specifically coronary heart disease) was a function of the interaction of job demands and decision latitude. Karasek (1979) proposed that job strain resulted not from a single aspect of work but rather the joint effects of job demands and decision latitude (i.e. worker control). This research sought to harmonize two contradictory traditions in industrial/organizational research: one tradition focusing on job decision latitude and the other focusing on job demands or stressors (Karasek, 1979).

A model proposed by Karasek to predict stress-related consequences of job characteristics was tested in a NIOSH funded project using prevalence data on heart disease from the 1961 Health Examination Study (1961), the 1972 National Health Interview Survey, and the 1971–1974 National Health and Nutrition Examination Survey. Hypotheses about job characteristics were tested by assigning job scores to occupations using U.S. Quality of Employment data from 1969, 1972 and 1977. Multivariate analyses (controlled for known CHD risk factors such as age, education, marital status, and ethnicity) showed that high job demands were associated with excess prevalence of myocardial infarction, as was low decision latitude. However, the combination of high job demands and low job control (i.e. the 'high strain group" which comprised 15% of the sample) was not significant in the regression model. On the other hand, high strain jobs (those with high demands and low decision latitude) did have a higher prevalence of myocardial infarction across age groups, especially after age 35. Psychological job demands were most consistently linked to high blood pressure, especially diastolic blood pressure, as was job decision latitude. High strain jobs tended to have slightly higher blood pressures across age groups, except for the 65+ group that showed the opposite pattern (Karasek, Schwartz & Theorell, 1982; Karasek, Theorell, Schwartz, Schnall, Pieper & Michela, 1988).

A second grant awarded by NIOSH to Karasek examined the prospective development of CHD risk factors in relationship to job characteristics and occupation using existing U.S. health databases. If job characteristics contribute to the ultimate development of CHD (as found in the first grant), they should affect the prospective development of conventionally measured CHD risk factors as well. However, almost no research has been undertaken in the prospective development of blood pressure, EKG, smoking, or Type A behavior linked to occupation or job characteristics. Such analyses would be of great potential value in occupational health research where the study of CHD risk factors could be accomplished with substantially smaller populations than are needed to study the prospective development of CHD itself. This study used a similar methodology to that employed in the first grant but was based on job title data available in the Western Collaborative Group Study, Exercise Heart, and Mr. Fit prospective databases, using adaptations of the existing job characteristics/occupation imputation methodology (Karasek, Theorell, Schwartz, Schnall, Pieper & Michela, 1988).

The NIOSH funding allowed these researchers to refine an occupational scoring system in which job characteristic scores were imputed to job titles and then to test associations between occupational scores and coronary heart disease. The findings reported in a 1982 grant report indicated the clear importance of decision latitude on myocardial infarction and of job demands on blood pressure, but tests of Demand × Control interaction terms were not always statistically significant (Karasek, Schwartz, Theorell, Pieper, Russell & Michela, 1982). Later research by other groups that tested Karasek's demand/control model would provide inconsistent results, some studies finding significant interactions while others did not find a significant interaction term. Still other NIOSH research partially supported a little tested aspect of the model; lower disability due to cardiovascular disease for 'active' jobs (Murphy, 1991). Active jobs represented the opposite of high strain jobs, that is, jobs with high demands but high decision latitude.

Of course, the lure of the demand/control hypothesis was its simplicity: workers will experience job strain whenever the demands of the work exceed their ability to control the demands. One advantage of Karasek's methodology was that issues of common method bias were avoided since the measures of job characteristics and health outcomes were not obtained from the same source. Rather, scores on job characteristics were imputed to occupations based on aggregated cores from selected items taken from the QES.

State of the Art Meeting on Worker Control and Health

As a follow-up to the demand/control research described above, NIOSH convened a special meeting of researchers to evaluate the state of knowledge on worker control and health (Sauter, Hurrell & Cooper, 1989). The meeting reviewed findings from the fields of industrial/organizational psychology, epidemiology, and psychophysiology and was organized around three major topics: (1) evidence for the effects of control on worker health; (2) methodological and theoretical concerns; and (3) control problems and solutions in modern work. A few highlights of the meeting are worth noting. For instance, Karasek (1989) agreed with other speakers that while studies routinely find main effects for demands and control, many do not find that the demand/control interaction term is statistically significant. He suggested, however, that the practical implications for job design remain the same whether separate main effects for demands and control are found or demand/control interactions are observed. Ganster (1989) suggested that control was often treated as a uni-dimensional construct when in fact there are likely to be specific domains of control that require measurement, such as control over tasks, pacing, scheduling, physical environment, decision making, interpersonal interaction, and job mobility. The idea that control is multi-dimensional was incorporated into the design of the NIOSH Generic Job Stress Questionnaire (described later in this chapter). Finally, Kasl (1989) concluded that ". . . fundamental questions regarding conceptualization, measurement, and supportive evidence remain unanswered . . ." with respect to worker control and health.

Stress Management

An important element in the initial five-year plan was research on stress reduction and prevention. This became more critical as more information on job stress and health was produced by the early NIOSH studies. The first NIOSH study in this area focused on the merits of biofeedback and muscle relaxation for reducing stress symptoms among hospital nurses (Murphy, 1983). This was followed by a study of highway maintenance workers (Murphy, 1984). The latter group was selected for study because research in this area had concentrated on white- and pink-collar workers. In both studies, stress management training was associated with improvements on measures of psychological function such as anxiety and perceived coping skills, but inconsistent effects on measures of somatic complaints (e.g. headaches, shortness of breath). Stress management did not produce consistent improvements in job/organization-relevant outcomes, such as absenteeism or job satisfaction. This is not surprising since the interventions did not focus on changing job-related sources of stress. The effects of stress management on physiological outcomes like muscle tension levels and hand temperature were positive but very small in magnitude (Murphy, 1983, 1984). These results agreed with prior and later studies showing that stress management training can improve individual-level measures of stress.

One outcome of this work was the preparation of a manual on stress management training (Murphy & Schoenborn, 1989) that presented available evidence on training effectiveness, raised warnings to organizations about focusing exclusively on changing individual workers while ignoring the work environment, and presented a prototype for comprehensive workplace stress reduction programs. Another outcome was a series of articles that reviewed the literature on the efficacy of occupational stress management programs (Murphy, 1984a, 1996). These reviews indicated that, as applied in work settings, stress management more often than not was being offered in a preventive, as opposed to curative, context. That is, participants were not recruited because of evident stress problems or health risks, but rather such training was open to all workers. Accordingly, these programs have a more compelling association with health promotion than with stress reduction. The reviews also highlighted substantial knowledge gaps in stress management research and recommended a more comprehensive approach to controlling job stress, one that combines stress prevention (via job redesign and organizational change) with stress management training.

Video Display Terminals (VDT)

In 1978, NIOSH received a request from the Labor Occupational Health Program, University of California at Berkeley for assistance in a study of stress and strain among video display terminal (VDT) operators. NIOSH provided advice on a draft questionnaire instrument developed by the Newspaper Guild and made recommendations for improving the nature and scope of the survey instrument. Based on this advice, NIOSH was formally asked to assist in the investigation of psychosocial factors and musculoskeletal disorders among VDT users. This investigation revealed a much higher prevalence of musculoskeletal symptoms among clerical VDT users (e.g. 56% for neck-shoulder pain) than among work peers who did not use VDTs (19% for neck/shoulder pain). Increased psychosocial demands (greater work pressure, reduced autonomy, and lower supervisory support) were also seen among the VDT users, suggesting a possible etiologic role of these factors (Smith, Cohen, Stammejohn & Happ, 1981).

A NIOSH-supported follow-up study at the University of Wisconsin resulted in findings nearly identical to effects seen in the West Coast study (Sauter, Gottlieb, Jones, Dodson & Rohrer, 1983). In this cross-sectional study, VDT users again reported increased work pressure and reduced support and personal control in their jobs compared with workers who did not use VDTS. Adding these factors (job control and social support) as predictor variables to regression models linking environmental factors to musculoskeletal outcomes substantially increased the explanatory power of these models. Three years later, NIOSH initiated a series of lab studies that sought to isolate stressful job and task characteristics of VDT operations. Although these studies did not detect changes in objectively measured visual function due to VDT use, subjective reports of visual and musculoskeletal complaints were more apparent in VDT operators. Other work in this area identified slow system response time as a source of stress for VDT operators (Schleifer & Amick, 1989) and examined the utility of end-tidal PCO_2 (peak concentration of carbon dioxide in a single exhaled breath) as a psycho-physiological indicator of stress in VDT work (Schleifer, 1994). In the presence of rapidly accumulating evidence that workplace psychosocial factors were instrumental in the development of musculoskeletal disorders in office and VDT work, NIOSH collaborated with Duke University in1993 to hold a state-of-the-art meeting that critically examined these factors and their influence (Moon & Sauter, 1996).

More recently, NIOSH has undertaken field interventions to evaluate the effectiveness of organizational interventions to reduce musculoskeletal disorders among VDT operators. In a controlled study of 100 data entry clerks at the Internal Revenue Service, reorganization of work schedules to provide more frequent rest breaks resulted in reduced discomfort in the neck, back, and upper extremity (Galinsky, Swanson, Sauter, Hurrell & Schleifer, 2000). It is noteworthy that these benefits occurred without any reductions in data-entry performance.

Stress Measurement Methodologies

The dominant methodology in job stress research had been a questionnaire survey approach in which workers were asked to rate job characteristics and also to provide information on the frequency of various health complaints. Problems with this methodology are well known, such as potential confounds between measures of stressors and strains (Kasl, 1978; Hurrell, Murphy, Sauter & Cooper, 1988). Perhaps the biggest problem was the absence of standardized scales to measure job characteristics, which prevented direct comparisons among studies but also prevented the development of a normative database.

The pressing need for a standardized set of reliable and valid scales to measure job stressors and strains across occupational settings prompted NIOSH to develop the Generic Job Stress Questionnaire (GJSQ). Working with outside experts (Dan Ganster and Neil Schmitt), NIOSH designed the GJSQ as a series of modules containing multi-item scales that addressed key features of the work environment and key health outcomes (Hurrell & McLaney, 1988). A general model of job stress and health (described in the succeeding section) was used to guide development of the GJSQ. Three criteria were used to select items and scales from existing instruments: (1) evidence of reliability and validity; (2) absence of confounding of stressors and strains; and (3) extensive use of the items in prior research. If no adequate measures for a particular construct could be found, then new items were created.

Table 2. NIOSH Generic Job Stress Questionnaire.

	Scale name	No. of items	Reliability (α)
(1)	Physical Environment	18	0.84
(2)	Role Conflict	8	0.82
(3)	Role Ambiguity	6	0.84
(4)	Intra-group Conflict	8	0.86
(5)	Inter-group Conflict	8	0.85
(6)	Job Future Ambiguity	4	0.65
(8)	Task Control	8	0.85
(9)	Decision Control	4	0.74
(10)	Physical Environment Control	2	0.79
(11)	Resource Control	2	0.82
(12)	Alternate Employment Opportunities	3	0.80
(13)	Social Support from Supervisor	4	0.88
(14)	Social Support from Coworkers	4	0.84
(15)	Social Support from Family	4	0.85
(16)	Quantitative Workload	7	0.85
(17)	Variance in Workload	3	0.86
(18)	Responsibility for People	4	0.62
(19)	Skill Underutilization	3	0.73
(20)	Mental Demands	5	0.75
(21)	Non-work Activities	7	*
(22)	Type A personality	16	0.85
(23)	Self-Esteem	10	0.85
(24)	Somatic Complaints	17	0.87
(25)	Job Satisfaction	4	0.83
(26)	Depression	20	0.88
	TOTAL	179	

* Data not available for this scale.

The final instrument contained 179 questions that were distributed across 26 scales (see Table 2), not counting demographic questions. All of the work scales demonstrated internal consistency with the exception of Responsibility for People (alpha = 0.62). Many of the scales assessed features of the work environment taken from commonly used instruments (e.g. Caplan et al., 1975) but in some areas, new scales had to be developed. One example is the topic of worker control. Instead of measuring global or facet-free control, four distinct dimensions of control were assessed (task, decision, physical environment, and resources) and multiple questions were generated for each dimension or domain of control.

As mentioned above, the selection of constructs to measure in the GJSQ was guided in part by the NIOSH model of job stress and health (see Fig. 2). This model built on the earlier frameworks offered by Caplan et al. (1975), Cooper and Marshall (1976), and Levi (1971). The model views job stress as a situation in which a working condition (stressor) or combination of working conditions interact with individual worker characteristics and result in acute disruption of psychological or physiologic homeostasis. These acute reactions, if prolonged, lead to a variety of illnesses. Three sets of factors are shown in the model to influence the stressor-strain relationship: individual factors, non-work situations, and buffers. These three sets of factors can lead to differences in the way workers exposed to the same stressors perceive or react to them. It is noteworthy that most job stress research examine only the link between stressors and acute outcomes, and few studies have tested the full model. A full test of the model would require the collection of records data on health and disability in addition to questionnaire data on stressors, strain, and mediating factors.

Work Schedules and Fatigue

A trend toward increased scheduling of workdays longer than eight hours, often in combination with night or rotating shift work, raised concerns about the degree of stress and fatigue produced by these schedules. Consequently, NIOSH initiated a series of laboratory and field studies in 1983 to examine these effects. A portable fatigue test battery was designed to measure fatigue development and accumulation across 8- and 12-hour work shifts and compressed workweeks (Rosa & Colligan, 1988), coupled with questionnaire assessments of perceived stress, mood, fatigue and sleepiness. Initial studies found decreased reaction time and grammatical reasoning performance and increased subjective fatigue after seven months of 12-hour shifts as compared to the previous 8-hour shift schedule. Daily sleep logs indicated a 1-hour sleep debt by the end of the

LAWRENCE R. MURPHY

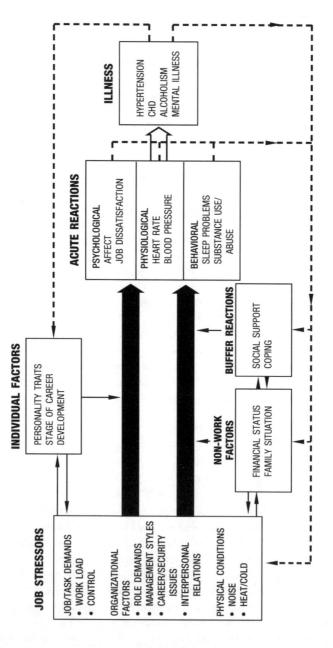

Fig. 2. NIOSH Model Used to Guide Job Stress Studies.

12-hour/3–4 day workweek. Performance did not deteriorate across the work-week, however, suggesting that the shorter workweek compensated somewhat for the longer work shift (Rosa, Colligan & Lewis, 1989). After 3.5 years on the 12-hour shift schedule, declines in alertness with time on-shift and reduc-tions in total sleep time were still apparent, and few improvements were observed relative to the 7-month test phase (Rosa, 1991). In a second worksite study at a natural gas utility, there were significant decrements in reaction time performance and subjective alertness 10 months after the change to a 12-hour shift schedule. Reductions in sleep across the workweek were most apparent on 12-hour night shifts (Rosa & Bonnet, 1993). Accumulated fatigue across consecutive workdays exemplified by progressive increases in choice reaction time were apparent across a 5-day week of 8-hour shifts and a 4-day week of 10-hour shifts in air traffic control specialists (Schroeder, Rosa & Witt, 1998).

The interaction of time of day and accumulated fatigue from hours of work was examined in a later laboratory study in which subjects were instructed to perform a manual work simulation at three repetition rates and to stop the work trial when they reached a given level of perceived muscular fatigue. The data showed that muscular fatigue increased during 12-hour shifts and fatigue increased more quickly across the night shifts compared to day shifts. Subjects were willing to work longer at slower repetition rates early in the shift but this difference among workloads was appreciably smaller by the end of the shift, especially night shift. The results indicated that extra hours of work added to the early-morning downturn in circadian arousal produced the greatest fatigue (Rosa, Bonnet, & Cole, 1998). A summary of the stress, fatigue, and perfor-mance effects of shift work was prepared by NIOSH and is available at: (*http://www.cdc.gov/niosh/pdfs/97–145.pdf*).

Top Ten Leading Causes of Work-Related Disease

In 1982, a list of leading work-related diseases and injuries was developed by the scientific leadership of NIOSH. Three criteria were used to select conditions or disorders for inclusion in the list: (a) the frequency of the condition; (b) the severity of the condition in the individual case; and (c) the "preventability" of the condition. NIOSH leadership identified 10 disorders that met these criteria and psychological disorders was one of them. The "top ten" list was intended to encourage deliberation and debate, to assist in setting national health priorities, and to disseminate the concerns of the NIOSH leadership and the focus of the institute (Millar, 1984).

In 1985 and 1986, symposia were held to establish national prevention strate-gies for the leading work-related diseases and injuries. Psychological disorders were addressed at the 1986 symposium held in Cincinnati, Ohio. Over 50 professionals from industry, business, trade unions, voluntary organizations, academia, and the professions attended the symposium. For each disorder, a team of internal and external experts was empanelled to prepare a national prevention strategy that described the scope of the problem, its work-relatedness, and recommendations for prevention and future research. The psychological disorders strategy document addressed four major areas: job design, surveillance, education and training, and mental health services (National Institute for Occupational Safety and Health, 1988). An expanded version of the psychological disorders national strategy later was published in the *American Psychologist* (Sauter, Murphy & Hurrell, 1990). The strategy examined current knowledge and practices and suggested initiatives for industry, labor, government, and academia to help promote the psychological health of workers. Key steps included measures to improve working conditions and employee mental health services, as well as research and surveillance to advance understanding of the problem. Within NIOSH, the strategy document was used to guide the research program and new projects were required to show relevance to research gaps identified in the strategy document.

In 1989, the American Psychological Association (APA), in collaboration with NIOSH, developed the APA/NIOSH Work and Well-Being Project, which used the NIOSH (1988) psychological disorders prevention document as its point of departure. This collaboration resulted in a national conference that was convened in November, 1990 (discussed later in this chapter).

Outside of NIOSH, the Institute of Medicine, National Academy of Sciences commissioned a special study of stress and human health. Panels were set up to address various aspects of stress and health, and one of those panels dealt with stress in organizational settings (Elliott & Eisdorfer, 1982). The panel reviewed the literature, presented a summary of the findings, and listed research needs including recommended interventions. Examples of recommendations were efforts to increase worker control of work arrangements, increasing worker participation in decision-making, avoiding monotonous machine-paced work, avoiding work overload, and facilitating communication among workers.

1990s: TO BE OR NOT TO BE

The 1990s are notable on several counts but the most memorable was the possibility that the NIOSH would be eliminated completely. Senate hearings held in the mid-1990s considered cutting 30% of the Occupational Safety and Health Administration budget and eliminating NIOSH and the Mine Safety and Health Administration as a federal agencies. In the end, this didn't occur but the threat of elimination certainly brought the issue of job stress close to NIOSH researchers! Ironically, funding for work organization and job stress research actually increased in the 1990s and this increase has continued in 2000. As the reader will see below, since the late 1990s, the number and scope of NIOSH job stress research projects rose dramatically in response to increased funding and support.

From a research perspective, the 1990s began with three new thrusts to the NIOSH job stress program. First, major funding initiatives were introduced throughout NIOSH and would become a stable part of the NIOSH funding mechanism in future years. Second, NIOSH would establish a long-term partnership with the American Psychological Association (APA) to sponsor international conferences on work, stress and health and to encourage more psychologists to pursue careers in occupational safety and health. Third, NIOSH developed a National Occupational Research Agenda to guide internal research and extramural funding and to provide general guidance for OS&H research.

Initiative-Driven Research

In 1990, the first targeted funding initiative appeared within NIOSH, earmarking special funds for HIV/AIDS research. In later years, initiatives dealing with Agriculture and Construction would appear and drive new project development. Still later, funding initiatives based on NORA would become more prominent. A few initiative-driven research efforts are described below.

HIV/AIDS Initiative

Although HIV/AIDS is not usually viewed from a job stress perspective, it was easily blended into the job stress research program from a safety management perspective. For instance, recommended work practices (e.g. not recapping used needles) to prevent occupational exposure to HIV/AIDS were incorporated into the OSHA blood-borne rule in 1992. Despite the wide dissemination of these recommendations, a substantial number of occupational exposures to contaminated blood and body fluids continue to occur, especially through needlestick injuries and cuts by sharp objects. Broadly speaking, failure to follow recommended work practices in any work environment is a safety issue, and a number of individual and organizational factors have been associated with the safety at work (e.g. Cohen, 1977; Zohar, 1980). These include strong management commitment to safety, provision of performance feedback to employees, humanistic management style, high worker involvement in safety, and good hygiene practices.

NIOSH adopted this safety perspective and awarded a cooperative agreement to Johns Hopkins School of Medicine to design a questionnaire study that assessed individual, job and organizational factors that influenced worker adherence to Universal Precautions (UP). Survey data were obtained from over 1,700 workers at three hospitals across the USA. Hierarchical regression analyses revealed that demographic factors and worker personal characteristics were not good predictors of adherence to UP. On the other hand, job/task factors, notably worker perceptions of job hindrances, were the best predictors of adherence to UP. Job hindrances included perceptions that job duties interfered with practicing UP, failure to follow UP because "patients needs come first," and perceptions that UP prevented workers from doing their job to the best of their abilities. Organization-level factors, such as management commitment to safety and performance feedback were good predictors of worker adherence to UP. In order to improve worker adherence to UP, it was suggested that organizations: (1) evaluate jobs/tasks to identify and then reduce hindrances to compliance; (2) insure top management commitment to safety; and (3) encourage managers to provide feedback and reinforcement to employees on their safety performance (Gershon, Murphy, Felknor, Vesley & DeJoy, 1995; DeJoy, Murphy & Gershon, 1995).

Agriculture Initiative
This initiative funded a wide range of projects dealing with health and safety issues in agricultural occupations. In the area of job stress, new research was funded that examined job stressors and health and safety consequences among farmers and farm families. NIOSH funded cooperative agreements to conduct in-depth interview and questionnaire studies of farm families. Intramural studies of farmer stress, health and safety were also designed (Kidd, Scharf & Veazie, 1996) and identified workload, hours of work, physical environment, mental demands, and work-family spillover as major job stressors in farming. Economic conditions, weather, lack of resources, and farm hazards also contributed to farmer stress levels. A structural model was developed that linked farm family stress and injury and provided ideas for future research. These findings led to additional and continuing research on health and safety interventions for farm families (Scharf, Kidd, Cole, Bean, Chapman, Donham & Baker, 1998).

Construction Initiative
Two new studies funded under this initiative examined job stress and strain among female construction workers. The first study involved interviews with tradeswomen and discovered that, compared to their male counterparts, tradeswomen felt that they were offered fewer opportunities to learn and use

new skills, they had to overcompensate to 'prove their worth' to male co-workers, and that they felt a responsibility for the safety of others at work. A follow-up telephone survey of 211 female construction workers found that skill underutilization, responsibility for the safety of others, sexual harassment, and gender-based discrimination were related to lower psychological health (Goldenhar, Swanson, Hurrell, Ruder & Deddens, 1998). A second study used a qualitative methodology to obtain information from construction owners and workers on work organization risk factors for health and safety (Grubb & Swanson, 1999). Hours of work and job demands were major risk factors for company owners, but not for contractors or line-workers. Poor safety climate emerged as a major risk factor that may have been due to the lack of formal safety training provided to workers. Safety regulations were viewed as "getting in the way" of doing the job and, from the owners point of view, not worth the monetary investment required. Front-line workers viewed safety as a matter of "common sense"; one learns what is not safe from the mistakes (i.e. accidents) of others.

NIOSH/APA Partnership

In 1990, NIOSH and the American Psychological Association (APA) began a partnership to address the concerns set forth in the National Strategy for the Prevention of Work-Related Psychological Disorders that was described earlier in this chapter (Sauter, Murphy & Hurrell, 1990). The partnership initially resulted in the joint sponsorship of a national conference on work and health in 1990 to present new research in the area of job stress and psychological disorders. Many topic areas for the planned conference were abstracted from the National Strategy document. The conference, entitled *Work and Well-Being: An Agenda for the 1990s*, brought together over 300 experts from the fields of psychology, occupational medicine, epidemiology, public health, and business. Participants included researchers, policy analysts, managers, and medical and human resource specialists representing industry, labor, government, and academia.

The conference had two major phases. The first phase involved the finaliza-tion of an action plan to protect the psychological health of workers. This plan was based upon more general formulations contained in the NIOSH National Strategy for Prevention of Work-Related Psychological Disorders. The NIOSH strategy emphasized the need to improve working conditions, to improve education and health service delivery pertinent to work-related psychological disorders, and to improve the surveillance of work-related psychological disorders and risk factors. Information dissemination, research, training, and policy development cross-cut each of these areas. The 1990 conference was followed by conferences in 1992, 1995, and 1998, each one being larger than the prior one. Proceedings from most of these conferences were published in a series of APA books (Gowing, Quick & Kraft, 1998; Keita & Sauter, 1992; Murphy, Hurrell, Sauter & Keita, 1995; Quick, Murphy & Hurrell, 1992; Sauter & Murphy, 1995).

Occupational Health Psychology

The second major outcome of the APA/NIOSH partnership was the development of a new discipline of study, occupational health psychology (OHP), which concerns the application of psychology to improving the quality of work life, and to protecting and promoting the safety, health and well-being of workers. The logic for this new discipline was that work organization and associated health and safety risks often fall into gaps between occupational health and psychology. The APA-NIOSH effort to promote the area of OHP, particularly to implement university programs and training in OHP, represents the first formal attempt by the psychology community to bring the expertise and resources of psychologists to the occupational safety and health field (Sauter, Hurrell, Fox, Tetrick & Barling, 1999).

In 1992, NIOSH entered into a cooperative agreement with the APA to develop university programs addressing these OHP training needs. To help ensure the quickest impact, OHP training under the APA-NIOSH cooperative agreement was supported initially at the postdoctoral level only and targeted principally to industrial/organizational psychologists for immediate application in teaching or professional practice in an organizational context. In the period 1994–1998, three university programs (Wayne State Department of Psychology, Duke University Medical Center, and the Johns Hopkins School of Public Health) served as training sites under the APA-NIOSH cooperative agreement. Program elements essential for selection as an OHP training site included: (a) faculty expertise in relevant areas such as work organization and health, job stress, etc.; (b) interdepartmental linkages which expose behavioral scientists to topics and methods in occupational safety and health, public health, epidemiology, labor studies, etc.; and (c) opportunities for projects, practical or internships with industry and labor organizations. Training sites were encouraged to develop a core OHP curriculum addressing the following topics:

• Organizational risk factors (management practices, job content, work roles and responsibilities, social/supervisory environment, etc.) for occupational stress, injury, and illness.

- Health aspects of stressful work, including physical and psychological health, and social and economic costs.
- Organizational interventions (e.g. work redesign) and programs (e.g. EAPS) for reduction of occupational stress, illness and injury.
- Research methods and practices in public/occupational health and epidemiology.

In 1998, training under the APA-NIOSH cooperative agreement was redirected to the graduate level in support of new course work, minor or major degree programs, or certificates in OHP in departments of psychology. Based on the same criteria for selection of postdoctoral training sites, three new universities (Kansas State University, University of Minnesota, and Bowling Green State University) were competitively selected as inaugural recipients of funding for support of graduate-level training in OHP, Subsequently, Bowling Green State University established a graduate minor in OHP as part of their existing industrial/organizational and clinical psychology programs, and Kansas State University developed a "concentration of courses and practica in OHP that would be offered to students in multiple psychology graduate programs, such as organizational psychology and human factors. Other universities funded from 1998–2001 were University of Minnesota, Clemson University, Tulane University, University of Houston, Portland State University, University of California-Los Angeles, Colorado State University, University of South Florida, and University of Texas at Austin (for details on the OHP program, see the NIOSH web page *http://www.cdc.gov/niosh/ohp.html*).

One of the most visible accomplishments of the APA/NIOSH partnership was the launching of the *Journal of Occupational Health Psychology* in 1996 as an APA publication. The journal addresses psychosocial factors related to the prevention of occupational health and safety problems and solicits research, theory, and public policy articles bearing upon occupational health psychology. The premier issue in January 1996 contained four state of the art reviews and five original research articles (*http://www.cdc.gov/niosh/ohp.html#johp*).

Downsizing and Health

Following the dissolution of the Soviet Union and the end of the nuclear arms race, the U.S. Department of Energy (DOE) and the nuclear defense industry embarked on a process of changing the agency's mission and determining appropriate staffing levels reflecting this change. Anticipating future layoffs, an approach was outlined in 1993 to plan and implement workforce layoffs consistently across the nuclear weapons industry. In 1995, Boston University School of Public Health was awarded a contract to examine the health and safety effects of downsizing in five selected DOE facilities across the U.S. The study used focus groups, a questionnaire survey, and measures of the downsizing rate aggregate measures of sick time usage and accidents. The survey was sent to a random selection of 10,646 workers at the five sites, and 55% of those responded to the survey ($N = 5,889$ respondents).

Compared to national norms, workers at four of the five DOE study sites had better physical health scores. This finding is consistent with many prior reports indicating that working populations generally are healthier than national samples of U.S. adults. However, the opposite was found for mental health and perceived stress, where scores for each DOE site were worse than the national norms (i.e. lower mental health and higher stress). Multi-level hierarchical regression analyses were conducted to examine relationships between down-sizing factors and worker health and well-being. Workers who felt that the downsizing process was fair, and that communication was open and honest, reported fewer medical symptoms (e.g. headaches, shortness of breath), fewer symptoms of downsizing survivor syndrome and more job security. Workers who were more directly involved with the downsizing process (i.e. delivered layoff notices) reported more medical symptoms. Finally, workers in jobs with high workload demands but with low decision-making authority reported higher levels of perceived stress and more job insecurity, more symptoms of survivor syndrome, and lower morale. It was suggested that the organizations: (1) implement processes and policies that emphasize fair procedures, and open, timely, and honest communication to employees in all work units; (2) assess workload demands following significant changes to a work unit or department; and (3) implement regular surveys of the organization, with particular attention to communication, workload, and management relations with the DOE (Murphy & Pepper, 2002).

National Occupational Research Agenda (NORA)

In 1996, NIOSH unveiled the National Occupational Research Agenda (NORA), a framework to guide occupational safety and health research into the next decade. NORA represented collaboration between NIOSH and 500 organizations and individuals and produced a list of 21 priority research areas, one of which was work organization (National Institute for Occupational Safety and Health, 1996). Work organization refers to the way work processes are structured and managed, and it deals with subjects such as the following: the scheduling of work (such as work-rest schedules, hours of work and shift work), job design (such as complexity of tasks, skill and effort required, and degree of worker control), interpersonal aspects of work (such as relationships with supervisors and coworkers), career concerns (such as job security and growth opportunities), management style (such as participatory management practices and teamwork), and organizational characteristics (such as climate, culture, and communications).

Many of these elements are sometimes referred to as "psychosocial factors" and have long been recognized as risk factors for job stress and psychological strain. But recent studies suggest that work organization may have a broad influence on worker safety and health and may contribute to occupational injury, work-related musculoskeletal disorders, cardiovascular disease, and other occupational health concerns such as indoor air quality complaints. For example, work organization factors such as monotonous work/time pressure, and limited worker control have been linked to upper-extremity musculoskeletal disorders in a number of studies. Similarly, it is widely believed that the combination of low worker control and high job demands is a risk factor for cardiovascular disease. However, the manner in which work organization factors affect these types of health problems is not well understood.

Work organization is influenced by factors such as economic conditions, technologic change, demographic trends, and changing corporate and employment practices. Information and service industries are replacing manufacturing jobs. The workforce is aging rapidly and becoming increasingly diverse. Re-engineering and downsizing continue unabated, and temporary or part-time jobs are increasingly common. These trends may adversely affect work organization and may result, for example, in increased workload demands, longer and more varied work shifts, and job insecurity. However, the actual effects of these trends on the conditions of work and on the well-being of workers have received little study.

Today's rapidly changing economy, with widespread corporate and government restructuring, has thrown the once low-profile issues of work organization into high relief, and has raised a host of research questions in need of additional study. For instance, if a factory or service operates around the dock to maximize productivity or attend to customer needs, what strategies will both assure productivity and prevent the adverse effects of night or extended shifts on injury rates or sleep disorders? What management approaches translate employer and employee concern about safety into actions that effectively prevent injury? How do 12-hour work shifts or "de-skilling" of certain jobs affect rates of sick leave, employee turnover, workers' compensation, and health care costs? How can such costs be avoided?

Definitive research is needed to clarify the relationship between psychosocial stressors associated with work organization and safety and health concerns ranging from substance abuse to musculoskeletal disorders. Also, a wide range of research is needed to identify successful interventions and models of work organization that promote safety and health and that meet current and future demands for increasing productivity.

Healthy Work Organizations

One of the goals of NORA was to develop partnerships with outside groups in the conduct of safety and health research. In the area of job stress, one such partnership is noteworthy. In 1993, NIOSH entered into an agreement with Corning Inc. to study job stress and stress prevention. No funds were exchanged; rather, NIOSH provided technical assistance to Corning, Inc. in the assessment of work stress while Corning Inc. allowed NIOSH to analyze its employee opinion survey data. The Corning employee survey data was anonymous and did not allow tracking of employee responses over time. However, access to the survey data provided NIOSH with an opportunity to develop and test a model of healthy work organizations (Sauter, Lim & Murphy, 1996).

The employee survey contained three major categories of questions relating to macro-organizational characteristics of work: management practices (e.g. leadership, strategic planning, employee performance rewards, career develop-ment), organizational culture/climate (e.g. innovation, empowerment, diversity, inter-group cooperation), core values (e.g. individual worker, total quality, leadership, integrity). Additionally, the survey was used to obtain data on perceived organizational performance (e.g. overall organizational effectiveness, work group performance, personal effectiveness) and on worker well-being (e.g. job satisfaction, stress, turnover intentions).

Multivariate, multiple regression analyses were performed to identify those organizational characteristics associated with both performance and health outcomes (Lim & Murphy, 1996). Three separate multivariate regressions were performed, one for each of the three categories of organizational characteris-tics (management practices, culture/climate, and values). Thus, regression analysis was multivariate with respect to the health and productivity outcomes, but not in terms of the organizational characteristics. The results identified specific factors from each of the three categories of organizational characteris-tics that were linked to the performance and health indicators. Management practices associated with both organizational effectiveness and perceived stress were continuous improvement at work (i.e. TQM), career development, fair pay/rewards, human resource planning, and strategic planning. The culture/climate factors associated with these two organizational health indicators were conflict resolution, diversity, and sense of belonging. Finally, the core values associated with these two organizational health indicators were commitment to technology, employee growth/development, and valuing the individual (Lim & Murphy, 1997).

These findings provide provisional support for an organizational health model that proposes that management practices create the culture and climate, which influence performance and employee satisfaction (see Fig. 3). The NIOSH healthy work organization model, along with some alternative models, is being tested via a cooperative agreement with the University of Minnesota, Carlson School of Business.

The research on healthy work organizations reflected a shift in focus away from a strictly pathogenic model of the work experience and towards a salutogenic model. The pathogenic models focuses on job stress, poor mental and physical health, and reduced performance as main measures. A salutogenic or health promoting model adds measures of worker growth and development, satisfaction, high performance, and teamwork and considers the organizational culture and climate as key influences (Murphy, 2000).

2000 AND BEYOND: SOMETHING OLD, SOMETHING NEW

NIOSH research in the current decade is just beginning but several trends are noteworthy. First, earlier work continues on several fronts. For instance, the NIOSH/APA collaboration continues with respect to the Occupational Health Psychology Fellowship Program (*http://www.cdc.gov/niosh/ohp.html*). Moreover, another international meeting on work stress and health is planned for 2003 in Toronto, Canada, with NIOSH co-sponsorship. And research on characteristics of healthy work organizations continues and a grant was awarded to the U. of Georgia to develop and test models of healthy work. Also, a book on international studies of healthy work organizations was co-edited by NIOSH to highlight ongoing efforts to design healthy work organizations (Murphy & Cooper, 2000). New work involves the preparation of a national research agenda for the field of work organization, new funding for a national quality of work life survey, a national survey of organizations, a large contract study of women, work and depression, and studies on the health of aging workers.

Work Organization Research Agenda

In one of its most ambitious efforts, NIOSH worked with representatives from industry, labor, academia, and government to formulate a national research agenda for work organization research (*http://www.cdc.gov/niosh/02-116pd.html*). The

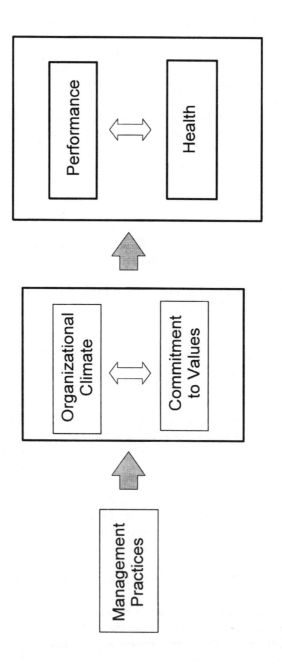

Fig. 3. NIOSH Provisional Model of Healthy Work Organizations.

agenda acknowledges that sweeping changes have occurred in the way jobs are designed and performed, in management and production methods, and in the human resource policies that accompany those changes. The changes include globalization, restructuring, flexible employment, longer hours of work, technological innovation, shifts in workforce demographics, and many other dynamics pertaining to work organization. The agenda recognized that such changes could have broad implications for worker health and safety, but they have occurred so quickly that they have outpaced scientists' ability to understand those implications. Consequently, researchers and others currently have only limited information for assessing the impacts.

Sauter, Brightwell, Colligan et al. (2002) proposed an ambitious plan to stimulate needed research to fill those gaps, including:

(1) Efforts to design and implement programs and systems for collecting data to better understand how the organization of work is changing.
(2) Increased study of potential safety and health risks associated with the changing organization of work.
(3) Increased research on interventions, examining ways to reorganize work to protect worker safety and health.
(4) Improvement of resources and training for researchers to help advance studies of work organization and occupational health and safety.

National Quality of Work Life Survey

It has been almost 30 years since NIOSH added questions on job stress to the 1972–1973 Quality of Employment Surveys, and 25 years since the last QES was administered. In light of the dramatic changes in the workplace since 1977, a nationally representative survey of the quality of work life (QWL) is long overdue. Organizational practices have changed dramatically in the past 15 years. To compete more effectively, many companies have restructured themselves and downsized their workforces, increased their reliance on non-traditional employment practices that depend on temporary workers and contractor-supplied labor, and adopted more flexible and lean production technologies. Women are disproportionately represented in jobs with restricted benefits and reduced flexibility, and they account for almost all of the growth in working hours. African-American women are twice as likely to be employed in temporary jobs than in traditional work arrangements, and (longer-tenured) older workers are at increased risk of displacement with greater earnings losses.

These changes have outpaced our understanding of their effects on worker safety and health and highlight the need for a national data collection effort to track major trends in organizational practices such as lean production and flexible manufacturing. Such a system also needs to acknowledge the changing workforce, which is increasingly populated by women, ethnic minorities, and older workers.

At the time of this writing (Spring 2002), information on the quality of work life are being collected by the National Opinion Research Center (NORC) from about 2,000 workers as part of the 2002 General Social Survey. The General Social Survey (GSS) is a biannual, personal interview survey of U.S. households conducted by NORC and partially funded by the National Science Foundation (NSF). The first survey took place in 1972 and since then more than 37,000 respondents have answered more than 3,500 different questions. The GSS contains a standard core of demographic and attitudinal variables, plus certain topics of special interest called "topical modules." Also, the GSS is part of the International Social Survey Program (ISSP), a continuing program of cross-national collaboration on surveys covering topics important for social science research. Over thirty countries are members of the ISSP.

A quality of work life (QWL) topic module was developed by NIOSH with advice from a multi-disciplinary panel that included industrial psychologists, sociologists, representatives from business, unions, and other federal agencies. A small group process was used to: (1) identify the key constructs that should be measured; (2) identify individual items to measure each construct; and (3) prioritize the items and constructs. The task turned out to be a classic good news, bad news scenario. The good news was that for the first time in 30 years, we could develop items for a national survey of workers. The bad news was that the items we selected had to fit into a 20-minute interview module. It was estimated that 60–80 questions could be administered in 20-minutes, depending on item wording and response scales used. By comparison, the 1977 QES contained over 300 items.

We began by identifying those items and constructs in the QES that were important and timely in the modern workplace. We were surprised at how many constructs from the QES were still relevant today (e.g. work-family issues, job security, hours of work). To this list was added new constructs that were not measured in the 1977 QES but were important and timely. Then we grouped the entire list of constructs into five broad categories: Job design/task characteristics, employee development/job future, organizational climate, individual/non-work factors, and outcomes. The distribution of items/constructs within each category was inspected to ensure adequate representation of each category. Next, multi-item scales (at least three items each) were created and then each participant rated the importance of each construct for inclusion in the module (a high, medium and low rating).

The module that resulted from this process was 120 items, fully 40 items more than our estimated maximum allotment. The size of the module was reduced first by retaining constructs, but dropping items within constructs. This produced a 90-item survey that was pre-tested in July 2001. The pre-test revealed that we needed to drop an additional 12 items from the module. As before, we decided to achieve the reduction by droppings items within constructs, not by dropping constructs. The final module consisted of 76 questions, half of which were taken directly from the 1977 QES. Topic areas covered by the module are shown in Table 3.

Table 3. List of Categories and Constructs Measured in the NIOSH Quality of Work Life Module to the 2002 General Social Survey.

Category name (No. of items)				
Job level (41 items)			*Culture/climate (11 items)*	
Workload	3		Safety climate	3
Autonomy	2		Discrimination	3
Pay/pay equity	3		Harassment	2
Skill utilization	2		Respect	1
Participation	2		Trust	1
Job future	2		Mgt. relationship	1
Repetitive work	2			
Resource adequacy	2		*Health outcomes (9 items)*	
Reward/recognition	2		Physical health	5
Skill utilization	2		Mental health	3
Supervisory behavior	2		Injuries	1
Coworker relations	2			
Promotions	2		*Other outcomes (6 items)*	
Variety	2		Performance	2
Occupation	2		Satisfaction	2
Job tenure	1		Intent to leave	1
Training	1		Job commitment	1
Layoffs	1			
Teamwork	1		*Hours of work (6 items)*	
Role clarity	1		Work at home	2
Role conflict	1		Overtime	2
Staffing	1		*Flexibility*	*1*
Safety and health	1		*Work/family*	*(4 items)*
Other/misc.	1		*Supervision*	*(3 items)*
			Benefits	*(1 items)*
			Union	*(1 items)*
			TOTAL =	76 Items

National Organizations Survey

To complement the QWL module, NIOSH is co-sponsoring a 3rd wave of the National Organizations Survey (NOS) that was first administered in 1991 (Kalleberg, Knoke, Marsden & Spaeth, 1996). The newest wave of the survey will be linked to the QWL module in that the sampling frame for the NOS will be based on the distribution of organizations represented in the 2002 GSS. The NOS will collect data on work practices and organizational programs and policies that the QWL module could not address (for reasons of limited size) and will be administered in the October-December 2002. In addition, NIOSH will add a special module to the NOS to gather data on the incidence of work-place violence and the presence and utility of violence intervention strategies. At the time of this writing, items for the NIOSH-sponsored modules for the NOS are being developed.

Depression, Cardiovascular Disease, and Work

A 5-year, prospective study has been funded to examine the relationship between depression, cardiovascular disease and work. The first component of the study examines the relationship between non-traditional work organization stressors (e.g. work-family conflicts, harassment, discrimination), traditional work organization stressors (e.g. job demands, control), and depression. Telephone survey data on non-traditional and traditional work organization stressors and depression will be collected from approximately 2,000 women and men working in administrative support positions (e.g. accounting, bookkeeping, clerical). Subjects will be drawn from 20 companies within two industries expected to vary with regard to work organization stressors (particularly non-traditional) and organizational policies, practices and programs. Data on absenteeism, disability and productivity will also be collected from personnel records. A Human Resources representative from each company will also provide infor-mation about specific HR policies and programs within their companies. It is hypothesized that workplace policies which prohibit discriminatory practices, and programs which promote career progression and work-family balance may attenuate the effects of work organization stressors on depression, especially among women workers.

A second effort investigates the prospective relationships between work organization (including job stressors) and depression among 10,000 men and 10,000 women. Job stressors will be assessed annually using both subjective and objective methods over a 5-year period. A questionnaire will be used that incorporates the NIOSH Generic Job Stress Questionnaire. This instrument captures a wide range of job stressors as well as factors (e.g. self-esteem, social support) thought to moderate or mediate the relationship between job stressors and their health consequences. The Center for Epidemiologic Studies Depression Scale (CES-D) will serve as the principal index of depression. An observational approach to assessing job stressors will also be employed which involve the use of a checklist and trained observers. An attempt will also be made to document all relevant information regarding objective stressor indicators (e.g. production quotas, staffing ratios, work pace rates). Two sources of stress (perceived discrimination and family-related demands) that are in part external to the work environment will also be assessed in this study.

Health of Aging Workers

Analyses of data from the Bureau of Labor Statistics, the Health and Retirement Survey, and the National Health Interview Survey are being performed to identify occupations/industries with the largest number of older workers during the next decade and the health conditions/risks that workers face as they grow older. An effort will be made to determine at what age health conditions or disabilities begin to change, with particular attention to those which appear to be further accelerated by work, or where the workplace might offer an opportunity to reduce rates of disease. In addition, NIOSH funded an occupational supplement to a four-year, multi-site study being conducted by the National Institute on Aging (NIA). The supplement will collect detailed occupation/industry information, work history and exposure to a variety of job stressors. In a related effort, physiological measures (e.g. changes in cortisol level) will be collected for subjects participating in a simulated work task at one of the NIA study sites.

SUMMARY

We've learned a great deal about job stress and health since the NIOSH stress research program was established in 1972. We learned that job stress was not merely a "fad" in the 1970s but has endured as a significant workplace concern. We learned that management and labor groups viewed stress from quite different perspectives; the former saw job stress as a personal problem while the latter viewed it as exclusively a workplace issue. We learned that while the research community had difficulty defining stress, workers rarely lacked for a definition and were adept at providing one if asked. We learned that job stress, unlike other workplace hazards (e.g. neurotoxic agents and ergonomic hazards), respects no occupational boundaries and so the potential for exposure to this class of health risks is ubiquitous. Finally, we learned that certain job conditions and work routines consistently produce health consequences (e.g. work overload, machine-pacing, rotating shift work, job insecurity, lack of control) but for other stressors (e.g. responsibility, cognitive demands), the relationship with health status is less consistent and probably moderated by individual and/or social factors or possibly by unmeasured work factors (e.g. organizational culture or climate).

On the other hand, there is a lot we haven't figured out about job stress and health relationships. For instance, we don't know much about the influence of worker self-selection and occupational 'drift' on job stress, in part because most studies have employed a cross-sectional design. We don't know enough about the contribution of objective job features vs. subjective perceptions in job stress and how these factors interact with organizational culture and climate to influence worker health and safety. Finally, although NIOSH routinely advocates job and organizational change interventions to reduce stress at work, we don't know with reasonable certainty which organizational change interventions will produce significant reductions in worker stress symptoms (see reviews by Parkes & Sparks, 1998; Van der Klink, Blonk, Schene & van Dijk, 2001), or if the reductions are larger than those seen after stress management training (Murphy, 1996). This latter point is especially challenging; either our job stress/health models are missing some important causal connections, or the link between job stressors and health is smaller than we thought, or the influence of non-work factors is larger than we thought. Much additional research is necessary to clarify job stress/health relationships.

The mission of NIOSH is to ensure safe and healthful working conditions for America's workers. The job stress research program has contributed to that mission by: (1) funding studies to identify job characteristics and working conditions that contribute to mental and physical health consequences for workers; (2) designing and testing interventions to prevent, reduce and manage stress at work; (3) disseminating the results of job stress studies to a wide audience; and (4) promoting job stress research in the private sector via grants, contracts and the sponsorship of national and international conferences.

REFERENCES

Althouse, R., & Hurrell, J. J., Jr. (1977). *An analysis of job stress in coal mining.* DHHS (NIOSH) Publication No. 77-217, Washington, D.C.: U.S. Government Printing Office.

Boxer, P. A., Singal, M., & Hartle, R. W. (1984). An epidemic of psychogenic illness in an electronics plant. *Journal of Occupational Medicine, 26,* 381–385.

Caplan, R. D., Cobb, S., French, J. R. P., Jr., Van Harrison, R., & Pinneau, S. R. (1975). *Job demands and worker health.* DHEW(NIOSH) Publication No. 75-160, Washington, D.C.: U.S. Government Printing Office.

Chadwick, J. H., Chesney, M. A., Black, G. W., Rosenman, R. H., & Sevelius, G. G. (1979). *Psychological job stress and coronary heart disease.* Final Report on Contract No. CDC-99-74-42, Washington, D.C.: U.S. Government Printing Office.

Cohen A. (1977). Factors in successful occupational safety programs. *Journal of Safety Research, 9,* 168–178.

Cohen, A., & Margolis, B. (1973). Initial psychological research related to the Occupational Safety and Health Act of 1970. *American Psychologist, 28,* 600–606.

Cobb, S., & Kasl, S. V. (1977). *Termination: The consequences of job loss.* DHHS (NIOSH) Publication No. 77-224, Washington, D. C. U.S. Government Printing Office.

Cole, L., Grubb, P., Sauter, S., Swanson, N., & Lawless, P. (1997). Psychosocial correlates of harassment, threats, and fear of violence in the workplace. *Scandinavian Journal of Work Environment and Health, 23,* 450–457.

Colligan, M. J., & Murphy, L. R. (1979). Mass psychogenic illness: An overview. *Journal of Occupational Psychology, 52,* 77–90.

Colligan, M. J., Pennebacker, J. W., & Murphy, L. R. (1982). *Mass psychogenic illness: A social psychological analysis.* Hillsday, New Jersey: Lawrence Erlbaum Associates.

Colligan, M. J., Smith, M. J., & Hurrell, J. J., Jr. (1977). Occupational incidence rates of mental heath disorders. *Journal of Human Stress, 3,* 34–39.

Cooper C. L., & Marshall J. (1976). Occupational sources of stress: A review of the literature relating to coronary heart disease and mental ill health. *Journal of Occupational Psychology, 49,* 11–28.

DeJoy, D., Murphy, L. R., & Gershon, R. M. (1995). The influence of employee, job/task, and organizational factors on adherence to Universal Precautions among nurses. *International Journal of Industrial Ergonomics, 16,* 43–55.

Elliott, G. R., & Eisdorfer, C. (Eds) (1982). *Stress and human health.* New York: Springer Publishing Company.

Galinsky, T., Swanson, N., Sauter, S. L., Hurrell, J. J., & Schleifer, L. M. (2000). A field study of supplementary rest breaks for data-entry operators. *Ergonomics, 43,* 622–638.

Ganster, D. (1989). Worker control and well-being: A review of research in the workplace. In: S. Sauter, J. J. Hurrell & C. L. Cooper (Eds), *Job Control and Worker Health.* Chichester: John Wiley.

Gershon, R. M., Murphy, L. R., Felknor, S., Vesley, D., & DeJoy, D. (1995). Compliance with Universal Precautions among health care workers. *American Journal of Infection Control, 23,* 225–236.

Goldenhar, L., Swanson, N., Hurrell, J. J., Ruder, A., & Deddens, J. (1998). Stressors and adverse health outcomes for female construction workers. *Journal of Occupational Health Psychology, 3,* 19–32.

Gowing, M. K., Quick, J. C., & Kraft, J. D.(1998). *The new organizational reality: Downsizing, restructuring and revitalization.* Washington, D.C.: American Psychological Association.

Grosch, J., & Murphy, L. R. (1998). Occupational differences in depression and global health: Results from a national sample of U.S. workers. *Journal of Occupational and Environmental Medicine, 40,* 153–164.

Grubb, P., & Swanson, N. (1999). Identification of work organization risk factors in construction work. In: A. Singh, J. Hinze & R. J. Coble (Eds), *Implementation of Safety and Health on Construction Sites.* Brookfield: Balkema, Rotterdam.

Hoiberg, A. (1982). Occupational stress and disease incidence. *Journal of Occupational Medicine, 24,* 445–451.

Hurrell, J. J., Jr. (1985). Machine-paced work and the Type A behavior pattern. *Journal of Occupational Psychology, 58,* 15–26.

Hurrell, J. J., Jr., & McLaney, M. (1988). Control, stress, and job satisfaction in Canadian nurses. *Work and Stress*, *2*, 217–224.

Hurrell, J. J. Jr., Pate, A., & Kliesmet, R. (1984). *Stress among police officers*. DHHS (NIOSH) Publication No. 84-108. Washington, D.C.: U.S. Government Printing Office.

Hurrell, J. J., Murphy, L. R., Sauter, S. L., & Cooper, C. L. (Eds) (1988). *Issues in occupational stress research* (p. 219). London: Taylor & Francis.

Kalleberg, A. L., Knoke, D., Marsden, P. V., & Spaeth, J. L. (1996). *Organizations in America: Analyzing their structures and human resource practices*. Newbury Park, CA: Sage.

Karasek, R. A. (1989). Control in the workplace and its health-related aspects. In: S. Sauter, J. J. Hurrell & C. L. Cooper (Eds), *Job Control and Worker Health*. Chichester: John Wiley.

Karasek, R. A. (1979). Job demands, decision latitude, and mental strain: Implications for job redesign. *Administrative Science Quarterly*, *24*, 285–307.

Karasek, R. A., Schwartz, J., & Theorell, T. (1982). *Job characteristics, occupation, and coronary heart disease*. Final Report on contract No. R-01-0H00906. Cincinnati, Ohio: NIOSH.

Karasek, R. A., Theorell, T., Schwartz, J. E., Schnall, P. L., Pieper, C. F., & Michela, J. L. (1988). Job characteristics in relation to the prevalence of myocardial infarction in the U.S. Health Examination Survey (HES) and the Health and Nutrition Examination Survey (HANES). *American Journal of Public Health*, *78*, 682–684.

Kasl, S. (1989). An epidemiological perspective on the role of control in health. In: S. Sauter, J. J. Hurrell & C. L. Cooper (Eds), *Job Control and Worker Health*. Chichester: John Wiley.

Kasl, S. V. (1978). Epidemiological contributions to the study of work stress. In: C. L. Cooper & R. Payne (Eds), *Stress at Work*. Chichester: John Wiley.

Kasl, S. V. (1987). Methodologies in stress and health: past difficulties, present dilemmas, future directions. In: S. V. Kasl & C. L. Cooper (Eds), *Stress and Health: Issues in Research Methodology*. New York: John Wiley and Sons.

Keita G. P., & Hurrell J. J. Jr. (Eds) (1994). *Job stress in a changing workforce*. Washington, D.C.: American Psychological Association.

Keita G. P., & Sauter S. L. (Eds) (1992). *Work and well-being: An agenda for the 1990s*. Washington, D.C.: American Psychological Association.

Kerckhoff, A., & Back, K. (1968). *The June bug: A study of hysterical contagion*. New York: Appleton-Century-Crofts.

Key, M. (1971). Responsibilities of the Department of Health, Education, and Welfare under Public Law 91-596. *Journal of Occupational Medicine*, *13*, 322–324.

Kidd, P. S., Scharf, T., & Veazie, M. A. (1996). Linking stress and injury in the farming environment: A secondary analysis of qualitative data. In: C. A. Heaney & L. M. Goldenhar (Eds), *Health Education Quarterly* (Vol. 23, pp. 224–237).

Kroes, W. H., & Hurrell J. J. Jr. (1976). *Job stress and the police officer: Identifying stress reduction techniques*. DHHS (NIOSH) Publication No. 76-187, Washington, D.C., U.S. Government Printing Office.

Kroes, W. H., Margolis, B., & Hurrell, J. J. Jr. (1974). Job stress in policemen. *Journal of Police Science and Administration*, *2*, 145–155.

Kroes, W. H., Hurrell, J. J. Jr., & Margolis B. (1974). Job stress in police administrators. *Journal of Police Science and Administration*, *2*, 381–387.

Levi L. (Ed.) (1971). *Society, stress, and disease*. London: Oxford University Press.

Lim, S. Y., & Murphy L. R. (1997). Models of healthy work organizations. In: P. Seppälä, T. Luopajärvi, C.-H. Nygård & M. Mattila (Eds), *From Experience to Innovation* (Vol. 1, pp 501–503). Helsinki, Finland: Finnish Institute of Occupational Health.

Lim, S. Y., & Murphy L. R. (1996). Stress: its impact on organizational effectiveness. In: O. Baron & H. W. Hendrick (Eds), *Human Factors in Organizational Design and Management*. Amsterdam, Netherlands: Elsevier Science.

McLean, A. (1970). *Mental health and work organizations*. Chicago, Illinois: Rand McNally and Company.

McLean, A. (1974). *Occupational stress*. Springfield, Illinois: Charles Thomas.

McLean, A. (1967). *To work is human: Mental health and the business community*. New York: The MacMillan Company.

McLean, A., Black, G., & Colligan, M. (Eds) (1978). *Reducing occupational stress*. DHHS (NIOSH) Publication No. 78-140, Washington, D.C.: U.S. Government Printing Office.

Margolis, B. L., & Kroes, W. H. (1974). Occupational stress and strain. *Occupational Mental Health, 2*, 4–6.

Margolis, B., Kroes, W. H., & Quinn, R. P. (1974). Job stress: An unlisted occupational hazard. *Journal of Occupational Medicine, 16*, 659–661.

Millar, J. D. (1984). Letter to the Editor. *Journal of Occupational Medicine, 26*, 340–341.

Moon, S. D., & Sauter, S. L. (Eds) (1996). *Beyond biomechanics: Psychosocial aspects of musculoskeletal disorders in office work*. London: Taylor and Francis, Ltd.

Murphy, L. R. (1983). A comparison of relaxation methods for reducing stress. *Human Factors, 25*, 431–440.

Murphy, L. R. (1991). Job dimensions associated with severe disability due to cardiovascular disease. *Journal of Clinical Epidemiology, 44*, 155–166.

Murphy, L. R. (2000). Models of healthy work organizations. In: L. R. Murphy & C. L. Cooper (Eds), *Healthy and Productive Work: An International Perspective*. London: Taylor-Francis.

Murphy, L. R. (1984a). Occupational stress management: A review and appraisal. *Journal of Occupational Psychology, 57*, 1–15.

Murphy, L. R. (1984b). Stress management in highway maintenance workers. *Journal of Occupational Medicine, 26*, 436–442.

Murphy, L. R. (1996). Stress management in work settings: A critical review of the research literature. *American Journal of Health Promotion, 11*, 112–135.

Murphy, L. R., & Cooper C. L. (2000). *Healthy and productive work: An international perspective*. London: Taylor-Francis.

Murphy, L. R., Hurrell, J. J., Sauter, S., & Keita, G. (Eds) (1995). *Job stress interventions*. Washington, D.C.: American Psychological Association.

Murphy, L. R., & Pepper, L. (2002). Effects of organizational downsizing on worker stress and health: A North American case study. In: C. Peterson (Ed.), *Work Stress: Studies of the Context, Content and Outcomes of Stress*. New York: Baywood Publishing Company.

Murphy, L. R., & Schoenborn, T. F. (Eds) (1989). *Stress management in work settings*. New York: Praeger Publishers.

National Institute for Occupational Safety and Health (1996). *National occupational research agenda*. DHHS (NIOSH) Publication No. 96-138. Washington, D.C.: U.S. Government Printing Office.

National Institute for Occupational Safety and Health (1980). *New developments in occupational stress*. DHHS (NIOSH) Publication No. 81-102. Washington, D.C.: U.S. Government Printing Office.

National Institute for Occupational Safety and Health (1978). *Occupational stress conference proceedings*. DHHS (NIOSH) Publication No. 78-156. Washington, D.C.: U.S. Government Printing Office.

National Institute for Occupational Safety and Health (1988). *Proposed national strategies for the prevention of work-related diseases and injuries.* DHHS (NIOSH) Publication number 89-137: Washington, D.C.: U.S. Government Printing Office.

O'Toole, J. (Ed.) (1974). *Work and the quality of life: Resource papers for Work in America.* Cambridge, MA: MIT Press.

Parkes, K., & Sparkes, T. J. (1998). *Organizational interventions to reduce work stress. Are They Effective? A Review of the literature.* United Kingdom: Health and Safety Executive, RR193/98 ISBN 0-7176-1625-8.

Public Law 91-596 (1970). 91st Congress, S. 2193. *Occupational Safety and Health Act.*

Quick, J. C., Murphy, L. R., & Hurrell, J. J. (1992). *Stress and well-being at work: Assessments and interventions for occupational mental health.* Washington, D.C.: American Psychological Association.

Quinn, R., Seashore, S., Kahn, R., Mangione, T., Campbell, D., Staines, G., & McCullough, M. (1971). *Survey of working conditions: Final report on univariate and bivariate tables.* Document No. 2916-0001. Washington, D.C.: U.S. Government Printing Office.

Quinn, R. P., & Shepard, L. J. (1974). *The 1972–1973 quality of employment survey.* Ann Arbor, Institute for Social Research, The University of Michigan.

Quinn, R. P., & Staines, G. L. (1979). *The 1977 quality of employment survey.* Ann Arbor, Institute for Social Research, The University of Michigan.

Rosa, R. R. (1991). Performance, alertness, and sleep after 3.5 years of 12-hour shifts: A follow-up study. *Work and Stress, 5,* 107–116.

Rosa, R. R., & Bonnet, M. H. (1993). Performance and alertness on 8-hour and 12-hour rotating shifts at a natural gas utility. *Ergonomics, 36,* 1177–1193.

Rosa, R. R., & Colligan, M. J. (1988). Long workdays vs. rest days: Assessing fatigue and alertness with a portable performance battery. *Human Factors, 30,* 305–317.

Rosa, R. R., & Colligan, M. J. (1997). *Plain language about shiftwork.* DHHS (NIOSH) Publication No. 97-145.

Rosa, R. R., Colligan, M. J., & Lewis, P. (1989). Extended workdays: Effects of 8-hour and 12-hour rotating shift schedules on performance, subjective alertness, sleep patterns, and psychosocial variables. *Work and Stress, 3,* 21–32.

Rosa, R. R., & Colligan, M. J. (1988). Long workdays vs. restdays: Assessing fatigue and alertness with a portable performance battery. *Human Factors, 30,* 305–317.

Rosenstock, L. (1997). Work organization at the National Institute for Occupational Safety and Health. *Journal of Occupational Health Psychology, 2,* 7–10.

Salvendy, G., & Smith, M. J. (1981). *Machine pacing and occupational stress.* London: Taylor and Francis, Ltd.

Sauter, S. L., Brightwell, W. S., Colligan, M. J., Hurrell, J. J., Jr., Katz, T. M., LeGrande, D. E., Lessin, N., Lippin, R. A., Lipscomb, J. A., Murphy, L. R., Peters, R. H., Keita, G. P., Robertson, S. R., Stellman, J. M., Swanson, N. G., & Tetrick, L. E. (2002). *The changing organization of work and the safety and health of working people: Knowledge gaps and research directions.* DHHS (NIOSH) Publication No. 2002-116. Washington, D.C.: U.S. Government Printing Office.

Sauter, S. L., Gottlieb, M. S., Rohrer, K. M., & Dodson, V. N. (1983). *The well-being of video display terminal users.* Final report on NIOSH on P.O. 79-0034, Cincinnati, Ohio (USA).

Sauter S., Hurrell, J. J., & Cooper, C. L. (Eds), 1989. *Job control and worker health.* Chichester: John Wiley.

Sauter, S. L., Hurrell, J. J., Fox, H. R., Tetrick, L., & Barling, J. (1999). Occupational health psychology: An emerging discipline. *Industrial Health, 37,* 199–211.

Sauter, S. L., Lim, S. Y., & Murphy, L. R. (1996). Organizational health: A new paradigm for occupational stress research at NIOSH. *Japanese Journal of Occupational Mental Health*, *4*, 248–254.

Sauter, S. L., & Knutson, S. J. (1984). *Ergonomic evaluation of VDT workplaces in New York State Departments of taxation and motor vehicles*. Final report on NIOSH P.O. 84-1929.

Sauter, S. L., & Murphy, L. R. (Eds) (1995). *Organizational risk factors for job stress*. Washington, D.C.: American Psychological Association.

Sauter S., Murphy, L. R., & Hurrell, J. J., Jr. (1990). Prevention of work-related psychological disorders: A national strategy proposed by the National institute for Occupational Safety and Health. *American Psychologist*, *45*, 1146–1158.

Scharf, T., Kidd, P., Cole, H., Bean, T., Chapman, L., Donham, K., & Baker, D. (1998). Intervention tools for farmers: Safe and productive work practices in a safer work environment. *Journal of Agricultural Safety and Health*, (Special issue)(1), 193–203.

Schmitt, N., & Fitzgerald, M. (1982). Psychogenic illness: Individual and aggregate data. In: M. J. Colligan, J. W. Pennebacker & L. R. Murphy (Eds), *Mass Psychogenic Illness: A Social Psychological Analysis*. Hillsday, New Jersey: Lawrence Erlbaum Associates.

Schleifer, L. M. (1994). End-tidal PCO_2 as an index of psychophysiological activity during VDT data entry work and relaxation. *Ergonomics*, *37*, 245–254.

Schleifer, L. M., & Amick, B. (1989). System response time and method of pay: Stress effects in computer-based tasks. *International Journal of Human-Computer Interaction*, *1*, 23–39.

Schroeder, D., Rosa, R. R., & Witt, A. (1998). Effects of 8- vs. 10-hour work schedules on the performance of air traffic control specialists. *International Journal of Industrial Ergonomics*, *21*, 307 321.

Sleight, R. B., & Cook, K. G. (1974). *Problems in occupational safety and health: A critical review of select worker physical and psychological factors*. DHHS (NIOSH) Publication No. 75-124. Washington, D.C.: U.S. Government Printing Office.

Smith, M. J., Hurrell, J. J., Jr., & Murphy, R. K., Jr. (1981). Stress and health effects in paced and unpaced work. In: G. Salvendy & M. J. Smith (Eds), *Machine Pacing and Occupational Stress*. London: Taylor and Francis Ltd.

Smith, M. J., Cohen, B. F. G., Stammerjohn, L., & Happ, A. (1981). An investigation of health complaints and job stress in video display operations. *Human Factors*, *23*, 387–400.

Smith, M. J., Colligan, M. J., Frockt, I. J., & Tasto, D. (1979). Occupational injury rates among nurses as a function of shift. *Journal of Safety Research*, *4*, 181–187.

Stahl, S., & Lebedun, M. (1974). Mystery gas: an analysis of mass hysteria. *Journal of Health and Social Behavior*, *14*, 44–50.

Stammerjohn, L., & Wilkes, B (1981). Stress/strain and line speed in paced work. In: G. Salvendy & M. J. Smith (Eds), *Machine Pacing and Occupational Stress*. London: Taylor and Francis Ltd.

Tasto, D. L., Colligan, M. J., Skjei, E. W., & Polly, S. J. (1978). *Health consequences of shiftwork*. DHHS (NIOSH) Publication No. 78-154. Washington, D.C.: U.S. Government Printing Office.

Van der Klink, J. J. L., Blonk, R. W. B., Schene, A. H., & van Dijk, F. J. H. (2001). The benefits of interventions for work-related stress. *American Journal of Public Health*, *91*, 270–276.

Wilkes, B., Stammerjohn, L., & Lalich, N. (1981). Job demands and worker health in machine-paced poultry inspection. *Scandinavian Journal of Work Environment and Health*, *7*, 12–19.

Work in America (1973). *Report of a special task force to the Secretary of Health, Education, and Welfare*. Cambridge, MA: MIT Press.

Zohar D. (1980). Safety climate in industrial organizations. Theoretical and applied implications. *Journal of Applied Psychology*, *65*, 96–102.

THE HEALTHY WORK ORGANIZATION MODEL: EXPANDING THE VIEW OF INDIVIDUAL HEALTH AND WELL BEING IN THE WORKPLACE

Robert J. Vandenberg, Kyoung-Ok Park,
David M. DeJoy, Mark G. Wilson and
C. Shannon Griffin-Blake

ABSTRACT

*With occupational stress representing just one example, different streams
of research have emerged over the past several decades to explain the
antecedents to and consequences of possessing a "healthy" workforce. A
positive characteristic of these seemingly independent efforts is that a
triangulation of results has emerged supporting the importance of attending
to the health and well being of the individual worker. A drawback to these
efforts, though, is that while utilizing at times the identical constructs, these
constructs are configured differently depending on the conceptual premises
of the focal framework. In an attempt to bring the different perspectives
together, a model of the "healthy work organization" is presented and
tested in this chapter. The model recognizes that there are higher-order*

Historical and Current Perspectives on Stress and Health, Volume 2, pages 57–115.
ISBN: 0-7623-0970-9

constructs characterizing many of the component constructs of the previous efforts, and it is at this level that much of the unification of those efforts is achieved. Utilizing structural equation modeling procedures, the healthy work organization model was supported.

INTRODUCTION

While referred to variously by different names (e.g. work stress, job stress, workplace stress, etc.), occupational stress has been unquestionably a prominent characteristic over the past three decades for describing a "healthy work organization" (Hendrix, Summers, Leap & Steel, 1995). As such, occupational stress has been the primary focus during this time period of much theoretical and empirical research resulting in a proliferation of models and frameworks describing both its content and its process (Beehr, 1995). Reinforcing its prominence as a research theme is the simple fact that occupational stress is not just the purview of one discipline or area. Rather, it is a frequently addressed topic in the top journals of many disciplines including medicine (e.g. Hallquivist, Diderichsen, Theorell, Reuterwall & Ahlbom, 1998), public health (e.g. Mausner-Dorsch & Eaton, 2000), epidemiology (e.g. Muntaner, Anthony, Crum & Eaton, 1995), health services (e.g. Cahill & Landsbergis, 1996), health education (e.g. Heaney, 1991), industrial/organizational psychology (e.g. Edwards & Harrison, 1993), management and organizational behavior (e.g. Xie & Johns, 1995), and labor relations (e.g. O'Brien & Stevens, 1981). Further, whole edited volumes, such as the one in which this chapter finds itself and others (e.g. Beehr & Bhagat, 1985; Cooper, 1998; Sauter & Murphy, 1995), are frequently published to promote current research and thinking. Finally, perhaps the ultimate benchmark of its importance is the number of funding initiatives devoted to a deepened understanding of the healthy workplace, such as the National Occupational Research Agenda, which provided support for the research reported in the current chapter.

Why has understanding occupational stress risen to such importance? One major reason is the estimated costs associated with occupational stress – not only to the individual suffering from high levels of stress but also to organizations, the insurance industry, and to society. The annual cost of occupational stress to U.S. businesses, for example, is estimated to be a very conservative $100 billion annually (Landsbergis & Vivona-Vaughan, 1995). Depression, the major psychological symptom of stress, alone is estimated to cost $44 billion annually due to its deleterious effects on absenteeism, job performance, and other workplace behaviors (Greenberg, Kessler, Nells, Finkelstein & Berndt, 1996; Kessler, Barber, Birnbaum, Frank, Greenberg, Rose, Simon & Wang,

1999). Other factors stemming from occupational stress and adding tremendously to the costs include medical expenditures related to disease, safety violations, accidents, and suicide. For example, psychological indices like depression contribute to the prevalence of cardiovascular disease. As is well known, cardiovascular disease is the leading cause of death among the adult population, and the total medical cost of cardiovascular disease is estimated at around $329 billion in the United States (American Heart Association, 2001). What is less commonly understood in the general population is that a greater portion of the variance in cardiovascular disease is accounted for by psychological factors (i.e. stress) rather than physical ones (Koslowsky, 1998; Theorell & Karasek, 1996). Understanding why occupational stress has emerged in importance is quite obvious when these costs are considered. Namely, by making it a priority research issue, it is hoped that the resulting knowledge will provide the basis around which to design interventions targeted toward its control, and ideally, its eradication.

Toward this end, several theoretical frameworks of occupational stress have emerged over the past three decades. Arguably, the three most prevalent and influential conceptual viewpoints are person-environment fit theory (French, Caplan & Harrison, 1982), the framework of occupational stress (House, 1981), and the demand-control-support model (Karasek, 1979). These three frameworks have been and continue to be foundations for research on occupational stress as evidenced by the fact that most contemporary researchers reference one or more of the frameworks when generating their specific research questions (e.g. Eden, 2002; Spector & Goh, 2002). As with all foundations, unless they are built upon, they offer only a limited perspective on the phenomenon of interest. For reasons articulated later in this chapter, we argue that stakeholder interest (e.g. the individual worker, medicine and health, organizational decision makers, labor unions, Federal and State agencies, etc.) is not just in occupational stress per se. Rather, their interests could be more generally characterized as wanting to identify the *healthy work organization* in which not only is occupational stress considered, but also other factors, such as health promotion and safety and risk management. Further, stakeholder interest is in the *work organization* because it brings a human capital orientation to workplace health and recognizes that there are important linkages between preserving and enhancing human capital and maximizing business strategy (Becker, Huselid, Pickus & Spratt, 1997; Goetzel & Ozminkowski, 2000).

The intent of this chapter is to introduce a conceptual model of the healthy work organization, and to provide empirical evidence supporting its validity. As will be seen shortly, while occupational stress is an important tenet underlying the proposed model, it is not the only perspective represented. We argue that this more general, healthy-work-organization perspective provides several needed extensions to the research in occupational stress:

• Despite *theoretical* claims for the existence of antecedents to the class of variables referred to as stressors in models of occupational stress (e.g. French et al., 1982), rarely are the antecedents included in actual empirical tests. The class of antecedents referred to here is the policies, beliefs and values transmitted by the *work organization* that support a "healthy" (i.e. less stressful) work environment. Thus, for reasons articulated in subsequent sections, the current test incorporates a set of antecedents referred to generally as organizational attributes.

• Even a cursory review of the empirical studies in occupational stress reveals that researchers operationalize "stressors" and "strains," and other model components using a host of variables. That is, there is no single operationalization of either a "stressor" or "strain" construct, or the other constructs within the occupational stress models. Stressors, for example, are commonly operationalized through measures of role conflict, job demands, autonomy, and a host of other variables in which the theme is on the requirements placed on workers through the job and its characteristics (e.g. Baker, Israel & Schurman, 1996). Strains are also variously operationalized through a multitude of constructs such as job satisfaction, organizational commitment, and anxiety (e.g. French et al., 1982; Spector & Goh, 2002). The point is that occupational stress researchers have adopted a multivariate perspective to operationalize the key components of their stress models with the assumption being that there is a common element underlying the component that ties the variables together. Yet, their actual empirical tests to date have not encompassed the assumption of there being a "higher-order" linkage among the variables characterizing a given model component. Rather, the tests of relationships have been primarily between one variable and another. A feature of the current healthy work organization model is that these higher-order components are isolated, and it is between them that the hypothesized relationships are examined.

• Another troublesome characteristic of the variables used to operationalize occupational stress model components is that they are identical to many of the same variables to operationalize components or linkages within many different conceptual frameworks of the organizational sciences. For example, Hackman and Oldham (1980) also propose linkages between job characteristics and outcomes like job satisfaction, and yet call this a "job characteristics model" and not an occupational stress model. Similarly, Hulin (1991) used many of the same variables as those in occupational stress models, and relationships among the variables, to define a theoretical model of employee work adjustment. A final example is the fact that Vandenberg, Richardson, and Eastman (1999) also used many of the same variables to test a model of high involvement work processes. Our point is not to imply that one configuration of the variables is more appropriate than another configuration. Rather, it is to recognize the need to take an integrative perspective – one that uses knowledge from many of these perspectives to accurately specify a model that captures the key points of all of these perspectives. To do so acknowledges the fact that regardless of the label used by the various researchers, the overarching concern among all of them is the work organization, and particularly, the need to create an environment that is "healthy" for all stakeholders. The healthy work organization model presented in the current chapter is an initial attempt at such integration.

The chapter is organized into four primary sections. The section immediately following is a very brief review of the three main conceptual frameworks in the occupational stress literature. The review is primarily context setting. The second section is a detailed presentation of the healthy work organization model, and the rationale underlying its design. The third section is the presentation of the tests of the models using over 3000 employees from 21 locations of the same corporation. The final section is discussion and conclusions.

MODELS OF OCCUPATIONAL STRESS

Since the 1960s, numerous models of occupational stress have been postulated in order to catch the entire picture of the relationship between work environment and workers' strain (Sparks & Cooper, 1999; Tetrick & LaRocco, 1987). As mentioned previously, the P-E fit theory (French, Rodgers & Cobb, 1974), the framework of occupational stress (House, 1981), and the demand-control-support model (Karasek, 1979) have had the largest overall impact with respect to driving occupational stress research. Each framework is reviewed briefly in the forthcoming paragraphs.

The Person-Environment (P-E) Fit Theory

The core premise of P-E fit theory is that stress arises from a misfit between person and environment, not from the two components separately (French, Rodger & Cobb, 1974). When people perceive that their work environments are not good or do not fit well with the needs, wants, and desires that they personally would like fulfilled from work, the discrepancies yield diverse strains, which are postulated to affect workers' health, well being, and work behaviors (Caplan, 1987; Caplan & Harrison, 1993; Edwards & Harrison, 1993). Figure 1 is a representative perspective within this stream of research.

Starting with "objective P-E fit" on the far left of Fig. 1, the assertion is that there is a "real" underlying fit between the objective environment of a position or job, and the objective attributes of the individual person holding that job. The objective environment places demands on the jobholder, which consist of quantitative and qualitative job requirements, role expectations, and group and organizational norms. Countering these demands are the individual's true abilities represented through the aptitudes, skills, training, time, and energy the person uses to meet the demands. Similarly, the objective environment also provides supplies consisting of the resources and rewards believed by the organization to meet adequate performance requirements in that position. The individual also has certain needs representing what is required to perform adequately, and encompassing physiological and psychological requirements of the job, values acquired through learning and socialization, and motives to achieve desired ends. The point is that the larger the discrepancy between the objective environment and the objective person, the greater the likelihood that a need for coping will arise (Edwards et al., 1998).

Whether that need for coping will eventually manifest itself in a person's behavioral and psychological responses at work (i.e. what is referred to as strains in Fig. 1) depends for the most part on the perceptual components of the model – the subjective environment and subjective person (Edwards & Harrison, 1993). Specifically, according to proponents of this perspective, stress is a subjective evaluation of whether perceived demands and supplies of the work environment are commensurate with the individual's perceptions of his/her own abilities and needs. If a large discrepancy is perceived, the individual may experience a great deal of strain, which simply defined are deviations from normal functioning in the individual's psychological, physical, and behavioral responses within the workplace (Edwards et al., 1998; Harrison, 1978). An important point of this perspective is just because a need for coping may exist based on "objective realities," it does not automatically mean that a person will experience stress and engage in defensive responding. Rather, whether strain is experienced at high levels depends on the subjective perceptions of the jobholder.

Over the years, a large quantity of research has been conducted on the P-E fit perspective. Representative is French et al.'s (1982) study using a using a random stratified sample of 318 workers in 23 occupations. The researchers operationalized both the subjective demands and supplies, and the subjective abilities and needs, and used 18 indices of psychological, physiological, and behavioral strains including job dissatisfaction, blood pressure, and smoking.

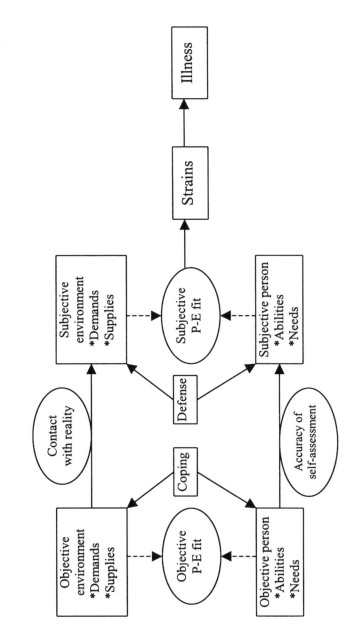

Fig. 1. A Model of Stress as Person-Environment Fit (Reprinted with permission from Edwards, Caplan & Harrison, 1998).

In general, they reported that subjective P-E fit was related most strongly to psychological strains, and to a lesser extent, physiological and behavioral strains. Depression was the most prominent psychological strain related to the P-E fit. Looking at the P-E fit literature collectively results in the following observations (Edwards, 1992). First, the relationships between P-E fit and various indices of strain have been well supported with the strongest associations occurring with psychological strain indices such as job dissatisfaction, anxiety, depressive symptoms, and somatic complaints. Second, because there are very few measures for objective P-E fit components (Harrison, 1985) and when used, there is little to no association with strains, most studies have only operationalized subjective P-E fit. Third, within the subjective P-E fit component, the majority of research has only operationalized the fit between perceived needs and supplies, and not between perceived demands and abilities.

The Framework of Occupational Stress

The framework of occupational stress (House, 1981) originated from the same theoretical foundation as that underlying the P-E fit perspective of occupational stress. That is, both models were based on French's (1963) programmatic social environment and mental health model. The framework of occupational stress shares two premises with P-E fit theory. One that stress arises from the misfit between person and environment, and the other is that subjective perceptions of work environments primarily determine strains. A major difference between House's framework of occupational stress and P-E fit theory is that House's entire framework together is occupational stress whereas P-E fit theory limits its focus on stress as arising only from the discrepancy between the subjective person and environment components. Figure 2 is a representative perspective within this stream of research.

The framework of occupational stress is based on a core definition, which is that occupational stress is a total process including the environmental sources of stress and the individual's perception of them as well as short-term and long-term physiological, psychological, and behavioral responses, and a number of modifying factors that influence the relationships among variables in the stress process (Israel, Schurman & House, 1989). Specifically, work stressors are the demands characterizing the individual's perceived role within the organization, and consist of such factors as role conflict, role ambiguity, underutilization, participation, and workload. Further, a combination of the work stressors determine individual perceived stress where perceived stress is cumulatively the individual's subjective negative feelings regarding the work environment such as job dissatisfaction. Perceived stress in turn shares a reciprocal relationship

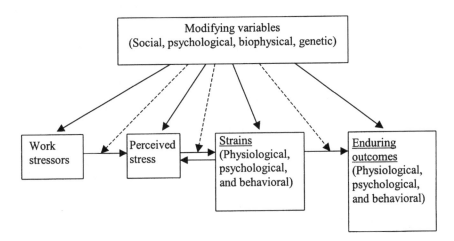

Fig. 2. The Framework of Occupational Stress (Reprinted with permission from Israel, Schurman & House, 1989).

with strains, which represent a class of relatively short-term responses such as depression, declines in performance, or excessive absences. The premise underlying the reciprocal association is that of a "snow-ball" effect where the negative feelings regarding work (stress) increase strains which in turn contribute even more to the negative feelings. The end result, however, is that the accumulation of physiological, psychological and behavioral strains will eventually result in long-term outcomes such as acute depression, alcoholism, unemployment, physiological problems (e.g. cardiovascular), and other costly results. The framework, however, recognizes that either the model components themselves or the associations between them could be tempered by a host of modifying factors such as social support, and the quality of interpersonal relationships within the work environment.

Like the P-E fit perspective, House's framework has been the subject of much research. Larocco, House, and French (1980), for example, confirmed the importance of social support by noting that it was negatively associated with one of their many strain measures, depression. Further, social support interacted with job satisfaction (an index of perceived stress) in explaining the impact of satisfaction on depression. Further, Israel, Schurman, and House (1989) reported that interpersonal relationships at work (a modifying factor in the model) explained 16% of the variance of work stressors and 13% of negative job feelings. In addition, depression was significantly associated with low perceived control, poor interpersonal relationships, and high-perceived work stressors.

In summary, the framework of occupational stress has been used to predict psychological strain and general health status as affected by the work environment. Job satisfaction, depression, and anxiety have been well predicted within the theoretical framework. However, most studies employing this framework to develop their research questions have examined only some parts or certain path relationships, and not the entire framework together.

The Demand-Control-Support Model

The demand-control-support model of occupational stress (Karasek, 1979) emphasizes the role of work content as the major source of stress. As such, Karasek divided job content into two components: (a) worker perceptions regarding the tasks that need to be completed in performing the job (job demands); and (b) worker perceptions about the degree of control or discretion they have in performing the job tasks (job control). Karasek (1979) conceptualized that the two constructs interacted with each other in affecting the amount of strain (i.e. mental and physical health) experienced by employees. The strongest levels of strain, and hence, the greatest levels of occupational stress were expected to occur in situations where there were extremely high demands, but very low control. Influenced by the research of House (1981), social support was added as a third component (Karasek & Theorell, 1990). While not eradicating strain totally, social support was predicted to buffer it to some degree even under high demand-low control conditions. Figure 3 is a representative perspective within this stream of research.

Karasek (1979) operationalized demands in Fig. 3 as a class of psychological stressors at work such as, and for example, requirements for working fast and hard, having a great deal to do, not having enough time, and having conflicting role and job demands. Job control was similarly operationalized as the individual's potential control over the tasks and the conduct of work and workflow. That is, Karasek regarded job control as a worker's latitude to have power over the diverse job demands. Social support was viewed as enlarging the latitude of job control even more, and as such, benefiting the individual in the same fashion as job control by reducing or buffering experienced strains. Social support has been typically operationalized through employees' perceptions of the amount of supervisor and/or coworker support. As indicated by the demand-control-support model in Figure 3, the highest level of strain would be expected in the "high strain, isolated" group. Workers in this group experience very high demands, and low control, and also perceive themselves as having no social support. Even with social support, low levels of psychological well being and fairly high levels of strain are still expected for those

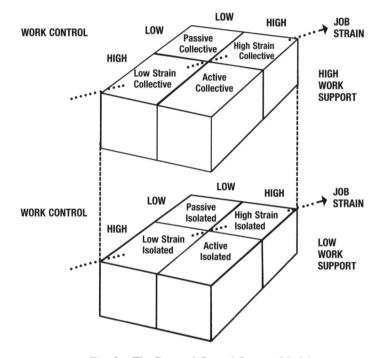

Fig. 3. The Demand-Control-Support Model
(Reprinted with permission from Johnson & Hall, 1988).

employees experiencing high demands and low control. As with the P-E fit model and the framework of occupational stress, researchers adopting the demand-control-support perspective have relied on multiple variables to operationalize the primary components of the model. For example, strain has been variously operationalized as cardiovascular disease, hypertension, anxiety, depression, somatic symptoms, and general mental well being (e.g. Karasek, Baker, Marxer, Ahlbom & Theorell, 1981; Mausner-Dorsch & Eaton, 2000). Research, however, has been generally supportive of the model. For example, more than one third of the published studies using the demand-control-support model have found clear effects of low job control, heavy job demands, and low support on elevated heart disease risk (Theorell & Karasek, 1996). Further, in a 9-year longitudinal study, Johnson, Hall and Theorell (1989) reported that men who belonged to the most favored 20% (low demand, high control, and high support) lived eight years longer on average than did the 20% of men in the least favored group (high demands, low control, and low support).

In summary, the demand-control-support model has been used primarily to predict psychological strain and cardiovascular disease risk, and has been very effective in this role. Further, research has generally supported many more main effects for demands, control, and support than interaction effects. Among the main effects, job control has emerged as the strongest factor determining strains (Kristensen, 1995).

Summary

All three perspectives have provided very solid foundations from which to address questions regarding occupational stress. Among the conclusions to be drawn from the review are the following. First, researchers have clearly not settled on one operationalization of any of the model components, but rather have relied on a host of variables to operationalize each component. Their approach, therefore, is very different from the traditional technique whereby a model component is typically anchored to a single operationalization. While there is nothing inherently wrong with adopting a multivariate approach for representing a given component, it presents some unique challenges that have yet to be addressed in this body of research. For one, it implies that there is possibly a common element, or higher-order latent construct linking together all of the variables operationalizing a given component. It would seem, therefore, that a more powerful test of the frameworks would be one that is conducted at this higher-order level. As it currently stands, even when researchers have appropriately applied multivariate statistical procedures, the results are still variable-to-variable. Therefore, there has not been a true test of these frameworks as specified by their respective proponents.

Another conclusion to be drawn from the review of the three models is that each has a narrow perspective. Underlying this observation is the fact that many of the same variables used in defining components for the occupational stress models are exactly the same as those used in proposing other models observed in the organizational sciences. Occupational stress researchers have largely ignored the research in other disciplines of the organizational sciences, and vice versa; that is, one field typically does not reference the work of the other field. The stance of the current authors is that it is absolutely fruitless to debate whether the configuration of the same variables under a pure occupational stress framework is better or worse than a different configuration driven from one of the other disciplines' frameworks. Rather, a more fruitful approach is to recognize the fact that each framework is devoted to understanding the elements of the work organization that promote the well being of not only the individual, but also the organization, and in a broad sense, society. Thus, there is a need to take an integrative perspective that combines the best elements of all frameworks. Taking an integrative approach whereby the elements from other disciplines are brought into the framework will provide some needed conceptual clarity. It is to that integrative approach, the healthy work organization, that the chapter now turns.

THE HEALTHY WORK ORGANIZATION

The following conceptual description of the healthy work organization borrows liberally from a manuscript written by two of the co-authors and that is currently unpublished (DeJoy & Wilson, 2002). Hence, foregoing having to continuously repeat the reference, DeJoy and Wilson (2002) are given primary credit for developing the perspective presented here.

The National Occupational Research Agenda (NIOSH, 1996) identified work organization as one of the national occupational safety and health research priority areas. Work organization was also highlighted in *Healthy People 2010* (U.S. Department of Health and Human Services, 2000) as an important factor in understanding the effects of conditions of employment on the health and well being of employees. Work organization generally refers to the way work processes are structured and managed, including, but not limited to, scheduling, job design, management style, organizational effectiveness, and employee work adjustment. The addition of the term "healthy" to work organization derives from the idea that it is possible to distinguish healthy from unhealthy work systems; that is, some work processes result in healthier outcomes than do other work processes. A key assumption of the healthy work organization is that creating and maintaining such organizations is good for all stakeholders – employees, shareholders (and others concerned with financial performance), and society in general.

Healthy work organization has several important implications for how we view the work-health relationship. First, placing emphasis on how work is structured and organized suggests that the very operational and functional fabric of the organization has a direct impact on employee health and well being (Danna & Griffin, 1999). Second, combining the term "healthy" with the term "work organization" connotes an integrative perspective bringing together viewpoints and findings from a number of disciplines and specialties, including not only traditional workplace health areas such as occupational stress and worksite health promotion, but also organizational behavior, human resources management, and economics (Danna & Griffin, 1999; Lindstrom, 1994; Sauter, Murphy & Hurrell,

1990). And third, healthy work organization brings a human capital orientation to workplace health and highlights potentially important linkages between pre-serving and enhancing human capital and maximizing business strategy (Becker et al., 1997; Goetzel & Ozminkowski, 2000; Smith, Kaminstein & Makadok, 1995). In short, there are parallel benefits in that "healthy" organizations should be better able to attract and retain productive workers, *and* they should be more successful in managing costs and competing in the marketplace than would "unhealthy" organizations. However, research progress toward testing these benefits has been hampered by isolated and fragmented efforts and the relative absence of testable conceptual models or frameworks (Cooper & Williams, 1994; Cox, 1988; Jaffe, 1995; Sauter, Lim & Murphy, 1996; Smith et al., 1995).

In order to address this shortcoming, we assembled and clarified the various conceptual and theoretical perspectives that converge on the concept of the healthy work organization. The end result of this work is the model presented in Fig. 4.

The model in Fig. 4 provides an overall architecture for portraying the substance or content of the healthy work organization, and provides context and direction for future research and practice. The model is based on our concep-tual definition of the healthy work organization as *one characterized by intentional, systematic, and collaborative efforts to maximize employee well being and productivity by providing well-designed and meaningful jobs, a supportive social-organizational environment, and accessible and equitable opportunities for career and work-life enhancement.*

To help the reader to understand the rationale underlying the model in Fig. 4, the section immediately following is devoted to discussing the five core conceptual themes underlying the model in general. Space constraints limit us to a summary of those themes at this point, but the interested reader is referred to DeJoy and Wilson (2002) for a detailed presentation. Following the summary, a lengthy presentation of each component and its constituent constructs is presented.

Core Perspectives Underlying the Healthy Work Organization

The job stress literature provides a rich underlying perspective for developing a model of healthy work organization (e.g. Cox, 1988; Cooper & Cartwright, 1994; Lindstrom, 1994), but several other research perspectives are also rele-vant. These include research related to: (a) human resources or organizational development (e.g. Jaffe, 1995; Rosen & Berger, 1991); (b) occupational safety and health (e.g. Cox & Howarth, 1990; DeJoy, Murphy & Gershon, 1995); and (c) integrative or multi-level health promotion (e.g. Goetzel, Jacobson, Aldana, Vardell & Yee, 1998; Pelletier, 1984; Pfeiffer, 1987).

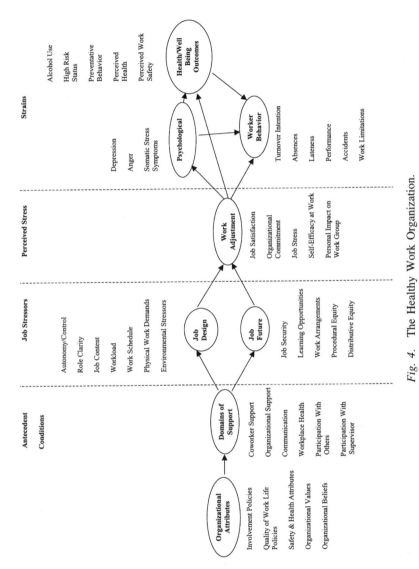

Fig. 4. The Healthy Work Organization.

Table 1 provides exemplars and summarizes the themes or defining aspects evident in these various core perspectives.

When viewed together, at least five broad themes emerge from the perspectives: (1) the increased salience of organizational factors in the work-health relationship; (2) the importance of organization-level action in producing positive change; (3) the need to modify the traditional employer-employee relationship in terms of increased opportunities for information exchange and employee involvement; (4) the view that healthy work organization involves multiple domains of work life; and (5) the expansion of organizational effectiveness to accommodate both employee and business outcomes. The far right column in Table 1 contains overall estimates of the prominence of each theme within each perspective.

The themes related to the role of organizational factors and to the importance of organizational change are highly apparent in each of the perspectives and suggests the need for some modification of the exchange relationship between employees and organizations in terms of increased levels of both upward and downward communication and enhanced levels of employee input and control. The theme that healthy work organization involves multiple domains of work life (theme 4) follows from the basic idea that healthy work organization is more than well-designed jobs. From the four perspectives, there would appear to be three fairly broad work domains. The first domain does involve the demands, characteristics, and requirements of the job itself. The second domain shifts attention to the interpersonal, social, and organizational environment at work, and the third domain addresses the overall employment relationship in terms of security, fairness, and access to opportunities. Finally, central to thinking about healthy work organization is the idea that organizational effectiveness is the end-result of healthy work organization (theme 5). However, this conceptualization of effectiveness should be expanded to include outcomes related to employee health and well being as well as more conventional indices of organizational success such as productivity, profits, shareholder value, and so forth. The interplay between these different but presumably related sets of effectiveness outcomes is a key aspect of healthy work organization. In summary, all of the core perspectives have a common element, and that is, that the healthy work organization recognizes that its basic operational and structural fabric (i.e. how its work is organized) can fundamentally facilitate or impair overall effectiveness in terms of both employee and business/mission performance.

Healthy Work Organization Model Components
In one way or another, all four perspectives call attention to six fairly distinct but interrelated components of work life (see Fig. 4): (a) core organizational

Table 1. Summary of Conceptual-Theoretical Perspectives Related to Healthy Work Organization

Core Perspective	Exemplars	Principal Themes
Human Resources/ Organizational Development	Healthy Companies/Organizations (e.g., Jaffe, 1995; Rosen & Berger, 1991); Learning Organizations (e.g., Senge, 1990); High Performance Work Systems (e.g., Huselid, 1995); High Involvement Work Processes (e.g., Lawler, 1992)	Importance of organizational context ***; Organizational change orientation ***; Employee participation/empowerment ***; Multiple domains of work life ***; Expanded view of organizational effectiveness **
Expanded Occupational Stress Model	Psychosocial Work Organization (e.g., Lindstrom, 1994); Organizational Stress/Comprehensive Stress Management (e.g., Cooper & Cartwright, 1994; Israel et al., 1989); Demand-Control Model (e.g., Karasek & Theorell, 1990)	Importance of organizational context ***; Organizational change orientation ***; Employee participation/empowerment **; Multiple domains of work life **; Expanded view of organizational effectiveness *
Organizational Safety and Health Management	Safety/Health Climate/Culture (e.g., Zohar, 1980); Human Error/Management Systems Failure (e.g., Hofmann et al., 1995); Self-Protective Behavior (e.g., DeJoy et al., 1995)	Importance of organizational context ***; Organizational change orientation ***; Employee participation/empowerment **; Multiple domains of work life *; Expanded view of organizational effectiveness *
Integrative Worksite Health Promotion	Integrative/Multi-Level Programming (e.g., Pelletier, 1984); Ecological Models (e.g., McLeroy et al., 1988); Health Promotive Environments (e.g., Stokols, 1992)	Importance of organizational context ***; Organizational change orientation ***; Employee participation/empowerment **; Multiple domains of work life **; Expanded view of organizational effectiveness **

Note: Asterisks are used to denote the extent to which the theme is evident within the particular theoretical-conceptual perspective: * = Low; ** = Moderate; *** = High.

attributes; (b) domains of support; (c) job design; (d) job future; (f) work adjustment; and (g) organizational effectiveness, including indices of individual well
being and work-related behavior and of organizational-level performance. Only
the three sets of individual indices are noted on Fig. 4, psychological outcomes,
work behaviors and health/well being outcomes, but the expectation is that
these would have collective influences upon organizational-level indices such
as financial performance, human resource costs (e.g. turnover, training), and
healthcare costs. The following paragraphs discuss each of the model
components, and their underlying operational variables moving from left to right
in Fig. 4.

Core organizational attributes. Core organizational attributes are portrayed as
the principal driving or enabling forces in the creation and maintenance of
healthy work organizations. On an objective level, attributes refer to both the
formal written policies and procedures of the organization, and the "unwritten"
ones that come in the form of organizational norms and that are simply
"understood." As is well documented in the organizational climate literature
(e.g. Vandenberg et al., 1999), though, it is not the actual "black-and-white"
statement of such policies or the simple presence of unwritten norms that
ultimately influence employee workplace attitudes and actions, but rather it is
the employees' interpretation of those attributes. At one extreme of interpretation is total unawareness of the attributes, and consequently, the attributes would
have no influence whatsoever on employee workplace behaviors and attitudes.
At the other extreme of interpretation is a perfect understanding of the
attributes, and letting workplace actions be guided solely by them. The reality,
however, is that employees have some level of awareness of these attributes,
and employees' interpretations of the attributes are filtered resulting in an
imperfect understanding of the "true" meaning of those attributes. It is this
perceived reality, nevertheless, that ultimately guides workplace behaviors and
attitudes. Thus, the focus of the healthy work organization model is on
employees' perceptions of the attributes, and not on some objective assessment
of the existence of those attributes. Using the literature underlying the four
perspectives as guide, we identified five sets of attributes that are relevant to a
healthy work organization.

Referring to Fig. 4, the three attribute sets – *involvement, quality of work
life (QWL), and safety and health* – are treated simultaneously, because they
refer to employees' perceptions of the policies defining each of those categories.
Polices and programs can be thought of as the surface manifestations of deeper
held organizational values and beliefs. Human resources-related policies impact
how employees experience life within an organization, and such policies are

among the more readily observable expressions of the organization's basic values and beliefs about its people. Jamieson and O'Mara (1991) argue that the encouragement of personal health within an organization requires policies in several important areas, including informing and involving people, and supporting lifestyle and life needs. Other researchers (e.g. Hale & Hovden, 1998; Hofmann et al., 1995) add "providing a safe and healthful work environment" as another broad policy area that expresses the organization's basic beliefs in maintaining a healthy work environment.

Turning to the *organizational-values* attribute set, we adopted Rokeach's (1979) conceptualization of values as being relatively lasting principles about the kinds of behaviors or end-states that are preferable to other entities such as the employing organization. Studies of successful companies suggest that these organizations typically have value systems that attend to all major stakeholders (e.g. Kotter & Heskett, 1992; Polley, 1987). Since the healthy work organization implicitly connotes an emphasis on the employee, there should be relatively strong values regarding the employees and their importance to the organization.

Organizational beliefs, the final attribute set, involve how the organization views its commitment to and responsibility for employee health and well being. At least two issues are important here. The first concerns general beliefs about the importance of healthy and satisfied employees to the overall success of the enterprise (Ribisl & Reischl, 1993). Of central importance is the idea that employees represent more than units of cost in the business equation. The second issue refers to a sense of shared responsibility for employee health and well being. This issue involves the idea that both individual behavior and organization-level action are important to protecting and enhancing worker health and well being (DeJoy & Southern, 1993; Sandroff, Bradford & Gilligan, 1990).

Domains of social support. As seen in Fig. 4, the core organizational attributes are expected to directly influence the second model component, domains of social support. The premise underlying this expectation is that a major outcome of perceiving sets of attributes that have the employees' health and well being at their core is a strong sense of support. That is, the employees sense that there are provisions for succeeding in their organizational roles, but in a manner conveying that they have an active role in that success. Specifically, the domains of social support emphasize interpersonal relations and the social/organizational environment at work. The healthy organization should provide opportunities for meaningful interpersonal interaction and communication, both for purposes of emotional support and for instrumental or tangible support in fulfilling job tasks and other assigned responsibilities. In comparison to job design (discussed below), evidence is less consistent for enumerating specific dimensions, however, organizational or management support appears to play a central role in shaping a healthy work organization (Cox & Howarth, 1990; Ribisl & Reischl, 1993; Zohar, 1980). There are also clear themes for the importance of meaningful employee participation and related needs for open and effective communication (DeJoy & Southern, 1993; Hale & Hovden, 1998; Karasek & Theorell, 1990). Based on the four perspectives presented in an above section (see Table 1), we identified five key dimensions – organizational support, coworker support, participation with others and supervision, communication, and safety and health climate.

The dimensions of *coworker and organizational support* may be defined as any action originating from these sources indicating a concern for the well being of the employee (Eisenberger, Huntington, Hutchison & Sowa, 1986; Jayaratne & Chess, 1984). Research has generally indicated that positive social relations, both at work and outside of the workplace, play a role in that the adverse effects of exposure to various job demands and hazards are likely to be more severe when these relationships provide little support (Karasek, Schwartz & Theorell, 1982; Stewart, 1989). Further, these forms of support, particularly organizational sources, connote a sense that there is a future within the organization. However, in terms of which source is expected to have the greatest impact, coworker support should be the strongest given that employees identify more closely with proximal relationships (i.e. among coworkers) than with distal relationships (i.e. the organization) (Larkin & Larkin, 1996).

Participation with others and with the supervisor refer to work situations in which an employee has meaningful input into job-related decision-making regardless of whether it is in interaction with the supervisor or with others such as coworkers (Vandenberg et al., 1999). The considerable literature on participation shows a wide range of effects in the fields of management, organizational behavior, industrial psychology, and communications. A significant majority of studies have emphasized job satisfaction, motivation, and productivity; however, participation in decision-making has also associated with diminished job stress, the use of active problem-solving strategies, and better mental health (Jackson, 1983; Spector, 1986). Participation in decision-making serves also to enhance employee understanding, perceived control, and communications (Ganster, 1989).

High quality *communication* from multiple sources has shown positive effects on role ambiguity, job performance, job stress, and worker satisfaction (Frone, Russell & Cooper, 1995). Performance feedback is especially important and includes both formal (i.e. performance appraisals and posted job requirements) and informal feedback (i.e. reminders of workplace norms and interaction of workers) from multiple sources including managers, supervisors, and coworkers (Hackman & Oldham, 1980). Studies have also linked effective communication and feedback to safety and health program effectiveness (Schurman & Israel, 1995), positive safety climate (DeJoy et al., 1995), and a variety of safety-related behaviors and outcomes (McAfee & Winn, 1989).

The perceptions of employees with respect to receiving support for their personal *safety and health* on the job have emerged as an important aspect of organizational climate. Indeed, attention to organizational factors supporting occupational safety and health has expanded to such an extent that Hale and Hovden (1998) regard it as the "third age of safety." Some of the evidence pointing to the importance of support factors includes research on safety program effectiveness (Cohen, 1977), workplace accidents and errors (Hayes, Perander, Smecko & Trask, 1998), and compliance with safe work practices and the use of personal protective equipment (DeJoy et al., 1995).

Job design. Job design involves the demands and other aspects of the specific job or work situation, or what DeJoy and Southern (1993) refer to as the immediate job-worker interface. As noted at the start of this chapter, the literature on occupational stress and health provides much of the basis for identifying the job-related factors associated with healthy work organization. That is, recent reviews of this literature (e.g. Cooper & Cartwright, 1994; Lindstrom, 1994; Sauter et al., 1990) reflect general agreement on the job or task factors, which are most important in preserving or enhancing worker health and well being. Further, the research reviewed in the section above on dimensions of organizational support, in addition to the cumulative research on House's (1981) and Karasek's (1979) occupational stress frameworks, makes it fairly clear that the dimensions of job design are strongly influenced by the domains of social support. Seven dimensions were selected to represent the job design component in Fig. 4. The healthy work organization provides jobs that involve reasonable workloads, meaningful and worthwhile tasks, and adequate levels of control, and clear job expectations. Work schedule also is an important element of job design, and jobs should be performed in a work environment that minimizes physical work demands, and exposure to environmental stressors.

Autonomy/control is the degree to which the job provides substantial freedom, independence, and discretion to the individual in scheduling work tasks and determining the procedures to be used in carrying them out (Hackman & Oldham, 1980). Employees who perceive high levels of control at work have tended to report higher levels of motivation, job satisfaction, involvement, and commitment, as well as lower levels of absenteeism, turnover, emotional distress, and physical symptoms, including exhaustion, headaches, and cardio-vascular disease than those employees with less control and autonomy (Greenberger, Strausser, Cummings & Dunham, 1989; Karasek et al., 1981; Spector, 1986). Evidence also suggests that job redesign interventions intended to increase autonomy/control can be effective at reducing many of the latter negative outcomes (e.g. Landsbergis & Viona-Vaugh, 1995).

Role clarity is often defined as the extent to which an employee's work goals and responsibilities are clearly communicated and the degree to which the individual understands the actions and processes required to achieve these goals such that there is minimum role ambiguity and role conflict (Hackman & Oldham, 1980). Occupational stress research has long supported that role ambiguity and conflict are stressful events because they add to the uncertainty of a work situation and reduce the extent to which workers have control over the job. Role conflict and ambiguity have been associated with burnout, increased job stress, work dissatisfaction and decreased productivity and commitment (e.g. Adkins, 1995). Adverse psycho-physiological responses such as increased heart rate and blood pressure have also been linked to low levels of role clarity (French et al., 1974; French et al., 1982).

Meaningfulness and skill utilization have been identified as important dimensions of *job content* (Hackman & Oldham, 1980). In general, tasks which are narrow, fragmented, highly repetitious, monotonous, and that otherwise provide for little stimulation or skill utilization, have been associated with job dissatisfaction, job stress, and poor mental health (Cox, 1988; Levi, 1981).

An employee's *workload* consists of the daily demands of the work situation or job design. Quantitative overload ("too much" work) and qualitative overload ("too difficult" work) have been associated with an assortment of psychological, physiological, and behavioral strain symptoms among employees (Frankenhaeuser & Johansson, 1986). Job satisfaction also appears closely linked to workload and job design (Greenberger et al., 1989). Strain may be most likely to occur when control is not commensurate with job demands, and social support is lowest (Karaek et al., 1981).

Employees who possess their preferred *work schedule* have been found to have increased job satisfaction, work commitment, and generally, positive work-related attitudes (Morrow, McElroy & Elliot, 1994). Further, day shift workers have been found to hold more favorable work-related attitudes than other shifts. In addition, higher levels of job satisfaction and organizational commitment have been shown for fixed shift workers as compared to rotating shift employees and for full-time vs. part-time employees (Lee & Johnson, 1991). Rotating shifts and permanent night work appear to be most problematic in terms of psychological, social, and physical well being.

A number of studies highlight the adverse impacts of *environmental stressors* and *physical work demands* on employee health and safety outcomes (e.g. Baker & Landrigan, 1990; Gustavsen, 1980). Environmental conditions can effect the employee's well being through exposure to such factors as loud noise, inadequate ventilation, bad lighting, variable temperatures, smoke and toxic chemicals (Rasanen, Notkola & Husman, 1997). Musculoskeletal symptoms and injuries due to physical work demands (e.g. highly repetitive tasks and frequent bending, twisting, and heavy lifting) have had similar influences on employee adjustment to work.

Job future. Based on reasoning from Sauter et al. (1990), we added a model component that shifts attention to job security and career development considerations. Our selection of the term 'job future' was intended to represent a multi-dimensional workplace domain that is more complex than simple job security. Specifically, the job future model component focuses on the employment or exchange relationship between employers and employees, and includes job security, equity, and related career development considerations. Previous attempts to model healthy work organization have either emphasized job demands and stressors to the relative exclusion of the other areas (Danna & Griffin, 1999), or have concentrated on the deeper structures of organizations (values or culture, etc.) without specific attention to how these fundamental attributes translate into specific job characteristics (Sauter et al., 1996). The underlying premise of job future is that employees in healthy work organizations should be clearly informed about opportunities for improving their job skills and career opportunities, as well as about the organizational and economic developments that may alter their employment situation (Sauter et al., 1990). Figure 4 indicates that the domains of social support are expected to have a direct association with job future. Since job future perceptions are shaped by the exchange relationship with the organization, it is the perceived support domains that convey the clearest message to employees as to what the organization is willing to give to them. Five dimensions are proposed for this model component: (a) job security; (b) procedural equity; (c) distributive equity; (d) learning opportunities; and (e) flexible work arrangements.

Job security has been defined as an employee's perception of a potential threat to continuity in his or her current job. Job security has been found to be positively related to job satisfaction, work commitment, quality of life, and mental and physical health (Heaney, Israel & House, 1994). *Learning opportunities* for increased job mastery and expanded skills for coping with change have assumed increasing importance in describing healthy work organization (Cooper & Cartwright, 1994; Lindstrom, 1994). In fact, such opportunities may represent an essential tradeoff in response to altered expectations about job security in the traditional sense. That is, today's workforce is very conscious about the "shelf-life" of knowledge and job positions, and that maintaining up-to-date knowledge, skills and abilities is needed for both internal movement within an organization, but most importantly, for obtaining positions with other organizations in the event that they are asked to leave their current workplace. Hence, most contemporary workers view learning opportunities as a mechanism to maintain their employability, and have a strong link to work adjustment indices such as job satisfaction and organizational commitment (Vandenberg et al., 1999).

Historically, perceptions of equity have been unquestionably the benchmark for operationalizing the fairness of the exchange process between employees and employers (Adams, 1963). From its long and rich research history, two forms of equity have emerged (Greenberg, 1986). *Distributive equity* represents the perceived fairness attached to the amount of rewards (e.g. merit pay increases) and their allocation along some performance criterion. *Procedural equity* entails the perceived fairness as to how the rules governing the reward system are applied across people. While the two forms of equity may have associations with different indices of employee work adjustment (Vandenberg & Lance, 1992), collectively between the two, they have associations with job satisfaction, organizational commitment, and perceptions of job stress.

Flexible work arrangements, including where one works, how much one works, and whether flextime is an option, allows the employee to have more control over his or her job. For many workers, flexible work arrangements provide the accommodations needed for managing child care, furthering education, and planning for retirement. Positive relationships have been found between flexible work arrangements and depression, anxiety, job satisfaction, and work-family conflict for both men and women (Morrow et al., 1994).

Work adjustment. The concept of employee work adjustment has an essential role within applied psychology and organizational behavior (Hulin, 1991; Lance, Vandenberg & Self, 2000; Vandenberg & Self, 1993). As applied in those disciplines and as used here, work adjustment refers to employees continuously interpreting, and when required, revising both the meaning of work as it pertains to a particular organization and the view of themselves as functioning members of their organizations (Vandenberg & Self, 1993). Positive adjustment occurs to the extent that the interpretations and possible revisions are mutually beneficial to both the person and the organization. Negative adjustment is reflected in a weakened linkage or bond between the person and organization (Lance et al., 2000; Vandenberg & Self, 1993).

The work adjustment component of the healthy work organization model underscores the importance of subjective evaluation and individual meaning in understanding the potential effects of job design and job future on employee health and well being (Lindstrom, 1994; Renn & Vandenberg, 1995). Briefly, as alluded to in the above sections on job design and job future, a great deal of research evidence has accumulated indicating that employees indices of work adjustment covary with the various indices of job design and job future. Using this research literature as a basis, work adjustment in the healthy work organization was defined through four indices, job satisfaction, organizational commitment, psychological empowerment (including workplace self-efficacy, and perceived impact on the work group), and experienced job stress. Job satisfaction pertains to the employee's general level of satisfaction with the nature and circumstances of his or her current job. Organizational commitment emphasizes affective commitment, or the emotional attachment of the employee to the organization. Psychological empowerment involves the worker's sense of control, self-efficacy, or mastery in the workplace. Job stress emphasizes the individual's appraisal of the work situation and demands, and thus, is perceived stress rather than stressful conditions or stress symptoms.

Organizational effectiveness. Perhaps the key assumption of healthy work organization is that healthy work organizations should benefit both employees and the business. As such, this component should contain sets of relevant outcomes related to both aspects. Decisions about specific measures to include as indices of organizational effectiveness are beyond the scope of the present paper, and would likely vary considerably from one situation to another (e.g. for profit vs. non-profit organizations). However, this component might easily contain a combination of both subjective and objective measures, and some measures would be at the level of the individual employee while others would be aggregate or organization-level measures. Following the view that health is more than the mere absence of disease, health measures could include indices of emotional and social health and well being as well as physical health per se. Candidate measures might include: general health status, vitality, life satisfaction, somatic symptoms, health conditions, health risk behaviors, self-care /preventive behaviors, health care utilization, depressive symptoms, anger-hostility, and general psychological well being. On the business side, measures could include profits, sales, defects/waste, customer/client satisfaction, return on equity, occupational injury and illness, productivity, absenteeism, and employee turnover.

As indicated on Fig. 4, we limited the current model to three categories of individual level variables. The first category, psychological outcomes, was defined through employees' levels of depression, anger and somatic stress. The second category consisted of several indices of employee health and well being. Specifically, alcohol use was defined as the total number of alcoholic beverages consumed per month per person. High-risk status was an index used to operationalize the degree to which an employee was at risk of contracting a severe disease or illness. It was created from several other measures tapping whether or not employees used tobacco products, whether or not they had high cholesterol, high blood pressure or other risk factors for major diseases, and whether or not they engaged in vigorous exercise. Preventive behaviors was also an index created from a composite of measures including whether or not they are screened regularly for cholesterol, high blood pressure and other risk factors (cancer, diabetes), and whether or not they protected themselves from exposure to the sun. The final indices, perceived health and perceived safety of the work environment, were intended to tap employees' own feeling of well being from both an internal (own health) and external (work environment) perspective.

We recognize that the psychological and health/well being outcomes are primarily driven by factors outside of the workplace. What cannot be denied, particularly with the research evidence accrued within the occupational stress arena, is that the workplace contributes significantly to those outcomes as well. Our intention in the model, therefore, is to indicate that while individuals may enter an organization with baseline levels of each outcome, those outcomes can vary either upward or downward as a function of the employee's own experience at work. Due largely again to the research in occupational stress (particularly those models relating perceived stress to short-term and long-term strains), the expectation is that these outcomes would vary with levels of employee adjustment to work. That is, employees who are highly satisfied, strongly committed, experience little job stress, and have strong self-control (positive work adjustment), are most likely to have less depression, anger and somatic stress than employees with negative work adjustment. Further, those with positive work adjustment are most likely to show reduced alcohol use, lower their high risk status and engage in more preventive behaviors.

The third category of individual-level outcomes in Fig. 4 is generally referred to as worker behaviors. It is characterized by a set of behaviors that are expected of employees in most situations. Namely, employees are expected to maintain longevity (i.e. have low turnover intentions), not abuse the absence or lateness policies, perform at an adequate level, engage in behaviors that minimize the risk of work-related accidents, and similarly not engage in any activity both in and out of the workplace that may limit a person's ability to perform at acceptable levels. As indicated on Fig. 4, this category is expected to be directly influenced by work adjustment, psychological outcomes and health/well being outcomes.

Summary

There is a set of labels (e.g. job stressors) at the top of Fig. 4 that are commonly used among occupational stress researchers to characterize the component constructs within that column. The use of the labels should not be construed as linking the healthy work organization model exclusively to an occupational stress research framework. We could have just as easily put labels from other conceptual models in those same places. For example, the label "core job characteristics" from Hackman and Oldham's (1980) job characteristics model could replace the current "job stressors" label. Our point is that regardless of the cause (e.g. disciplinary "siloing," purposeful ignorance of ongoing research in other disciplines, etc.), there has been a great deal of conceptual redundancy across research streams in that the same constructs are being used to characterize components within different conceptual models. This would not be an issue if occupational stress researchers, for example, had a single construct labeled "job stressors," or "perceived stress," and developed a single operationalization of that construct. However, it is understandable that they have not done so because their overriding concern is in determining how individual experiences within the workplace (and as captured in constructs such as support, job demands, job satisfaction, etc.) collectively come together to determine whether the individuals are working productively in a manner that is not only "good" for the organization, but also for those individuals, and society as a whole. The "good" in this case refers not only to performance (i.e. number of units produced, contacts made, etc.), but also to the fact that the work experiences can affect the health of individuals, and therefore, determine health costs. Thus, unlike Selye (1983) who coined the term "stress" to refer to a specific individual reaction, the term "occupational stress" is used to characterize a process model.

The main thrust of the healthy work organization model is to highlight the fact that regardless of the discipline, the central focus of all models in which these constructs are components, is the health and well being of the individual. Further, the argument given to organizations as to why they should be concerned with individual health and well being is that not doing so has tremendous costs to the organization. Given that many organizations have little advantage over competitors in terms of goods and services, and therefore, operate within small profit margins, they compete at the level of costs; that is, those organizations that control costs will be the industry leader in terms of profits (Vandenberg et al., 1999). The following pages present an empirical test of the healthy work organization model.

TEST OF THE HEALTHY WORK ORGANIZATION MODEL

The intent of the following analyses is to present evidence that the healthy work organization model is a viable framework in which to test and generate hypotheses regarding individual responses to the workplace. This section is organized much like the methods and results sections of traditional journal articles. That is, the next sub-section is a condensed methods overview beginning with a description of the sample and research sites, and ending with an overview of the analytical procedures. Some of the material is condensed to conserve space, but in all cases, the interested reader may contact the authors to receive additional information. Following the methods sub-section is a sub-section devoted to the outcomes of the analyses.

Methods

Respondents
The sample consisted of 3930 employees from 21 stores of one retail organization. The stores were located in the Southeastern United States, and varied in size from 150 to 375 employees. The 3,930 respondents represented over 50% of all employees in the 21 locations. Surveys were administered onsite at each store during two consecutive workdays. Questionnaire responses were completely anonymous and participation was encouraged but voluntary. As an incentive, employees were given time on the clock to participate, and provided a relatively quiet environment (a training room) in which to complete the survey. Completed questionnaires were deposited in locked storage boxes by the respondent to reinforce the confidentiality of the information. Within the sample, 24% had supervisory responsibilities, 54% had worked for the organization two or more years, 65% were male, 57% were married or cohabitating with a partner, 97% had a high school education or higher, and 73% were Caucasian. Further, they worked an average of 40 hours per week.

Survey Development
To conserve space, a detailed presentation of the survey development process is not given here, but is available upon request from the authors. Briefly, standard survey development procedures (Hinkin, 1995; Lance & Vandenberg, 2002) were strictly adhered to, and included: (a) item selection/generation based on a

comprehensive review of the research literature; (b) presentation of items to subject matter experts for sorting into appropriate conceptual categories; (c) administration of preliminary item set to a small sample for purposes of exploratory factor analysis; (d) after refining item set based on step (c), items were presented to a large sample for purposes of confirmatory factor analysis; and (e) item set was presented to another large sample six months later for purposes of cross-validation. The final step, (e), consisted of fixing the factor loadings of the second sample to those of the first CFA sample (step (d)) to determine if there is a significant loss in model fit. Collectively, the results at all steps supported the validity of the survey instrument. The end result was a survey instrument with nearly 200 items representing approximately 30 first-order constructs.

Measures
The description of the scales below follows the order of the categories from left to right on Fig. 4. That is, it begins with the organizational attributes and ends with the outcome variables under worker behaviors. All items are scaled on five-point Likert scales unless otherwise noted.

Organizational attributes. Values refer to the internalized normative beliefs, which guide behavior and desired end-states within organizations (Rokeach, 1979). While there are different "value sets" (e.g. people, production, etc.), the current focused on what O'Reilly, Chatman and Caldwell (1991) referred to as values with an employee orientation (e.g. tolerance). The six-item measure asked respondents: "thinking about your company or organization as a whole, how characteristic are each of the following traits," and they were subsequently presented with the six traits (alpha = 0.89). *Beliefs* entail employees' perceptions as to how strongly the organization views its commitment to and responsibility for employee health and well being (Ribisl & Reischl, 1993). An example from the nine-item scale includes "employees should have a say in decisions that affect how they do their jobs" (alpha = 0.90).

An important attribute to reinforcing organizational values is the *organizational policies and practices* perceived by employees as the true boundary conditions in the sense that their actions are guided or bounded by them. This study focused on three themes underlying policies and practices, which were based largely on the work of Jamieson and O'Mara (1991), and of Vandenberg et al. (1999). All items regardless of theme asked respondents "to what extent does your company or organization as a whole have specific policies and/or programs in place for . . .". The first theme was policies and practices for high involvement work practices and consisted of 10 items ("incorporating changes or innovations suggested by employees or employee groups"; alpha = 0.93). The second theme focused on policies and practices facilitating employees' abilities to balance work and non-work issues ("offering EAPs to help employees deal with stress, family problems, substance abuse, etc."; alpha = 0.85). The third theme was policies and practices reinforcing safety and health practices ("providing applicable occupational safety and health training"; alpha = 0.90). The scales for both the last two themes consisted of four items each.

Domains of social support. Organizational support involves the actions undertaken at the organizational level that encourage, bolster, or assist the employees in undertaking their tasks and responsibilities. Eisenberger et al.'s (1986) nine-item global measure was used in this study (e.g. "the organization really cares about my well being"; alpha = 0.91). *Coworker support* focuses on the informal social/interpersonal relationships that develop among peers. Ribisl and Reischl's scale (1993) was used to measure this construct ("my coworkers care about me as a person"; alpha = 0.92). Participation, in general, refers to a workplace in which employees are encouraged to involve themselves in some meaningful way with the people in the organization. The three-item *participation with supervisor* scale (Vroom, 1959) included items such as "do you feel you can influence decisions of your immediate supervisor regarding things about which you are concerned?" (alpha = 0.77). The three-item *participation with others* scale (Caplan, Cobb, French, Harrison & Pinneau, 1975) included items such as "I take part with others at my workplace in making decisions that affect me" (alpha = 0.88).

Communication is the extent to which employees see an effective information exchange within the organization. The eight-item communication scale used in the current study was adapted from Vandenberg et al. (1999), and included items such as "management gives enough notice to employees before making changes in policies and procedures" (alpha = 0.86). Finally, *safety and health support* involves the degree to which the safety and health of employees is promoted in the work environment. The seven-item scale used in the current study was a version of the NIOSH Safety Climate Scale (DeJoy et al., 1995). An example item is "there are no significant shortcuts taken when workplace safety and health are at stake" (alpha = 0.90).

Job design. Seven dimensions derived largely from reviews of the job stress literature (Cooper & Cartwright, 1994; Lindstrom, 1994; Sauter et al., 1990) were included as part of the job design component. An employee's *workload* consists of the daily demands of the work situation. This construct was measured with four items taken from a task demand scale developed by Klitzman, House, Israel and Mero (1990). An example of items included: "I am asked to do an excessive amount of work" (alpha = 0.78).

Autonomy (control) is the degree to which the job provides substantial freedom, independence, and discretion to the individual in scheduling the work and in determining the procedures to be used in carrying it out. The three-item scale contained in the Job Diagnostic Survey (Hackman & Oldham, 1980) were used in the current study (e.g. "my job permits me to decide on my own how to go about doing the work"; alpha = 0.77). *Job content* is the extent to which the job is viewed as being meaningful, valuable, and worthwhile. A six-item scale (House, McMichael, Wells, Kaplan & Landerman, 1979) was used to represent this construct ("I have an opportunity to develop my own special skills and abilities"; alpha = 0.80).

Role clarity is the extent to which an employee's work goals and responsibilities are clearly communicated and whether the individual understands the processes required to achieve these goals. The four-item scale adopted to measure this construct was adapted from Rizzo, House, and Lirtzman (1970). An example item is "there are clear, planned goals and objectives for my job" (alpha = 0.82).

Based both on the work of Johansson, Johnson, and Hall (1991), and "walk-throughs" of the store's work environment conducted by the authors, two scales were created to assess *environmental stressors* and *physical work demands*, respectively. The seven-item environmental stressors scale encompassed employees' perceptions of the potential hazards found in their immediate work areas such as the noise and poor lighting (alpha = 0.84). The five-item physical work demands scale assessed factors such as lifting and repetitive motions (alpha = 0.82). The five-item *work schedule* scale used in this study consisted of items from Morrow et al. (1994), with additional items developed by the investigators to reflect scheduling issues unique to the participating company "my work hours are unpredictable from one week to the next"; alpha = 0.84).

Job future. Five dimensions were included in the job future component. *Job security* consists of the employees' perceptions about the likely continuity of their employment with the organization. A five-item scale (Kuhnert, Sims & Lahey, 1989) was used to measure this variable ("I am afraid of losing my job"; alpha = 0.79). From the long and rich research history on equity, two forms have emerged as important in the study of organizations. *Distributive equity* represents the perceived fairness attached to the amount of rewards (e.g. merit pay increases) and their allocation along some performance criterion. *Procedural equity* entails the perceived fairness as to how the "rules" are applied across people. The current study used a four-item distributive equity scale, and a six-item procedural equity scale (Greenberg, 1986). An example distributive equity item is "I am fairly rewarded considering my responsibilities" (alpha = 0.95). In contrast, the procedural equity scale included items such as "when pay and promotion decisions are made, all sides affected by the decisions have a say" (alpha = 0.95).

Learning opportunities entail employees' beliefs about available opportunities to learn new skills or keep current skills updated. Five items adapted from Vandenberg et al. (1999) were used to assess this dimension ("I am given a real opportunity to improve my knowledge and skills"; alpha = 0.90). *Flexible work arrangements* variable involves the extent to which job requirements limit employees' ability to fulfill various non-work obligations and activities. Bohen and Viveros-Long's (1981) six-item scale was used to measure this construct ("how easy or difficult was it to arrange time to do each of the following on a typical workday" with items including "go to a health care appointment" and "respond to the needs of your children or other family members"; alpha = 0.87).

Work adjustment. Job satisfaction examines how satisfied employees are with their specific work situation, tasks, demands, and responsibilities. The five-item scale used in the current study (Hackman & Oldham, 1980) included items such as "generally speaking, I am very satisfied with my job" (alpha = 0.81). While the latter scale focuses narrowly on the attributes of the job itself, *organizational commitment* represents the strength of employees' attachment to the company as whole. The nine-item version of the Organizational Commitment Questionnaire (Mowday, Steers & Porter, 1979) was used to measure this construct ("I am willing to put in a great deal of effort beyond that normally expected in order to help this organization be successful"; alpha = 0.92).

Efficacy, in general, refers to a person's sense of mastery and confidence in their work role, and is typically considered an index of positive work adjustment. Adapting Spreitzer's (1995) perspective, we utilized two forms of efficacy in the current study. *Self-efficacy* refers to a person's own sense of confidence in his/her ability to effectively work at the job. This was measured with Spreitzer's three-item scale ("I am confident about my ability to do my job"; alpha = 0.81). The second form, *impact*, refers to a person's perception about their ability to meaningfully influence his/her workgroup or team. Again, Spreitzer's (1995) three-item measure was used ("my impact on what happens in my workgroup is large"; alpha = 0.88).

Job stress focuses on the employee's perceptions and reactions to stressors at work. The six-item scale was adapted from Cohen, Kamarck, and Mermelstein (1983), and included items such as "in the last month, how often have you been upset because of something that happened unexpectedly at work" (alpha = 0.88).

Effectiveness indices. As seen in Fig. 4, there were 3 categories of outcome variables: (a) psychological outcomes; (b) health/well being outcomes; and (c) worker behaviors. Three measures were used to represent the *psychological outcomes.* The first two measures, adapted from Ilfeld (1978), assessed depressive symptoms, and anger/hostility. Depressive symptoms were represented using seven-items (e.g. feel downhearted and blue, feel lonely; alpha = 0.86), and anger was operationalized with four items (e.g. feel easily annoyed, feel critical of others; alpha = 0.87). Respondents were asked to report how often they had experienced these symptoms or feelings during the past month, using a four-point scale: "never," "once in a while," "fairly often," "very often." The third measure, somatic symptoms, included seven symptom states generally associated with stress and/or anxiety (e.g. headache, heart beating hard, sweaty hands). Respondents indicated how often they had experienced these symptoms during the past month (alpha = 0.89).

The second category, health and well being outcomes, included five variables. The two variables used to assess alcohol consumption and high-risk status were adapted from the U.S. Centers for Disease Control and Prevention's Behavioral Risk Factor Surveillance Survey. The *alcohol measure* provided an overall measure of alcohol consumption during a 30-day period. It was the combination of responses to drinking frequency (number of days alcohol consumed per month) multiplied by quantity (number of drinks typically consumed on a day that alcoholic beverages were consumed). *High-risk status* was also created from a combination of responses to items including tobacco product use, and whether or not they have been diagnosed with high blood pressure, with high cholesterol or with diabetes. Higher scores denoted higher risk status.

A similar procedure was used to create an index of *preventive behaviors.* Briefly, both genders were asked how frequently they were examined by medical professionals for high blood pressure and cholesterol (1 = never had an exam to 5 = within the past 12 months). Similarly, both sexes were asked whether they protect themselves from sun exposure and had flu shots. For males, their responses to the latter four "baseline" questions plus another denoting whether they were screened for testicular cancer were averaged together. For females, their responses to the latter "baseline" questions were averaged also with their responses to questions regarding the frequency with which they had pap smears, breast examinations, and mammograms. Responses were coded such that the higher the score, the greater their engagement in preventive behaviors.

The remaining two variables, *perceived health* and *perceived exposure to safety and health hazards*, were designed to tap individuals' perceptions of their own well being. Perceived health ranged from 1 (poor) to 5 (excellent).

Similarly, perceived exposure to safety and health ranged from 1 (very unsafe) to 5 (very safe).

The final category of outcome variables (Fig. 4), worker behaviors, was represented by six variables. *Turnover intention* asked respondents to rate the probability that they are leaving the company in the next 12 months (1 = 0 to 20% to 5 = 81 to 100%). *Absences* were measured by asking respondents to denote how many days they were absent when scheduled to work but to not count scheduled days off in their calculations. The scale for the latter measure ranged from 1 (no days missed when scheduled to work) to 5 (four or more days missed when scheduled to work). *Lateness* was measured by asking individuals to rate how frequently they are late for work in an average month (1 = never to 5 = almost daily). *Performance* was operationalized by asking respondents to note how their supervisors rated their performance on their last appraisal (1 = unsatisfactory to 5 = outstanding). *Accidents* were represented by having respondents note how many accidents they were involved in on the job over the past 12 months. Finally, *work limitation* was created from responses to two items. The first item simply asked "yes" or "no" if the individual's capacity to work (either the kind of work or the amount) had been limited by some injury or health condition. Those responding "yes" were then asked whether the injury or health condition was caused by their job. A work limitation score of zero was given to all who responded "no" to the first question. A score of one was given to those who responded "yes" to the first question but "no" to the second. The highest work limitation score, two, was given to those who responded "yes" to both questions.

Analytical Procedures

There were two phases to the data analysis: (a) treatment of missing data; and (b) the test of the model.

Treatment of missing data. While it is common practice to use list-wise deletion to deal with missing data, doing so in the present case would have reduced the usable number of respondents by nearly 50%. The dramatic reduction in sample size is a severe problem with list-wise deletion and a reason why it has come under serious question (Little & Schenker, 1995). This is due to the fact that it eliminates a case if there is a missing response on even one item. For the present sample, only approximately 3% of the total number of responses (760,000 which is the total number of respondents times the number of items in the survey) was missing. Alternatively, experts recommend determining how much of the missing data is random vs. systematic, and then imputing values for those cases where data are randomly missing (Little &

Schenker, 1995; Muthén, Kaplan & Hollis, 1987; Roth, 1994). Applying this practice requires three steps. The first step is to eliminate cases where there are missing data on objective measures or single-item measures. For example, it is not viable to impute a value for someone who did not respond to whether they smoke or not, or who refused to specify the likelihood that they may leave the organization in the next 12 months. In other words, items that are best candidates for imputation are items from multi-item scales where all items are required to operationalize the construct (i.e. the total item set represents the content domain of the construct). This assumes of course that the scale begins with strong validity and reliability. In the present study, this first step indicated that 3063 cases out of the 3930 had responses on all single-item and objective measures used in the current study.

The second step requires an examination of the remaining cases to determine whether there are systematic vs. random patterns to missing responses. Unfortunately, no firm rules exist as to what constitutes one or the other pattern. An obvious "systematic case" would be a person who refused to answer any items of a particular scale. Thus, the data were examined for such cases, but none were found. Less obvious, though, is determining how many items have to have missing values to define a systematic pattern of "missingness" for a particular scale. Experts recommend a conservative 2/3rds rule (Roth, 1994). That is, a case is not considered missing at random if the respondent answered less than 2/3rds of the item set for a scale. In the current study, none of the 3063 respondents fell into that category.

The third and final step is to apply an imputation method to the missing values. It is beyond the scope of this manuscript to discuss the advantages and disadvantages of the different methods (excellent treatments may be found in Little & Schenker, 1995; Muthén et al., 1987; Roth, 1994). Given that our model was ultimately examined using structural equation modeling procedures, the expected maximization (full information maximum likelihood) multiple imputation procedure (LISREL Version 8.5; Du Toit & Du Toit, 2001) was applied to impute missing values.

Test of the model. The model in Fig. 4 was tested using a structural equation modeling approach. Again, only a brief overview of the technique is presented here, but a more detailed explanation is available upon request from the authors. Referring to Fig. 4, all of the variables listed in association with a model component were represented at the item level. "Involvement policies," for example, was actually a 1st-order latent variable defined through its respective 10 items. Similarly, and again for illustration, organizational commitment was construed as a 1st-order latent variable defined through its nine items.

Collectively, therefore, 31 1st-order latent variables (all of the variables listed with the model components except health and well being outcomes and worker behavior) were specified using 194 items. In turn, the 31 1st-order variables were used to define six 2nd- or higher order variables. For example, the 2nd-order "psychological outcomes" latent variable was defined through the 1st-order variables, depression, anger and somatic stress. Similarly, the 2nd-order "job future" variable was represented through its five 1st-order variables, job security, learning opportunities, communication, workplace health, participation with others, and participation with supervisors. Thus, excluding health and well being and work behavior outcomes for the moment, the hypothesized associations between ellipses on Fig. 4 were examined between these higher-order constructs.

Given no compelling conceptual reason to expect a 2nd-order latent variable to underlie the work behavior and health and well being outcomes, we treated each of the variables for those components as independent entities. As a result and for example, there were in reality six additional paths emanating respectively from the 2nd-order work adjustment latent variable and the 2nd-order psychological outcomes latent variable to the six worker behavior variables. There were an additional five paths from each of those 2nd-order constructs to each of the variables characterizing the health and well being component. Finally, there were 30 paths emanating from the health and well being component representing the hypothesized associations between worker behavior and health and well being.

Inferring support for the hypotheses was a two-step process. The first step was to examine the overall fit of the model to the data. This is an omnibus test that in practical terms asks whether or not the specification of the paths as conceptually supported is a reasonable reflection of the theoretical process underlying the variables. Assuming that it is, then the second step is to examine the statistical significance of each of the hypothesized paths to infer direct support for each expectation. It does not make sense to infer the statistical significance of the hypothesized paths without first asking whether the model itself is reasonable.

The issue of overall model fit, however, is itself complex and opinions vary (Lance & Vandenberg, 2001). While there are hosts of available fit measures, no single index of fit exists which unequivocally results in a clear fit/no fit interpretation. This is due to the fact that each fit index is characterized by its own strengths and weaknesses that in turn vary as a function of the characteristics of the model itself (e.g. sample size, model complexity, degrees of freedom, etc.). As a consequence, researchers typically select a number of different fit indices that accommodate the characteristics of their particular study, and judge overall fit on the pattern of outcomes across all of those indices. The primary characteristics of the current study were sample size, and model complexity with correspondingly large degrees of freedom. While sample size was obvious, model complexity refers to the fact that the model test included almost 200 items representing 31 1st-order variables, six 2nd-order variables, and the 11 single-item responses making up the health and well being outcomes and worker behavior component. This meant that there was over 15,000 degrees of freedom in the model test. Taking this into consideration, six fit indices were selected. The first index was the traditional chi-square goodness of fit test – the only true statistical test of fit. In an ideal world, strong fit is reflected in a non-significant chi-square. However, the chi-square test is rarely statistically non-significant with large samples and complex models even when all of other fit indices indicate strong fit (Bollen & Long, 1993). Therefore, some have suggested calculating the chi-square to degrees-of-freedom ratio as a supplement to chi-square test. While no set standard exists as to what constitutes an appropriate (i.e. to infer fit) ratio, ratios of five have been viewed as a lower bound limit, and ratios of three or less as indicators of excellent fit (Wheaton, Muthén & Summers, 1977). In fact, a chi-square value less than 3.84 and with one degree of freedom is statistically non-significant.

The third and fourth fit indices examined the residuals (i.e. the difference between the observed covariance matrix and the one predicted on the basis of the model parameters). The standardized root mean square residual (SRMSR) is a sample-based index reflecting the average squared difference between the observed and predicted matrices. Ideally, it should be 0, but acceptable fit may inferred with values up to 0.10. Since the SRMSR doesn't adjust for model parsimony, it cannot get any better as model complexity increases, but it should also not get any worse. The fourth measure of fit was the root mean square error of approximation (RMSEA). Unlike the other indices, the RMSEA does not require a null model in its calculation and does not conflict with the requirements for parsimony (Browne & Cudeck, 1993). The RMSEA addresses how well a model would fit the population covariance matrix if it were available and with optimally chosen parameter values (Browne & Cudeck, 1993). Ideally, this index should reflect that there is no model error, but values up to 0.08 are considered acceptable errors of approximation in the population with values of 0.05 or less indicating excellent fit.

The fifth and sixth indices were the Tucker-Lewis Index (TLI) and the Relative Noncentrality Index (RNI). The TLI and RNI are not systematically related to sample size, and both reflect systematic variation in model misspecification. While good fit is inferred when values are 0.90 or greater (excellent fit is indicated by values of 0.94 or greater), it is reasonable to expect that this value could drop somewhat below 0.90 for complex models with high degrees of freedom, due to the fact that these indices heavily penalize model complexity and reward model parsimony.

Finally, it should be noted that adding tremendously to the model complexity was the inclusion of several covariates into the analysis. Specifically, variables representing individuals' ages, organizational tenure, hours worked per week, whether or not they had supervisory responsibility, education level, marital status, gender and race were included as controls. All variance due to these variables in association with all of the 1st-order variables, and the 11 single item measures constituting the worker behavior component and the health and well being outcomes was controlled for simultaneously while estimating the hypothesized paths in Fig. 4. Therefore, we could preface each of the inferences regarding the hypothesized outcomes with the statement, "all else being equal in terms of age, race, etc." Controlling for these variables was particularly important for the outcome components given that, for example, education is positively correlated with engagement in preventive behaviors, or that younger individuals have higher turnover intentions than older people. Overall, we could simply be more confident that the observed results are representing true associations between the constructs and are less likely due to extraneous sources.

Results

Turning first to overall fit of the model, the fit indices indicated strong support for the healthy work organization model in Fig. 4. While the chi-square goodness-of-fit test was statistically significant ($\chi^2 = 63077.7$, d.f. = 17994, $p < 0.0001$), the chi-square to degree of freedom ratio was quite small (3.51) and within the limits associated with strong fit. Further, both the SRMSR (0.06) and RMSEA (0.03) values were well below the maximum thresholds for inferring good fit (0.10 and 0.05, respectively). In contrast, the TLI (0.87) and RNI (0.88) were somewhat below the 0.90 standard to infer strong fit. The values for the TLI and RNI were not wholly unexpected as these indices heavily penalize complex models. However, the research literature on fit indices provides no agreed upon standards for how much of a drop in those two indices is required before observing true model misspecification (the aspect these indices are purportedly sensitive to) vs. a sensitivity of these indices to anomalous study characteristics (model complexity in this case). Given that the drop was not dramatic (perhaps less than 0.85), and that the other fit indices indicated strong model fit, we felt confident that the model fit the data quite well, and we could proceed with the interpretation of the specific findings.

Once more for the sake of conserving space, the results associated with the 1st-order measurement models are not presented here, but are available upon request from the authors. In general, however, the measurement model associating item-level data to the 1st-order constructs was strongly supported. The results for the measurement model representing the higher-order constructs are presented in Table 2.

Table 2. Measurement Model for the 2nd-Order Latent Variables.

Parameter	Estimate (Standard Error)	*t*-value
Standardized Factor Loadings of the 2nd-Order Latent to 1st-Order Latent Constructs		
Attributes to Values	0.84 (RI)	
Attributes to Beliefs	0.29 (0.02)	13.28
Attributes to Involvement Policies	0.93 (0.04)	31.48
Attributes to Balance Policies	0.83 (0.04)	29.53
Attributes to Safety Policies	0.71 (0.03)	27.82
DOS to Organizational Support	0.91 (RI)	
DOS to Coworker Support	0.62 (0.02)	27.70
DOS to Involvement with Others	0.60 (0.03)	28.63
DOS to Involvement with Supervision	0.67 (0.03)	28.29
DOS to Communication	0.83 (0.03)	33.01
DOS to Health/Safety	0.71 (0.02)	28.45
Job Design to Job Content	0.84 (RI)	
Job Design to Autonomy	0.68 (0.03)	29.65
Job Design to Work Schedule	0.62 (0.03)	26.19
Job Design to Role Clarity	0.68 (0.03)	27.74
Job Design to Workload	-0.42 (0.03)	-18.40
Job Design to Physical Demands	-0.26 (0.03)	-12.71
Job Design to Environmental Conditions	-0.55 (0.03)	-20.08
Job Future to Job Security	0.61 (RI)	
Job Future to Procedural Equity	0.76 (0.06)	22.77
Job Future to Distributive Equity	0.74 (0.07)	23.57
Job Future to Learning Opportunities	0.84 (0.06)	23.84
Job Future to Flexible Work Arrangements	0.53 (0.05)	18.94
Work Adjustment to Job Satisfaction	0.96 (RI)	
Work Adjustment to Org. Commitment	0.85 (0.02)	28.40
Work Adjustment to Self-Efficacy	0.27 (0.01)	13.54
Work Adjustment to Impact	0.56 (0.02)	27.00
Work Adjustment to Stress	-0.65 (0.02)	-32.48
Psychological Out. to Somatic Symptoms	0.66 (RI)	
Psychological Out. to Depression	0.81 (0.05)	22.73
Psychological Out. to Anger	0.81 (0.04)	22.47

Note: RI = reference indicator; DOS = domains of support; Psychological Out. = psychological outcomes; *t*-values exceeding 1.96 are statistically significant.

As evident in Table 2, all of the hypothesized associations from the higher-order constructs to each of their respective component 1st-order constructs were statistically significant and in the appropriate direction. Thus, there was clear support for our expectation that the six sets of 1st-order dimensions have a common higher-order element that is over and above the uniqueness of each of those dimensions. Given this support meant as well that the associations from one higher-order construct to the next (and representing the substantive tests), and from them to the individual outcome measures could be meaningfully tested. These results are summarized in Tables 3 and 4. As a reminder, the results should be interpreted with a prefacing statement somewhat like, "all else being equal with respect to respondents age, education, race, marital status, hours worked, supervisory responsibility and gender."

Looking first at the top half of Table 3, clear support is indicated for the associations among the higher-order constructs. As expected, organizational

Table 3. Hypothesized Outcomes With the 1st-Order Health and Well Being Outcomes Associations Between the 2nd-Order Latent Variables and Between the 2nd-Order Work Adjustment and Psychological

Parameter	Estimate (Standard Error)	t-value
Standardized Path Coefficients Between the 2nd-Order Constructs		
Attributes to Domains of Support	0.92 (0.04)	31.42
Domains of Support to Job Design	0.91 (0.02)	33.89
Domains of Support to Job Future	0.97 (0.03)	23.84
Job Design to Work Adjustment	0.63 (0.06)	13.20
Job Future to Work Adjustment	0.31 (0.08)	7.56
Work Adjustment to Psychological Outcomes	−0.46 (0.01)	−17.53
Standardized Path Coefficients from Work Adjustment and Psychological Outcomes to the 1st-order Health and Well-Being Outcomes		
Work Adjustment to Alcohol Use	−0.02 (1.1)	ns
Psychological Outcomes to Alcohol Use	0.14 (2.3)	5.75
Work Adjustment to High Risk Status	0.03 (0.01)	ns
Psychological Outcomes to High Risk Status	0.16 (0.01)	7.30
Work Adjustment to Preventive Behaviors	−0.01 (0.02)	ns
Psychological Outcomes to Preventive Behaviors	−0.16 (0.05)	−5.00
Work Adjustment to Perceived Health	−0.02 (0.03)	ns
Psychological Outcomes to Perceived Health	0.01 (0.06)	ns
Work Adjustment to Perceived Work Safety	0.43 (0.02)	20.40
Psychological Outcomes to Perceived Work Safety	−0.08 (0.05)	−3.11

Note: ns = statistically non-significant; t-values equal to or greater than absolute values of 1.96 are statistically significant at $p < 0.05$ or lower.

Table 4. Effects of Work Adjustment, Psychological Outcomes and Health and Well Being Outcomes on Worker Behaviors.

| | Predictor Variables | | | | | | | | | | | | | |
| | Work Adjustment | | Psychological Outcomes | | Alcohol Use | | High Risk Status | | Preventive Behaviors | | Perceived Health | | Perceived Safety | |
Criterion Variables	Est. (se)	t-value	Est. (se)	t-value	Est. (se)	t-value	Est. (se)	t-value	Est. (se)	t-value	Est. (se)	t-value	Est. (se)	t-value
Turnover Intention	-0.60 (0.03)	-27.11	0.00 (0.06)	ns	0.05 (0.00)	2.70	-0.03 (0.08)	ns	-0.03 (0.02)	ns	0.01 (0.02)	ns	0.05 (0.02)	3.27
Absences	-0.05 (0.03)	-2.49	0.27 (0.06)	8.39	0.01 (0.00)	ns	-0.02 (0.08)	ns	-0.03 (0.02)	ns	0.00 (0.02)	ns	-0.01 (0.02)	ns
Lateness	-0.02 (0.02)	ns	0.24 (0.05)	7.84	0.04 (0.00)	2.51	-0.07 (0.06)	-2.19	-0.11 (0.02)	-3.63	0.03 (0.01)	ns	-0.02 (0.02)	ns
Performance	0.26 (0.03)	10.54	-0.02 (0.05)	ns	-0.01 (0.00)	ns	-0.03 (0.07)	ns	0.01 (0.02)	ns	-0.01 (0.02)	ns	-0.01 (0.02)	ns
Accidents	0.00 (0.01)	ns	0.13 (0.03)	4.78	-0.01 (0.00)	ns	0.02 (0.04)	ns	-0.01 (0.01)	ns	-0.02 (0.01)	ns	-0.11 (0.01)	-5.24
Work Limitations	-0.04 (0.02)	ns	0.18 (0.03)	6.00	-0.03 (0.00)	ns	0.02 (0.05)	ns	0.05 (0.01)	ns	-0.02 (0.01)	ns	-0.05 (0.01)	-2.81

Note: Est. (se) = standardized parameter estimates (standard error); *t*-values greater than or equal to 1.96 are statistically significant at the $p < 0.05$ level or lower.

attributes were positively associated with the domains of social support, which in turn had positive associations with both the job design and job future components. In turn, both job design and job future had positive associations with the work adjustment component. The association from the job future component to work adjustment was much weaker, though, than that for job design. Further, as expected, the negative relationship between work adjustment and psychological outcomes indicated that the stronger individuals' adjustment to the workplace, the less likely they are at psychological risk for depression, anger and somatic stress.

Turning now to the bottom half of Table 3, much clearer support was obtained for the hypothesized paths between psychological outcomes and health and well being than between work adjustment and health and well being. That is, the greater individuals' psychological risks for depression, anger and somatic stress: (a) the greater their use of alcohol (unstandardized coefficient was approximately 13 more drinks per month); (b) the higher their health risk status; (c) the less likely they are to engage in preventive behaviors; and (d) the more likely they are to perceive their well being as threatened by exposure in the workplace to safety and health hazards. In contrast, work adjustment possessed only its expected positive association with perceived exposure to safety and health hazards (i.e. the more adjusted individuals are, the safer they perceived the work environment). Given, though, the very strong association between work adjustment and psychological outcomes meant that the work adjustment component had indirect effects on the other health and well being outcomes through the psychological outcomes. Indeed, the unstandardized indirect effect from work adjustment to alcohol use was -8, meaning that work adjustment could reduce alcohol use through its influence on psychological outcomes.

Attending now to Table 4, it should be noted first that not a single worker behavior outcome was left unaccounted for by the set of predictors embodied through work adjustment, psychological outcomes, and the set of health and well being measures. Specifically, turnover intention was, as expected, negatively influenced by work adjustment, and appeared to be promoted through increasing levels of alcohol use. Similarly, while lower levels were associated with work adjustment, absences appeared to increase with increasing psychological risks for depression, anger and somatic stress. Lateness was also similarly associated with the psychological outcomes, but in addition, appeared to increase with increasing use of alcohol. Also, as expected, work adjustment had strong positive associations with individuals' perceptions as to how their supervisors rated their job performance. Finally, incidents of accidents and whether a person's work capacity was limited appeared to increase with increasing psychological risks for depression, anger and somatic stress. However, offsetting the latter associations was the fact that accidents and work limitations decreased as individuals' perceived well being in the workplace was not threatened by safety and work hazards.

Somewhat disappointing in Tables 3 and 4 were the results around perceived health. It was neither predicted by work adjustment and psychological outcomes (Table 3) nor was predictive of any outcome in Table 4. Similarly, while high-risk status and preventive behaviors were predicted by psychological outcomes (Table 3), neither variable had a very strong presence as predictors of work behaviors. Given that the common theme in all three variables is health, perhaps the selected predictors and outcomes were not sensitive to their variability. For example, all three might be expected to predict health claims, or behaviors associated with exercise.

DISCUSSION AND CONCLUSIONS

Collectively, the results were very supportive of the healthy work organization model. The omnibus test of fit indicated that the specification of the parameters as presented in Fig. 4 were reasonable and representative of the data. Further, the results for the specification of the high-order constructs indicated that many of the variables used in tests of occupational stress frameworks, and other frameworks such as work adjustment models have a common element. Most important is the fact that the hypothesized associations among the higher-order constructs or common elements were strongly supported adding criterion-related validity to the model specification. In addition, the set of individual behaviors, which we know collectively influences organizational objective performance (Vandenberg et al., 1999), was successfully predicted through the model.

In as much as the model test represents an omnibus examination, it does not inform us, however, as to what specific variables of each of the higher-order components was driving the associations at the higher-levels. Such information may be useful, for example, if there was interest in designing targeted interventions for this specific sample. The term "specific" in the last sentence is important to recognize because it concedes that a different application of the healthy work organization model may yield similar higher-order results, but a different pattern of results when it comes to examining the associations among the specific variables. In this analysis, another model was specified, but there were no 2nd-order variables (the covariates were included). Rather, all of the paths from all of the variables in one component to all of the variables in another component were freely and simultaneously estimated. For example, there were now 30 paths representing the associations between the five organizational attribute variables and the 6 variables for domains of social support. Similarly,

66 paths were specified representing the associations between the variables for domains of social support and the 11 variables making up job design and job future. It should also be noted that the fit of this model was poorer than that obtained for the omnibus test ($\chi^2 = 68717.15$, $d.f. = 17888$; $\chi^2/d.f. = 3.86$; $SRMSR = 0.08$; $RMSEA = 0.03$; $TLI = 0.85$; $RNI = 0.86$). Further, using the Akaike information criterion to compare the two models indicates that the omnibus model utilized the information in the database (AIC = 64919.7) better than did the current model test (AIC = 70971.2). However, we contend that model fit in the current test is not entirely relevant given that strong model fit was obtained in the omnibus test, and that the goal of the current analysis was to explore what was driving the omnibus test – not to confirm a set of expected associations.

The results from these analyses are organized in Tables 5 through 10. Given that the purpose of the supplementary analyses helps sharpen and clarify the results, the following discussion will work backwards through the model starting with the outcome variables.

We will leave it to the individual reader to struggle with the specifics of the information in Tables 5 through 10. While one may perhaps weave several stories from the results, we believe the most representative one underlying the omnibus test is as follows, and as summarized in Fig. 5. Simply put, we identified those dimensions within each component that were the strongest drivers of, most frequently associated with, dimensions in the adjoining components. For example, between the two, job satisfaction and anger had associations with *all* six of the worker behavior variables (our most distal outcomes) (Table 5), job stress was significantly associated with all three psychological dimensions (Table 7), and so forth.

Further, as seen in Fig. 5, the pattern of positive and negative (+ and –) signs between the variables are completely consistent with what one would expect. For example, job satisfaction was negatively associated with turnover intentions and frequency of job-related accidents. In contrast, generalized anger was positively associated with the frequency of job-related accidents and the degree to which the individual had work limitations. Interestingly, anger also was positively associated with the per-month frequency of alcohol use which in turn promoted levels of turnover intentions and how often individuals were late for work. In addition to the direct effects of job satisfaction (negative) and anger (positive) on accidents and work limitations, both variables also had indirect effects on those outcomes through their positive (job satisfaction) and negative (anger) associations with the degree to which employees felt their well being was protected from safety and health hazards in the workplace. The latter variable, in turn was negatively associated with accidents and work limitations.

Table 5. Summary of Effects of the 1st-Order Health/Well-Being Outcomes, Psychological Outcomes and Work Adjustment Dimensions on the 1st-Order Worker Behavior Dimensions.

Predictor Variables	Outcome Variables: Worker Behaviors					
	Turnover Intentions	Absences	Lateness	Performance	Accidents	Work Limitations
Health/Well-Being Outcomes						
Alcohol Use	0.05		0.04			
High Risk Status						
Preventive Behaviors			-0.07			
Perceived Health						
Perceived Work Safety	0.04				-0.10	-0.05
Psychological Outcomes						
Depression	0.05				-0.05	
Anger		0.08	0.18		0.03	0.05
Somatic Stress		0.14			0.10	0.17
Work Adjustment						
Job Satisfaction	-0.31			0.12	-0.07	-0.10
Organizational Commitment	-0.32				0.06	0.07
Job Stress			-0.07			
Self-Efficacy at Work	0.10		-0.05	0.07		
Personal Impact on Work Group	0.05			0.12		-0.04

Note: All coefficients are standardized values, and only those that were statistically significant, $p < 0.05$ or less, are reported; blank cells = not statistically significant.

Table 6. Summary of Effects of the 1st-Order Psychological Outcomes and Work Adjustment Dimensions on the 1st-Order Health and Well Being Outcomes.

Predictor Variables	Outcome Variables: Health and Well Being Outcomes				
	Alcohol Use	High Risk Status	Preventive Behaviors	Perceived Health	Perceived Work Safety
Psychological Outcomes					
Depression	-0.05		-0.05		0.07
Anger	0.13		-0.07		-0.09
Somatic Stress		0.11			
Work Adjustment					
Job Satisfaction			-0.06		0.28
Organizational Commitment			0.10		0.05
Job Stress			-0.03		-0.11
Self-Efficacy at Work	-0.07	-0.05			
Personal Impact on Work Group	0.04		-0.05		

Note: All coefficients are standardized values, and only those that were statistically significant, $p < 0.05$ or less, are reported; blank cells = not statistically significant.

Table 7.   Summary of Effects of the 1st-Order Work Adjustment
Dimensions on the 1st-Order Psychological Outcomes.

Predictor Variables	Criterion Variable		
	Depression	Anger	Somatic Stress
Psychological Outcomes			
Job Satisfaction	−0.04		
Organizational Commitment			0.06
Job Stress	0.40	0.53	0.40
Self-Efficacy at Work	−0.07		−0.11
Personal Impact on Work Group			

Note: All coefficients are standardized values, and only those that were statistically significant, $p < 0.05$ or less, are reported; blank cells = not statistically significant.

Also of interest is the fact that job stress was positively associated with anger. Job stress was itself negatively influenced by individuals' feelings of job security and job content, which in turn, had positive associations with job satisfaction. The two primary positive drivers from the domains of social support for job content and job security were organizational support and the level of participation with the supervisor (Table 9). Finally, among the organizational attributes, the degree to which high involvement work policies were perceived and the amount the organization values the individual had positive associations with both organizational support and participation with the supervisor (Table 10).

Lest we become bogged down in the details of the latter findings, the goal of the chapter was to present a model of healthy work organization, and empirical data supporting (at least initially) its validity. The healthy work organization model represents an integrative perspective utilizing some of the strongest attributes from the many frameworks proposed over the decades which have used many of the same variables. However, it should be apparent at this point that the core of the healthy work organization model draws heavily from an occupational stress frame of reference. This is due to the fact that the major occupational stress frameworks, as with the current model, have as their central focus the health and well being of the individual. In doing so, they have been quite successful in linking a configuration (albeit narrow) of work environment characteristics to actual physiological and psychological indicants of individual well being – something the other core perspectives do not do. However, the occupational stress frameworks have not taken advantage of thinking and findings in these other areas to expand the frameworks.

Table 8. Summary of Effects of the 1st-Order Job Design and Job Future Dimensions on the 1st-Order Work Adjustment Dimensions.

Predictor Variables	Outcome Variables: Work Adjustment Dimensions				
	Job Satisfaction	Organizational Commitment	Job Stress	Self-Efficacy at Work	Personal Impact on Work Group
Job Design					
Autonomy		-0.05		-0.06	0.24
Role Clarity				0.12	0.10
Job Content	0.47	0.43	-0.15	0.17	0.09
Workload	-0.04		0.33		0.10
Work Schedule	0.17	0.08	-0.07		0.05
Physical Work Demands		0.07	-0.04	0.07	
Environmental Stressors	-0.07	-0.05	0.16		
Job Future					
Job Security	0.16	0.20	-0.15	0.18	0.14
Learning Opportunities	0.11	0.16		0.05	
Work Arrangements	0.09		-0.09		0.09
Procedural Equity				-0.09	0.05
Distributive Equity	0.14	0.07	-0.10	-0.09	0.06

Note: All coefficients are standardized values, and only those that were statistically significant, $p < 0.05$ or less, are reported; blank cells = not statistically significant.

Table 9. Summary of Effects of the 1st-Order Dimensions for Domains of Support With the 1st-Order Dimensions for Job Design and Job Future.

| Predictor Variables | Job Design Dimensions | | | | | | | Job Future Dimensions | | | | |
	Autonomy/ Control	Role Clarity	Job Content	Workload	Work Schedule	Physical Work Demands	Environmental Stressors	Job Security	Learning Opportunities	Work Arrangements	Procedural Equity	Distributive Equity
Coworker Support	-0.06	0.07		-0.13		-0.06	-0.07	-0.05				0.06
Organizational Support	0.35	0.26	0.57	-0.15	0.33	-0.07	-0.15	0.24	0.45	0.17	0.35	0.44
Communication		0.17	0.09	-0.17	0.10		-0.11		0.19	0.20	0.29	0.16
Workplace Health		0.09			-0.04		-0.19	0.09	0.14		0.04	-0.05
Participation With Others	0.21	0.09	0.10	0.17	0.08	0.07	0.10			0.06		
Participation With Supervisor	0.25	0.12	0.13	-0.15	0.17	-0.17	-0.15	0.23	0.13	0.17	0.10	0.17

Note: All coefficients are standardized values, and only those that were statistically significant, $p < 0.05$ or less, are reported; blank cells = not statistically significant.

Table 10. Summary of Effects of the 1st-Order Organizational Attributes Dimensions on the 1st-Order Dimensions for Domains of Support.

Predictor Variables: Organizational Attributes	Coworker Support	Organizational Support	Communication	Workplace Health	Participation With Others	Participation With Supervisor
Involvement Policies	0.37	0.53	0.55	0.21	0.43	0.42
Quality of Work Life Policies		0.11	0.05			0.08
Safety and Health Attributes	0.08	-0.04	0.11	0.49		
Organizational Values Regarding People	0.27	0.52	0.39	0.35	0.23	0.37
Organizational Beliefs Regarding Safety and Health			-0.05	0.09		

Criterion Variables

Note: All coefficients are standardized values, and only those that were statistically significant, $p < 0.05$ or less, are reported; blank cells = not statistically significant.

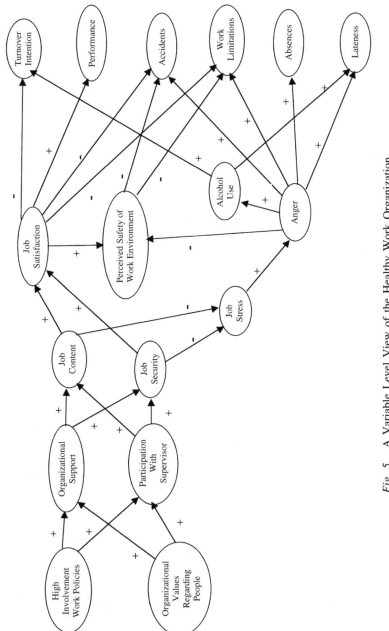

Fig. 5. A Variable Level View of the Healthy Work Organization.

The healthy work organization model is an attempt to do so. Included among the extensions is a recognition that much of what gets done in an organization, and how work is organized, is driven by the core attributes of the organization, and what support is available. These antecedent components were clearly supported in the current study. Also, supported was the fact that while researchers have variously operationalized the same components using different variables, there is a common, higher-order element among those variables that possess meaningful associations with one another. It was also shown, though, that this more omnibus view may be driven by a specific pattern of associations among the variables underlying the higher-order elements, and that this specific pattern may vary from sample-to-sample. The latter observation may also be the reason why researchers have not always obtained the same patterns of findings when using the same sets of variables in tests of occupational stress and other frameworks. Finally, the healthy work organization model was anchored to a set of individual behaviors that are commonly recognized as being ones that have an impact on objective measures of organizational effectiveness (e.g. financial performance).

The current test was not without some recognized limitations. For one, it was cross-sectional. However, we quickly point out that by including so many covariates and by conducting the tests at the higher-order level (and thereby controlling also for each individual variable), many of the concerns with cross-sectional data were probably mitigated. The second limitation was the fact that many model components have an "organizational perspective." This is particularly true for the two antecedents, organizational attributes and domains of social support. The third limitation is that we did not include any organizational-level effectiveness indices such as financial performance or turnover. Both of the latter limitations imply the need to address the model through a multilevel perspective. Data currently being collected in this project will eventually enable us to do just that. In the meantime, encouraging is the fact that as a preliminary analysis, hierarchical linear modeling supported that there is significant between unit differences on all of the variables underlying all six of the 2nd-order components in Fig. 4. Despite these limitations, the healthy work organization model was strongly supported and provides a viable framework for framing our research questions.

The concept of healthy work organization, particularly as delineated in the proposed model, has several implications for how organizations view and approach the welfare of their employees and the enterprises themselves. With leaner organizations and more aggressively competitive markets, the end effects have been to increase employee workloads, decrease workforce size, and reduce job security. These factors are just examples of occupational stress that continue to grow and be mounting problems facing American workers in an ever-changing work environment. Taking a more proactive approach to addressing the organizational stress process would tend to require that organizations engage in some form of systematic self-analysis in order to address such work conditions and job stressors. Thus, ongoing, critical analysis is central to our working definition of healthy work organization. The proposed model requires organizations to examine their innermost workings; specifically, how work processes are structured and managed and how employees are viewed and treated in the course of day to day operations. Via this diagnostic audit, not only can work conditions and stressors be identified but organizations may use this information as a springboard to identify and determine the most appropriate interventions needed to address those issues. The healthy work organization model presented in this chapter not only represents an integrative perspective employing salient attributes from various frameworks utilized over the past few decades but also appears to be conceptually supported based on our own research findings.

ACKNOWLEDGMENTS

This work was supported in part by the National Institute for Occupational Safety and Health (NIOSH) and the U.S. Centers for Disease Control and Prevention (CDC). However, its contents are solely the responsibility of the authors and do not necessarily represent the official views of NIOSH or CDC.

REFERENCES

Adams, J. C. (1963). Toward an understanding of inequity. *Journal of Abnormal and Social Psychology, 67*, 422–436.

Adkins, C. (1995). Previous work experience and organizational socialization: A longitudinal examination. *Academy of Management Journal, 38*, 839–862.

American Heart Association (2001). *2002 heart and stroke statistical update*. Dallas, TX: American Heart Association.

Baker, E., Israel, B., & Schurman, S. (1996). Role of control and support in occupational stress: An integrated model. *Social Science and Medicine, 43*, 1145–1159.

Baker, D. B., & Landrigan, P. J. (1990). Occupationally related disorders. *Environmental Medicine, 74*, 441–460.

Becker, B. E., Huselid, M. A., Pickus, P. S., & Spratt, M. F. (1997). HR as a source of shareholder value: Research and recommendations. *Human Resources Management, 36*, 39–478.

Beehr, T. (1995). *Psychological stress in the workplace*. New York: Routledge.

Beehr, T. A., & Bhagat, R. S. (1985). *Human stress and cognition in organizations*. New York: Wiley.

Bohen, H., & Viveros-Long, A. (1981). *Balancing jobs and family life*. Philadelphia: Temple University Press.

Bollen, K. A., & Long, J. S. (1993). *Testing structural equation models*. Newbury Park, California: Sage.

Browne, M. S., & Cudeck, R. (1993). Alternative ways of assessing fit. In: K. A. Bollen & J. S. Long (Eds), *Testing Structural Equation Models*. Thousand Oaks, CA: Sage.

Cahill, J., & Landsbergis, P. A. (1996). Job strain among post office mail handlers. *International Journal of Health Services, 26*, 731–750.

Caplan, R. D. (1987). Person-environment fit in organizations: Theories, fact, and values. In: A. W. Riley & S. J. Zaccaro (Eds), *Occupational Stress and Organizational Effectiveness* (pp. 103–140). New York: Praeger.

Caplan, R. D., Cobb, S., French, T. R. P., Harrison, R. V., & Pinneau, S. R. (1975). *Job demands and worker health*. Washington, D.C.: U.S. Government Printing Office.

Caplan, R. D., & Harrison, R. V. (1993). Person-environment fit theory: Some history, recent developments and future directions. *Journal of Social Issues, 49*, 253–275.

Cohen, A. (1977). Factors in successful occupational safety programs. *Journal of Safety Research, 9*, 168–178.

Cohen, S., Kamarck, T., & Mermelstein, R. (1983). A global measure or perceived stress. *Journal of Health and Social Behavior, 24*, 385–396.

Cooper, C. L. (1998). *Theories of organizational stress*. New York: Oxford University Press.

Cooper, C. L., & Cartwright, S. (1994). Healthy mind, healthy organization-A proactive approach to occupational stress. *Human Relations, 47*, 455–471.

Cooper, C. L., & Williams, S. (Eds) (1994). *Creating healthy work organizations*. New York: John Wiley and Sons.

Cox, T. (1988). Editorial: Organizational health. *Work & Stress, 2*, 1–2.

Cox, T., & Howarth, I. (1990). Organizational health, culture, and helping. *Work & Stress, 4*, 107–110.

Danna, K., & Griffin, R. W. (1999). Health and well being in the workplace: A review and synthesis of the literature. *Journal of Management, 25*, 357–384.

DeJoy, D. M., Murphy, L., & Gershon, R. M. (1995). The influence of employee job/task, and organizational factors on adherence to universal precautions among nurses. *International Journal of Industrial Ergonomics, 16*, 43–55.

DeJoy, D. M., & Southern, D. J. (1993). An integrative perspective on worksite health promotion. *Journal of Occupational Medicine, 35*, 1221–1230.

DeJoy, D. M., & Wilson, M. G. (2002, under review). Work and health: Delineating a model of healthy work organization. *Health Education and Behavior*.

Du Toit, M., & Du Toit, S. (2001). *Interactive LISREL: User's Guide*. Lincolnwood, IL: Scientific Software International.

Eden, D. (in press). Job Stress and respite relief: Overcoming high-tech tethers. In: P. L. Perrewé & D. C. Ganster (Eds), *Research in Occupational Stress and Well Being* (Vol. 1). Greenwich, CT: JAI Press.

Edwards, J. R. (1992). A cybernetic theory of stress, coping, and well being in organizations. *Academy of Management Review, 17*, 238–274.

Edwards, J. R., Caplan, R. D., & Harrison, R. (1998). Person-Environment fit theory: conceptual foundation, empirical evidence, and directions for future research. In: C. L. Cooper (Ed.), *Theories of Organizational Stress* (pp. 28–67). New York: Oxford University Press.

Edwards, J. R., & Harrison, R. V. (1993). Job demands and worker health: Three-dimensional reexamination of the relationship between person-environment fit and strain. *Journal of Applied Psychology, 78*, 628–648.

Eisenberger, R., Huntington, R., Hutchison, S., & Sowa, D. (1986). Perceived organizational support. *Journal of Applied Psychology, 71*, 500–507.

French, J. R. P. (1963). The social environment and mental health. *Journal of Social Issues, 19,* 39–56.

French, J. R. P., Rodgers, W. L., & Cobb, S. (1974). Adjustment as person-environment fit. In: G. Coelho, D. Hamburg & J. Adams (Eds), *Coping and Adaptation* (pp. 316–333). New York: Basic Books.

French, J. R. P., Caplan, R. D., & Harrison, R. V. (1982). *The mechanisms of job stress and strain.* New York: Wiley.

Frone, M. R., Russell, M., & Cooper, M. L. (1995). Job stressors, job involvement, and employee health: A test of identity theory. *Journal of Occupational and Organizational Psychology, 68,* 1–11.

Ganster, D. C. (1989). Worker control and well being: A review of research in the workplace. In: S. L. Sauter, J. J. Hurrell & C. L. Cooper (Eds), *Job Control and Worker Health* (pp. 3–23). New York: John Wiley & Sons.

Goetzel, R. Z., Jacobson, B. H., Aldana, S. G., Vardell, K., & Yee, L. (1998). Health care costs of worksite health promotion participants and non-participants. *Journal of Occupational and Environmental Medicine, 40,* 341–346.

Goetzel, R. Z., & Ozminkowski, R. J. (2000). Health and productivity management: Emerging opportunities for health promotion professionals for the 21st century. *American Journal of Health Promotion, 14,* 211–214.

Greenberg, J. (1986). Determinants of perceived fairness of performance evaluations. *Journal of Applied Psychology, 71,* 340–342.

Greenberg, P. E., Kessler, R. C., Nells, T. L., Finkelstein, S. N., & Berndt, E. R. (1996). Depression in the workplace: an economic perspective. In: J. P. Feighner & W. F. Boyer (Eds), *Selective Serotonin Re-uptake Inhibitors: Advances in Basic Research and Clinical Practice* (2nd ed., pp. 327–363). New York: Wiley & Sons.

Greenberger, D. B., Strausser, S., Cummings, L. L., & Dunham, R. B. (1989). The impact of personal control on performance and satisfaction. *Organizational Behavior & Human Decision Processes, 43,* 29–51.

Gustavsen, B. (1980). Improving the work environment: A choice of strategy. *International Labour Review, 119,* 271–286.

Hackman, J. R., & Oldham, G. R. (1980). *Work redesign.* Reading: MA: Addison-Wesley.

Hale, A. R., & Hovden, I. (1998). Management and culture: The third age of safety – a review of approaches to organizational aspects of safety, health, and environment. In: A. M. Feyer & A. Williamson (Eds), *Occupational Injury: Risk, Prevention, and Intervention* (pp. 129–165). London: Taylor-Francis.

Hallquivist, J., Diderichsen, F., Theorell, T., Reuterwall, C., & Ahlbom, A. (1998). Is the effect of job strain on myocardial infarction risk due to interaction between high psychological demands and low decision latitude? Results from Stockholm Heart Epidemiology Program (SHEEP). *Social Science and Medicine, 46,* 1405–1415.

Harrison, R. V. (1985). The person-environment fit and the study of job stress. In: T. A. Beehr & R. S. Bhagat (Eds), *Human Stress and Cognition in Organizations* (pp. 23–55). New York: Wiley.

Hayes, B. E., Perander, J., Smecko, T., & Trask, J. (1998). Measuring perceptions of workplace safety: Development and validation of the work safety scale. *Journal of Safety Research, 29,* 145–161.

Heaney, C. A. (1991). Enhancing social support at the workplace: Assessing the effects of the caregiver support program. *Health Education Quarterly, 18,* 477–494.

Heaney, C. A., Israel, B. A., & House, J. S. (1994). Chronic job insecurity among automobile workers: Effects on job satisfaction and health. *Social Science and Medicine, 38,* 1431–1437.

112   ROBERT J. VANDENBERG ET AL.

Hendrix, W. H., Summers, T. P., Leap, T. L., & Steel, R. P. (1995). Antecedents and organizational effectiveness outcomes of employee stress and health. In: R. Crandall & P. L. Perrewe (Eds), *Occupational Stress* (pp. 73–92). Washington, D.C.: Taylor & Francis.

Hinkin, T. R. (1995). A review of scale development practices in the study of organizations. *Journal of Management, 21*, 967–988.

Hofmann, D. A., Jacobs, R., & Landy, F. (1995). High reliability process industries: Individual, micro, and macro organizational influences on safety performance. *Journal of Safety Research, 26*, 131–149.

House, J. S. (1981). *Work stress and social support.* Massachusetts: Addison-Wesley Publishing Company.

House, J. S., McMichael, A. J., Wells, J. A., Kaplan, B. H., & Landerman, L. R. (1979). Occupational stress and health among factory workers. *Journal of Health and Social Behavior, 20*, 139–160.

Hulin, C. L. (1991). Adaptation, persistence, and commitment in organizations. In: M. D. Dunnette & L. M. Hough (Eds), *Handbook of Industrial and Organizational Psychology* (2nd ed., Vol. 2, pp. 445–505). Palto Alto, CA: Consulting Psychologists Press.

Huselid, M. A. (1995). The impact of human resource management practices on turnover, productivity, and corporate financial performance. *Academy of Management Journal, 38*, 635–672.

Ilfeld, F. W. (1978). Psychologic status of community residents along major demographic dimensions. *Archives of General Psychiatry, 35*, 716–724.

Israel, B. A., Schurman, S. J., & House, J. S. (1989). Action research on occupational stress: Involving workers as researchers. *International Journal of Health Services, 19*, 135–155.

Jackson, S. E. (1983). Participation in decision making as a strategy for reducing job-related strain. *Journal of Applied Psychology, 68*, 3–19.

Jaffe, D. T. (1995). The healthy company: Research paradigms for personal and organizational health. In: S. L. Sauter & L. R. Murphy (Eds), *Organizational Risk Factors for Job Stress* (pp. 13–29). Washington, D.C.: American Psychological Association.

Jamieson, D., & O'Mara, J. (1991). *Managing workforce 2000: Gaining the diversity advantage.* San Francisco: Jossey-Bass.

Jayaratne, S., & Chess, W. A. (1984). The effects of emotional support on perceived job stress and strain. *Journal of Applied Behavioral Science, 20*, 141–153.

Johansson, G., Johnson, J. V., & Hall, E. M. (1991). Smoking and sedentary behavior as related to work organization. *Social Science and Medicine, 32*(7), 837–846.

Johnson, J. V. & Hall, E. M. (1988). Job strain, workplace social support, and cardiovascular disease: A cross-sectional study of a random sample of the Swedish working population. *American Journal of Public Health, 78*, 1336–1342.

Johnson, J., Hall, E., & Theorell, T. (1989). The combined effects of job strain and social isolation on the prevalence and mortality incidence of cardiovascular disease in a random sample of the Swedish male working population. *Scandinavian Journal of Work and Environmental Health, 15*, 271–279.

Karasek, R. A. (1979). Job demands, job decision latitude, and mental strain: Implications for job redesign. *Administrative Science Quarterly, 24*, 285–308.

Karasek, R. A., Baker, D., Marxer, F., Ahlbom, A., & Theorell, A. (1981). Job decision latitude, job demands, and cardiovascular disease: A prospective study of Swedish men. *American Journal of Public Health, 71*, 694–705.

Karasek, R. A., Schwartz, J., & Theorell, T. (1982). *Job characteristics, occupation and coronary heart disease.* Department of Industrial Engineering and Operations Research, Columbia University. Final report to the National Institute for Occupational Safety and Health, U.S. Department of Health and Welfare (Contract No. R-01-0H00906).

Karasek, R. A., & Theorell, T. (1990). *Healthy work: Stress, productivity and the reconstruction of working life.* New York: John Wiley & Sons.

Kessler, R. C., Barber, C., Birnbaum, H. G., Frank, R. G., Greenberg, P. E., Rose, R. M., Simon, G. E., & Wang, P. (1999). Depression in the workplace: Effects on short-term disability. *Health Affairs, 18,* 163–171.

Klitzman, S., House, J. S., Israel, B. A., & Mero, R. P. (1990). Work stress, non-work stress, and health. *Journal of Behavioral Medicine, 13,* 221–243.

Koslowsky, M. (1998). Theories of organizational stress. In: M. Koslowsky (Ed.), *Modeling the Stress-Strain Relationship in Work Settings* (pp. 8–29). London: Routledge.

Kotter, J., & Heskett, T. (1992). *Corporate culture and performance.* New York: Free Press.

Kristensen, T. S. (1995). The demand-control-support model: Methodological challenges for future research. *Stress Medicine, 11,* 17–26.

Kuhnert, K., Sims, R. R., & Lahey, M. A. (1989). The relationship between job security and employee health. *Group & Organization Studies, 14,* 399–410.

Lance, C. E., & Vandenberg, R. J. (2002). Confirmatory factor analysis. In: F. Drasgow & N. Schmitt (Eds), *Measuring and Analyzing Behavior in Organizations: Advances in Measurement and Data Analysis* (pp. 221–256). San Francisco: Jossey-Bass.

Lance, C. E., Vandenberg, R. J., & Self, R. M. (2000). Latent growth models of individual change: The case of newcomer adjustment. *Organizational Behavior and Human Decision Processes, 83,* 107–140.

Landsbergis, P. A., & Vivona-Vaughan, E. (1995). Evaluation of an occupational stress intervention in a public agency. *Journal of Organizational Behavior, 16,* 29–48.

Larkin, T. J., & Larkin, S. (1996). Reaching and changing frontline employees. *Harvard Business Review, 74,* 95–104.

LaRocco, J. M., House, J. S., & French, J. R. P. (1980). Social support, occupational stress, and health. *Journal of Health and Social Behavior, 21,* 202–218.

Lawler, E. E., III. (1992). *The ultimate advantage: Creating the high involvement organization.* San Francisco: Jossey-Bass.

Lee, T. W., & Johnson, D. R. (1991). The effects of work schedule and employment status on the organizational commitment and job satisfaction of full vs. part time employees. *Journal of Vocational Behavior, 38,* 208–224.

Levi, L. (1981). *Preventing work stress.* Reading, PA: Addison-Wesley.

Lindstrom, K. (1994). Psychosocial criteria for good work organization. *Scandinavian Journal of Work and Environmental Health, 20,* 123–133.

Little, R. J. A. & Schenker, N. (1995). Missing data. In: G. Arminger, C. C. Clogg & M. E. Sobel (Eds), *Handbook of Statistical Modeling for the Social and Behavioral Sciences* (pp. 39–75). New York: Plenum.

Mausner-Dorsch, H., & Eaton, W. W. (2000). Psychosocial work environment and depression: Epidemiologic assessment of the demand-control model. *American Journal of Public Health, 90,* 1765–1770.

McAfee, R. B., & Winn, A. R. (1989). The use of incentives/feedback to enhance workplace safety: A critique of the literature. *Journal of Safety Research, 20,* 7–19.

McLeroy, K. R., Bibeau, D., Steckler, A., & Glanz, K. (1988). An ecological perspective on health promotion programs. *Health Education Quarterly, 15,* 351–377.

Morrow, P. C., McElroy, J. C., & Elliot, S. M. (1994). The effect of preference for work-status, schedule, and shift on work-related attitudes. *Journal of Vocational Behavior, 45,* 202–222.

Mowday, R. T., Steers, R. M., & Porter, L. W. (1979). The measurement of organizational commitment. *Journal of Vocational Behavior, 14,* 224–247.

Muntaner, C., Anthony, J. C., Crum, R. M., & Eaton, W. W. (1995). Psychological dimensions of work and the risk of drug dependence among adults. *American Journal of Epidemiology*, *142*, 183–190.

Muthén, B., Kaplan, D., & Hollis, M. (1987). On structural equation modeling with data that are not missing completely at random. *Psychometrika*, *52*, 431–462.

National Institute for Occupational Safety and Health (1996). *National Occupational Research Agenda* (NIOSH Publication No. 96-115). Washington, D.C.: National Institute for Occupational Safety and Health.

O'Brien, G. E., & Stevens, K. (1981). The relationship between perceived influence and job satisfaction among assembly line employees. *Journal of Industrial Relations*, *23*, 33–48.

O'Reilly, C. A., Chatman, J., & Caldwell, D. F. (1991). People and organizational culture: A profile comparison approach to assessing person-organization fit. *Academy of Management Journal*, *34*, 487–516.

Pelletier, K. R. (1984). *Healthy people in unhealthy places: Stress and fitness at work*. New York: Delacorte Press.

Pfeiffer, G. J. (1987). Corporate health can improve if firms take an organizational approach. *Occupational Health & Safety*, *86*, 96–99.

Polley, R. B. (1987). Exploring polarization in organizational groups. *Group and Organization Studies*, *12*, 424–444.

Rasanen, K., Notkola, V., & Husman, K. (1997). Perceived work conditions and work-related symptoms among employed Finns. *Social Science and Medicine*, *45*, 1099–1110.

Renn, R. W. & Vandenberg, R. J. (1995). The Critical Psychological States: An Underrepresented Component in Job Characteristics Model Research. *Journal of Management*, *21*, 279–303.

Ribisl, K. M., & Reischl, T. M. (1993). Measuring the climate for health at organizations: Development of the worksite health climate scales. *Journal of Occupational Medicine*, *35*, 812–824.

Rizzo, J. R., House, R. J., & Lirtzman, S. I. (1970). Role conflict and ambiguity in complex organizations. *Administrative Science Quarterly*, *20*, 150–163.

Rokeach, M. (1979). From individual to institutional values: With special reference to the values of science. In: M. Rokeach (Ed.), *Understanding Human Values* (pp. 47–70). New York: Free Press.

Rosen, R. H., & Berger, L. (1991). *The healthy company: Eight strategies to develop people, productivity, and profits*. New York: G. P. Putnam's Sons.

Roth, R. L. (1994). Missing data: A conceptual view for applied psychologists. *Personnel Psychology*, *47*, 537–560.

Sandroff, D. J., Bradford, S., & Gilligan, V. F. (1990). Meeting the health promotion challenge through a model of shared responsibility. *Occupational Medicine: State of the Art Review*, *5*, 677–690.

Sauter, S. L., Lim, S. Y., & Murphy, L. R. (1996). Organizational health: a new paradigm for occupational stress research at NIOSH. *Occupational Mental Health*, *4*, 248–254.

Sauter, S. L., & Murphy, L. R. (1995). *Organizational risk factors for job stressors*. Washington, D.C.: American Psychological Association.

Sauter, S. L., Murphy, L. R., & Hurrell, J. J. (1990). Prevention of work-related psychological disorders. *American Psychologist*, *45*, 1146–1158.

Schurman, S. J., & Israel, B. A. (1995). Redesigning work systems to reduce stress: A participatory action research approach to creating change. In: L. R. Murphy, J. J. Hurrell, S. L. Sauter & G. P. Keita (Eds), *Job Stress Interventions* (pp. 235–252). Washington, D.C.: American Psychological Association.

Selye, H. (1983). The stress, concept: Past, present, and future. In: C. L. Cooper (Ed.), *Stress Research: Issues for the Eighties* (pp. 1–20). New York: John Wiley & Sons.

Senge, P. (1990). *The fifth discipline.* New York: Doubleday Currency.

Smith, K. K., Kaminstein, D. S., & Makadok, R. J. (1995). The health of the corporate body: Illness and organizational dynamics. *Journal of Applied Behavioral Science, 31,* 328–351.

Sparks, K., & Cooper, C. L. (1999). Occupational differences in the work-strain relationship: Towards the use of situation-specific models. *Journal of Occupational and Orgainzational Psychology, 72,* 219–229.

Spector, P. E. (1986). Perceived control by employees: A meta-analysis of studies concerning autonomy and participation at work. *Human Relations, 39,* 1005–1016.

Spector, P. E., & Goh, A. (in press). The role of emotions in the occupational stress process. In: P. L. Perrewé & D. C. Ganster (Eds), *Research in Occupational Stress and Well Being* (Vol. 1). Greenwich, CT: JAI.

Spreitzer, G. M. (1995). Psychological empowerment in the workplace: Dimensions, measurement, and validation. *Academy of Management Journal, 38,* 1442–1465.

Stewart, M. J. (1989). Social support: Diverse theoretical perspectives. *Social Science & Medicine, 28,* 1275–1282.

Stokols, D. (1992). Establishing and maintaining healthy environments: Toward a social ecology of health promotion. *American Psychologist, 47,* 6–22.

Tetrick, L. E., & LaRocco, J. M. (1987). Understanding, prediction, control as moderators of the relationships between perceived stress, satisfaction, and psychological well being. *Journal of Applied Psychology, 72,* 538–543.

Theorell, A. & Karasek, R. (1996). Current issues relating to psychosocial job strain and cardio-vascular disease research. *Journal of Occupational Health Psychology, 1,* 9–26.

U.S. Department of Health and Human Services. (2000). *Healthy People 2010* (Vol. 2). Washington, D.C.: U.S. Government Printing Office.

Vandenberg, R. J., & Lance, C. E. (1992). Examining the causal order of job satisfaction and organizational commitment. *Journal of Management, 18,* 153–167.

Vandenberg, R. J., Richardson, H., & Eastman, L. (1999). High involvement organizations: Their antecedents and consequences. *Groups & Organizations Management, 24,* 300–339.

Vandenberg, R. J., & Self, R. M. (1993). Assessing newcomers' changing commitments to the organization during the first 6 months of work. *Journal of Applied Psychology, 78,* 557–568.

Wheaton, B., Muthén, B., Alwin, D. F., & Summers, G. F. (1977). Assessing reliability and stability in panel models. In: D. R. Heise (Ed.), *Sociological Methodology* (pp. 84–136). San Francisco: Jossey-Bass.

Xie, J. L. & Johns, G. (1995). Job scope and stress: Can job scope be to high? *Academy of Management Journal, 38,* 1288–1309.

Zohar, D. (1980). Safety climate in industrial organizations: Theoretical and applied implications. *Journal of Applied Psychology, 65,* 96–102.

INDIVIDUAL AND ORGANIZATIONAL HEALTH

Lois E. Tetrick

ABSTRACT

Individual health and organizational health have been conceptualized in several ways. This chapter discusses some of these conceptualizations of health including both the medical model, which characterizes health as the absence of illness, and other models, which characterizes health as optimal functioning not just the absence of illness. It is proposed that the literature on occupational stress, positive psychology, and the emerging literature on emotions in the work environment may be useful in extending our understanding and conceptualization of individual and organizational health. The literatures on pay structure and dispersion as well as organizational learning are reviewed. It is posited that these two organizational phenomena can be used to develop theoretical and empirical support for understanding organizational health, individual health, and the linkage between the two from both a positive health and ill health perspective.

Historical and Current Perspectives on Stress and Health, Volume 2, pages 117–141.
Copyright © 2002 by Elsevier Science Ltd.
All rights of reproduction in any form reserved.
ISBN: 0-7623-0970-9

INTRODUCTION

Stress is perhaps the most frequently used paradigm or theoretical framework for understanding individual employees' health and well being as a function of their interactions with their work environments (Spector & Goh, 2001). In 1975, Selye defined stress as the non-specific response to any demand. Although there has been considerable debate as to this definition, he suggested that this is a useful definition allowing one to distinguish between events (e.g. stressors) and the results or reactions to these events or stressors such as eustress and distress. According to Selye, eustress was a positive experience challenging people to grow and adapt. Alternatively, distress was a negative experience resulting in worry and anxiety. Eustress appears to reflect positive emotions, which McGuire (2001) suggested reflect a means to an end and are relatively short-lived. Distress, on the other hand, is undesirable and associated with negative emotions, which frequently persist for longer periods of time. This lingering effect may explain the negative impact of distress and negative emotions on physical health.

Despite this distinction between eustress and distress almost three decades ago, the preponderance of research on stress, especially occupational stress, has focused on distress (Nelson & Simmons, in press). Recently, there has been a call for more consideration of positive psychology (Seligman & Csikszentmihalyi, 2000) focusing on human strengths and optimal functioning. With the "re-emergence" of positive psychology, the term positive psychology was first used by Maslow in 1954 according to Resnick, Warmoth and Serlin (2001), it would appear timely to reconsider the positive as well as the negative impact of stress. The purpose of this chapter is to discuss the concept of health and well being arguing that health is more than merely the absence of illness. This conceptualization of health allows an integration of the stress literature with positive psychology to more fully address the notion of occupational health, not just occupational ill health, incorporating the role of positive and negative emotions in individual health. This chapter then discusses the concept of organizational health and attempts to draw a link between individual and organizational health based on rewards and learning. More specifically, the role of pay structures and organizational learning are discussed as they relate to both individual and organizational health.

CONCEPTUALIZATION OF HEALTH

At one level almost everyone has an understanding of what is meant by health (Larson, 1999). However, when one attempts to actually define health it becomes less apparent what is actually meant. There are several different conceptualizations of health. This holds true whether one is talking about the health of individuals or the health of organizations although conceptualizations of organizational health and individual health generally have appeared in separate literatures. This section presents several models of individual health incorporating positive psychology as well as the stress literature. Then the literature on organizational health is presented and similarities and differences in the models discussed.

Individual Health

"When we are healthy we don't notice our health but concentrate on other things. Health is, as it were, transparent, whereas illness and disease is opaque" (Downie & Macnaughton, 1998, p. 823). Downie and Macnaughton (1998) suggest that one of the challenges in trying to move beyond defining health as the absence of illness to a more positive, balanced perspective on health is the lack of a clear identity. That is, defining health as *not* just the absence of illness still doesn't provide a clear definition of what it *is*. It may be that Nietzsche was correct when he wrote "For there is no health as such, and all attempts to define anything that way have been miserable failures. Even the determination of what health means for your body depends on your goal, your horizon, your energies, your drives, your errors, and above all the ideals and phantasms of your soul" (as cited in Downie & Macnaughton, 1998, p. 824). Faced with this challenge, I nevertheless will review recent attempts to expand our perspective on health beyond that of the medical model.

Larson (1999) conceptualized health according to four models: the medical model, the World Health Organization (WHO) model, the wellness model, and the environmental model. The medical model essentially focuses on health as the absence of illness or disease. This is probably the most predominant view of health and one that Seligman and Csikszentmihalyi (2000) criticized as unduly influencing psychology with its focus on ill health rather than examining human strengths and optimal functioning.

The remaining three models are distinctly different from the medical model but somewhat more difficult to differentiate among themselves. In contrast to the medical model, the World Health Organization in their constitution defined health as a state of complete physical, mental, and social well being (World Health Organization, 1946). The importance of this model in addition to reflecting a positive orientation is that it includes not only physical and mental well being but also social well being, a dimension that generally was not considered in the medical model. The wellness model incorporates the idea of people having a reserve of health, which allows them to overcome illness and progress toward optimal human functioning. This model includes the importance of well being, energy, and the ability to work. Thus, the wellness model clearly incorporates a positive psychology perspective perhaps more explicitly than the WHO model although certainly consistent with the WHO model. The last model Larson (1999) suggested was the environmental model. This model focuses on individuals' adaptation to their physical and social environments. This model, perhaps more so than the wellness model, emphasizes the effective performance of the roles individuals have, including their roles as employees and family members by adapting to the demands of the environment.

These models are not without their criticisms (see Hofmann & Tetrick, forthcoming); however, they do offer some insights into the conceptualization of health. First, these conceptualizations of health all rely on values. This is consistent with Nietzsche's contention that conceptualizing health necessarily requires consideration of individual's motives and goals. It is also consistent with Ryff's (1995) contention that defining states of "complete social well being" or "optimal human functioning" requires addressing basic values and ideas. Secondly, these conceptualizations when taken together clearly incorporate physical, psychological, and social environmental factors in not only avoiding ill health but also in adapting and growing within various roles and environments.

One concern about these models, because of their reliance on values to define health, is that there may not be a similar meaning of health across various groups or cultures. Although an open question, there is some evidence to suggest that people do distinguish between health and ill health and that there may be some core conceptualizations of health. For example, Schmidt and Frohling (2000) examined lay persons' definitions of health by asking German children aged 5, 8, 12, or 16 and some of their mothers what "health" meant to them. These individuals did not have difficulty making a distinction between health and ill health. They defined health as being in a positive mood, having energy, feeling good, being strong and fit, feeling happy, being satisfied, taking pleasure in activities, and being able to do things such as playing, doing sports, or just getting out of the house. These aspects of health are strikingly similar to those included by the WHO, wellness, and environmental models of health, and clearly are consistent with the focus of positive psychology. Therefore, there may be more agreement in the basic values reflecting positive health than some have predicted.

A review of the literature identified several perspectives of what has been viewed as constituting health and well being. These range from Maslow's (1954) conceptualization of self-actualization to Rogers (1963) notion of fully functioning to Antonovsky's (1993) sense of coherence to a variety of additional dimensions or indicators of health and well being. For example, Seligman and Csikszentmihalyi (2000) suggested hope, wisdom, creativity, future mindedness, courage, spirituality, responsibility, and perseverance should be the foci of positive psychology in order to enhance our understanding of optimal human functioning and human strengths. Ryff and Singer (1998, 2000) define psychological well being as including autonomy, personal growth, self-acceptance, life purpose, mastery, and interpersonal flourishing. Ryan and Deci (2001) in their review of well being added from self-determination theory psychological growth, integrity, well being, vitality, and self-congruence; and Pajares (2001) included optimism and feelings of authenticity, while Snyder and McCullough (2000) included love, forgiveness, gratitude, humility, wisdom, control and hope as indicators of well being. Salovey et al. (2000) included positive affect, meaningfulness, manageability and hope. Recently, Luthans (2002) presented six concepts that met his criteria for positive organizational behavior (e.g. self-efficacy, hope, optimism, happiness or subjective well being, and emotional intelligence). Each of these positive organizational behavior concepts has been mentioned by other scholars as indicators of health and well being with the possible exception of emotional intelligence. Emotional intelligence is typically considered an individual difference which differentiates among people although it develops over the life span and can be changed somewhat with training (Ashkanasy & Daus, 2002). To the extent emotional intelligence is a stable individual difference then it probably should not be considered an indicator of health and well being.

There are undoubtedly other indicators of health and well being that have been proposed; however, I believe that it is clear to the reader that the dimensions of health and well being are numerous, raising a variety of issues. First, the stress literature has identified several illnesses and negative emotions resulting from distress, and while we may not have as large an empirical base of research, we do have multiple aspects of health and well being that may result from eustress. The question is whether we can link specific events or stressors to positive emotions and well being. For example, Cropanzano, Weiss, Suckow and Grandey (2000) review the literature linking perceptions of injustice to negative emotions with anger being one of the primary negative emotions. Anger and hostility have been recognized as precursors of ill health. Alternatively Basch and Fisher (2000) report in their test of Affective Events Theory (Weiss & Cropanzano, 1996) that while making mistakes and company policies were related to negative emotions, learning, recognition, and goal achievement were linked to positive emotions. In a similar vein, Larsen, Diener and Lucas (2002), citing Frederickson, indicate that there is a positive relation between positive emotions and creativity. This may provide a basis for the experience of flow discussed by Csikszentmihalyi (1997) and for timelessness as discussed by Mainemelis (2001). The emerging literature does appear to link both positive and negative emotions with subsequent health and ill health, although the mechanisms are not yet fully understood.

Secondly, the question arises whether the positive end of the health continuum is just the opposite end of the health continuum from negative, ill health. Based on the research on positive and negative affect (Watson & Clark, 1992; Watson, Clark & Telegen, 1988), it would be unlikely for this to be true, at least for a number of the concepts that have been considered to be indicators of ill health and positive health. There is some evidence to support that positive health and ill health are distinct and may involve different processes. For example, Krueger, Hicks and McGue (2001) looked at altruism (one indicator of positive health) and antisocial behavior (one behavioral reaction to distress). They found that altruism and antisocial behavior were indeed orthogonal and had different sources. Therefore, while health may be considered as a continuum ranging from ill health to positive health, it would be unwise to consider the aspects of health to be simply the obverse of ill health. For example, Weiss (2002) indicated that the effects of emotions on cognitive processes differ depending on the specific emotion aroused. Also, both Spector and Goh (2001) and Frederickson (2001) have posited that positive emotions can actually affect negative emotions. Therefore, it seems likely that the mechanisms underlying the relation between distress and ill health are different from the mechanisms underlying the relation between eustress and positive health. It also may be that these mechanisms are interconnected at some stages to the extent that positive emotions affect negative emotions or vice versa.

The third issue is that there does not seem to be a coherent framework for organizing the array of constructs that have been considered to reflect positive health. This isn't necessarily an exclusive problem with the conceptualization of positive health, as Weiss (2002) indicated that there also isn't agreement as to which emotions are "basic," although there is some agreement on happiness, surprise, fear, sadness, anger, and disgust. The question is whether there seems to be any convergence as to the indicators of positive health. Many of the concepts purported to reflect positive health have been described as virtues, as Snyder and McCullough (2000) did, for example; others clearly reflect values. Still other indicators of positive health appear to be more closely associated with emotions reflective of eustress; for example, Salovey et al. (2000) included three positive psychological states to reflect positive health, specifically mean-ingfulness, manageability, and hope. There also appears to be a parallel in the positive health literature with Spector and Goh's (2001) model of the stress process. In Spector and Goh's model negative emotions are posited to result from the perception of a stressor. These negative emotions then result in behav-ioral, physical, and psychological strains. If we use Spector and Goh's framework in the positive psychology realm, then it would be suggested that eustress, or the positive emotions experienced as a result of an environmental event, would result in health and well being reflected by behavioral, physical, and psychological responses.

Frederickson (2001) offers a somewhat different explanation for the connection between positive emotions and health and well being in her broaden-and-build theory of emotions. According to Fredrickson the specific action tendencies for positive emotions are more vague and less specified than the action tendencies for negative emotions. Therefore, positive emotions like joy, contentment, and love, although conceptually distinct, all broaden people's "momentary thought-action repertoires and build their enduring personal resources, ranging from physical and intellectual resources to social and psychological resources" (Frederickson, 2001, p. 219). Negative emotions, on the other hand, focus on the behavioral responses. Based on this theoretical perspective, Fredrickson found that positive emotions actually speeded recovery of cardiovascular reactivity to enduring negative emotions. Berk, Felten, Tan, Bittman and Westengard (2001) provided further evidence for the beneficial health effects of positive emotions. In this instance, humor operationalized as mirthful laughter was found to positively affect neuroimmune parameters. Therefore, Frederickson (2001) and Berk et al. (2001) support a connection between positive emotions and physical health consistent with an extension of Spector and Goh's (2001) framework although the linkages between positive emotions and health may be somewhat less specific than the linkages between negative emotions and ill health. From these studies, it is clear that positive emotions play a significant part in understanding this extended perspective of health and well being as well as negative emotions and behavioral strains.

Organizational Health

From the above it can be seen that health has primarily been viewed from a negative perspective – the absence of illness. However, this appears to be changing. The question is do we find the same focus on negative aspects when examining organizational health? Based on a review of the literature on organizational health it does appear to have a somewhat more positive focus, although one might argue that the concern for organizational health often stems from organizational ill health.

Historically, there has been a focus on problem solving and adaptability as a means for organizational survival in the long-term (Bennis, 1962; Miles, 1969). Several other characteristics or properties of healthy organizations have been proposed. These include goal focus, communication adequacy, optimal power/equalization, resource utilization, cohesiveness, innovativeness, and meeting goals (see Bennett, Cook & Pelletier, in press; Hofmann & Tetrick, forthcoming; Newell, 1995 for reviews). Interestingly, there has been a more recent trend in defining organizational health in light of the health of the employees within the organization. That is, it has been recognized that in order for organizations to be healthy the health of their employees needs to be considered (Cooper & Cartwright, 1994; Newell, 1995; Quick, 1999). For example, Quick (1999) reported that the characteristics of a work environment signifying a healthy organization were high levels of employee satisfaction, low levels of grievances, low absenteeism, low turnover, few accidents and an absence of workplace violence.

As suggested above, there are indicators of organizational ill health as well as indicators of organizational health. These range from the more traditional financial indicators such as poor return on investment to more behavioral indicators like downsizing, high levels of turnover or absenteeism among employees, and frequent grievances. It can be seen that several of the indicators of "organizational health" suggested by Quick (1999) and others do focus on ill health similar to the medical model conceptualization of individual health. Newell (1995) extended the list of aspects of organizational health by arguing that organizations need to be concerned about social and moral responsibility to prevent ill health. Organizations that develop reputations as bad places to work will have difficulty recruiting top talent. Further, if they act without concern for the communities in which they operate, then community members can affect the viability of the organization by bringing legal action or by boycotting the organization's products or services. She further argued that to achieve quality, flexibility, innovation and responsibility (characteristics of a healthy organization), organizations need employees who are competent, empowered, and committed to the organization. Masterson (2001) actually demonstrated that employees' perceptions of organizational justice was related to customers' attitudes toward the organization, suggesting subsequent organizational consequences, although she did not directly assess the impact of the customers' reactions to the organization to actual organizational health indicators.

Cooper and Williams (1994), among other scholars, have argued that organizational health and employee health are co-dependent, and there is some tangentially related empirical support for this. Direct empirical tests, however, are scarce usually only addressing one aspect of individual or organizational health such as downsizing. For example, Tetrick (2000) reviewed the literature on downsizing and found that the evidence suggests that downsizing was generally not effective in restoring organizational health, with organizations repeatedly reducing their workforce without improving organizational functioning. Further, Landsbergis, Cahill and Schnall (1999) found that not only did downsizing have a negative impact on workers, downsizing was indicative of a failure to thrive for the organization.

Many studies of organizational health have focused on a single indicator of health as indicated above. However, a recent empirical study by McHugh and Brotherton (2000) examined multiple indicators of organizational health. They compared four organizations, two of which had been determined to be healthy and two of which had been determined to be unhealthy based on traditional financial indicators such as return on capital, return on sales, sales per employee, and gross profit margin. There were differences between the healthy and unhealthy organizations in the levels of support present, with financially healthy organizations having greater supports and lower constraints. But surprisingly considering the occupational stress literature, the financially healthy organizations did not differ from the financially unhealthy organizations in the levels of job demands, self-esteem, stress and psychological well being. McHugh and Brotherton reported that the unhealthy organizations were unhealthy for different reasons based on contextual information obtained through interviews with key personnel in the organizations. They therefore concluded that financial indicators of health did not adequately capture organizational health.

When these results are considered in conjunction with prior conceptualizations of organizational health (Cooper & Cartwright, 1994; Masterson, 2001; Newell, 1995; Quick, 1999), there does appear to be support for the contention that a healthy organization is also one in which the employees' work environment is healthy. This argument is further bolstered by the literature on knowledge management and the management of intellectual capital in organizations (DeNisi, Jackson & Hitt, in press). One of the basic premises of knowledge management is the development and maintenance of a work environment that encourages individuals to learn and share their knowledge. The knowledge or intellectual capital in organizations is posited to be unique and difficult to duplicate. This uniqueness gives organizations that manage their intellectual capital effectively a competitive strategic advantage. However, there is little empirical evidence at this time to support the theoretical propositions. Clearly, there needs to be more empirical research to address the relation between employees' health and organizational health.

Several questions arise in increasing our understanding of organizational health and the linkage between organizational health and individual health. For example, do the processes underlying organizational health mimic those underlying individual health? If so, can the stress framework help us inform the potential linkages between individual and organizational health? For example, Mayrhofer (1997) argued that balance must be achieved between conflicting goals that exist when organizations attempt to sustain flexibility and hence organizational health. This call for balance mirrors, at least in part, the work-life balance issue that is found in the stress literature (see Frone, in press). It also reflects the perspective of many other scholars that health is a balance between a drain on resources to fight off illness and the development of a reserve of resources for growth and adaptation (Downie & Mcnaughton, 1998; Hofmann & Tetrick, forthcoming). As was the case with the relation between eustress and positive health and between distress and ill health (see above), it is not clear that the mechanisms underlying health are the same at the organizational level and at the individual level. In fact, it appears that cross-level effects are likely although they have not been studied. Given this lack of research, we should proceed with caution before assuming that what is good for the organization is necessarily good for the employees or vice versa.

LINKING ORGANIZATIONAL AND INDIVIDUAL HEALTH

A brief examination of two literatures offers some theoretical and empirical support for understanding organizational health, individual health, and the linkage between the two from both a positive health and ill health perspective. First, I will discuss pay structure and its relation to organizational and individual health. Interested readers are referred to Gerhart (2000) and Gerhart and Rynes (forthcoming) for a more detailed discussion on pay structures within organizations; the focus here will be on how pay structure may relate to organizational and individual health. Secondly, I will discuss organizational learning as an adaptive response to the environment and its parallel, individual learning, drawing the relation to the stress and well being literature.

Pay Structure

Pay is a key component in the employment relationship. The income earned from employment has long been considered to be a factor in individuals' health and well being (Jahoda, 1982; Warr, 1987). In general there has been an assumption that lack of pay is harmful and receipt of pay is good. In fact, Warr (1987), in his vitamin model of work and well being, described the availability of financial rewards as a vitamin in which deficiencies are harmful to one's well being. Further, like vitamins C and E, more pay is not considered to be toxic to one's well being. Somewhat surprisingly, there has been little research investigating the relation of pay with safety and health (Sinclair & Tetrick, in press). There has been considerable research, however, on the effects of unemployment and on the relation between social economic status and health.

The sociological and epidemiological literature has established the existence of a health gradient relating lower social economic status with poorer health (Adler & Ostrove, 1999). This relation has been observed in several countries especially in the developed countries and is typically steeper within countries than between countries suggesting that the gradient is not a function of health care systems or other economic or cultural differences (Marmot, 1999). Also, Adler and Ostrove (1999) concluded that there is more evidence suggesting that social economic status impacts health than there is evidence suggesting that health affects social economic status. Therefore, one would conclude that income as a component of social economic status is an important factor in understanding people's health.

The relation between income and health, however, is complex. For example, studies examining the relation between social economic status and the incidence of disease and mortality have shown that the health gradient does not exist for all diseases. Adler and Ostrove (1999) report "there is strong and consistent evidence of the health gradient for cardiovascular disease, diabetes, metabolic syndrome, arthritis, tuberculosis, chronic respiratory disease, gastrointestinal disease, and adverse birth outcomes as well as for accidental and violent deaths" (p. 8). Strikingly, several of these diseases have been related to the experience of distress and occupational distress specifically. In fact, Marmot (1999) suggests that stress may be the underlying mechanism that links social economic status and ill health. Having to cope with limited resources to meet the events of daily living may explain the relation between position in the social hierarchy and allostatic load, which refers to the effect on the body of maintaining balance or stability in response to stressors (McEwen & Seeman, 1999). Thus, the coping and reacting to limited resources may explain the resulting relation between social economic status and health.

Work has been described as one social structure that generates social inequalities (Wilkinson, 1999). Most organizations have some level of hierarchy that is related to occupational prestige, control and decision latitude. These typically parallel the pay levels within the organization such that individuals who have more status and control receive greater pay. It is interesting to note that Wilkinson (1999) reported that greater income differences in communities were related to more violence, less trust and less cohesiveness among residents. The question remains whether this same relation between income dispersion and violence, trust, and cohesiveness holds within organizations. If the health gradient does operate within organizations as it does in communities, cities, and countries, there are important implications for the degree of pay dispersion in organizations' pay structures and its relation to organizational and individual health.

A review of the literature found only a few studies at the individual level of analysis that addressed the relation between pay structure and well being. Adelmann (1987) as cited in Danna and Griffin (1999) found that personal income was positively related to psychological well being, where psychological well being was operationalized as happiness, self-confidence, and lack of vulnerability. Also, there has been some support that aspects of pay structure can have adverse effects on well being. For example, Schleifer and Okogbaa (1990) found that incentive pay was related to increased blood pressure and decreased heart rate variability among people who were performing a data entry task. Further, they observed that when people performed this task over a longer period of time, heart rate decreased and heart rate variability increased. They suggested that this longer-term effect may have been the result of increased mental fatigue. Shirom, Westman and Melamed (1999) also found that monotony on the job mediated the effect of the pay system on well being. In their study, they found that blue-collar employees who worked under a performance-contingent pay system had higher levels of depression and somatic complaints than blue-collar workers who worked under a pay-for-time-worked system. Therefore, these studies suggest that not only the amount of pay one receives, but also the structure of the pay system, such as whether pay is contingent on performance, may be related to the health effects of employment on workers.

In addition to the sociological and epidemiological literature on the health gradient discussed above, a potential link between pay dispersion within organizations and ill health can also be hypothesized drawing on the organizational justice literature. Distributive justice is concerned with the fairness of the distribution of outcomes with pay being one of the most frequently studied outcomes (Cropanzano & Ambrose, 2001). This literature would suggest that to the extent people feel that their pay is not fair relative to others then they will experience injustice and the negative emotions that accompany such cognitive appraisals (Cropanzano, Weiss, Sickow & Grandey, 2000). The question is who are the others that one might use for comparison purposes. The literature on pay satisfaction would suggest that it would be individuals in similar jobs rather than the full organizational hierarchy. However, it is possible that pay dispersion throughout the organization may contribute to perceptions of distributive justice. Also, it is not known what factors individuals might consider in judging inequalities as unfair. Woodward and Kawachi (2000) suggested that inequalities are unfair when the basis for the inequalities is unjust such as a lack of equal opportunity and education; however, research is clearly needed to address judgments of fairness in pay dispersion. Judgments of the fairness of pay dispersion may reflect organizational and societal cultural values.

Shaw and Gupta (2001) found support for a link between pay fairness and employees' reports of life satisfaction, depression, and somatic complaints. Fairness was positively related to positive health (e.g. life satisfaction) and negatively related to ill health (e.g. depression and somatic complaints) as would be expected. In addition, pay fairness was related to higher performance, less absenteeism, and lower turnover, suggesting a link between pay structure and organizational health as well as individual health. Shaw, Gupta, and Delery (in press), in a subsequent study, found evidence for a relation between pay dispersion and physical health. In a study of truck drivers who worked very independently, pay dispersion was strongly positively related to accident frequency ratios when there were relatively low levels of individual incentives and the opposite was found under high levels of individual incentives. Therefore, in independent jobs, high levels of individual incentives, which lead to high pay dispersion, resulted in safer performance, higher productivity, and higher perceived organizational performance. However, in the concrete pipe plants where people had to work with others, Shaw et al. (in press) found that high pay dispersion was dysfunctional resulting in higher accident rates, lower productivity, and lower perceived organizational performance. Shaw et al. (in press) argue that high levels of pay dispersion foster competition and lack of cooperation, which is counter to the climate needed in interdependent work.

These results are consistent with other research examining the pay dispersion and organizational performance relation. High levels of pay dispersion among executives were detrimental to organizational performance in high-tech firms (Hambrick & Siegel, 1997). This decline in performance was thought to be the result of a decrease in collaboration within the executive teams and less communication among team members. Since communication is considered to be critical for a healthy organization, reduction in communication would be expected to result in lower organizational performance. Bloom (1999) in his study of baseball teams also found that high pay dispersion was negatively related to individual and organizational performance. However, players who had high levels of pay (were at the top of the pay distribution) performed better than players who had lower levels of pay. This supports my earlier contention that high levels of pay dispersion can result in the perception of distributive injustice and hence negative emotions (Cropanzano et al., 2000) and lack of well being. These results also suggest that level within the pay dispersion may reflect higher status and recognition at higher levels in the pay dispersion and lack of status and recognition at lower levels of the pay dispersion.

The empirical research, thus, suggests that pay dispersion can have negative effects on individual and organizational health. Bloom and Michel (2002) found additional evidence of the negative effects of high levels of pay dispersion among executives using two different samples of managers across two different periods of time. Increased levels of pay dispersion were related to lower levels of managerial tenure suggesting higher levels of turnover in companies with greater pay dispersion, again signifying an association between high levels of pay dispersion and lower levels of organizational health. Similar to Bloom and Michel, Guthrie (2000), in a study of New Zealand companies, found that the use of skill-based pay plans was negatively related to turnover. He interpreted this as indicating that investment in employees' skills and knowledge base results in a stronger bond between employees and their organizations. He also found that group-based pay plans were associated with increased turnover rates and this relation was stronger as group size increased. Thus, the potential bene-fits of group-based pay plans, like increased group productivity, may be offset by increased turnover. This would be especially detrimental to organizational health if the people who are leaving are high performers.

Although the empirical evidence is limited, it does appear that pay structure can affect both individuals' and organizations' health. The relation is not straightforward, depending, among other things, on the degree of interdepen-dence among individuals in the organization, the degree of monotony involved in the tasks that individuals are supposed to perform, and perceptions of fair-ness of the pay system. It also appears that the pay structure can be a source of both eustress (e.g. connoting status and recognition) or distress (e.g. a source of injustice). As was evident above, individual health and organizational health are complex, multidimensional concepts. Similarly, pay systems are also complex and multidimensional. Future research needs to develop a theoretical framework for the effect of pay on individual and organizational health drawing on the work that has already been done. To test this theoretical framework will require the examination of the effects of specific aspects of the pay system on individuals' and organizations' health.

Organizational Learning

There are other aspects of organizational systems that have the potential to affect individual and organizational health and well being than the pay system.

The indicators of organizational health reviewed above have considerable overlap with generally recognized dimensions of organizational culture and climate. For example, autonomy, communication, flexibility, innovation, openness, risk and trust were found to be among the 26 dimensions of organizational climate suggested by Cook, Hepworth, Wall and Warr's (1981). A later review by Koys and Decotiis (1991) suggested the dimensions of organizational climate to be autonomy, cohesion, fairness, innovation, pressure, recognition, support, and trust. The debate as to the number of climate dimensions is unsettled much as the debate as to the number of basic emotions (Weiss, 2002) or what constitutes health and well being (see above). However, it does appear that fairness, trust and innovation are among the key dimensions.

These aspects of the climate also appear to be critical for fostering organizational learning (Tetrick & Da Silva, in press). There are several definitions of organizational learning. According to Fiol and Lyles (1985), organizational learning is a process of improving actions through understanding and knowledge, or as suggested by Garvin (1993), organizational learning reflects an organization's ability to adapt its behavior to improve organizational performance by the creation, acquisition, and transfer of knowledge. Birleson (1998) described a learning organization as one "enabling communication, removing restraints to learning, creating synergy between the interests of the organization and its members, nurturing creativity and reflection, functioning in a coherent and integrated manner, and maintaining a focus on service improvement" (p. 215). Therefore, one might visualize organizational learning as a culture that promotes adaptation to the external environment through the strategic management of knowledge (DeNisi, Jackson & Hitt, in press; Tetrick & Da Silva, in press).

Organizational learning thus defined then reflects an organization's response to an environmental event. Organizational learning theorists have assumed that organizational learning will lead to improved organizational performance and hence organizational health; however, there is little empirical evidence to support this assumption (e.g. Lundberg, 1995; Slater & Narver, 1995). Also, some theorists have suggested that organizational learning may not always lead to improved organizational health. For example, Crossan, Lane, White and Djurfeldt (1995) suggested that organizational learning might have a negative effect on performance, at least in the short-run. This was posited to occur because individuals would need to unlearn familiar ways of doing things and implement new, unfamiliar practices. Fiol (in press) also notes that unlearning is an important aspect of organizational learning that often is more difficult. For example, once knowledge is codified it is difficult to remove or replace this knowledge with new knowledge. Unfortunately, empirical research addressing these propositions is lacking.

Many organizational learning theorists have argued that organizational learning will create a competitive advantage for the organization through the ability to acquire and apply new knowledge effectively (e.g. Slater & Narver, 1995), although it has been argued that this may not always be the case. For example, Cohen and Leventhal (1990), drawing on human cognition, argued that organizations need to have some prior related knowledge in order to be able to assimilate and use new knowledge; they referred to this as absorptive capacity. Developing this absorptive capacity requires individual learning as well as organizational learning or knowledge management. Therefore, individual learning is considered a necessary, but not sufficient, condition for organizational learning (Lundberg, 1995). Again, there is little empirical evidence relating organizational learning to improved organizational effectiveness through the ability to acquire and apply new knowledge effectively, although Hitt, Bierman, Shimizu, and Kochhar (2001) did find support for a direct and moderating relation between management of human capital and company financial performance. Based on their review of the literature on absorptive capacity, Zahra and George (2002) concluded that greater understanding of the processes of acquiring, assimilating, transforming, and exploiting knowledge is needed to be able to develop and sustain organizations' competitive advantage.

In addition to the limited number of empirical studies at the organizational level, there have been only a few studies conducted at the individual level. These studies have looked at the relation between perceptions of the climate for organizational learning and employee job performance (Da Silva, Tetrick, Slack, Etchegaray, Latting, Beck & Jones, 2002), job stress (Mikkelsen, Saksvik & Ursin, 1998), and psychological well being (Tetrick, Da Silva, Jones, Etchegaray, Slack, Latting & Beck (2000). As expected, perceptions of a climate for organizational learning were related to improved job performance and psychological well being as well as reduced perceptions of job stress. Therefore, it is not clear whether organizational learning enhances organizational performance. However, it does appear that a climate for organizational learning provides the communities of practice and a sense of trust that are necessary for individual and collective learning to occur (Fiol, in press; Noe, Colquitt, Simmering & Alvarez, in press). Further, this climate for organizational learning is positively related to individual well being.

As has been the case with organizational learning, it has generally been considered that learning is good for individuals. Sirgy, Efraty, Siegel, and Lee (2001) suggested that there were seven aspects of life that were needed to capture the full domain of the quality of work life. These were health and safety needs, economic and family needs (pay and job security), social needs (collegiality at work and leisure time off work), esteem needs (recognition and appreciation of work within the organization and outside the organization), actualization needs (realization of one's potential within the organization and as a professional), knowledge needs (learning to enhance job and professional skills), and aesthetic needs (creativity at work as well as personal creativity and general aesthetics). According to Sirgy et al.'s (2001) formulation of the quality of work life, learning is a cornerstone for well being. Similarly, Mainemelis (2001) included a sense of mastery as one of the experiences that link timelessness to creativity. He argued, however, much like Mayrhofer (1997) did at the organizational level, that there is a need for balance between challenges of the tasks and one's skills. Given this balance, experts achieved a sense of peak performance, heightened competence, and total control over the task. This is consistent with Theorell's (in press) perspective that learning reflects a sense of control and thus would be expected to reduce the experience of distress. Further the literature on learning goal orientation has shown that a mastery orientation results in positive responses and enhanced performance (Dweck & Leggett, 1988; Jagicinski & Strickland, 2000; Kozlowski, Gully, Brown, Salas, Smith & Nason, 2001; VandeWalle, Ganesan, Challagalla & Brown, 2000). A mastery orientation has also been found to reduce emotional exhaustion (Jacobsson, Pousette & Thylefors, 2001). Therefore, learning appears to be a key factor in not only reducing distress and ill health but promoting eustress and positive health.

Considering the literature on organizational learning and individual learning, it appears that there may be a synergistic effect of learning. Individual learning results in a heightened sense of control and self-efficacy, which leads to enhanced health and well being. Additionally, individual learning is a necessary, but not sufficient, condition for organizational learning to occur (Fiol & Lyles, 1985). Organizational learning is a social process where individuals interact with each other in a collaborative effort sharing their experiences and knowledge (Mohrman, in press). The effectiveness of organizational learning in enhancing organizational health remains undocumented but there is some support for a positive relation between organizational learning and individual health and well being. Future research needs to explicitly examine the relations between learning and positive health at both the individual and organizational levels.

SUMMARY AND FUTURE RESEARCH DIRECTIONS

In this chapter, it was argued that health and well being encompass more than simply the absence of illness both in considering individual health and organizational health. Certainly, much of the literature on occupational stress and well being has focused on negative aspects of health such as physical and mental illnesses. However, drawing on the concept of eustress, it is apparent that health and well being can include positive aspects of health such as happiness and optimal human functioning. While there has been a noticeable negative bias in discussions of individual health, there seems to be a somewhat more neutral perspective on organizational health, although as theorists considered employees' health as indicators of organizational health, the negative bias seemed to reappear. Extending the conceptualization of health to include positive health as well as the absence of illness and ill health extends our thinking about the relation among these three aspects of health as well as the interrelations between individual and organizational health.

A review of the literature suggests that we know more about the antecedents and consequences of ill health from both an individual and an organizational perspective than we know about positive health. The literature suggests a relation between individual positive health and ill health. The question remains whether a similar relation also exists between organizational positive health and ill health. Consistent with Seligman and Csikszentmihalyi (2000) and Luthans (2002), theory development is needed to distinguish between positive health and ill health. One place to start might be the development of a theoretical framework for organizing the various indicators of positive health and ill health. Refreshing Selye's (1975) concepts of eustress and distress may be useful in this regard.

Another major question is whether ill health and positive health are simply opposite ends of the continuum with similar underlying mechanisms or whether they actually operate according to different underlying mechanisms. I have argued that ill health is not likely to be the obverse of positive health, drawing heavily on the positive and negative affect literature. This literature as well as other literature on emotions suggests that positive health may have effects on ill health further supporting a distinction between positive health and ill health rather than positive health and ill health being opposite ends of the same continuum. Integration of positive and negative emotions explicitly in theories of occupational stress may provide theoretical mechanisms for these relations. Fortunately, there is a rapidly emerging literature on emotions in the workplace that may facilitate the development of these theoretical mechanisms.

Although the empirical evidence is indeed anemic, there does appear to be a connection between individual health and organizational health. An examination of the literature on pay structure and organizational learning provides two theoretical perspectives on this linkage with some empirical research to support these positions, although neither literature is extensive. At least theoretically, these two literatures suggest a two-way connection with organizational health affecting individual health and individual health affecting organizational health. In this chapter, each of these literatures was examined separately. However, it doesn't take much extension to posit a connection between pay structures and organizational and individual learning since in many instances pay is tied to skills and competencies. Therefore, it becomes clear that a general systems perspective (Kozlowski & Klein, 2000) is needed to more fully understand individual and organizational health.

The occupational stress literature may be able to inform a general systems perspective on individual and organizational health. Much of the occupational stress literature has focused on proximal aspects of the work environment such as job demands and control (Karasek & Theorell, 1990) or effort-rewards imbalance (Bakker, Killmer, Siegrist & Schaufeli, 2000; Siegrist, 1996). These approaches are clearly important; however, it is time for us to broaden our perspectives and address the context in which individuals find themselves. That is to say we need to examine the total context recognizing that individuals reside within organizations and these organizations have a variety of human resource policies and practices that may jointly affect individuals' health and well being. These human resource policies and practices, as well as other systems within organizations, are connected. In addition, individuals' inputs and health can affect the organization's health. Given these connections between individual employees and their organization, a multi-level perspective is needed to develop a more comprehensive theoretical perspective on the relation between individual and organizational health (Kozlowski & Klein, 2000). Though only two organizational phenomena were discussed in this chapter, readers are encouraged to consider other systems within organizations to more thoroughly explore linkages between individual and organizational health.

REFERENCES

Adler, N. E., & Ostrove, J. M. (1999). Socioeconomic status and health: What we know and what we don't. In: N. E. Adler, M. Marmot, B. McEwen & J. Stewart (Eds), *Socioeconomic Status and Health in Industrial Nations: Social, Psychological, and Biological Pathways* (pp. 3–15). New York, NY: The New York Academy of Sciences.

Antonovsky, A. (1993). *Unraveling the mysteries of health.* San Francisco: Jossey-Bass.

Ashkanasy, N. M., & Daus, C. S. (2002). Emotion in the workplace: The new challenge for managers. *Academy of Management Executive, 16,* 76–86.

Bakker, A. B., Killmer, C. H., Siegrist, J., & Schaufeli, W. B. (2000). Effort-reward imbalance and burnout among nurses. *Journal of Advanced Nursing, 31,* 884–891.

Basch, J., & Fisher, C. D. (2000). Affective events-emotions matrix: A classification of work events and associated emotions. In: N. J. Askanasy, C. E. J. Härtel & W. J. Zerbe (Eds), *Emotions in the Workplace: Research, Theory, and Practice* (pp. 36–47). Westport, CN: Quorum Books.

Berk, L. S., Felton, D. L., Tan, S. A., Bittman, B. B., & Westengard, J. (2001). Modulation of neuroimmune parameters during eustress of humor-associated mirthful laughter. *Advances in Mind – Body Medicine, 17*, 200.

Bennett, J. B., Cook, R., & Pelletier, K. R. (in press). Toward an integrated framework for comprehensive organizational wellness: Concepts, practices, and research in workplace health promotion. In: J. C. Quick & L. E. Tetrick (Eds), *Handbook of Occupational Health Psychology* (pp. 69–95). Washington, D.C.: American Psychological Association.

Bennis, W. (1962). *Beyond bureaucracy: Essays on the development and evolution of human organization*. San Francisco, CA: Jossey-Bass.

Birleson, P. (1998). Learning organisations: A suitable model for improving mental health services. *Australian and New Zealand Journal of Psychiatry, 32*, 214–222.

Bloom, M. (1999). The performance effects of pay dispersion on individuals and organizations. *Academy of Management Journal, 42*, 25–40.

Bloom, J., & Michel, J. G. (2002). The relationships among organizational context, pay dispersion, and managerial turnover. *Academy of Management Journal, 45*, 33–42.

Cohen, W. M., & Levinthal, D. A. (1990). Absorptive capacity: A new perspective on learning and innovation. *Administrative Science Quarterly, 35*, 128–152.

Cook, J. D., Hepworth, S. J., Wall, T. D., & Warr, P. B. (1981). *The experience of work: A compendium and review of 249 measures and their use*. London: Academic Press.

Cooper, C. L., & Cartwright, S. (1994). Healthy mind; healthy organization: A proactive approach to occupational stress. *Human Relations, 47*, 455–471.

Cooper, C. L., & Williams, S. (1994). *Creating healthy work organizations*. Chichester: John Wiley.

Cropanzano, R., & Ambrose, M. L. (2001). Procedural and distributive justice are more similar than you think: A monistic perspective and a research agenda. In: J. Greenberg & R. Cropanzano (Eds), *Advances in Organization Justice* (pp. 119–151). Palo Alto: Stanford University Press.

Cropanzano, R., Weiss, H. M., Suckow, K. J., & Grandey, A. A. (2000). Doing justice to workplace emotion. In: N. M. Ashkanasy, C. E. J. Härtel & W. J. Zerbe (Eds), *Emotions in the Workplace: Research, Theory, and Practice* (pp. 49–62). Westport, CT: Quorum Books.

Crossan, M. M., Lane, H. W., White, R. E., & Djurfeldt, L. (1995). Organizational learning: Dimensions for a theory. *International Journal of Organizational Analysis, 3*, 337–360.

Csikszentmihalyi, M. (1997). *Creativity: Flow and the psychology of discovery and intervention*. New York: HarperPerennial.

Da Silva, N., Tetrick, L. E., Slack, K. J., Etchegaray, J. M., Latting, J. K., Beck, M. H., & Jones, A. P. (2002, April). Employees' psychological climate for organizational learning and supervisory performance. Paper presented at the annual conference of the Society for Industrial and Organizational Psychologists, Toronto, CA.

Danna, K., & Griffin, R. W. (1999). Health and well being in the workplace: A review and synthesis of the literature. *Journal of Management, 25*, 357–384.

DeNisi, A., Jackson, S., & Hitt, M. A. (in press). The knowledge-based approach to sustainable competitive advantage In: S. Jackson, M. Hitt & A. DeNisi (Eds), *Managing Knowledge for Sustained Competitive Advantage: Designing Strategies for Effective Human Resource Management*. San Francisco, CA: Jossey-Bass.

Downie, R. S., & Macnaughton, R. J. (1998, March 14). Images of health. *Lancet, 351*, 823–826.

Dweck, C. S., & Leggett, E. L. (1988). A social-cognitive approach to motivation and personality. *Psychological Review, 95*, 256–273.

Fiol, C. M. (in press). Designing knowledge work for competitiveness: About pipelines and rivers. In: S. Jackson, M. Hitt & A. DeNisi (Eds), *Managing Knowledge for Sustained Competitive Advantage: Designing Strategies for Effective Human Resource Management*. San Francisco, CA: Jossey-Bass.

Fiol, C. M., & Lyles, M. A. (1985). Organizational learning. *Academy of Management Review, 10*, 803–813.

Fredrickson, B. L. (2001). The role of positive emotions in positive psychology: The broaden-and-build theory of positive emotions. *American Psychologist, 56*, 218–226.

Frone, M. (in press). Work-Family Balance. In: J. C. Quick & L. E. Tetrick (Eds), *Handbook of Occupational Health Psychology* (pp. 143–162). Washington, D.C.: American Psychological Association.

Garvin, D. A. (1993, July/August). Building a learning organization. *Harvard Business Review, 71*, 78–91.

Gerhart, B. (2000). Compensation strategy and organizational performance. In: S. L. Rynes & B. Gerhart (Eds), *Compensation in Organizations: Current Research and Practice* (pp. 151–194). San Francisco, CA: Jossey-Bass.

Gerhart, B., & Rynes, S. L. (forthcoming). *Compensation: Theory, evidence, and strategic implications*. Palo Alto, CA: Sage.

Guthrie, J. P. (2000). Alternative pay practices and employee turnover: An organization economics perspective. *Group and Organization Management, 25*, 419–439.

Hambrick, D. C., & Siegel, P. A. (1997). Pay dispersion within top management groups: Harmful effects on performance of high-technology firms. *Academy of Management Proceedings*, 26–29.

Hitt, M. A., Bierman, L., Shimizu, K., & Kochhar, R. (2001). Direct and moderating effects of human capital on strategy and performance in professional service firms: A resource-based perspective. *Academy of Management Journal, 44*, 13–26.

Hofmann, D. A., & Tetrick, L. E. (forthcoming). On the etiology of health: Implications for "organizing" individual and organizational health. In: D. A. Hofmann & L. E. Tetrick (Eds), *Health and Safety in Organizations: A Multilevel Perspective*. Jossey Bass.

Jacobsson, C., Pousette, A., & Thylefors, I. (2001). Managing stress and feelings of mastery among Swedish comprehensive school teachers. *Scandinavian Journal of Educational Research, 45*, 37–53.

Jagicinski, C. M., & Strickland, O. J. (2000). Task and ego orientation: The role of goal orientations in anticipated affective reactions to achievement outcomes. *Learning & Individual Differences, 12*, 189–208.

Jahoda, M. (1982). *Employment and unemployment: A social psychological analysis*. Cambridge: Cambridge University Press.

Karasek, R., & Theorell, T. (1990). *Healthy work: Stress, productivity, and the reconstruction of working life*. New York: Basic Books.

Koys, D. J., & DeCotiis, T. A. (1991). Inductive measure of psychological climate. *Human Relations, 44*, 265–285.

Kozlowski, S. W. J., Gully, S. M., Brown, K. G., Salas, E., Smith, E. M., & Nason, E. R. (2001). Effects of training goals and goal orientation traits on multidimensional training outcomes and performance adaptability. *Organizational Behavior & Human Decision Processes, 85*, 1–31.

Kozlowski, S. W. J., & Klein, K. J. (2000). A multilevel approach to theory and research in organizations: Contextual, temporal, and emergent processes. In: K. J. Klein & S. W. J. Kozlowski (Eds), *Multilevel Theory, Research, and Methods in Organizations: Foundations, Extensions, and New Directions* (pp 3–90). San Francisco: Jossey-Bass.

Krueger, R. F., Hicks, B. M., & McGue, M. (2001). Altruism and antisocial behavior: Independent tendencies, unique personality correlates, distinct etiologies. *Psychological Science, 12,* 397–402.

Landsbergis, P. A., Cahill, J., & Schnall, P. (1999). The impact of lean production and related new systems of work organization on worker health. *Journal of Occupational Health Psychology, 4,* 108–130.

Larsen, R. J., Diener, E., & Lucas, R. E. (2002). Emotion: Models, measures, and individual differences. In: R. G. Lord, R. J. Klimoski & R. Kanfer (Eds), *Emotions in the Workplace: Understanding the Structure and Role of Emotions in Organizational Behavior* (pp. 64–106). San Francisco: CA. Jossey-Bass.

Larson, J. S. (1999). The conceptualization of health. *Medical Care Research and Review, 56,* 123–136.

Lundberg, C. C. (1995). Learning in and by organizations: Three conceptual issues. *International Journal of Organizational Analysis, 3,* 10–23.

Luthans, F. (2002). Positive organizational behavior: Developing and managing psychological strengths. *Academy of Management Executive, 16,* 57–72.

Mainemelis, C. (2001). When the muse takes it all: A model for the experiences of timelessness in organizations. *Academy of Management Review, 26,* 548–565.

Marmot, M. (1999). Epidemiology of socioeconomic status and health: Are determinants within countries the same as between countries? In: N. E. Adler, M. Marmot, B. McEwen & J. Stewart (Eds), *Socioeconomic Status and Health in Industrial Nations: Social, Psychological, and Biological Pathways* (pp. 16–29). New York, NY: The New York Academy of Sciences.

Maslow, A. H. (1954). *Motivation and personality.* New York: Harper.

Masterson, S. S. (2001). A trickle-down model of organizational justice: Relating employees' and customers' perceptions of and reactions to fairness. *Journal of Applied Psychology, 86,* 594–604.

Mayrhofer, W. (1997). Warning: Flexibility can damage your organizational health. *Employee Relations, 19,* 519–534.

McEwen, B. S., & Seeman, T. (1999). Protective and damaging effects of mediators of stress: Elaborating and testing the concepts of allostatis and allostatic load. In: N. E. Adler, M. Marmot, B. McEwen & J. Stewart (Eds), *Socioeconomic Status and Health in Industrial Nations: Social, Psychological, and Biological Pathways* (pp. 20–47). New York, NY: The New York Academy of Sciences.

McGuire, J. G. (2001). Synthesizing the relationship between homeostasis and health. *Journal of School Health, 71,* 77–79.

McHugh, M., & Brotherton, C. (2000). Health is wealth: Organisational utopia or myopia? *Journal of Managerial Psychology, 15,* 744–770.

Mikkelsen, A., Saksvik, P. O., & Ursin, H. (1998). Job stress and organizational learning climate. *International Journal of Stress Management, 5,* 197–209.

Miles, M. B. (1969). Planned change and organizational health: Figure and ground. In: F. D. Carver & T. J. Sergiovani (Eds), *Organizations and Human Behavior* (pp. 375–391). New York: McGraw-Hill.

Mohrman, S. A. (in press). Designing work for knowledge-based competition. In: S. Jackson, M. Hitt & A. DeNisi (Eds), *Managing Knowledge for Sustained Competitive Advantage: Designing Strategies for Effective Human Resource Management.* San Francisco, CA: Jossey-Bass.

Nelson, D. L., & Simmons, B. L. (in press). Health psychology and work stress: A more positive approach. In: J. C. Quick & L. E. Tetrick (Eds), *Handbook of Occupational Health Psychology* (pp. 97–119). Washington, D.C.: American Psychological Association.

Newell, S. (1995). *The healthy organization: Fairness, ethics and effective management.* London: Routledge.

Noe, R. A., Colquitt, J. A., Simmering, M. J., & Alvarez, S. A. (in press). Knowledge management: Developing intellectual and social capital. In: S. Jackson, M. Hitt & A. DeNisi (Eds), *Managing Knowledge for Sustained Competitive Advantage: Designing Strategies for Effective Human Resource Management.* San Francisco, CA: Jossey-Bass.

Pajares, F. (2001). Toward a positive psychology of academic motivation. *Journal of Educational Research, 95,* 27–35.

Quick, J. C. (1999). Occupational health psychology: The convergence of health and clinical psychology with public health and preventive medicine in an organizational context. *Professional Psychology: Research and Practice, 30,* 123–128.

Resnick, S., Warmoth, A., & Serlin, I. A. (2001). The humanistic psychology and positive psychology connection: Implications for psychotherapy. *Journal of Humanistic Psycology, 41,* 73–102.

Rogers, C. (1963). The actualizing tendency in relation to "motives" and to consciousness. In: M. R. Jones (Ed.), *Nebraska Symposium on Motivation* (Vol. 11, pp. 1–24). Lincoln: University of Nebraska Press.

Ryan, R. M., & Deci, E. L. (2001). On happiness and human potentials: A review of research on hedonic and eudaimonic well being. *Annual Review of Psychology, 52,* 141–166.

Ryff, C. D. (1995). Psychological well being in adult life. *Current Directions in Psychological Science, 4,* 99–104.

Ryff, C. D., & Singer, B. (1998). The contours of positive human health. *Psychological Inquiry, 9,* 1–28.

Ryff, C. D., & Singer, B. (2000). Interpersonal flurishing: A positive health agenda for the new millennium. *Personality and Social Psychology Review, 4,* 30–44.

Salovey, P., Rothman, A. J., Detweiler, J. B., & Steward, W. T. (2000). Emotional states and physical health. *American Psychologist, 55,* 110–121.

Schleifer, L. M., & Okogbaa, O. G. (1990). System response time and method of pay: Cardiovascular stress effects in computer-based tasks. *Ergonomics, 33,* 1495–1509.

Schmidt, L. R., & Frohling, H. (2000). Lay concepts of health and illness from a developmental perspective. *Psychology and Health, 15,* 229–238.

Seligman, M. E. P., & Csikszentmihalyi, M. (2000). Positive psychology: An introduction. *American Psychologist, 55,* 5–14.

Selye, H. (1975). Confusion and controversy in the stress field. *Journal of Human Stress, 1,* 37–44.

Shaw, J. D., & Gupta, N. (2001). Pay fairness and employee outcomes: Exacerbation and attenuation effects of financial need. *Journal of Occupational and Organizational Psychology, 74,* 299–320.

Shaw, J. D., Gupta, N., & Delery, J. E. (in press). Pay dispersion and work force performance: Moderating effects of incentives and interdependence. *Strategic Management Journal.*

Shirom, A., Westman, M., & Melamed, S. (1999). The effects of pay systems on blue-collar employees' emotional distress: The mediating effects of objective and subjective work monotony. *Human Relations, 52,* 1077–1098.

Sinclair, R. R., & Tetrick, L. E. (in press). Pay and benefits: The role of compensation systems in workplace safety. In: J. Barling & M. Frone (Eds), *The Psychology of Workplace Safety.* Washington, D.C.: American Psychological Association.

Siegrist, J. (1996). Adverse health effects of high effort – low reward conditions. *Journal of Occupational Health Psychology, 1,* 27–41.

Sirgy, M. J., Efraty, D., Siegel, P., & Lee, D. J. (2001). A new measure of quality of work life (QWL) based on need satisfaction and spillover theories. *Social Indicators Research, 55,* 241–302.

Slater, S. F., & Narver, J. C. (1995). Market orientation and the learning organization. *Journal of Marketing, 59,* 63–74.

Snyder, C. R. & McCullough, M. E. (2000). A positive psychology field of dreams: "If you build it, they will come . . ." *Journal of Social and Clinical Psychology, 19,* 151–160.

Spector, P. E., & Goh, A. (2001). The role of emotions in the occupational stress process. In: P. Perrewe & D. Ganster (Eds), *Research in Occupational Stress and Well Being: Exploring Theoretical Mechanisms and Perspectives* (Vol. 1, pp. 195–232). Stamford, CT: JAI Press, Inc.

Tetrick, L. E. (2000). Linkages between organizational restructuring and employees' well being. *Journal of the Tokyo Medical University, 58,* 357–363.

Tetrick, L. E., & Da Silva, N. (in press). Assessing culture and climate for organizational learning. In: S. Jackson, M. Hitt & A. DeNisi (Eds), *Managing Knowledge for Sustained Competitive Advantage: Designing Strategies for Effective Human Resource Management.* San Francisco, CA: Jossey-Bass.

Tetrick, L. E., Da Silva, N., Jones, A. P., Etchegaray, J. M., Slack, K. J., Latting, J. K., & Beck, M. H. (2000, April). Organizational learning: Does it lead to employee well being. Paper presented at the annual conference of the society for industrial and organizational psychologists, New Orleans.

Theorell, T. (in press). To be able to exert control over one's own situation: A necessary condition for coping with stressors. In: J. C. Quick & L. E. Tetrick (Eds), *Handbook of Occupational Health Psychology* (pp. 201–219). Washington, D.C.: American Psychological Association.

VandeWalle, D., Ganesan, S., Challagalla, G. N., & Brown, S. P. (2000). An integrated model of feedback-seeking behavior: Disposition, context, and cognition. *Journal of Applied Psychology, 85,* 996–1003.

Warr, P. (1987). *Work, unemployment and mental health.* Oxford: Oxford University Press.

Watson, D., & Clark, L. A. (1992). Affects separable and inseparable: On the hierarchical arrangement of the negative affects. *Journal of Personality and Social Psychology, 62,* 489–505.

Watson, D., Clark, L. A., & Tellegen, A. (1988). Development and validation of brief measures of positive and negative affect: The PANAS scale. *Journal of Personality and Social Psychology, 54,* 1063–1070.

Weiss, H. M. (2002). Conceptual and empirical foundations for the study of affect at work. In: R. G. Lord, R. J. Klimoski & R. Kanfer (Eds), *Emotions in the Workplace: Understanding the Structure and Role of Emotions in Organizational Behavior* (pp. 20–63). San Francisco: Jossey-Bass.

Weiss, H. M., & Cropanzano, R. (1996). Affective Events Theory: A theoretical discussion of the structure, causes and consequences of affective experiences at work. In: B. M. Staw & L. L. Cummings (Eds), *Research in Organizational Behavior: An Annual Series of Analytical Essays and Critical Reviews* (Vol. 18, pp. 1–74). Stamford, CT: JAI Press, Inc.

Wilkinson, R. G. (1999). Health, hierarchy, and social anxiety. In: N. E. Adler, M. Marmot, B. McEwen & J. Stewart (Eds.) *Socioeconomic Status and Health in Industrial Nations: Social, Psychological, and Biological Pathways* (pp. 48–63). New York, NY: The New York Academy of Sciences.

Woodward, A., & Kawachi, I. (2000). Why reduce health inequalities? *Journal of Epidemiologyand Community Health, 54,* 923–929.

World Health Organization (1946). *Constitution.* New York: WHO.

Zahra, S. A., & George, G. (2002). Absorptive capacity: A review, reconceptualization, and extension. *Academy of Management Review, 27,* 185–203.

CROSSOVER OF STRESS AND STRAIN IN THE FAMILY AND WORKPLACE

Mina Westman

ABSTRACT

*Studies investigating the crossover of job stress and strain between part-
ners have shown that job demands are transmitted from job incumbents
to their partners, affecting their psychological and physical health. Based
on the crossover literature and on models of job stress and the work-family
interface, this chapter develops a comprehensive framework to integrate
the literature conceptually, delineating the mechanisms that underlie
the crossover process. Three main mechanisms that can account for the
apparent effects of a crossover process are specified. These mechanisms
include common stressors, empathic reactions, and an indirect mediating
process. Gaps in the literature are identified, recommendations for future
research are proposed, and the implications for organizational theory and
practice are discussed.*

INTRODUCTION

There is ample evidence that job stress has an impact on workers' mental and
physical well being (Kahn & Byosiere, 1992). However, less attention has been
paid to individuals' reaction to the job stress experienced by those with whom

Historical and Current Perspectives on Stress and Health, Volume 2, pages 143–181.
Copyright © 2002 by Elsevier Science Ltd.
All rights of reproduction in any form reserved.
ISBN: 0-7623-0970-9

they interact regularly. This phenomenon has been labeled in the work family literature "contagion" or "crossover."

CURRENT MODELS OF WORK-FAMILY INTERACTION

Scholars in the work-family domain rely on models such as segmentation, compensation, and spillover, to characterize the process by which work and family are linked (Evans & Bartolome, 1980; Piotrkowski, 1979, Wilensky, 1960; Zedeck, 1992). Segmentation refers to the separation of work and family, such that experiences in the two domains do not influence one another (Zedeck, 1992). Compensation represents efforts to offset dissatisfaction in one domain in seeking satisfaction in another domain (Zedeck, 1992). Spillover refers to the transfer of attitudes, feelings and behaviors from one domain to the other (Lambert, 1990). A fourth process that links family and work is crossover (Bolger, DeLongis, Kessler & Wethington, 1989).

In the present chapter I follow the differentiation of Bolger et al. (1989) and of Wethington (2000) between two situations in which stress is carried over. The first is *spillover*, a within-person across-domains contagion of demands and consequent arousal from one area of life to another. Thus, in spillover, stress experienced in one domain of life results in stress in the other domain for the same individual. The second type of situation is *crossover*, which involves contagion across people, whereby demands and their consequent arousal cross over between closely related or otherwise linked individuals. Thus, in crossover, stress experienced in the workplace by the individual leads to stress being experienced by the individual's spouse at home. Whereas spillover is an *intra-individual* transmission of stress or strain, crossover is a dyadic, *inter-individual* transmission of stress or strain.

According to current research, spillover occurs from home to work and from work to home within the individual, whereas crossover occurs from an individual at the workplace to his or her spouse at home. Thus, crossover research is based upon the prepositions of the spillover model, recognizing the fluid boundaries between work and family life. However, the crossover model adds another level of analysis to previous approaches by adding the intra-individual level, specifically the dyad, as an additional focus of research.

I broaden Bolger et al.'s (1989) definition of crossover to also include situations whereby stress and strain experienced by one employee leads to the experience of stress and strain by another employee in the same job environment. Therefore, in this chapter, crossover is treated as an inter-individual dyadic process where stress and strain experienced by an individual generate similar reactions in another individual, both in the family and in the workplace.

This chapter integrates prior crossover research, stimulates additional inquiry into the phenomenon of crossover, and proposes a comprehensive theoretical framework that extends our understanding of work and family life. The proposed framework aspires to guide research by clarifying how the crossover process is initiated and maintained and what are its consequences. First, the theoretical perspective for studying crossover is introduced. Second, core mechanisms of the model are proposed, and the relevant empirical findings are presented. Finally, theoretical, methodological, and practical implications are discussed.

A THEORETICAL PERSPECTIVE

Several experts in the field of work-family research have criticized the "state of the art" of work-family models. Barnett (1998) and Zedeck (1992) have criticized their atheoretical basis, and Lambert (1990) found work-family theories inadequately conceptualized, neither delineating well-specified causal models nor capturing all of the processes that link work and home.

Drawing upon systems theory, Bronfenbrenner (1977) criticized the lack of systematic research on work-family that adopts a dynamic, interpersonal, and social system perspective. He pointed out that components within the system tend to interrelate and affect each other; therefore, processes operating in different settings are not independent of each other. Nevertheless, most researchers in the work-family arena focus on individual outcomes. The proposed crossover model starts with the individual level and moves to the dyadic level, thereby benefiting from incorporating multiple levels of the work-family systems. Examining the crossover effects of stress and strain using the dyad as the unit of analysis contributes to our understanding of the complexities of multiple roles in different domains. This framework enables the investigation of the ripple effect of stress as it starts at the workplace, crosses over to the spouse, who in turn conveys the consequences to the co-workers, who transmit it to their spouses at home and so on. This expansion shows how stress, generated either at home or at the workplace, moves from the micro-level (couple, family) to meso-level social systems (workplace-management, team-group), thereby potentially impacting the entire organization. To date, there is no single theoretical perspective that encompasses crossover. Most crossover studies are descriptive or inductive, offering post-hoc explanations. In the current chapter I present a model that embeds the crossover process into a job-stress model and anchors it in role theory (Kahn, Wolfe, Quinn, Snoek & Rosenthal, 1964). The usefulness of role theory as a basis for crossover research lies in underscoring the interrelations between a focal person and his or her role senders in the work settings and in other settings where the individual functions. Role theory is a sound basis for crossover research, as first, it relates both to the person and to his or her role senders, thus encompassing spouses and coworkers and the interaction between them and second, because it focuses on a wider role stress paradigm than the work-family interface models.

Kahn et al. (1964) defined a "role" as a set of expectations applied by the role senders to the incumbent, the role receiver, within and beyond organizational boundaries. These expectations can result in perceived role stress. Role conflict, role overload, and role ambiguity are the most widely researched job stressors and have been associated with job dissatisfaction, job-induced tension, and propensity to leave the organization (Fisher & Gittelson, 1981; Jackson & Schuler, 1985). As can be seen from the reviewed literature1 (See Table 1), these role stressors are the main antecedents of the crossover process.

According to role theory, the work and family settings are involved in continuous and elaborate interchanges with their social environments. This conceptualization allows us to view family members as intimately connected coworkers and vice versa. The role episode model depicts the interpersonal process between the focal person and the role senders that occurs over time, incorporating interpersonal and personal factors. These factors may affect the role episode by influencing the focal person, the role senders, or the relationship between them. The model delineated in Fig. 1 uses role theory as an anchor for theoretical development in the work-family domain. The model can guide research to determine how experiences and processes in the work and family domain are linked and how the crossover effect is likely to vary for workers characterized by different personality attributes and by the interaction between the partners.

CORE CONSTRUCTS AND THE RELATIONSHIPS AMONG THEM

The conceptual model classifies a selected array of perceptions of stress and strain as antecedent influences of the crossover process. Furthermore, the model posits interpersonal variables as possible mediators of the crossover process and personal attributes as possible moderators of this process.

The core assumption of the model is that one's stress or strain has an impact on others in different settings, indicating a complex causal relationship between stress and strain in the individual arena and between the stress and strain of dyads. In light of the accumulated findings of crossover research (e.g. Jones & Fletcher, 1993a; Long & Voges, 1987), it is reasonable to posit that variables reflecting job and family demands are the main antecedents of the crossover process. Most researchers have defined job stress in terms of negative characteristics of the individual-organizational interface using stressors such as

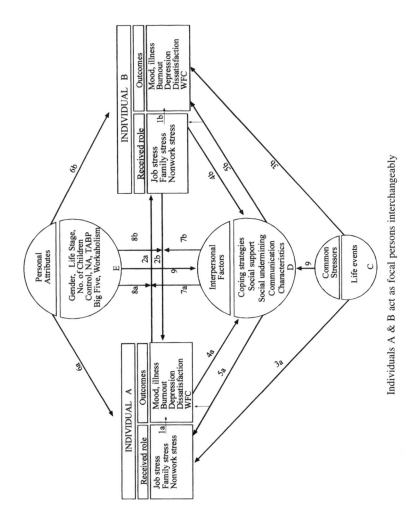

Individuals A & B act as focal persons interchangeably

Fig. 1. Crossover Model of Stress and Strain.

overload, role conflict, and role ambiguity (e.g. Kahn et al., 1965). Job-related strains, according to Jex and Beehr (1991), are behavioral, psychological, or physical outcomes resulting from the experience of stress. Most crossover research focuses on the path between a sender and a receiver.

Figure 1 distinguishes between five dimensions of the crossover process: job and family stress, psychological and physiological strains, life events, the inter-personal factors, and personal attributes. Starting at the left, the model shows that the received role of the individual generates stress that may lead to the response of strain (Boxes A & B, arrows 1a, 1b). The experienced stress and strain of one individual – the sender – may cause stress and strain in the other individual – the receiver (Arrows 2a & 2b).

An important issue in crossover research is determining where stress and strain originate and how they flow between domains inside and outside the family. Do the stress and strain originate in the job, outside the job, or in the family? Currently most findings pertain to the job as the source of stress and strain in the family, focusing on the relationship between the demands of a worker's job and the resulting psychological strain for the spouse or co-habiting partner. For example, Jackson and Maslach (1982) investigated crossover of stress from police officers to their wives and found that officers with high levels of stress were more likely to display anger, spend time away from home, and be less involved in family life, whilst their wives showed a corresponding increase in distress and dissatisfaction. Similarly, Burke, Weir, and DuWors (1980) found that wives of correctional facility administrators reported less marital and life satisfaction, decreased social participation, and increased psychosomatic problems and negative feelings when their husbands reported greater occupational demands. Long and Voges (1987) also found that demands of prison officers' jobs adversely affected their wives' well being.

In the following paragraphs I review literature concerning stress and strain in the crossover process and the mediating and the moderating variables affecting it. I then suggest a few possible mechanisms underlying the crossover process. Some of the linkages in the proposed model are very well supported empirically, whereas others require further support and several of the variables have not yet been investigated in crossover research.

Stress and Strain (Boxes A and B)

The current chapter is based on empirical studies that investigated the crossover process from different angles. Some have focused on the crossover of job *stress* from the individual to the spouse (e.g. Burke et al., 1980), some have exam-ined the process whereby *job stress* of the individual affects the *strain* of the

Table 1. Summary of Characteristics and Findings of Crossover Studies.

Study/Sample	Crossover of[a]	Direction of Crossover[a]	Mediating Variables[a]	Design/Data Collection /Analyses	Findings[a]
Barnett et al. (1995) 210 dual-earner couples	Distress	H to W W to H	Commitment	Longitudinal, three waves data collection	Increase in distress over time of one partner was mirrored in the changes in distress of the other.
Bakker & Schaufeli (2000) 154 high school teachers	Burnout	Colleagues to individual	Susceptibility to emotional contagion	Cross sectional	Perceived burnout among colleagues was related to teacher's burnout. Susceptibility to emotional contagion moderated the relationship between perceived burnout of colleagues and teacher's burnout
Bakker et al. (2001) 507 general practitioners	Burnout	Colleagues to individual	Susceptibility to emotional contagion	Cross sectional	Perceived burnout among colleagues was related to GP's burnout. Susceptibility to emotional contagion moderated the relationship between perceived burnout of colleagues and GP's burnout
Beehr & Johnson (1995), 177 male and female police officers and their spouses	Coping strategies to spouses' well being	Police officers to spouses		Cross-sectional, vignettes	P.O.'s coping strategies were positively related to spouse's well being.
Bolger et al. (1989) 166 married couples	Job stress to Home stress	H to W		Longitudinal, daily diaries	Spouse's job stress affected the other spouse stress at home.

Table 1. Continued.

Study/Sample	Crossover of[a]	Direction of Crossover[a]	Mediating Variables[a]	Design/Data Collection /Analyses	Findings[a]
Booth (1977) 560 couples	W's occupational status on H's marital satisfaction.	W to H	Tenure, division of labor	Cross-sectional	Ws' employment had no impact on Hs' well being.
Burke et al. (1980) 85 senior administrators of correctional institutes and spouses	Occupational demands to strain	H to W	W's life demands W's received social support	Cross-sectional	Hs' occupational demands were related to wives' dissatisfaction, decreased social participation and increased psychosomatic symptoms.
Chan & Margolin (1994) 59 dual earner couples	Work mood and affect at home	H to W W to H		Two consecutive work days	Ws' negative work mood and work fatigue on H's reactions at home. Ws' home affect on partners subsequent work mood.
Dew et al (1987) 104 couples	Employment status to distress	H to W	H's distress	Longitudinal, five measurement in 54 months	Hs' employment status affected his distress which, in turn, affected his W's distress.
Eckenrode & Gore (1981), 356 women	Significant other's life event on women's health	Significant others to women	Demographic variables	Cross-sectional	Frequency of significant others' life events affected women's health status and health behavior
Fletcher (1983) Information on 1.088.995 death cases	Male occupational mortality on wives mortality	H to W	Domestic psychological environment	Retrospective	Job risks of H affect life expectancy of H and W.
Fletcher (1988) 324.822 British men in 556 occupations and 35.915 wives	H's occupation stress on W's life expectancy	H to W	Shared domestic environment Psychological mechanisms, social class.	Retrospective	Ws' life expectancy and their cause of death are associated with the occupational mortality risk of their H.

Table 1. Continued.

Study	Variables	Direction	Measures	Design	Findings
Greenhaus & Parrasuman (1987) 425 couples	W's employment status on H's job satisfaction and quality of life	W to H	Time commitment, Hs' level of satisfaction with their work and their marriage	Cross-sectional	Ws' employment was positively related to Hs' job satisfaction and quality of life.
Hammer, Allen & Grigsby (1997) 399 couples	Work-family conflict (WFC)	W to H and H to W	Career priority, Involvement in work and family activities	Cross-sectional	Ws' WFC had an effect on Hs' WFC and Hs' WFC had and effect on Ws' WFC.
Haynes, Eaker & Feinleib (1983) 269 couples	W's profession - H's heart disease.	W to H		Longitudinal (10 years)	Hs of employed Ws in white-collar jobs were over three times more likely to develop CHD than those married to blue-collar workers or house-wives.
Jackson & Maslach (1982) 142 police officers and spouses	H's job stress on W's dissatisfaction and distress.	H to W	Family interactions, anger, withdrawal	Survey, Cross-sectional	Hs' stress affected their coping and distress and dissatisfaction of W.
Jackson, Zedeck & Summers (1985) 95 Plant operators and spouses	H's job experiences to W's physical, affective and behavioral symptoms.	H to W		Cross-sectional	Emotional interference caused by job experiences was related to spouses' quality of life and dissatisfaction with employee's job.
Jones & Fletcher (1993a), 60 working couples	Job and domestic stresses to evening mood: mental well being.	H to W and W to H	Accuracy of perception of each other's job stress.	Cross-sectional	Spouses have accurate perceptions of their partners' jobs. Transmission of stress from H to W especially H in high-stress jobs.

Table 1. Continued.

Study/Sample	Crossover of[a]	Direction of Crossover[a]	Mediating Variables[a]	Design/Data Collection /Analyses	Findings[a]
Jones & Fletcher (1993b)	Work stress to psychological and physical health	H to W and W to H	Marital communication about work	Diaries every evening for three weeks. Longitudinal	Daily fluctuations in work stresses affect both partners.
Katz, Beach, & Joiner (1999) 105 dating couples	One's depression to the other's depression	Boyfriend to girlfriend Girlfriend to boyfriend	Reasurance seeking	Cross-sectional	Contagion of depressive symptoms between partners. Reassurance seeking tendencies moderated contagion within couples.
Long & Voges (1987) 301 prison officers and their wives	H's job stress to well being of W	H to W	Communication	Cross-sectional	Hs' stress is related to Ws' stress and strain.
Mauno & Kinnunen (2002) 387 couples	Economic stress to partners' job insecurity	H to W and W to H		Cross-sectional	Hs' economic stress crossed over to Ws' job insecurity and vice versa
Mitchel, Cronkite & Moos (1983) 157 couples	Negative events and on going strain to partners' depression	H to W		Cross-sectional	Partners' events and strain were related to partners' depression.
Morrison & Clements (1997) 82 naval couples	Job stressors on partners' well being	H to W		Longitudinal	The well being of sea-going partners. Fluctuates as a function of the deployment and the mariners' job characteristics

Table 1. Continued.

Study	Relationship	Direction	Variables	Design	Findings
Parasurman, Greenhuas & Granose (1992) 119 couples	Role stressors and WFC to partners' family satisfaction	W's to H's		Cross-sectional. Moderated regression analysis	Females' family role stressors had a significant negative relationship with their spouses' family satisfaction. Males' work and family stressors and WFC did not affect their spouses' family satisfaction.
Pavett (1986) 149 spouses of CPA's	Job stress to burnout	Spouse to spouse	Type A, social support	Cross-sectional	CPA's stress affected spouses' physical and psychological symptoms of burnout
Riley & Eckenrode (1986) 314 women	H's life events to W's distress	H to W	Personal resources	Cross-sectional	Women with lower levels of personal resources were distressed by the life events of their significant others.
Roberts & O'Keefe (1981) 752 couples	W's occupational status on H's stress levels	W to H	Income, education and occupation	Cross-sectional	Ws' employment status had little or no effect on H's stress experience
Rook, Dooley & Catalano (1991) 1383 married females (a second interview with a subset of 92)	H's stress to W's emotional health (psychological distress)	H to W	Marital tension, social support wives' life events	Longitudinal, telephone interviews.	Hs' job stress was associated with W's distress.
Rosenfield (1980) 60 married couples	W's occupational status to H's distress	W to H		Cross-sectional	Ws' employment was positively related to Hs' distress (psychosomatic symptoms, anxiety, sadness, immobilization.

Table 1. Continued.

Study/Sample	Crossover of[a]	Direction of Crossover[a]	Mediating Variables[a]	Design/Data Collection /Analyses	Findings[a]
Rosenfield (1992) 60 married couples	W's occupational status to H's well being	W to H	Income, share in domestic labor	Cross-sectional	Ws' employment was negatively related to Hs' well being only when wives' employment decreased Hs' relative income and increased their share of domestic labor.
Staines et al. (1986) 408 husbands to housewives, 208 husbands to wives working for pay	W's employment status on H's job and life satisfaction	W to H	Husbands' adequacy as breadwinner	Cross-sectional	Hs of employed Ws registered lower job and life satisfaction than Hs of housewives.
Thompson & Bolger (1999) 68 couples in which one member was preparing for the Bar examination.	Examinees' depression to partners' feelings about the relationship and partners' feelings toward examinees' depression	Examinees to partners and partners to examinees		Diary studies for 5 weeks, concurrent and prospective analyses.	Examinees' depression was related to partners' feeling less positive and more negative about the relationship.
Vinokur et al. (1996) 815 job-seekers and their spouses	Depression	H to W and W to H	Economic hardship, transactions between couples	Longitudinal, SEM	The depression of both partners is the result of common stressors and non-supportive and undermining transaction.
Westman & Etzion (1995) 101 career officers and their working wives	Burnout	W to H and H to W	Partner's job stress, sense of control, social support	Cross-sectional, SEM	Symmetric crossover effects of burnout from husbands to wives and vice versa.

Table 1. Continued.

Westman & Vinokur (1998) 232 couples	Depression	W to H and H to W	Social undermining	Longitudinal, SEM	Direct crossover of depression. Life events had an impact on the crossover process. Social undermining mediated the crossover process.
Westman et al (2001) 98 couples	Burnout	H to W and W to H	Social undermining	Cross-sectional, SEM	Direct crossover of burnout from H to W but not from W to H.
Westman, Etzion & Segev. (2002)	Work-family conflict	H to W and W to H	Social support	Cross-sectional	Direct crossover of work-family conflict from H to W and from W to H.
Westman et al. (2002b)	Marital dissatisfaction	H to W and W to H	Social undermining, economic hardship	Longitudinal, SEM	A strong crossover effect of marital dissatisfaction from Hs' to Ws' but no effect from Ws' to Hs'.

[a] H – husbands; W – wives.

spouse (Jones & Fletcher, 1993a; Long & Voges, 1987), and others have studied how psychological *strain* of one partner affects the *strain* of the other (Mitchell, Cronkite & Moos, 1983; Westman & Etzion, 1995).

Katz, Monnier, Libet, Shaw and Beach (2000) relate to two types of stress crossover effects. Direct crossover effects occur when a target individual's experience of stress leads to the experience of stress in others. Indirect crossover effects occur when an individual's experience of stress leads to distress in others. Indirect crossover effects of stress from an individual to a spouse may depend on the individual's own stress response. That is, when stressors have a strong impact on a target individual's well being, the individual's own well being may affect the spouses' well being. Katz et al. (2000) found that medical students perceived that stress had negative effects on their own well being in addition to the well being of their spouses.

Similarly, Dew, Bromet and Schulberg (1987) studied indirect crossover effects among women whose husbands had recently lost their jobs. They found that husbands' unemployment led to husbands' emotional distress. In turn, husbands' distress led to wives' distress. These findings suggest that a person's strain may account for the effect of the person's experience of stress on a spouse's strain. Accordingly, an individual's level of perceived stress may affect a spouse's strain only to the extent that perceived stress negatively affects the individual's own strain. These findings demonstrate the importance of incorporating the sender's stress and strain into crossover models, as the sender's strain may mediate the crossover from one's stress to the other's stress and strain.

It is noteworthy from Table 1 that most crossover researchers (e.g. Burke et al., 1980; Pavett, 1986; Long & Voges, 1987) have used some kind of chronic job stress, defined as the "enduring problems, conflicts, and threats that many people face in their daily lives" (Pearlin, 1989, p. 245). However, a few (e.g. Eckenrode & Gore, 1981; Riley & Eckenrode, 1986) have used life or job events, defined by Wheaton (1996) as discrete, observable, and "objectively" reported events that require some social or psychological adjustment on the part of the individual. The Table also demonstrates that the following strains have been frequently investigated: burnout (Bakker, Schaufeli, Sixma & Bosweld, 2001; Pavett, 1986), depression (Katz, Beach & Joiner, 1999; Vinokur, Price & Caplan, 1996), dissatisfaction (Westman, Vinokur, Hamilton & Roziner 2002), and physical health (Jones & Fletcher, 1993b).

Mediating and Moderating Variables (Box D)

Two important issues in crossover research are: (a) what are the moderators of crossover, or what variables buffer or intensify the crossover process; and (b) what are the variables that mediate the crossover process. Whereas research has identified several antecedent influences on the crossover process, the psychological process mediating these linkages needs to be explored. Detecting the main underlying mechanisms of the crossover process is a basis for developing a systematic theoretical and empirical approach in this domain. Therefore, the suggested model includes a group of mediators. This implies that the job stress and accompanying strain of the sender (Person A) may have an effect on the stress and strain of the receiver (Person B) through their effects on interpersonal factors such as coping strategies and the social interaction. For reasons of parsimony, some of the model's recursive processes involving feedback loops have been omitted from Fig. 1.

HYPOTHETICAL MECHANISMS FOR THE CROSSOVER PROCESS

The crossover literature is not characterized by a systematic theoretical and empirical approach that distinguishes between the possible explanations of crossover effects. Few researchers consider how job demands of job incumbents get translated into poor well being of the spouses and how one's strain affects the partner's strain (arrows 2a & 2b in the model). Without an understanding of these mechanisms, a model that accurately captures the complexities of the work/family nexus cannot be specified and tested. A better understanding of these processes will enable identifying effective strategies for coping with the stress crossover. Westman and Vinokur (1998) specify three main mechanisms that can account for the apparent effects of a crossover process: empathic reactions, common stressors, and a mediating process.

Direct Empathetic Crossover (Arrows 2a & 2b)

The first claim of the model is that direct crossover of stress occurs from one partner to the other. *Direct empathetic crossover* implies that stress and strain are transmitted from one partner to another directly as a result of empathic reactions. The basis for this view is the finding that crossover effects appear between closely related partners who care for each other and share the greater part of their lives together. According to Lazarus (1991, p. 287), empathy is regarded as "sharing another's feelings by placing oneself psychologically in that person's circumstances." The core relational theme for empathy would have to involve a sharing of another person's emotional state, distressed or otherwise. Accordingly, strain in one partner produces an empathetic reaction in the other that increases his or her own strain.

158   MINA WESTMAN

This view is supported by social learning theorists (e.g. Bandura, 1969; Stotland, 1969), who have explained the transmission of emotions as a conscious processing of information. They suggest that individuals imagine how they would feel in the position of another and thus come to experience and share the other's feelings.

Eckenrode and Gore (1981) demonstrated that men's life events increased the amount of stress their wives experienced. These findings show that although life events research considers stress as an individual level variable, one's stressful events can affect the stress level of another. On the basis of their findings they argued that stressful life events influence the entire network of close ties. They suggested that the effect of the one's life events on the spouse's distress may be the result of empathy expressed in reports such as "We feel their pain is our own" (p. 771).

However, in order to establish and support the "direct-empathy" explanation for the crossover process, it is suggested to add measures of empathy to crossover research. This will support the attribution of a direct crossover effect to empathy and rule out the possibility that some other processes are operating.

A similar mechanism by which crossover is suggested to operate is emotional contagion. Emotional contagion has been defined as "The tendency to automatically mimic and synchronize facial expressions, vocalizations, postures, and movements with those of another person and, consequently, to converge emotionally" (Hatfield, Cacioppo & Rapson, 1994, p. 5). As the definition implies, the emphasis is on noconscious emotional contagion. However, contagion may also occur via a conscious cognitive process of tuning in to the emotions of others. As a few researchers base their crossover model on emotional contagion theory (Bakker & Schaufeli, 2000; Bakker et al., 2001), it is important to clarify whether emotional contagion is an additional possible mechanism of the crossover process

Uni- and Bi-Directional Crossover
The literature shows that crossover may be unidirectional (Arrows 2a or 2b) or bi-directional (Arrows 2a & 2b). Most stress crossover studies have been unidirectional, examining and finding effects of husbands' job stress on the well being of their wives (Burke et al., 1980; Jackson & Maslach, 1982; Long & Voges, 1987; Pavett, 1986; Rook, Dooley & Catalano, 1991). These studies related to the wives as the passive recipients of stress and strain from their husbands, neither assessing nor controlling wives' job and life stress, and in some cases had mixed samples of working and non-working wives. Therefore, we cannot rule out the possibility that what appears as direct crossover of stress from husbands to wives is at least partially an outcome of the wives' job.

Despite the significant increase in the number of women who have joined the workforce at all job levels, no published research has focused exclusively on the crossover of stress from wives to husbands. Some researchers have investigated the impact of women's employment, but not their job stress, and found negative effects of wives' employment status on husbands' strain (e.g. Booth, 1977; Greenhaus & Parasurman, 1987; Haynes, Eaker & Feinleib, 1983; Roberts & O'Keefe, 1981; Rosenfield, 1980, 1992; Staines, Pottic & Fudge, 1986). These studies did not specify which element of the wives' employment caused crossover, nor did they eliminate the possibility that it is their own job stress that causes their strain.

The paths of crossover are not always equal or circular. Rather they are often unidirectional and nonreciprocal. Crossover of stress and strain appears to flow from husbands to wives more than from wives to husbands (Bolger et al., 1989; Jones & Fletcher, 1993a; Westman, Etzion & Danon, 2001). Recent studies focus on both spouses and examine bi-directional crossover of stress or strain. Jones and Fletcher (1993a) found transmission of husbands' job demands on wives' anxiety and depression after controlling wives' job stress. However, they did not find such an effect from wives to husbands, perhaps because the women in their sample did not experience high levels of stress. Similarly, Westman et al. (2001) found crossover of burnout from husbands to wives but not from wives to husbands. In the same vein, a recent longitudinal study of officers in the Russian army and their wives Westman et al. (2002b) detected strong crossover effects of marital dissatisfaction from husbands to wives but no significant crossover from wives to husbands. Larson and Almeida (1999) maintain that the finding that wives are more frequently the receivers in the crossover process may reflect their deliberate efforts to be empathic toward their husbands and a general tendency to have more preamble boundaries than men.

Yet a few bi-directional crossover studies found symmetric crossover effects between partners. Westman and Etzion (1995) demonstrated crossover of burnout from career officers to their spouses and vice versa, after controlling husband's and wife's own job stress. Similarly, Katz, Beach, and Joiner (1999) found contagion of depression within dating couples after controlling the relationship satisfaction. The intensity of the contagion effects was similar among men and women. Hammer, Allen & Grigsby (1997) also found bi-directional crossover of work family conflict from husbands to wives and vice versa. Similarly, Westman, Etzion and Segev (2002) found crossover of work-family conflict from women in the Air Force to their spouses and vice versa. Whereas these were cross-sectional studies, the bi-directional nature of the crossover effect also was demonstrated in studies using longitudinal designs. Barnett, Raudenbush, Brennan, Pleck and Marshall (1995) and Westman and Vinokur

(1998), found bi-directional crossover of distress from husbands to wives and from wives to husbands.

Spuriousness – Common Stressors (Circle C)

The common stressors mechanism suggested by Westman and Vinokur (1998) refers to common stressors in a shared environment that increase both partners' strain. Such findings should be considered spurious cases of crossover. What appears to be a crossover effect is the result of common stressors in a shared environment increasing the strain in both partners (Arrows 3a & 3b). *Common stressors* affecting both partners will impact the strain of both partners, and the similarity in the strain appears as crossover. This suggests that people in close relationships may experience shared stressors (e.g. economic hardship).creating psychological strain in both of them. Hobfoll and London (1986) suggested that many stressors make simultaneous demands on both individuals in a dyad.

One common stressor that may affect both partners is stressful life events. Unfortunately, most crossover studies focus on job stress and do not include life events as possible common stressors that might affect both spouses. A close exception is Rook et al. (1991), who used husbands' life events as their measure of stress, although these stressful events were reported by their wives. The validity of such a measure is questionable, as it is an indication of the way wives perceive their husbands' life events and how it affects them. Morrison and Clements (1997) used life events as a control for non-job related stress but did not investigate its role in the crossover process. Vinokur, Price & Caplan (1996) found that family financial strain had an impact on the crossover process and on the supportive and undermining transactions between the partners. Similarly, Westman and Vinokur (1998) found that common life events affected the crossover process by increasing each partner's depression. The explanation of the appearance of crossover based on common stressors that have adverse effects on both partners' strain was not supported in Westman et al. (2002b) study. None of the common stressors in that study had an impact on *both* husbands' and wives' marital dissatisfaction. In light of the inconsistency of the results to date, future research should examine which common stressors produce spurious crossover effects by affecting general strains or specific ones, such as marital dissatisfaction.

Crossover as a Mediated Process (Circle D)

The following section focuses on the mediating effect of coping mechanisms, social support, and undermining in the crossover process.

Coping strategies represent efforts to prevent or reduce the negative effects of stress. Numerous studies suggest that problem-focused strategies are positively related to well being, whereas the emotion-focused ones are negatively related to well being (Westman & Shirom, 1995). Most of these studies have examined the direct effect of coping on one's well being or the moderating effects of coping on the relationship between stress and strain (Edwards, Baglioni & Cooper, 1990). However, a few studies have examined the relationship between one's coping and the other person's well being. One's strain can affect one's own coping strategies and the partner's coping strategies. Therefore, coping can be viewed as a predictor of one's strain and of the spouse's (Arrows 5a & 5d) strain (Beehr, Johnson & Nieva, 1995) or as a mediator (Arrow 4d & 4b) of the relationship between one's stress and the spouse's stress or strain (Jackson & Maslach, 1982).

Researchers have provided two main directions of the relationships between one's coping and the partner's well being. Monnier and Hobfoll (1997) demonstrated the impact of one's coping on the spouse's well being. They found that active coping by respondents was negatively related to the partner's depression and that active, prosocial coping was inversely related to future depression, demonstrating that it may have some long-term ameliorative crossover effects. The other view, proposed by Burke et al. (1980) and Kahn, Coyne, and Margolin (1985), is that one's strain may determine the spouse's coping strategies (Arrows 4a & 4b). Burke et al. (1980) found that wives whose husbands reported high job demands used more emotion-focused coping strategies, such as distraction, explosive outbursts, and talking to others. However, they used problem-focused coping strategies when their husbands reported lower job demands. Kahn et al.'s (1985) findings that spouses of depressed persons used more aggressive strategies support this direction. The results supporting the second perspective may imply that women who use less constructive coping experience greater crossover of stress from their husbands than women using problem-focused strategies. The possibility that one's stress may exhaust the partner's coping capacity, thereby increasing the partner's vulnerability to stress, has not been investigated.

The two main views of whether depression affects the partner's coping or whether coping affects his or her depression are not contradictory and may even be reciprocal, suggesting a feedback loop. The process may commence at either points of one's coping or depression. The important issue is the spiral that starts when one role sender's state and actions affect the partner and vice versa. Only experimentation and longitudinal studies can unravel the initiation of the process. Another area that merits further research is the impact of coping strategy on the focal respondent's partner, that is, whether certain patterns of the partners' coping strategies attenuate or strengthen the crossover process. Certain coping strategies may simultaneously enhance the well being of the coper and result in worse outcomes for partners. To illustrate, withdrawal from stressful episodes may be functional for the individual adopting such a strategy, but it may involve delegating communal responsibilities to a partner who may not be prepared to assume the added burdens. In the long run, such coping strategies may also result in negative psychological outcomes for the coper. The possibility that problem-focused coping may negatively affect those close to the focal respondent has been considered only recently (Hobfoll, Dunahoo, Ben-Porat & Monnier, 1994). Therefore, it is important to investigate how the interaction process affects both of the partners. It will require longitudinal designs to detect changes in coping and their effects over time.

Communication Characteristics refer to what people say to each other or how they react to events that happen to them. The literature supporting this explanation implies the need to focus on the couple's communication pattern in terms of the kinds of interaction likely to enhance the partners' experience of stress or strain. Several investigators have addressed the nature of information communicated between the partners as mediating the crossover process. Jones and Fletcher (1993b) suggested that communication may mediate the relationship between the partners' moods. They found that the woman's mood was affected by her partner's communication pattern: it was more positive when her husband offloaded worries and frustrations, but more negative when he became withdrawn or distracted.

Accurate knowledge of the spouse's job stress may be an important mechanism in the crossover process. The amount and kind of discussion are not necessary conditions for crossover, as partners can learn about their spouses' stress and strain from other venues. Pearlin and Turner (1987) found that many interviewees tried to segregate stress arising in the workplace from the family domain, explaining that their distress would only anguish the spouse, the spouse would blame them for the problems, or that the spouse would give them unwanted or inappropriate advice. Whatever the reason, people rarely succeeded in barricading distress generated at work from the family domain. Spouses indicated they could tell when their partners were stressed, regardless of whether the partner related to it. Mood changes, shifts in activities, and other clues aroused awareness to the distress of their partners, even when they did not know the reason for it. Attempts to screen stresses from the family and the uncertainty created by such attempts were additional sources of strain. These findings show that attempts at segmentation are rarely successful and may even intensify the crossover process.

The Social Interaction Process

Social support refers to transactions with others that provide emotional and instrumental support, appraisal, and information (House, 1981). Antonovsky (1979) found that inadequate social support in stressful situations may increase vulnerability to distress. Therefore, an interaction style that does not provide enough support, or demands support from a spouse unable to provide it, can produce a crossover effect and also affect the crossover process. Jones and Fletcher (1993a) suggested that lack of social support might lead to a greater tendency to transmit stress to the other, although they did not investigate social support in this context. Repetti (1989) found that spouse's support moderated the association between workload and marital withdrawal. Higher levels of with-drawal were followed by an increase in social withdrawal and less expression of anger in evenings when wives were supportive. These associations were not observed on relatively low supportive evenings.

Kessler and McLeod (1984) found that caring for a wide network of people was an additional burden for women, and this support translated into trans-mission of stress from their network to themselves. Similarly, Riley and Ekenrode (1986) noted that significant others are influenced by each other's distress indirectly, via the other's reduced social support, noting that demand for social support caused a drain in others in the dyad or in the social group. They underscored two processes: the transaction of support, whereby individ-uals share their resources with the needy, and diminished resources experienced by the providers of social support, both because their resources are shared and because they empathetically experience the demands of the needy. These find-ings indicate that stress experienced by one partner creates demands to provide support and, when unable to meet these expectations, the other is apt to feel anxious or guilty. Conversely, a crisis experienced by a close partner may diminish the social support available to the individual. In the same vein, Hobfoll and London (1986), studying Israeli women whose relatives were mobilized to serve during wartime, found that social support aided the recipients but depleted the resources of the donors at a time when they also needed their stress resistance resources. The indications are that social support is a finite resource and that people compete for in a zero-sum game. Therefore, the expected donor experiences strain either because of his or her inability to provide support or because of his or her depleted resources.

According to Hobfoll et al. (1994), many researchers demonstrating the beneficial effects of social support have focused on the recipient, thereby overlooking its impact on the donor. The role of the donor in the interaction may be one of the keys to the crossover process. Thus, support providers may be adversely affected via stress crossover effects.

As suggested above, an indirect mediating crossover process is a transmission mediated by interpersonal exchange. Thus, an increase in the strain of one partner is likely to trigger provocative behavior or exacerbate a negative interaction sequence with the other partner, often expressed as a social undermining behavior toward the other person and perceived as such by the partner (Vinokur and van Ryn, 1993).

Social undermining is referred to in the literature as social hindrance, social conflict, and negative social support. According to Vinokur and van Ryn (1993), social undermining consists of behaviors directed toward the target person that express negative affect, convey negative evaluation or criticism, or hinder the attainment of instrumental goals. Researchers have shown that social conflict is symptomatic of the stress and strain of cohabiting partners (Abbey, Abramis & Caplan, 1985; Kahn, Coyne & Margolin, 1985; Vinokur & van Ryn, 1993). Furthermore, Duffy, Ganster & Pagon (2002) have demonstrated that supervisors' and coworkers' social undermining is related to employee's somatic complaints. The explanation that the crossover process is mediated by negative social interactions is supported by empirical findings from two lines of research. First, research documents that frustration is often an outcome of stressful conditions that trigger aggression (Berkowitz, 1989). Second, the literature on family processes also reports that stressed couples exhibit high levels of negative conflictual interactions (Schaefer, Coyne & Lazarus, 1981).There are two main views on the relationship between social undermining and depression concerning the initiation of the crossover process. Some researchers (Coyne & Downey, 1991; Russel & Curtona, 1991; Vinokur & van Ryn, 1993) have shown that social undermining increases the stress and strain of partners (Arrows 5a, 5b). Vinokur and van Ryn (1993) found in a longitudinal study that an increase in social undermining produced a change for the worse in the respondents' mental health. In the same vein, Shinn, Lehaman, and Wong (1984) suggested conceptualizing negative interpersonal relationships as a stressor leading to strain.

There are also advocates, however, of the inverse view (Arrows 4a, 4b) that depression precedes conflicting interactions (Nelson & Beach, 1990; Schmaling & Jacobson, 1990). For example, MacEwen, Barling, and Kelloway (1992) found that overload resulted in anxiety and depression, which in turn resulted in more negative marital interactions. Similarly, Crouter, Perry-Jenkins, Huston, and Crawford (1989) found that high levels of stress at work were related to increased negative marital interactions at home. The cross-sectional design of most of the studies precludes concluding whether social conflict is an antecedent or consequence of changes in well being. To illustrate, Abbey et al. (1985) found positive correlations between social conflict and anxiety and depression among students. They concluded that "the greater the amount of social conflict respondents reported receiving from the person closest to them, the greater their depression and anxiety" (p. 119). However, they noted in their discussion that, though for theoretical reasons they interpret these relations in terms of causal pathways, neither their research design nor existing research evidence preclude the rival hypothesis that the greater the depression and anxiety, the higher the degree of social conflict. This causal inconclusiveness is typical of crossover research.

These seemingly contradicting findings lead us to propose that crossover of stress and strain is mediated by the negative interaction between the partners. Westman and Vinokur (1998) supported the mediating role of undermining in the crossover process. They showed that the correlation in depression symptoms in couples was due primarily to crossover via negative social interaction. Women's depression at both waves of their longitudinal study increased their undermining behaviors toward their husbands (Arrow 4a), which in turn increased the husbands' depressive symptoms (Arrow 5b). In sum, some studies have found that depression precedes conflictual interactions and others have found that conflictual interactions precede depression. Though there is more theoretical justification for the hypothesis that undermining leads to the other person's depression, there is also theoretical justification for the rival hypothesis. It is our conclusion that social undermining increases the partner's depression, which in turn, tends to foster an environment characterized by social undermining. Thus, I suggest both directions of influence between depression and undermining, i.e. recursive relationships of social undermining acting as an antecedent of strain for one person and as a consequence of depression for the other. Feedback loops may occur between undermining and depression, triggering a vicious circle in which one amplifies the other.

PERSONAL ATTRIBUTES AS MODERATING VARIABLES (CIRCLE E)

There is no systematic empirical evidence on the contribution of personal attributes to the crossover process. They can influence stress and strain directly as exogenous variable (Arrows 6a & 6b) and indirectly (Arrows 8a & 8b) as moderators that interact with Person A's job stress and strain in explaining Person B's stress and strain. Some crossover researchers have considered demographic characteristics. However, the conceptual links to crossover are weak and the causality is ambiguous. The most frequently investigated characteristics include gender, life stage, and number of children, and they have generally been weakly related to crossover.

One personality characteristic found to be related to strain in the crossover process is sense of control (Westman & Etzion, 1995; Westman & Vinokur, 1998). Researchers have rarely looked into other personality attributes that might help explain crossover. This lack is noteworthy considering the importance of personality in stress research (Spector & O'Conell, 1994). Future crossover research should include personal attributes such as the Big Five trait dimensions (Digman, 1990), Type A Behavior Pattern (Edwards & Baglioni, 1991), and workaholism that would help to fill an important gap in crossover research.

A personal trait relevant to crossover research is negative affectivity (NA), defined by Watson and Clark (1984) as a stable tendency to experience negative emotions across time and situations. Though many studies have concluded that NA may be associated with over-reporting of job stress and strain (Burke, Brief & George, 1993), none has examined the impact of NA in explaining the crossover process. Only Morrison and Clements (1997) used the NA of both spouses as a control variable. They found that female's NA was a significant predictor of her reported well being across each of the three dependent measures they used (physical health, depression, and GHQ). However, NA affected only physical health amongst the males. The impact of NA of one partner may affect his or her report on stress and strain, and the "crossover" detected may be spurious. Furthermore, couples may influence each other's perceptions of their social environment. What is considered stress crossover may be crossover of NA. By not controlling NA, crossover research may have overestimated the effect of one's job stress on spouse's well being.

Several Processes Operating in Conjunction
Another possibility is that more than one explanation is appropriate to explain the crossover process, and that some of the proposed explanations operate in conjunction. Vinokur et al. (1996), for example, found that financial strain, representing common stressors, increased symptoms of depression in the job seeker and in the partner. These depressive symptoms increased the partners' undermining behavior, which increased depressive symptoms in the job seeker, indicating an indirect effect. Westman and Vinokur (1998) found a direct crossover effect of depression between spouses. In addition, social undermining was a strong mediating factor, indicating an indirect effect of crossover. Finally, life events representing common stressors were found adversely to affect the depression of both partners, which increased social undermining and further increased depression. These findings highlight the possibility that several mechanisms may concurrently explain the crossover process. Furthermore, it is possible that crossover begins with one mechanism, such as empathy, but, as the stress and strain continue, the spouse may demonstrate undermining behavior

that increases the strain of the partner. Or, the process may start with under-mining behavior, but, despite this behavior which initiates the crossover process, the spouse also feels empathy toward the other, which intensifies the crossover process.

NEW TOPICS FOR CROSSOVER RESEARCH

Crossover in the Workplace

As previous crossover research was based on the work-family interface, researchers focused only on the family as the "victim" of the job incumbent's stress. However, when the crossover framework is based on role theory we can broaden the scope of research and investigate the crossover of stress from home to the workplace and among role senders in the work setting. As the simplest level of crossover is the dyadic process that transpires between two individuals, the same principle can be applied to interactions in other organizations. What happens to one member of a dyad, whether a family member or a work-group member, affects the other. This approach is consistent with Moos's (1984) theory that people are part of a social system and should be understood in these systems. The family is one such system and the workgroup is another. Each member is linked to other members, and change in one will affect change in others. Just as the conditions that people experience in the workplace can have pronounced effects on the transmission of stress within the family, the conditions experienced in the family may cross over to the others in the workplace. As Kanter (1977) argued, "if emotional climate at work can affect families, so can the family's emotional climate and demands affect members as workers" (p. 56). Furthermore, individuals in the work team who share the same environment may start a crossover chain of stress and strain among themselves, whether the source of stress is in the family or at the workplace.

Bolger et al. (1989) suggested that conflicts with persons in ongoing, non-family relationships might be particularly distressing, because they have continuity and usually lack sufficient intimacy and understanding to prevent arguments from being perceived as a major threat. In an exploratory investigation of the work domain, Westman and Etzion (1999) found crossover of work-induced strain from school principals to teachers and vice versa, after controlling their job stress. Further studies should investigate the impact of supervisors' stress and strain on their subordinates' strain and vice versa, and the impact of colleagues' stress and strain on one another in an effort to detect and identify distressed teams and workplaces.

Whereas Westman & Etzion (1999) detected crossover of strain from school principals to teachers and vice versa in accordance with their crossover model, other researchers have started to investigate the crossover of burnout of colleagues. Two studies have focused on burnout contagion in the workplace (Bakker & Schaufeli, 2000; Bakker, Schaufeli, Sixma & Bosveld, 2001), integrating the literature on emotional contagion and burnout to develop a burnout contagion model. The two studies involved a representative sample of 507 general practitioners (Bakker et al., 2001) and 154 high school teachers (Bakker & Schufeli, 2000). Their main hypothesis was that burnout arises as a result of perceived burnout complaints among colleagues and susceptibility to emotional contagion. They also hypothesized that burnout is contagious in a work group where people collaborate extensively and communicate their negative attitudes toward clients (e.g. patients, pupils).

Using LISREL, they found support in both studies for the burnout contagion model. Furthermore, susceptibility to emotional contagion moderated the relationship between perceived burnout complaints among colleagues and the individual's burnout. However, their measure of perceived burnout complaints from the group was problematic, as the researchers themselves indicated that among other methodological limitations, cognitive dissonance may operate and magnify the perception of the number of burnt out colleagues. Some additional issues that have to be dealt with include the questions of what initiates the emotional contagion process and what fuels it. Is it long term or short term? What are the processes that affect the contagion of burnout? Is it the intensity of the complaints? Is it the frequency of complaints? Or perhaps the closeness of people who complain? More conceptual work is needed to tease out the varieties of contagion.

If these findings are replicated and alternative explanations are ruled out, one could claim that the crossover phenomenon does not necessarily start with one's stress that results in strain, but that being in constant contact with people who declare their burnout is contagious. The question remains as to whether the intensity and duration of contagious burnout is similar to burnout experienced by people who either empathize with a burnt out partner or develop burnout as a result of undermining behavior from a burnt out partner.

If the findings reported in this section are replicated, and stress and strain in the workplace are contagious, this might lead to burnout or a depressive climate in organizations. The new trends in structuring work, including the increase in the use of team-based production and greater interdependency, will only increase the possibility and frequency of crossover, thus creating a "strain climate." Researchers and managers should identify the processes leading to this phenomenon and suggest ways to prevent and manage it at the individual, dyad, and team levels.

The proposed model delineates the feedback process between focal persons in various role sets. The reciprocal relationship between the work and family settings can precede recursively from the work domain to the family domain or from the family domain to the work domain. After its initiation, the crossover process unfolds as a spiral in various directions, dictated by the setting and the other role players.

High-Stress Occupations and Situations

Some crossover researchers have focused on husbands with stressful jobs, such as prison officers and career officers (Burke et. al., 1980; Jackson & Maslach, 1982; Katz et al., 2000; Long & Voges, 1987; Pavett, 1986; Westman & Etzion, 1995). Others have investigated highly stressed respondents. Jones and Fletcher (1993b), for example, found a stronger bivariate relationship between husbands' job stress and wives' well being only in a sub-sample of husbands reporting higher levels of stress. The small size of this sub-sample and the similarity between spouses' mood, which may be either a cause or a result of crossover, call for replication. Furthermore, Hatfield, Cacioppo and Rapson (1994) indicate that the more intense the emotions, the more influential they are on the emotions of the spouse. These findings indicate that stressful occupations and stressful demands can potentially have a dual impact upon the individual and his or her family. Organizations should be aware because of the high price that stress exacts from the individuals and those close to them. We need comparisons of crossover in samples of stressful and less stressful occupations. Furthermore, we need to investigate crossover in the same sample under stressful and non-stressful conditions to determine whether fluctuations in stress affect the crossover process and whether we can detect tranquility transmission. It is also important to compare couples having one partner reporting high stress to couples having one partner reporting low stress, in order to investigate whether there is a critical point at which stress crossover starts. Such research should assess the job stress and resources of both partners and have a design that enables investigation of the variation in spousal well being as a function of differential stress. Identification of potentially stressful events or stressful occupations that enhance the crossover process will help management in finding preventive measures.

Following Westman's (2001) recommendation to investigate fluctuations in stress, Etzion and Westman (2001) conducted two longitudinal studies. They examined the impact of acute job stress and low to moderate stress on the crossover of burnout between couples. They sought evidence for different levels of crossover of strain between partners during two points in time characterized by high and low stress. In the first study they examined the effect of a two-week organized tour abroad on perceived job stress and burnout of 25 couples in a before-after quasi-experiment. The participants in the second study were 32 couples in which one of the partners was a student in an Executive MBA program. The questionnaires were completed by both spouses at the beginning of the program and during the end-of-term examinations, characteristically a period of acute stress. In both studies, strain crossed over from one partner to the other under the stressful conditions (i.e. before vacation and during exams), but no significant crossover was found during the more relaxed period (i.e. immediately after the vacation and at the beginning of the course). They interpreted the results as showing that crossover of burnout occurred on stressful occasions but not during the more tranquil ones.

These results need replication in order to capture the full range of the crossover phenomenon. Furthermore, if these findings are replicated, then salutogenic interventions geared toward facilitating cross-partner relief (e.g. reducing a wife's strain in order to facilitate a reduction in the husband's strain) may be worthwhile during stressful times but would be of no value during a respite.

Focusing on a similar situation, Thompson and Bolger (1999) using a diary technique, investigated carryover of depression from role senders studying for the bar exam, a very stressful event, to their conjugal partners. The diary technique enabled detecting the time when crossover was highest and lowest. They found that examinees' depression was related concurrently and prospectively to the partners' less positive and more negative feelings about the relationship. However, the association declined as the examination approached and vanished on the day of the exam. They interpreted these findings as suggesting that when the source of negative emotion is attributable to a justified cause (the bar exam), spouses act in ways that prevent the transmission of depression. Thus, partners preserved their ability to supply support when examinees needed it most. Crossover throughout most of this period was mainly uni-directional. However, while during most of the period there was little evidence that partners' feelings about the relationship predicted changes in the examinees' depression, immediately before the exam, the partners' positive feelings about the relationship predicted a decline in the examinee's depression. These findings highlight the contribution of diary studies to better understanding regarding the unfolding of the crossover process, as the intensity of transmission can change several times over the course of the stressful event. The issue of fluctuations in stress and strain should be further explored.

Gender Differences in the Crossover Processes

Neither theory nor empirical evidence provides adequate guidance regarding the role of gender in the crossover process. However, gender is a potential moderator of the impact of one's stress on the spouse's strain because of differences in the traditional role demands and expectations for men and women (Lambert, 1990). There is some indication that women are more susceptible than men to the impact of stressors affecting their partners (Kessler, 1979). Kessler and McLeod (1984) showed that events happening to significant others are more distressing for women than for men. They suggested that because of their greater involvement in family affairs, women become more sensitive not only to the stressful events that they experience but also to those that affect other family members. Furthermore, research on social support has increasingly characterized support seeking, giving, and utilization as processes that involve men and women differently (Etzion, 1984).There is also evidence that people differ in the way they can read others. Haviland and Malatesta (1981) found that women were more vulnerable to emotional transmission than men. Conger, Lorenz, Edler, Simons and Xiaojia (1993), highlighting another angle, found different responses to financial stress in the form of greater hostility among men. This increasing hostility has the potential for undermining toward the spouse, thereby increasing spouse's depressive symptoms.

Evidence concerning gender differences in the crossover effects is mixed. Several of the reviewed articles related to bi-directional crossover. Of these, a few studies found a bi-directional crossover effect of a similar magnitude from husbands to wives and from wives to husbands (Barnett et al., 1995; Hammer et. al., 1997; Westman & Etzion, 1995; Westman & Vinokur, 1998; Westman, 2002a). An exception is Parasurman, Greenhouse and Granrose's (1992) finding that whereas men's work and family stressors and WFC did not affect their wives' family satisfaction, women's family role stressors had a significant negative relationship with their husbands' family satisfaction. Contrary to these findings, Jones and Fletcher (1993a) reported a crossover effect of men's job demands on women's psychological health but found no effect of women's job demands on men's psychological health. One explanation for the contradictory findings may be the wives' occupations. The wives in Jones and Fletcher's original study did not report high levels of job stress.

Morrison and Clements (1997) investigated the impact of husbands' job characteristics on spouses' well being. Both spouses completed questionnaires, however, only husbands-to-wives crossover was investigated while controlling for wives' stress. Interestingly, these researchers found that wives' stress had a lower impact on their health than their husband's job characteristic. A possible explanation of this finding is that the wives' jobs were less stressful, which would render this finding similar to that of Jone's and Fletcher's (1993a), who found stronger relationships between male partners' job stress and female partners' well being when examining men in more stressful occupations. Westman et al. (2001) and Westman et al. (2002b) also found, in two different populations and different designs, a uni-directional crossover of strain from husbands to wives but not from wives to husbands.

Earlier studies tended to focus on crossover effects in homogenous and male-dominated professions (e.g. police officers, prison officers, military personnel, air traffic controllers), which are occupations associated with specific and intense types of stress. Most studies have focused on the male partner as the primary worker and "transmitter" of stress within the couple. There is a need for further investigation of the crossover process, both in more heterogeneous and representative occupational samples, and also in samples of couples where both male and female partner have equivalent status in the workplace and similar sources of occupational stress.

There are several aspects of the relationship between gender and crossover that merit further research because of their societal implications. One is the impact of stress on gender roles and the impact of the crossover process on the entire family. As the number of women affected by stress, strain, and the crossover process increases, the need for a thorough study of its effects becomes urgent. Information about the contribution of gender will enrich our knowledge of the crossover process and facilitate preventive measures for the individual and for the family.

Positive Crossover

All the reviewed studies investigated negative crossover, such as when job stress of one spouse affects the stress or strain of the other spouse. However, just as stressful demands or a bad day at work have a negative impact on the partner's well being, positive job events may also cross over to the partner and have a positive effect on his or her well being. Whereas crossover is usually defined as a transmission of stress, we can broaden the definition into transmission of positive events or feelings as well. Positive experiences and feelings are not merely the absence of stress but qualitatively different experiences.

One possible reason for the neglect of the investigation of positive crossover is that stress research relies heavily on medical models, with their emphasis on negative effects, just as negative affectivity was investigated for many years before researchers broadened their interest to positive affectivity. Although the emphasis in the analysis of empathy, which is one of the underlying mechanisms of crossover, tends to be placed on another's distress or on the tragic, empathy could just as easily involve the sharing of another's positive emotions and the conditions that bring them about.

One can think of many instances of positive crossover, such as enjoyable experiences at one's job leading to job satisfaction crossover and eliciting a good mood in the partner at home. Similarly, a person whose workgroup is in a good mood because of getting a bonus or recognition for a job well done may transmit this good mood to the spouse. Conversely, family life can support, facilitate, or enhance work life. Supportive family relationships and attitudes can create positive crossover to the work set. Investigating positive crossover can enhance theoretical thinking and make practical contributions to cross over literature. In the work arena, management should be aware that their positive actions could reverberate with additional positive outcomes that they did not originally plan. Just as crossover at the workplace can cause a burnout climate in the organization, we can think of "positive contagion," whereby relaxed people create an unperturbed organization. One possible antecedent for such a climate may be frequent positive events (e.g. vacations).

RESEARCH DESIGNS

The pioneering crossover studies were either qualitative or cross-sectional and retrospective, demonstrating ambiguous findings so that further research designed more rigorously was required. However, several studies employed designs of daily repeated measures of stress and strain from both husbands and wives (Bolger et al., 1989; Chan & Margolin, 1994; Jones & Fletcher, 1993b; Jones & Fletcher, 1996). These designs enabled researchers to study the dynamics within situations that appear static in conventional cross-sectional studies (Bolger et al., 1989). The daily diaries help to solve measurement problems associated with retrospective recall by allowing family members or people in the workplace to report experiences and interactions nearer to the time they occur. Furthermore, such measurement is constructive for capturing information about the dynamics of strains instead of the static information from cross-sectional designs.

A few studies have employed a longitudinal design with two measures of about a year apart (Barnett et al., 1995; Vinokur et al., 1996; Westman & Vinokur, 1998). Barnett et al. (1995) found in a longitudinal study of dual-earner couples that changes in job experiences of one partner affected the distress level of the other partner. Furthermore, they found that change over time in one partner's distress was a function of his or her own job stress and of the partner's job stress and distress. Morrison and Clements used a longitudinal design of navy couples with two measurements a month apart. They found that well being of partners who remained at home fluctuated as a function of the deployment status and the job characteristics of their partners.

Very little is known as to which variables are antecedents, consequences, or mediators in the crossover process because so little attention has been paid to causal relationship. Because of the longitudinal design and the use of SEM, the studies of Vinokur et al. (1996), Westman and Vinokur (1998), and Westman et al. (2002b) ruled out rival hypotheses concerning direction of causation, with relatively internally valid findings. One of the most pressing research needs is to illuminate more specifically how the crossover process occurs. A longitudinal research strategy would seem appropriate to study crossover effects and causality more rigorously, by analyzing covariation across time. Such designs are instrumental to examining how a spouse's well being varies as a function of fluctuations in intensity of the jobholder's stress. Examining the unfolding dynamics of stress over time will help to complement and integrate the important insights that researchers have already uncovered regarding crossover.

Knowledge of moderators will provide a more dynamic picture of family processes. In order to advance crossover research it is advisable to combine the insights of qualitative research with data derived from empirically rigorous quantitative designs.

Future crossover studies should investigate the amount of variance in the partners' distress explained by their own job demands, by their partners' demands, and by their dispositions. Yet another important issue involves the multiple levels of analysis that must be employed when investigating the work-family interface: individuals, partners, families, teams, and organizations. The clear advantage of crossover research is that it is based on observation of two partners. Collecting data from both partners avoids confounding and enables controlling each partner's stress. Bi-directionality is a crucial issue in the study of crossover as it enables investigation of symmetric models. Some of the crossover researchers collected data from both partners concerning one's job stress; some collected data from one spouse about engaging in social undermining while the spouse related to received undermining, enabling a measure of the amount of undermining in the interaction. Still we need more measures at a higher level of analysis such as at the family level (e.g. rate at which arguments between partners escalate) and at the organizational level (conflict in teams). Finally, there is a need for triangulation of data sources concerning indicators of crossover.

THEORETICAL IMPLICATIONS

The proposed model has interesting theoretical implications. A stressful event that starts at work is transferred from the employee to the spouse and to other employees, then from the spouse to others in the family. The literature reviewed supports the theoretical and practical relevance of the proposed model. Overall, the proposed model seems feasible based on the existing evidence, although additional research is needed to test it more directly, particularly with regard to some of the moderators. To investigate the crossover process thoroughly we have to investigate three phases of relationships in the causal chain: the relationships between the individual's stress and strain; the work-family links – the level of spillover for the same individual; and the crossover of one's stress to his or her partner or to the group. Each phase is a necessary but not sufficient condition for the next because of the mediating variables that may intervene in each relationship. As our model and findings show, individual differences as moderators and the social interaction as a mediator are important factors in the crossover process. Though investigating all these relationships sequentially within one study is an ambitious undertaking, it will shed light on the crossover process. To date, no study has employed a longitudinal design to assess all the direct and indirect relationships among the constructs specified by the model. A comprehensive understanding of the crossover process will elicit ample opportunities to buffer this chain of influence, whether in the two intraindividual phases or at the interindividual level.

Although crossover is defined as movement of demands between individuals *across borders*, I have suggested that it can occur between individuals in the same domain, as when stress generated in the workplace affects other job incumbents through a crossover process (Westman & Etzion, 1999). However, stress can generate at home and cross over into the work setting. Crossover research has to focus on its effect on the individual, the family, the work-team and the organization.

Furthermore, findings of crossover reinforce the idea that a complete understanding of the relationship between family and work stress may be achieved through changing the unit of study from the individual to the family and the work team. Information about the dyad adds to our understanding of well being in husbands and wives above and beyond that provided by information about the individual. Thompson and Walker (1982) point out that for research to be dyadic, the problem must be conceptualized at the level of the relationship and the analysis must be interpersonal, focusing on the responses between the two individuals. Crossover research suffers from a lack of systematic research of the individual and societal conditions under which one or another form of crossover is more likely to emerge. A contingency theory of crossover can be developed once a typology of mediating and moderating variables has been specified.

The effect of job demands and/or life events may be multiple, affecting the individual, a spouse, family members, friends, managers, coworkers, and subordinates. Pursuing those challenges as outlined in this chapter will not only go a long way toward clarifying stress and strain crossover, but will also make important contributions to role theory as a whole, in particular to our understanding of the role episode. By understanding the crossover of stress and strain, it becomes possible to revisit some of the basic assumptions in role theory about the various role sets of which the focal person is a member, and how the expectations emanating from those sets interactively create the role episode that is at the center of this process.

Five broad themes emerge from this chapter: (1) links between the workplace and the family are exceedingly complex, requiring us to specify the multiple underlying pathways of influence; (2) identifying and testing theoretically based moderators of these processes remain an important task; (3) exploring the psychological process mediating the linkages between the antecedent's influences and the crossover process is crucial to further developing crossover theory and for practical implications; (4) distinguishing between possible explanations of crossover effects is a promising direction for theory development; and (5) the challenges of combining work and family life are not limited to any one country, as the contributions from scholars in Australia, England, Canada, Finland, Israel, the Netherlands, Russia, and the United States demonstrate.

NOTE

1. Table 1 presents empirical crossover research published between 1977 and 2002, screened out of a computer search using the keywords *crossover, carry-over, contagion, transfer, transference*, and *transmission*.

REFERENCES

Abbey, A., Abramis, D. J., & Caplan, R. D. (1985). Effects of different sources of social support and social conflict on well being. *Basic and Applied Social Psychology, 6,* 111–129.

Antonovsky, A. (1979). *Health, stress and coping.* San Francisco: Jossey-Bass.Bakker, A. B., & Schaufeli, W. B. (2000). Burnout contagion process among teachers. *Journal of Applied Social Psychology, 30,* 2289–2308.

Bakker, A. B., & Schaufeli, W. B. (2000). Burnout contagion process among teachers. *Journal of Applied Social Psychology, 30,* 2289–2308.

Bakker, A. B., Schaufeli, W. B., Sixma, H. J., & Bosweld, D. (2001). Burnout contagion among general practitioners. *Journal of Social and Clinical Psychology, 20,* 82–98.

Bandura, A. (1969). *Principles of behavior modification.* New York: Holt, Rinehart, & Winston.

Barnett, R. C. (1998). Toward a review and reconceptualization of the work/family literature. *Genetic, Social, and General Psychology Monographs, 124,* 125–182.

Barnett, R, C., Raudenbush, S. W., Brennan, R. T., Pleck, J. H., & Marshall, N. L. (1995). Changes in job and marital experience and change in psychological distress: A longitudinal study of dual-earner couples. *Journal of Personality and Social Psychology, 69,* 839–850.

Beehr, T. A. (1995). *Psychological stress in the workplace*. London: Routledge.

Beehr, T. A., Johnson, L. B., & Nieva, R. (1995). Occupational stress: Coping of police and their spouses. *Journal of Organizational Psychology, 16*, 3–25.

Berkowitz, L. (1989). Frustration-aggression hypothesis: Examination and reformulation. *Psychological Bulletin, 106*, 59–73.

Bolger, N., DeLongis, A., Kessler, R., & Wethington, E. (1989). The contagion of stress across multiple roles. *Journal of Marriage and the Family, 51*, 175–183.

Booth, A. (1977). Wife's employment and husband's stress: A replication and refutation. *Journal of Marriage and the Family, 39*, 645–650.

Bronfenbrenner, U. (1977). Toward an experimental ecology of human development. *American Psychologist, 32*, 513–531.

Burke, R. J., Brief, A. P., & George, J. M. (1993). The role of negative affectivity in understanding relations between self-report of stressors and strains: A comment on the applied psychology literature. *Journal of Applied Psychology, 78*, 402–412.

Burke, R. J., Weir, T., & DuWors, R. E. (1980). Work demands on administrators and spouse well being. *Human Relations, 33*, 253–278.

Chan, C. J., & Margolin, G. (1994). The relationship between dual-earner couples daily work mood and home affect. *Journal of Social and Personal Relationships, 11*, 573–586.

Conger, R. D., Lorenz, R. O., Edler, G. H., Simons, R. L., & Xiaojia, G. E. (1993). Husband and wife differences in response to undesirable life events. *Journal of Health and Social Behavior, 34*, 71–88.

Coyne, J. C., & Downey, G. (1991). Social factors and psychopathology: Stress, social support, and coping processes. *Annual Review of Psychology, 42*, 401–425.

Crouter, A. C., Perry-Jenkins, M., Huston, T. L., & Crawford, D. W. (1989). The influence of work-induced psychological states on behavior at home. *Basic and Applied Social Psychology, 10*, 273–292.

Dew, M., Bromet, E., & Schulberg, H. (1987). A comparative analysis of two community stressors' long-term mental health effects. *American Journal of Community Psychology, 15*, 7–184.

Digman, J. M. (1990). Personality structure: Emergence of the five-factor model. *Psychological Assessment, 41*, 417–440.

Duffy, M., Ganster, D., & Pagon, M. (2002). Social undermining in the workplace. *Academy of Management Journal, 45*, 331–351.

Eckenrode, J., & Gore, S. (1981). Stressful events and social support: The significance of context. In: B. Gottlieb (Ed.), *Social Networks and Social Support* (pp. 43–68). Beverly Hills, CA: Sage.

Edwards, J. R., & Baglioni, A. J. (1991). Relationship between Type A behavior pattern and mental and physical symptoms: A comparison of global and component measures. *Journal of Applied Psychology, 76*, 276–290.

Edwards, J. R., Baglioni, A. J., & Cooper, C. L. (1990). Stress, Type-A, coping, and psychological and physical symptoms: A multi-sample test of alternative models. *Human Relations, 43*, 919–956.

Etzion, D. (1984). The moderating effect of social support on the relationship of stress and burnout. *Journal of Applied Psychology, 69*, 615–622.

Etzion, D., & Westman, M. (2001). Vacation and the crossover of strain between spouses – Stopping the vicious cycle. *Man and Work, 11*, 106–118.

Evans, P., & Bartolome, F. (1980). *Must success cost so much?* New York: Basic Books.

Fisher, C. D., & Gittelson, R. (1983). A meta analysis of the correlates of role conflict and ambiguity. *Journal of Applied Psychology, 68*, 320–333.

Fletcher, B. (1983). Marital relationships as a cause of death: An analysis of occupational mortality and the hidden consequences of marriage – some U.K. data. *Human Relations, 36,* 123–134.

Fletcher, B. (1988). Occupation, marriage, and disease specific mortality concordance. *Social Science and Medicine, 27,* 615–622.

Greenhaus, J. H., & Parasurman, S. (1987). A work-nonwork interactive prospective of stress consequences. *Journal of Organizational Behavior Management, 8,* 37–60.

Hammer, L. B., Allen, E., & Grigsby, T. D. (1997). Work-family conflict in dual-earner couples: Within individual and crossover effects of work and family. *Journal of Vocational Behavior, 50,* 185–203.

Haviland, J. M., & Malatesta, C. Z. (1981). The development of sex differences in non-verbal signals: Fallacies, facts and fantasies. In: C. Mayo & N. M. Henley (Eds), *Gender and Nonverbal Behavior* (pp. 183–208). New York: Springer-Verlag.

Hatfield, E., Cacioppo, J., & Rapson, R. (1994). *Emotional contagion.* New York: Cambridge University Press.

Haynes, S. G., Eaker, E. D., & Feinleib, M. (1983). Spouse behavior and coronary heart disease in men: Prospective results from the Framingham heart study. *American Journal of Epidemiology, 118,* 1–22.

Hobfoll, S. E., Dunahoo, C. L., Ben-Porat, Y., & Monnier, J. (1994). Gender and coping: The dual-axis model of coping. *American Journal of Community Psychology, 22,* 49–82.

Hobfoll, S. E., & London, (1986). The relationship of self concept and social support to emotional distress among women during war. *Journal of Social Clinical Psychology, 12,* 87–100.

House, J. S. (1981). *Job stress and social support.* Reading, MA: Addison Wesley.

Jackson, S. E., & Maslach, C. (1982). After-effects of job-related stress: Families as victims. *Journal of Occupational Behavior, 3,* 63–77.

Jackson, S. E., & Schuler, R. (1985). A meta-analysis and conceptual critique of research on role ambiguity and role conflict in role settings. *Organizational Behavior and Human Decision Processes, 36,* 16–78.

Jackson, S. E., Zedeck, S., & Summers, E. (1985). Family life disruptions: Effects of job-induced structural and emotional interference. *Academy of Management Journal, 28,* 574–586.

Jex, S. M., & Beehr, T. A. (1991). Emerging theoretical and methodological issues in the study of work-related stress. *Research in Personnel and Human Resources Management, 9,* 311–365.

Jones, F., & Fletcher, B. (1993a). An empirical study of occupational stress transmission in working couples. *Human Relations, 46,* 881–902.

Jones, F., & Fletcher, B. (1993b). Transmission of occupational stress: A study of daily fluctuations in work stress and strain and their impact on marital partners. In: H. Schroder, K. Rescke, M. Johnston & S. Maes (Eds), *Health Psychology: Potential Indiversity* (pp. 328–338). Regensburg: Roderer Verlag.

Jones, F., & Fletcher, B. (1996). Taking work home: A study of daily fluctuations in work stressors, effects on mood and impact on marital partners. *Journal of Occupational and Organizational Psychology, 69,* 89–106.

Kahn, R. L., & Byosiere, P. (1992). Stress in organizations. In: D. Dunnette & L. M. Hough (Eds), *Handbook of Industrial and Organizational Psychology* (pp. 571–651). Palo Alto, CA: Consulting Psychology Press.

Kahn, R. L., Wolfe, D. M., Quinn, R. P., Snoek, J. D., & Rosenthal, R. A. (1964). *Organizational stress.* New York: Wiley.

Kahn, J. P., Coyne, J. C., & Margolin, G. (1985). Depression and marital disagreement: The social construction of despair. *Journal of Social and Personal Relationships, 3,* 447–461.

Kanter, R. M. (1977). *Work and family in the United States*. New York: Russel Sage Foundation.

Katz, J., Beach, S., & Joiner, T. (1999). Contagious depression in dating couples. *Journal of Social and Clinical Psychology, 18*, 1–13.

Katz, J., Monnier, J., Libet, J., Shaw, D., & Beach, S. (2000). Individual and crossover effects of stress on adjustment in medical student marriages. *Journal of Marital and Family Therapy, 26*, 341–351.

Kessler, R. C. (1979). A strategy for studying differential vulnerability to the psychological consequences of stress. *Journal of Health and Social Behavior, 20*, 100–108.

Kessler, R. C., & McLeod, J. D. (1984). Sex differences in vulnerability to undesirable life events. *American Sociological Review, 49*, 620–631.

Lambert, S. J. (1990). Processes linking work and family: A critical review and research agenda. *Human Relations, 43*, 239–257.

Larson, R., & Almeida, D. (1999). Emotional transmission in the daily lives of families: A new paradigm for studying family processes. *Journal of Marriage and the Family, 61*, 5–20.

Lazarus, R. S. (1991). *Emotion & adaptation*. New York: Oxford.

Long, N., & Voges, K. (1987). Can wives perceive the sources of their husbands' occupational stress? *Journal of Occupational Psychology, 60*, 235–242.

MacEwen, K., Barling, J., & Kelloway, K. (1992). Effects of short-term role overload on marital interactions. *Work and Stress, 6*, 117–126.

Mauno, S., & Kinnunen, U. (2002). Perceived job insecurity among dual-earner couples: Do its antecedents vary according to gender, economic sector and the measure used? *Journal of Occupational and Organizational Psychology, 75*, 295–314.

Mitchell, R., Cronkite, R., & Moos, R. (1983). Stress, coping and depression among married couples. *Journal of Abnormal Psychology, 92*, 433–448.

Monnier, J. & Hobfoll, S. (1997). Crossover effects of communal coping. *Journal of Social and Personal Relationships, 14*, 263–270.

Moos, R. (1984). Context and coping: Toward a unifying conceptual framework. *American Journal of Community Psychology, 12*, 5–25.

Morrison, D., & Clements, R. (1997). The effects of one partner's job characteristics on the other partner's distress: A serendipitous, but naturalistic, experiment. *Journal of Occupational and Organizational Psychology, 70*, 307–324.

Nelson, G., & Beach, S. (1990). Sequential interaction in depression: Effects of depressive behavior on spousal aggression. *Behavior Therapy, 21*, 167–182.

Parasurman, S., Greenhaus, J. H., & Granrose, C. S. (1992). Role stressors, social support and well being among two-career couples. *Journal of Organizational Behavior, 13*, 339–356.

Pavett, C. M. (1986). High-stress professions: Satisfaction, stress, and well being of spouses of professionals. *Human Relations, 39*, 1141–1154.

Pearlin, L. (1989). The sociological study of stress. *Journal of Health and Social Behavior, 30*, 241–256.

Pearlin, L., & Turner, H. A. (1987). The family as a context of the stress process. In: S. Kasl & C. Cooper (Eds), *Stress and Health: Issues in Research Methodology*. New York: Wiley.

Piotrkowski, C. (1979). *Work and the family system: A naturalistic study of the working-class and lower-middle-class families*. New York: The Free Press.

Repetti, R. (1989). Effects of daily workload on subsequent behavior during marital interaction: The roles of social withdrawal and spouse support. *Journal of Personality and Social Psychology, 57*, 651–659.

Riley, D., & Eckenrode, J. (1986). Social ties: Costs and benefits within different subgroups. *Journal of Personality and Social Psychology, 51*, 770–778.

Roberts, R., & O'Keefe, S. J. (1981). Sex differences in depression re-examined. *Journal of Health and Social Behavior*, *22*, 394–400.

Rook, S. K., Dooley, D., & Catalano, R. (1991). Stress transmission: The effects of husbands' job stressors on emotional health of their wives. *Journal of Marriage and the Family*, *53*, 165–177.

Rosenfield, S. (1980). Sex differences in depression: Do women always have higher rates? *Journal of Health and Social Behavior*, *22*, 394–400.

Rosenfield, S. (1992). The cost of sharing: Wives employment and husbands' mental health. *Journal of Health and Social Behavior*, *33*, 213–225.

Russell, D. W., & Cutrona, C. E. (1991). Social support, stress, and depressive symptoms among the elderly: Test of a process model. *Psychology and Aging*, *6*, 190–201.

Schaefer, C., Coyne, J. C., & Lazarus, R. S. (1981). The health-related functions of social support. *Journal of Behavioral Medicine*, *4*, 381–406.

Schmaling, K., & Jacobson, N. (1990). Marital interaction and depression. *Journal of Abnormal Psychology*, *99*, 229–236.

Shinn, M., Lehmann, S., & Wong, N. W. (1984). Social interaction and social support. *Journal of Social Issues*, *40*, 55–76.

Spector, P. E., & O'Connell, B. J. (1994). The contribution of personality traits, negative affectivity, locus of control and Type A to the subsequent reports of job stressors and job strains. *Journal of Occupational and Organizational Psychology*, *67*, 1–12.

Staines, G. L., Pottic, K. G., & Fudge, D. A. (1986). Wives' employment and husbands' attitudes toward work and life satisfaction. *Journal of Applied Psychology*, *71*, 118–128.

Stotland, E. (1969). Exploratory investigations of empathy. In: L. Berkowitz (Ed.), *Advances in Experimental Social Psychology* (Vol. 4, pp. 271–314). New York: Academic Press.

Thompson, A., & Bolger, N. (1999). Emotional transmission in couples under stress. *Journal of Marriage and the Family*, *61*, 38–48.

Thompson, L., & Walker, A. J. (1982). The dyad as a unit of analysis: Conceptual and methodological issues. *Journal of Marriage and the Family*, *44*, 889–900.

Vinokur, A., Price, R. H., & Caplan, R. D. (1996). Hard times and hurtful partners: How financial strain affects depression and relationship satisfaction of unemployed persons and their spouses. *Journal of Personality and Social Psychology*, *71*, 166–179.

Vinokur, A., & van Ryn, M. (1993). Social support and undermining in close relationships: Their independent effects on mental health of unemployed persons. *Journal of Personality and Social Psychology*, *65*, 350–359.

Watson, D., & Clark, L. E. (1984). Negative affectivity: The disposition to experience aversive emotional states. *Psychological Bulletin*, *96*, 465–498.

Westman, M. (2001). Stress and strain crossover. *Human Relations*, *54*, 557–591.

Westman, M. (2002). Gender asymmetry in crossover research. In: D. Nelson & R. Burke (Eds). *Gender, Work Stress and Health*. Washington: American Psychological Association.

Westman, M., & Etzion, D. (1995). Crossover of stress, strain and resources from one spouse to another. *Journal of Organizational Behavior*, *16*, 169–181.

Westman, M., & Etzion, D. (1999). The crossover of strain from school principals to teachers and vice versa. *Journal of Occupational Health Psychology*, *4*, 269–278.

Westman, M, Etzion, D., & Danon, E. (2001). Job insecurity and crossover of burnout in married couples. *Journal of Organizational Behavior*, *22*, 467–481.

Westman, M., Etzion, D., & Segev, K. (2002a). The crossover of work-family conflict from one spouse to another. Working Paper No. 1/2002. The Israel Institute of Business Research, Tel Aviv University.

Westman, M., & Shirom, A. (1995). Dimensions of coping behavior: A proposed conceptual framework. *Anxiety, Stress, and Coping, 8*, 87–100.

Westman, M., & Vinokur, A. (1998). Unraveling the relationship of distress levels within couples: Common stressors, emphatic reactions, or crossover via social interactions? *Human Relations, 51*, 137–156.

Westman, M., Vinokur, A., Hamilton, L., & Roziner, I. (2002b). Crossover of marital dissatisfaction during downsizing: A study of Russian Army officers and their spouses. Working Paper No. 6/2002. The Israel Institute of Business Research, Tel Aviv University.

Wethington, E. (2000). Contagion of stress. *Advances in Group Processes, 17*, 229–253.

Wheaton, B. (1996). The domains and boundaries of stress concepts. In: H. Kaplan (Ed.), *Psychological Stress: Perspectives on Structure, Theory, Life Course, and Methods* (pp 29–70). San Diego, CA: Academic Press.

Wilensky, H. L. (1960). Work, careers and social integration. *International Social Science Journal, 12*, 543–560.

Zedeck, S. (1992). Introduction: Exploring the domain of work and family concerns. In: S. Zedeck (Ed.), *Work, Families and Organizations* (pp. 1–32). San Francisco: Jossey-Bass.

ALTERNATIVE WORK ARRANGEMENTS AND EMPLOYEE WELL BEING

Julian Barling, Michelle Inness and
Daniel G. Gallagher

ABSTRACT

One significant trend in human resource practice that dominated the 1990s was the move away from traditional, full-time employment toward a variety of different forms of alternative work arrangements. Accompanying this trend was a growing concern about the effects of alternative forms of work for well being. We first review the different forms of alternative work arrangements, which vary in terms of temporal, numerical and locational flexibility. Thereafter, the effects of different forms of alternative work arrangements (e.g. part-time employment, job-sharing, outsourcing) on psychological and physical well being, and occupational safety and health are evaluated. We conclude by noting that alternative work arrangements do not necessarily exert uniformly negative effects on well being. Instead, the importance of the volitionality with which individuals assume alternative work arrangements must be considered: When individuals choose such arrangements because they want to, any potential negative effects are minimized. In contrast, when individuals assume such work arrangements because of a lack of perceived alternatives, there is a greater risk for negative effects. Finally, the need for future research which more

Historical and Current Perspectives on Stress and Health, Volume 2, pages 183–216.
ISBN: 0-7623-0970-9

rigorously accounts for the conceptual differences across alternative work arrangements is noted.

INTRODUCTION

Researchers who focus upon the study of employment, organizations, worker-organizational relationships, and employee well being have become trapped by a stereotypical image of the world of work, assuming that "normal," "standard" or "typical" work exists in the form of a cyclical Monday through Friday work schedule, with a morning starting time, lunch break, and a late afternoon or early evening commute back home, with rest and relaxation relegated to week-ends and public holidays. In contrast, the reality is that within the U.S. and Canada, less than one-third of the workforce is employed in jobs that fit the Monday through Friday, full-time, day shift stereotype (Fenwick & Tausig, 2001). Thus, frequently utilized terms like "non-standard" or "atypical" employment, which appear in the management and organizational psychology literature, are in many respects ambiguous, if not inappropriate. If less than a third of the workforce falls within the definition of traditional work arrange-ments, then what precisely is "standard" or "typical" employment?

More than a decade ago, Pfeffer and Baron (1988) noted that existing theories and perspectives of organizational theory are based upon bureaucratic models of organizational control. Within such models, there exists the underlying assumption of a clear delineation of manager-employee responsibilities, a relationship where satisfactory performance is rewarded by continued employ-ment, with work being crucial to personal and social identity. More recently, Gallagher and McLean Parks (2001) raised questions concerning the extent to which such commonly accepted and tested constructs as organizational commitment, work involvement, or an identifiable employer have meaning to workers performing jobs outside standard models of employment. Given recent changes in the world of work, we believe it is now an opportune time to open the door both to theoretical and practical questions concerning the extent to which models of occupational stress and employee well being are applicable to the majority of workers and work arrangements which are outside the stereotyped and bureaucratic world of "regular" employment, and the aim of this chapter is to initiate such thinking.

We begin this chapter with a detailed overview of the many employment arrangements that exist outside of the traditional full-time, nine-to-five world of work. Attention will be given not only to the underlying structural charac-teristics of "atypical" work arrangements, but also, where applicable to the factors that have contributed to their increased emergence.

THE NATURE OF ALTERNATIVE WORK ARRANGEMENTS

Rethinking the Image of Employment Contracts and Working Schedules

In recent years there has been a considerable focus within academic and practitioner literatures on the changing nature of employment contracts (Cooper & Burke, 2002; Kalleberg, 2000; Tetrick & Barling, 1995; Vosko, 2000; Zeytinoğlu, 1999). For the most part, writers have sought to document the decline of the "traditional" or ongoing employer – employee relationships, and the growth of alternative working arrangements. Very visible in these discussions of the new working relationships has been the increased presence and growth of "contingent," "temporary," or "fixed-term" contracts. The transition from more permanent to contingent or transitory employment contracts has been repeatedly associated with employer concerns about increasingly competitive product markets, the availability of new information technologies and managerial strategies which can minimize the fixed costs associated with people (Cappelli, 1999). For many employers, the mantra at the start of the new century has become organizational "flexibility" (Sparrow, 1998; Drucker, 2002), and in many circles "flexibility" has become a code word for employer-driven efforts to restructure the way in which work is performed and the basic characteristics of the employment contract.

From the organizational perspective, human resource flexibility can be achieved in a number of ways. At the organizational or micro level, flexibility may be numerical, functional, temporal, locational, or financial in focus (Reilly, 1998). Numerical flexibility has been frequently characterized as the ability of the employer to readily adjust the size of the workforce to meet the cyclical needs of the business. Numerical flexibility may not only be focused on the ability to adjust required levels of employment at a particular phase of operations, but could also involve large scale adjustments in the size of the organization's immediate workforce through the "outsourcing" or "subcontracting" of work previously performed within the organization (Brewster et al., 1997). Temporal flexibility also relates to organizational interests in matching staffing levels with the daily or immediate production or services schedules of the organization (Reilly, 1998). Temporal staffing flexibility is frequently achieved through shift work schedules, "flextime" arrangements (i.e. variable starting and finishing times), and compressed or flexible working weeks. Especially in service industries, temporal flexibility is often achieved through the practice of employing workers on part-time contracts. Functional flexibility is relevant in the context of how an organization internally associates labor within the organization. Firms that are functionally flexible strive to reduce the lines of demarcation between different jobs within the organization, and improve productivity by moving employees among different tasks within the organization. Functional flexibility is also often achieved through initiatives such as cross training and skill-based pay plans. While functional flexibility is focused internally, locational flexibility is directed toward ways of using workers outside of the normal workplace (Reilly, 1998). Locational strategies may include the use of home-based workers, outworkers, and the increased use of workers on "teleworking" arrangements (Duxbury & Higgins, 2002). Finally, employers may also seek financial flexibility through variable pay systems that attempt to link labor costs with organizational performance. Through gain sharing (and also loss sharing) and other forms of performance-based pay, the goal is to place a larger share of the employee's compensation at risk.

We now turn our attention to a description of the different forms of alternative work arrangements. It is important to note that many of these arrangements are not new, but have been used for many years (see Capelli, 1999). What is more novel and under-developed is the empirical attention focused on these work arrangements.

Temporal Flexibility

Full-Time Work
From a statistical perspective, full-time work is usually indicated by holding a job, or employment with a particular organization, for between 35 to 40 hours of paid employment per week. However, being a "full-time" employee should not be mistaken for the stereotypical view of the Monday-to-Friday, nine-to-five worker. Being a full-time worker could very well include a variety of scheduling or alternative temporal work arrangements. For example, temporal flexibility has traditionally focused on employer interests concerning when the work is performed. As a function of extant technologies or customer generated demand, full-time work is often performed on a *shift work* basis. Most notably, full-time work is engaged in, but such work may be performed during nights or early morning "graveyard" shifts. To a large degree, shift work may be predictable and regular in scheduling, (i.e. an ongoing evening shift). In many respects it can be a fixed work schedule, but not necessarily the nine-to-five day shift.

Alternatively, shift work may itself be variable in terms of scheduling. Variability may exist as to whether workers remain on a selected shift, or whether they are moved or rotated between shifts. Shifts may also differ in both length and days of the week. For example, in some occupations, particularly those associated with public safety (police, fire, health care), "normal" work schedules may well fall outside the assumed standard of eight hour shifts, and in fact may sometimes extend as long as 12–24 hours. In essence, full-time work, and nine-to-five employment are no longer synonymous.

Part-Time Work
Although differences exist between countries with regard to the legal or statistical definition, part-time employment is generally defined as scheduled work that is performed for fewer than 35 hours per week. Within many countries, part-time work represents a significant share (i.e. in excess of 20%) of all paid employment. Younger workers (16–24 years of age), middle-aged women, and older workers transitioning into retirement are disproportionately represented among part-time workers.

Part-time work has long been a scheduling mechanism used by organizations to achieve temporal flexibility. Used mainly in the service and retail trade sectors, part-time work schedules are a cost-efficient means for appropriate staffing at peak customer demand hours. From the employee's perspective, part-time work arrangements are usually undertaken on a voluntary basis, and in many circumstances represents a way for workers to balance work (income and work experience) and non-work interests (school and/or family demands, Barling & Gallagher, 1996).

Job Sharing
Job sharing represents a nexus between the worlds of full- and part-time employment. Job sharing arrangements have been promoted primarily as a means of allowing workers in career-oriented professions to maintain on-going employment within an organization, while simultaneously being placed on a reduced hour or part-time schedule. Most workers in job sharing arrangements are women with children at home, and are more likely than "regular" part-time workers to hold university degrees.

Temporary Employment
For many organizations, the employment of workers on temporary or "fixed-term" contracts provides a way of maximizing numerical flexibility within increasingly competitive environments. Under the terms of *direct-hire* temporary work arrangements, workers are recruited to the organization's own "in-house" pool of temporary employees. In situations where the organization needs to secure staffing on an unexpected basis (e.g. because of absences) or to meet expanded production or service demands, workers are drawn from the "in-house" pool. Perhaps the most commonly recognized means of

securing workers under fixed-term employment contracts, however, is through the use of temporary help staffing firms (e.g. Manpower, Adecco, Kelly Services).

Historically, temporary staffing has been associated with providing client organizations with workers for short-term assignments in the areas of office support work (i.e. clerical) and manual unskilled laborers. However, the temporary help industry has evolved to include the short-term placement of workers in a broad range of technical and professional services. This increased professionalization of skills available through temporary help firms also affords employer or client organizations access to increased functional flexibility. In particular, employers may be able to contract workers with specific skill sets that are needed only on a short term basis through temporary help firms. From the employee's perspective, being registered with and dispatched through the services of temporary help firms offers a way to transition in and out of the labor force, and a method of gaining and applying job related skills. In many cases temporary work is seen as a means of access to more permanent employment arrangements with a particular client or employer organization.

Seasonal Contracts

Within certain industries, there is a substantial need by organizations to make regular numerical adjustments in the size of their workforces. Most visible of such types of organizations are those that are highly seasonal in nature (e.g. agriculture, tourist resorts). In many respects, seasonal contracts represent a hybrid of full-time and part-time employment contracts. Employees are often employed to work full-time schedules on a weekly or monthly basis, but the contracts are simultaneous part-time in the respect that they are only for a part of the calendar year. As noted by Alder and Alder (2001), some seasonal work (e.g. service-focused resort industries) requires excessively long workdays and frequent rescheduling of work shifts to meet service and weather conditions. In other contexts, seasonal contracts may be fairly stable, for example where the employer is using workers on seasonal or short-term contracts to meet numerical staffing needs created by "regular" employees on summer vacations. Seasonal employment contracts are also exemplified in the form of migrant labor contracts that are common in large-scale agricultural business. The work involves excessive hours (often exempted from prevailing labor laws), and the contracts are of fixed duration. Most forms of seasonal employment have explicit starting and termination dates associated with the employment relationship. Although successful performance of the job may imply an expectation of a future contract, the employment deal is clearly fixed in time or task completion.

Self-Employed and Independent Contractors
Approximately 8% of the workforce is self-employed (Bregger, 1996; Gardner, 1995), and many of these workers operate as *independent contractors* or free-lance workers. In the broader context of organizational downsizing, many professional workers have turned toward self-employed consulting as a means of personally restructuring and re-establishing their own careers, often after being laid off from a traditional job in an organization (Barling, 1999). For many organizations, independent contractors represent an identifiable form of functional flexibility in which they are able to secure required professional expertise without making the commitment of an on-going relationship. Most independent contractor arrangements are established on a project basis, rather than on actual hours of work. Independent contractors technically operate in a world where a single employer is replaced with multiple "client" arrangements (Gallagher & McLean Parks, 2001).

Locational Flexibility

In addition to understanding the underlying structure of employment contracts (e.g. full-time, part-time, temporary, seasonal), jobs can also be viewed from the perspective of locational flexibility, i.e. where they are performed.

Home-Based Work and Teleworking
From a locational perspective, employment (at least in the context of an industrial society) has invariably been viewed as taking place in a location away from home. For an increasing number of self-employed workers or independent contractors, the home and the office are now one and the same, a trend that has increased since the 1980s (Edwards & Field-Hendrey, 1996). Although it is difficult to closely measure the number of workers who electronically commute to work via *teleworking* arrangements, telework has become an increasing prevalent form of "locational" flexibility for both employers and workers, with advantages including reduced travel time, reductions in work related costs, greater flexibility is scheduling work hours, as well as the potential for a better balance of work-family interests (Duxbury & Higgins, 2002). Teleworking can be structured in a number of different ways. Telework is not necessarily always performed from home; telework may be performed outside the home and office, but at designated "telecenters" or other "hoteling" or remote worksite arrangements. The combined growth of both self-employed independent contractor arrangements and teleworking arrangements has also been accompanied with a change in the gender profile of home-based workers, with a continued rise in the number of men electing to work from home.

A substantial number of workers are employed in "outworker" arrangements. While "outworking" is in many respects the same as "home-based" employment, the term and practice of "outworking" has long been associated with self-employed garment trade workers. Women and immigrants are disproportionately involved in telework. More technically-sophisticated "outworking" jobs with piece rate or commission-based payments now exist in the form of home-based "call-centers".

Outsourcing

Managerial decisions to *subcontract* or *outsource* certain products or services has become increasingly common in the context of organization strategies aimed at retaining direct control and responsibility over only those functional areas which represent an organization's "core competences" (Greer, Youngblood & Gray, 1999). In many cases, outsourcing is a cost-benefit based employment strategy founded on the belief that services currently performed in the organization (e.g. food services, payroll, accounting, marketing) can be performed more efficiently by "external providers".

As an increasingly popular approach to organizational re-staffing, outsourcing has the potential to change the social dynamics of the workplace. For example, in some cases, the workforce of an entire functional area may be terminated as a result of a decision to outsource the work. However, the same workforce may be hired by the new firm which provides the outsourcing service. For the discharged workers, their basic tasks and responsibilities remain the same, but their employment-contract is now with another employer. Such arrangements may be particularly perplexing to workers from a locational perspective when the job itself is performed on the premises of the past employer.

Numerical Flexibility

Analogous to the increasing desire of organizations to maximize different forms of flexibility, workers may also seek to contract or expand their own levels of paid work. *Overtime work*, *moonlighting*, and *multiple job holding*, represent three long established approaches through which workers can expand their own paid work time. Although the availability of overtime work hours is not normally controlled by workers, individual employees may signal to the organization their interest and availability to perform such work when it is available.

Moonlighting refers to those situations in which individuals have a primary job or employer organization to which they are attached, but seek additional working time at a different organization. In contrast, *multiple-job holding* occurs where individual workers take on varying amounts of work at different organizations in order to construct the hourly equivalent of a full-time job. In many cases, multiple job holding may be motivated by the inability of workers to find suitable full-time employment, and are thus forced for economic reasons to construct a full-time work schedule from part-time positions. In fact, financial factors represent a major factor cited in the reasons why people seek and hold a second job (Stinson, 1990; Amirault, 1997). In contrast, there is evidence to support the counter-intuitive suggestions that people who moonlight tend to be relatively well paid and better educated than individuals who hold only one job (Amirault, 1997), and moon-lighters may seek out additional work to minimize undesirable domestic relationships (Hochschild, 1997). In both the case of moonlighting and multiple job holding, however, the structural and social aspects of work may add a degree of complexity that would be otherwise absent in a single employment relationship.

Summary

Perhaps the strongest force for alternative working arrangements is the need for employers to meet temporal or schedule-based demands, which results in increased interest in, and emphasis on shift work, part-time hours, and seasonal work by employers. For many organizations, the perceived need to become more flexible in terms adjusting staffing levels (temporal) and acquiring specific skills on short notice (functional flexibility), has contributed to a sizable increase in the number of employment relationships which not only have become more flexible in terms of when work is performed, but also changed the duration of employment from a fixed term to a temporary basis. As in the past, the home also remains a place of paid employment. In the current technological environment, the nature of the types of jobs that can be performed at home and the ability of employers to increase options in terms of where the work is performed has dramatically increased.

Employees themselves are also often seeking alternative working arrangements which more effectively fit their own needs. This search can include multiple job holding or performing work for multiple clients. The flexibility of being able to work fewer or more hours, to share a job with another worker, or to work from home are all flexibility-based considerations which are driven by worker interests and not simply imposed upon the worker.

However, as suggested above, the variety that exists in how hours can be scheduled, the duration of the workweek, the location of the work, and the permanency of the work contract, make it extremely difficult to establish clear or non-overlapping categories of "alternative" work arrangements.

THE CONSEQUENCES OF ALTERNATIVE WORK ARRANGEMENT FOR EMPLOYEE WELL BEING

Thus far, we have presented a framework within which to understand alternative forms of employment. Before attempting an understanding of the consequences of alternative forms of employment for work stress and well being, several conceptual issues require explanation, including the use of the terms "work stress" and "psychosocial work factors", a description of psychosocial work factors, and how alternative work factors affect employee well being.

First, we explicitly choose not to use the term "work stress". Ever since Kahn et al.'s (1964) classic study on role stressors, the topic of "work stress" (or "work stressors") has received a tremendous amount of attention, from empirical researchers, practitioners and the lay public alike. On the one hand, this attention is obviously beneficial, given the body of knowledge that has been generated. However, as the topic of "work stress" has gained in popularity, it may have been used so broadly that its consensual meaning has become diffused (see Barling, 1990; Sauter, Murphy & Hurrell, 1990), with concomitant negative consequences for construct validity. For this reason, we choose to avoid the term.

Instead, we choose to focus on the subjective experience of work (Barling, 1990), or the perceived psychosocial work environment (Sauter et al., 1990) for several reasons. First, as Sauter et al. (1990, p. 1150) suggest, the term "psychosocial factors" highlights the focus on the experiences of individual workers, including the social environment at work, organizational aspects of the job, and the content . . . of the tasks performed". Second, a focus on psychosocial characteristics of the workplace is gaining increasing acceptance in the organizational literature (e.g. Elovainio, Kivimäki & Vahtera, 2002; Hurrell, 2002). Third, objective events at work (e.g. a move from traditional to alternative employment arrangements) initially influence the subjective experience of work. In turn, it is the subjective experience of work that influences psychological, psychosomatic and behavioral outcomes (Barling, 1990; Pratt & Barling, 1988).

Finally, Warr (1987) notes that the relationship between work and mental health is not linear. Instead, he argues that mental health will be affected by environmental factors in the same way that vitamins affect physical health. To pursue this analogy, vitamins do not exert a uniform, linear effect on physical health. Extremely high levels of vitamins A and D, for example, may not only fail to provide benefits, but can be detrimental, and Warr (1987) argues that the same principle holds true for what we term psychosocial work factors. We suggest that control or autonomy may function similarly to vitamins A and D, where too much control or autonomy may be detrimental. Schaubroeck, Jones and Xie's (2001) research suggests that high levels of control may be used ineffectively, and experienced as distressing, by people who have a propensity for self-blame for negative outcomes, or low self-efficacy beliefs.

Warr's (1987) vitamin model is important because it reminds us that changes in forms of employment can exert positive as well as negative effects, and that a singular focus on deficiencies in the psychosocial work environment will lead to a truncated body of knowledge. What is required instead is a focus that allows us to understand the negative consequences of changes in work arrangements, but also positive outcomes as well (Turner, Barling & Zacharatos, 2002). One example of the impact of an exclusively problem-oriented focus is illustrative. Until the mid-1980s, virtually all research on the effects of maternal employment found that it yielded negative consequences. However, the surveys that were being conducted primarily asked questions about the potentially deleterious effects of maternal employment. Only when researchers began to look for any possible benefits of maternal employment were any positive effects found (Barling, 1990).

A comprehensive description of various components of the psychosocial work environment experienced by employees in traditional and alternative forms of employment can be captured in ten different elements. Sauter et al. (1990) initially identified six of these psychosocial workplace factors (and their article contains a more comprehensive discussion of these factors), including work-load and pace, work scheduling, role clarity, employment security, positive interpersonal relationships and high quality jobs.

The issue of *work load and pace* has been of interest to researchers for several decades, and recent meta-analytic findings (Sparks, Cooper, Fried & Shirom, 1997) confirm their importance. Likewise, *work scheduling* has been an issue to employees ever since the invention of electricity allowed work to take place on a 24 hour cycle. The nature, meaning, and consequences of role stressors have been recognized since Kahn et al.'s (1964) classic research (see Jackson & Schuler, 1985). Sauter et al. (1990) include "role stressors" in their conceptualization, as do we and others (Warr, 1987). However, while incorporating this idea, we focus on "*role clarity*" (rather than role stressors or role ambiguity) to reflect the positive nature of the psychosocial work factors. Next, we include *employment security*. While we accept the importance of Sauter et al.'s (1990) notion of "career" security, we focus on employment security for a number of reasons: (a) when employees are insecure, long-term career development assumes less importance than short-term aspirations for security; (b) employment security is more realistic in a market-driven economy than job security; and (c) employment security forms a major part of current conceptualizations of high performance work systems (e.g. Pfeffer, 1998). People seek work for many reasons, and the opportunity for *positive interpersonal relationships* is one of the most important (Jahoda, 1982; Warr, 1987). Poor relationships with people at work is an important source of dissatisfaction. By contrast, social support from people at work enhances performance and well being. Lastly, Sauter et al. (1990) include job content, and note how narrow, fragmented jobs that provide little challenge and skill use are associated with dissatisfaction and diminished well being. In keeping with a positive focus on psychosocial factors, we incorporate *high quality jobs* (see Barling, Kelloway & Iverson, in press), which include skill development (e.g. training) and empowerment (e.g. skill use, autonomy).

In trying to understand the consequences of new forms of employment on psychosocial work factors, however, we go beyond the six factors identified by Sauter et al. (1990), and include four additional components of the psychosocial work environment, namely personal control at work, perceived fairness, financial compensation and status volition.

Currently, a tremendous amount of empirical attention is focused on the nature and amount of *personal control* that employees can exert on their jobs, with findings consistently showing its positive effects on performance and well being (e.g. Ganster, Fox & Dwyer, 2001), and personal control forms a central part of several theories of "healthy work" (e.g. Karasek & Theorell, 1990; Warr, 1987). Personal control also assumes considerable importance in a workplace environment experiencing changes. *Perceived justice* is an issue that had attracted considerable attention in the last two decades, and exerts widespread and robust effects on different organizational attitudes and behaviors (Colquitt, Conlon, Wesson, Porter & Ng, 2001). With changes in the nature of employment, perceived justice (especially procedural and interpersonal justice) assumes considerable importance in the perceptions of the workplace environment. Next, we agree that there is some debate about the merits of financial compensation as a motivating factor (Pfeffer, 1999). Nonetheless, we believe that the specific nature of changing employment conditions mandates the inclusion of *pay and benefits* as one of the core psychosocial work factors, because changing employment conditions can mean a decrease (e.g. a move to part-time employment) or an increase (e.g. moonlighting) in financial compensation. The importance of compensation is also supported by Warr (1987), who includes the "availability of money" as one of the critical features in the psychosocial work environment. Lastly, we include *volition*, which reflects the extent to which individuals have been free to choose their particular employment type. This is different from job control, which reflects the control *within* one's job. In contrast, volition reflects the degree of control over the work arrangements *about* the job. In an environment of changing employment characteristics, volition assumes considerable importance.

Because work is a central activity for most adults, the various psychosocial experiences employees have at work can exert critical implications for their well being (Tausig, 1999). Empirical examinations of the impact of work experiences on employee well being have focused on three central themes: Psychological well being, physical well being, and the physical safety of employees. Several observations in the literature on occupational influences on well being are relevant. First, both mental and physical *wellness* have typically been defined in 'negative' terms, whereby general well being is defined as the absence of negative physical or psychological symptoms (Jamal, Baba & Tourigny, 1998). Second, psychological and physical well being are often related, and may be reciprocally caused (Jamal, 1999). Third, and most importantly from our perspective in this chapter, most theoretical formulations on the impact of work on well being are based almost entirely on data gathered from employees involved in traditional work arrangements (e.g. Karasek & Theorell, 1990; Hackman & Oldham, 1976), only extending to other forms of employment more recently. Given the variety of forms of alternative employment and their corresponding psychosocial experiences, each form of alternative employment may have a unique set of consequences for the general well being of employees.

We now turn our attention to a review of the research on well being associated with many of the forms of alternative employment. Specifically, we will now consider the consequences of the different alternative work arrangements for psychological and physical health, and occupational safety. In doing so, however, it will become apparent that there is a paucity of empirical data relating to many of the alternative work arrangements. As such, this discussion is grounded both on available empirical data on alternative work arrangements, as well as results of research generated on employees in traditional work arrangements.

Part-time Employment

Part-time work has attracted considerable empirical attention (Barling & Gallagher, 1996), a situation that was probably stimulated initially by calls to focus on part-time employees, who had been described as the "missing persons of organizational research" (Rotchford & Roberts, 1982). However, part-time workers no longer warrant the title of the "missing persons". Part-time employment is probably the most prevalent of the different forms of alternative work arrangements, and has attracted perhaps more attention than any of the other alternative work arrangements.

Psychological Well Being
The research that followed Rotchford and Roberts' early challenge to the omission of part-time workers in empirical examinations can be divided into several phases. In the first phase, numerous studies were conducted that focused on potential differences between full-time and part-time employees' job attitudes (e.g. job satisfaction, organizational commitment). The results of these studies either yielded no substantial differences in job attitudes between these groups, or inconsistent findings, with some showing that part-time employees manifested more or less positive job attitudes (see Barling & Gallagher, 1996; Lee & Johnson, 1991). With the exception of the finding that part-time employees manifest higher levels of turnover than their full-time counterparts, most studies that focused on job-related behaviors (absenteeism, turnover and job performance) did not yield significant differences between these two groups. Overall, with a few exceptions (see for e.g. Dubinsky & Skinner, 1984; Steffy & Jones, 1990), much literature suggests that being employed on a part-time basis may have few unique implications for employees' subjective well being (Barling & Gallagher, 1996).

As a consequence of these findings, Barling and Gallagher (1996) suggested that the next logical question is whether there are meaningful differences *within* part-time employees. To answer this question they turned to a large body of research focusing mainly on the quantity of work performed by teenagers who are employed on a part-time basis while still at high school. Initial hypotheses suggested that the number of hours these teenagers worked was critical to diverse aspects of their well being (Steinberg, Fegley & Dornbusch, 1993), and this is important to a discussion of part-time workers given that number of hours worked is the most obvious factor on which part-time and full-time workers differ. Subsequent findings, however, suggest no consistent differences between part-time and full-time employment. Research on teenage part-time employees shows that the quantity of employment (and by extension, employment status) is an insufficient explanation of any subsequent effects, and that the quality of employment is much more important (Barling, Rogers & Kelloway, 1995; Loughlin & Barling, 1998). Part-time employees exposed to high quality work react in much the same way as do full-time employees. Similarly, full-time employees exposed to poor quality jobs can be expected to respond in the same manner as their part-time counterparts. Thus, these results suggest that specific temporal characteristics of alternative work arrangements may be less important than the quality of the job.

What appears to be more critical to part-time employees' well being is whether their involvement in part-time employment is voluntary. Voluntary part-time employment may not only pose little threat to well being, but may even offer certain lifestyle benefits over full-time employment. Enjoying a preferred work schedule, and a sense of control over personal scheduling may increase part-time workers' job satisfaction, organizational commitment, and general well being, relative to full-time employees (Krausz, Sagie & Biderman, 2000). Voluntary part-time employment may be particularly beneficial for certain groups of workers such as women and elderly workers. These data also showed that part-time workers experienced less stress or depression than the other two groups, and that married couples in which the wife was employed on a part-time basis reported less marital conflict and lesser reductions in intimacy compared with couples in which the wife worked full-time (Olds, Schwartz, Eisen & Betcher, 1993). Hock and DeMeis' (1990) examined the issue of maternal employment status and showed that employed and non-employed mothers did not differ in terms of depressive symptomatology. However, women who would have preferred to be employed but remained at home manifested higher levels of depressive symptomatology. Similarly, Barling, Fullagar and Marchl-Dingle (1987) showed that mothers' employment status preference moderated the effects of employment status on their children's behaviors.

Research comparing full-time and part-time employees has extended these findings, showing that status congruence (i.e. preference to be employed part-time vs. full-time) is a significant predictor of work attitudes (e.g. Keil, Armstrong-Stassen, Cameron & Horsburgh, 2000; Holtom, Lee & Tidd, in press; Krausz, Sagie & Biderman, 2000; Morrow, McElroy & Elliott, 1994). Holtom et al. (in press) have extended these findings to show that work status congruence is also associated with employee retention and performance.

Thus, part-time employment per se would appear to be of minimal significance with respect to the psychosocial work environment, and well being. Instead, the research findings to date suggest that it is the quality of one's employment, and the degree of volition in choosing the work status, that makes a difference. Given observations that increases in part-time employment mostly occur during recessionary periods, and can often be assumed to be involuntary, is of some concern regarding the psychosocial work environment encountered by part-time employees and their well being (Barling, 1999; Nardone, 1995). Future research, however, should address further whether there are meaningful differences within groups of part-time employees more directly. In addition, issues related to employment security, positive interpersonal relationships and personal control may be especially salient given the nature of part-time employment.

Physical Well Being
There are several reasons why part-time employment may be both positively and negatively associated with physical well being. With respect to a positive

impact of part-time employment on well being, many work-related illnesses result from cumulative exposure to a dangerous or unhealthy work environment. The reduced working hours that define part-time employment correspond with less exposure to illness-inducing agents, and may therefore act as a buffer against such illnesses (Castillo, Davis & Wegman, 1999). However, part-time employees may suffer other vulnerabilities. For instance, within part-time employees as a group, two subgroups of workers who may have an above average vulnerability for health problems are young employees and shift workers (Furnham & Hughes, 1999). While there is a growing literature on the psychosocial experiences of teenagers who are employed on a part-time basis (Barling & Kelloway, 1999), little is known about the extent to which youth may suffer physical symptoms or illness as a result of work-related exposure. It is of interest, however, that for young people, part-time work has been associated with alcohol and drug use, at least partially because holding a part-time job provides access to financial resources with which to acquire these substances (Frone, 1999). Second, though shift workers can be full or part-time, many part-time employees are also shift workers, and shiftwork may be particularly threatening to employee health. Some research has suggested that within two to three years of commencing employment, as many as 20 to 30% of shift workers quit because of health concerns (Mykletun & Mykletun, 1999), and for workers with rotating shifts, the negative health effects may be even more pronounced (Jamal & Baba, 1992, 1997; Martens, Nijhuis, Van Boxtel & Knottnerus, 1999). These negative effects may be especially pronounced for backward rotating shifts (Sauter et al., 1990).

A number of factors may mediate the relationship between shift work and health, including the quality of the employee's social life, family relationships, the employee's adjustment to shift work, and the employee's initial physical fitness. Despite these seemingly bleak data on part-time employee's physical well being, it remains difficult to ascertain the direction of causality of the relationship between part-time work and illness, as some people may choose part-time employment because of the presence of a pre-existing health condition (Mykletun & Mykletun, 1999). In such cases, the ability to work part-time would in itself be a critical consideration for subsequent well being.

Occupational Safety
There is very little research addressing the occupational safety of part-time employees, and no studies providing a direct comparison of full and part-time employees' occupational safety (e.g. Sherer & Coakley, 1999). However, one potential threat to part-time worker health and safety is that part-time workers are less likely to have received occupational health and safety training

(Barker, 1995; Sherer & Coakley, 1999), and are therefore less familiar with the safety and operating procedures in their work, as compared to their counterparts in more traditional employment relationships. As such, their lesser understanding of safety procedures may not only pose a threat to the safety of themselves, but also to their coworkers (Sverke, Gallagher & Hellgren, 1999).

Other characteristics of part-time work may exacerbate occupational safety problems. First, part-time workers who do shift work late at night and in small numbers may be particularly vulnerable to violent assaults (Castillo, 1998). Second, the reduced work hours of part-time employees may hamper their socialization, and hence, communication with coworkers about work-related topics, including issues of health and safety (cf. Goodman & Garber, 1988). Finally, injuries caused from reduced attention associated with boredom may be especially problematic for part-time adolescent workers (Frone, 1998).

Temporary Employment

There is considerable debate surrounding the issue of whether the number of people involved in temporary employment has increased in recent years. Irrespective of the nature of this debate, we do not believe that temporary employment will diminish in the near future given the flexibility offered to both employers (with practices such as just-in-time production) and employees alike. Accordingly, an understanding of the psychosocial work environment encountered by temporary workers is necessary.

Psychological Well Being

Initial attempts to understand the nature of temporary employment have treated temporary employment as a homogeneous experience (see Ellingson, Gruys & Sackette, 1998). Subsequent research, however, has challenged this view. Like part-time employment, a major factor in the way in which temporary employment is experienced is whether it is assumed on a voluntary or involuntary basis (Ellingson et al., 1998). Research suggests that voluntary temporary employees rated their opportunities for learning and personal development, and the quality of their physical work more highly than did either involuntary temporary workers or permanent workers (Kraus, Brandenwein & Fox, 1995). Moreover, although voluntary temporary employees were less satisfied with the extrinsic rewards of their job, they were also lower in their desire for extrinsic rewards than either of the other two groups, and had higher levels of intrinsic reward. Also like part-time work, temporary work offers short-term, flexible employment, which may be particularly attractive to certain groups of people such as mothers and older workers who, for lifestyle reasons, do not choose to hold permanent or consistent employment (Feldman, Doepinghaus & Turnley, 1995).

However, not all people who accept temporary employment do so to accommodate lifestyle needs or develop new skills. People also enter temporary employment if permanent employment is unavailable to them. U.S. data suggest that 63% of temporary workers indicated that they would prefer more traditional employment, and 40% were actively seeking full-time employment (Cohany, 1996). That temporary employment may be considered for some a less desirable alternative is also evidenced by the demographics of temporary workers who are younger than their counterparts in more permanent forms of employment, less educated, and more likely to be members of minority groups. Temporary workers also typically garner lower wages, receive fewer benefits, and lack job security relative to permanent workers, and have a more difficult time qualifying for unemployment benefits or workers' compensation (Chen, Popovich & Kogan, 1999).

When individuals have little choice but to accept temporary employment, they may enjoy little control over either the type of work they are asked to perform or the conditions of their work environment. Temporary workers may feel compelled to tolerate unsatisfactory job experiences including abusive work situations to maintain their chances of being hired again in the future (Rogers, 1995). Importantly, labor legislation designed to protect the interests of workers often does not extend to temporary employment, and temporary employees may find it difficult to gain a voice in order to express health and safety concerns to the organization (Aronsson, 1999).

However, there are other aspects of temporary employment that are relevant to the psychological experience of work. First, irrespective of choice to enter temporary employment, temporary employees are often paid lower wages, and routinely receive fewer benefits, than employees who enjoy traditional work arrangements (e.g. Nollen, 1996). This might have considerable implications for pay and benefits, and perceptions of justice (especially distributive justice), both of which are core aspects of the psychosocial work environment. Second, temporary workers may be marginalized (Feldman et al., 1994) and alienated from traditional workers (Rogers, 1995). Chattopadhyay and George (2001), for example, showed the internal workers who find themselves in groups dominated by temporary employees experience lower levels of work-based self-esteem, trust, attraction and altruism, but the same is not true for temporary employees who find themselves in groups dominated by traditional internal employees. This may well make it more difficult for temporary employees to derive the benefits of positive interpersonal and social relationships at work.

Physical Well Being

There have been no research studies of which we are aware addressing the physical well being of temporary employees. One experience common to temporary employees, however, will be the bouts of unemployment experienced between temporary work assignments. We suggest that an understanding of whether employees assume this work arrangement voluntarily or not will predict their response to being without work. When individuals choose temporary employment, periods with no work between jobs will more likely be seen as respite. In contrast, individuals engaged in temporary employment because of a lack of alternatives, may be more likely to experience the time between jobs as unemployment, and under such conditions, we would predict that physical well being would be threatened.

Occupational Safety

Because temporary workers are likely to change their work environments more frequently than people in most other kinds of work relationships, they may be more likely to lack familiarity with the job, and be unaware of potential work hazards. This is important because research on full-time employees has shown that familiarity with the job and with coworkers is an important predictor of safety (Goodman & Garber, 1988), and as such, it is reasonable to suggest that temporary employees may be prone to more workplace injuries. Efforts to reduce such injuries must include educating new or inexperienced workers about the hazards associated with the job, and training them to negotiate these environments (Cooke & Blumenstock, 1979). Unfortunately, however, just as with part-time workers, temporary employees may be less likely to receive adequate safety training as compared to permanent employees (Aronsson, 1999), and research suggests that temporary workers have more exposure to poor working conditions (Benavides, Benach, Diez-Roux & Roman, 2000).

In addition, the ease with which temporary employees can be replaced (Barker, 1995; Beard & Edwards, 1995), and employee concerns about missing the possibility of obtaining employment in the future, may encourage employees to behave in more dangerous ways. Employees may be motivated to increase their productivity by working quickly, less carefully, and by taking less time to attend to personal protection (Aronsson, 1999; Collinson, 1999), and may fear that registering safety complaints could harm their chances of future employment with the organization (Aronsson, 1999). Thus, while there is no direct research evidence available, we suggest that the extent to which temporary employment is engaged in by choice or not will strongly moderate any effects on well being.

Self-employed Workers

Psychological and Physical Well Being
One defining characteristic of self-employment is the amount of discretion inherent in the work. Self-employed individuals can exert relatively more control over the type of work activities that are performed, when the work is performed, and the pace at which the work is done, all of which are factors associated with mental health (Ettner & Grzywacz, 2001). Steptoe, Evans and Fieldman's (1997) experimental study is instructive in providing some indication of the subjective meaning of self-employment. They assigned 132 individuals aged between 30 and 65 either to a self-paced or an externally-paced experimental condition. Both systolic blood pressure and electrodermal activity were higher in the externally than the self-paced group, despite the fact that the pace was identical in the two groups. While no differences were yielded with respect to diastolic blood pressure, or heart rate, these findings do indicate that if anything, self-employment may have some beneficial consequences, presumably because of increases in work-based and personal control associated with self-employment.

A second defining characteristic of self-employment, however, is the high level of demands (Bleach, 1997) and increased numbers of hours of work per week encountered by self-employed individuals (Barling, 1999; Personick & Windau, 1995). Other concerns salient to self-employed workers are economic uncertainty, market fluctuations, and the threat of loss of assets, all of which can impose considerable stress and encourage behaviors detrimental to health (Lewin-Epstein & Yuchtman-Yaar, 1991). Consequently, we predict that while the increased amount of work engaged in by self-employed individuals might be associated with negative outcomes (Sparks et al., 1997), the enhanced control offered by self-employment might well buffer any negative effects. Aside from the frequent loss of benefits associated with a move from regular, full-time employment to self-employment, one other noticeable demographic aspect that characterizes self-employment is the marked increase in work hours (Gardner, 1995). This is important because of the link between longer work hours and physical and psychological well being (Sparks et al., 1997).

Occupational Safety
While there is little research on the psychological and physical well being associated with self-employment, Personick and Windau (1995) reviewed the incidence of injuries among self-employed workers, and compared these rates to that of wage and salary workers. Data indicate that self-employed workers represent one in every five fatal injuries at work. Several factors might account

for this. While self-employed workers may confront the same health and safety challenges as other workers in similar occupations, many self-employed workers lack the protection of government oversight and safety regulations. In addition, self-employed individuals may not have the resources to afford safety training and protective equipment. Further, the longer working hours characteristic of self-employment and the concomitant physical fatigue may increase the likelihood of injuries at work, while simultaneously increasing the duration with which the employee is exposed to these hazards.

Home-based Employment

Traditionally, employment has taken place in a location away from the home. One of the substantive changes in employment arrangements has been the growth in the U.S. in the number of home-based workers since the early 1980s, which reversed the pattern of the previous two decades in which the number of home-based workers had declined (Edwards & Field-Hendrey, 1996). Given advances in computing and communications technology, Edwards and Field-Hendrey (1996) predict that the growth in home-based workers is likely to continue, leaving it important to understand the subjective work experience of these workers.

Psychological Well Being

For some, home-based work offers the benefits of enhanced flexibility over the number and hours of work, the time of day in which to work, autonomy over the tasks of work, and freedom from supervision. For others, home-based work may have been an undesirable but more easily obtainable alternative for employment. This points to a major variation between different types of home-based employment. Both highly paid, well-qualified consultants and poorly paid, relatively powerless employees may choose to work from home, often for different reasons and with different outcomes.

The nature of working from home is such that it may have meaningful effects on the perceived psychosocial work environment. The normal protections that are available to employees within a traditional workplace (such as the accessibility of social support, geographic closeness to a supervisor, physical safety) are not as readily accessible when working from home (Barling, Rogers & Kelloway, 2001). In addition, Standen, Daniels and Lamond (1999) point both to potentially positive aspects associated with home-based work (specifically, telework) such as temporal flexibility, and family support, as well as negative aspects, for example the loss of valued social contacts, which is critical for well being (Jahoda, 1982). This points to the diverse way in which home-based work is experienced, and the need for further research to understand this hetero-geneous phenomenon.

There are differential predictions about the subjective experience of home-based work. On the one hand, home-based work is seen as emancipatory, in as much as it can provide employees with greater opportunities for autonomy and flexibility. At the same time, there is equal concern about the possibility for exploitation associated with home-based work, because home-based work could increase job insecurity and result in a lower standard of living (see Jurik, 1998). We add to these concerns the possibility for greater work-family conflict.

Several qualitative studies have been reported that focused on the subjective experience of home-based employment. Home-based workers who see clients in their home experience frequent intrusions at home in terms of daily tele-phone-calls (Fitzgerald & Winter, 2001). In addition, data derived from qualitative studies suggest that working at home also makes maintaining a separation between home and work more difficult (Fitzgerald & Winter, 2001; Steward, 2000). In contrast, data from quantitative research do not replicate this phenomenon: Using a quasi-experimental design and qualitative analyses, neither Hill, Miller, Weiner and Colihan's (1998) qualitative nor quantitative analyses showed any effects of telework on work/life balance. Both sets of analyses in the Hill et al. (1998) study, however, suggested that teleworkers experience greater flexibility than traditional office workers, and this is consis-tent with Frone and Yardley's (1996) finding that the perceived importance of work-at-home policies are associated with the extent to which family affects work, but not the extent to which work interferes with family. Drawing broad conclusions from these studies, therefore, would be premature, difficult and hazardous.

Nonetheless, we believe that research will continue to focus on home-based workers, and particularly on certain groups of home-based workers. One partic-ular group of home-based workers that have received attention in recent years is that of 'teleworkers' or 'telecommuters.' Teleworkers are typically more highly skilled employees, frequently professionals, who work from home (Schneider de Villegas, 1990). While empirical findings suggest that telecom-muting may have a positive impact on worker productivity, job performance, work morale, and flexibility (Hill et al., 1998), the impact of telecommuting on job satisfaction yields more mixed findings. One study that directly compared the job satisfaction of telecommuters to that of a control group found no differences between these groups on job satisfaction (Kraut, 1987). In addition, despite the fact that many people enter into various kinds of home-based work to balance work and family life, research suggests that these roles often become more blurred than balanced (Jones, 1997).

Physical Well Being and Occupational Safety
There does not appear to be any data pertaining to the physical health and occupational safety of homeworkers. However, the dominant feature of homework is that it takes place outside the formal workplace. This is important, because when work takes place in a private setting, such as an individual's residence, there is less monitoring for health and safety standards, and few, if any health and safety inspections by external regulators (see Barling et al., 2001). Indeed, it is not even certain that all workplace standards and requirements apply to home offices and workplaces. As a result, we would predict that there is an increased risk for health problems and injuries, especially for those homeworkers who have not chosen this option voluntarily.

"Moonlighting"

Psychological Well Being
The data suggest that there may be something of a demographic profile associated with the decision to moonlight. First, financial obligations represent a major factor cited in the reason for seeking and holding a second job, a situation that has not abated recently (Stinson, 1990; Amirault, 1997). It does not follow from this, however, that the majority of people holding second jobs, earn relatively less in their primary jobs. Instead, recent data show that moonlighters are more likely to be relatively well paid and better educated than individuals who hold one job only (Amirault, 1997). What this indicates is that it may be more likely that individuals choose to engage in moonlighting, rather than feel compelled to do so, and differential consequences follow from each of these two possibilities. Negative consequences would be associated with moonlighting in those situations where individuals felt compelled to accept this arrangement, while more positive outcomes would ensue if individuals engaged in moonlighting more freely.

Studies conducted in both Canada and the United States have contrasted the "job stress", or psychosocial work factors, experienced by moonlighters and single job holders. Sinclair, Martin and Michel's (1999) study revealed no differences between moonlighters and those holding down a single, full-time job with respect to job satisfaction, a valuable proxy for the psychosocial work environment. Sinclair et al. (1999) also assessed pay equity (which reflected both pay satisfaction and fairness), and again revealed no between group differences. Their study provides initial support for the notion that moonlighters do not experience the psychosocial work environment differently from employees who enjoy traditional employment arrangements.

Research conducted in Canada replicates and extends these findings. Jamal and Baba (1992) showed that despite their greater time investment in work, moonlighters were more active participants in social and voluntary organizations. In a subsequent study, Jamal, Baba and Rivière (1998) showed that moonlighters experienced significantly less burnout and job stress than non-moonlighters. They ascribe an energic/opportunity hypothesis to account for these findings, suggesting that moonlighters are "a special breed" (p. 196) who experience more energy and higher social expectations. We suggest that an alternative explanation is equally plausible. Specifically, in the extent to which moonlighters choose employment arrangement, they exert volition which would protect their well being, and this hypothesis awaits explicit empirical scrutiny.

Future research on moonlighters' job experiences should focus on an additional issue. The studies reported here focus on a single work environment (presumably their primary job) for moonlighters, and contrast moonlighters and non-moonlighters. This strategy does not make it possible to compare the psychosocial work environment of the two different jobs held by the same person. It is possible, however, that moonlighters do not experience their different jobs the same, and several research questions are raised. For example, one possibility that emerges is whether there are additive effects with respect to the psychosocial environment if both jobs are experienced very positively, or very negatively. Perhaps even more interestingly, there could be differential consequences for well being if perceptions of the psychosocial work environment are markedly different across the two jobs.

Physical Well Being and Occupational Safety
We know of only a few studies that have examined the physical health of moonlighters, and are aware of no studies examining the physical safety of this population. Based on the findings that suggest that moonlighters may enjoy superior energy levels than average, it is not likely that the longer hours worked by moonlighters will render them more fatigued or stressed than the average single job holder. As such it may not be reasonable to expect differences in illness or injury between moonlighters and workers in traditional employment relationships. Research that has directly compared the health of moonlighters with that of single job holders suggests that there are no detrimental health or safety consequences for people who moonlight (Jamal et al., 1998), presumably because of their greater energy.

Job Sharing

The last two decades saw management being exhorted and even expected to do whatever is feasible to help employees balance work and family responsibilities (Barling, 1990). Job sharing was introduced and promoted within this environment as one way by which two employees could share the responsibilities associated with one full-time job. Job sharing is recognized by many administrators as one of the more complex forms of flexible work options (Solomon, 1994). As such, while organizations that have introduced job sharing arrangements may be viewed as model employers, the move in this direction is more often demand-driven (Stanworth, 1999).

Psychological Well Being

There remains very little empirical data on job-sharing. What is known is that the perceived importance of job sharing is significantly associated with the degree to which family responsibilities conflict with work demands (but not the degree to which work demands conflict with family responsibilities (Frone & Yardley, 1996). Seib and Muller's (1999) analysis of 44 employed mothers suggests that job-sharing was more effective than either part-time employment, or flextime in balancing work and family demands. These results should perhaps be expected, because job-sharing would result in a dramatic reduction in hours of work. Perhaps more importantly, though, job-sharing would almost always be engaged in on a voluntary basis, which itself would be expected to exert a positive effect on the psychosocial workplace environment and well being.

Physical Well Being and Occupational Safety

We are not aware of research examining the impact of job sharing on physical health and safety. To the extent that the work environment of people participating in a job sharing program is the same as people in traditional work arrangements, no unique threats to health and safety should be expected. However, it is possible that when job sharing entails different work hours from one day to the next, any changes in sleep patterns from day to day, as well as social and domestic disruptions may increase the likelihood of chronic health problems (Smith, Robie, Folkard, Barton, McDonald, Smith, Spelten, Tollerdell & Costa, 1999). An additional factor for consideration is that job sharing could result in less familiarity between workers, which could heighten safety risks (Goodman & Garber, 1988).

Outsourced Employment

As organizations continue to emphasize cost containment, which includes an attempt to retain as few permanent employees as possible, and to reduce costs such as employee benefits, outsourcing will continue to remain a perceived competitive advantage to employers. Despite the prevalence of this alternative form of employment, there remains little behavioral research on the psychosocial work environment experienced by people employed on an outsourcing basis. This is important, because with the potential loss of pay and benefits, and power and control that would accompany outsourcing, it is possible to suggest that there would be negative effects for the psychosocial work environment.

Psychological and Physical Well Being

Another area in which research on alternative work arrangements and well being is relatively sparse is in the effects of outsourcing on physical and mental well being. This issue was examined in one study that directly compared the psychosocial and physiological outcomes of outsourced and direct-hire bus drivers (Netterstrom & Hansen, 2000). Despite equivalent baseline levels of physical and mental health, after a year of work, the outsourced workers could be distinguished from the direct-hire workers on the basis of seeing the job as having low levels of predictability and meaningfulness, low colleague support and low job satisfaction as compared to the direct-hire workers. Physiological measures indicated that as compared to direct-hire workers, outsourced workers showed higher levels of biological responses to increased stress including increased cortisol levels in urine, blood pressure, and HDL/cholesterol ratios.

Another finding of some significance is that within eight months of the outsourcing, seven of the 20 bus drivers in Netterstrom and Hansen's (2000) outsourced group were no longer with the new organization due to dissatisfaction with their working conditions. While it is not possible to make large inferences based on such small numbers, this finding should at least alert researchers to the possibility of a potentially negative workplace environment associated with the practice of outsourcing.

Occupational Safety

For several reasons, one specific group of outsourced workers, subcontracted workers, tend to receive inadequate on-site safety training (Rebitzer, 1995). First, in the absence of a clearly identifiable sole employer, the issue of who bears responsibility for safety training is often unclear. Second, although subcontracted workers have typically had some general occupational health and safety training, they may not receive *site-specific* health and safety training (O'Brien,

1999). This is important, because specific safety training raises employees' safety awareness, teaches skills for coping with work-related hazards, and establishes opportunities for an open flow of communication about safety issues (Rebitzer, 1995; Roughton, 1995). Not surprisingly, therefore, while research suggests that subcontractors have higher accident rates than do direct hires, this difference may be especially pronounced for employees with less than one year of experience (Rebitzer, 1995), perhaps highlighting the long-term benefits of on-the-job learning when more formal opportunities such as training are not available.

Seasonal and Migrant Employment

Our focus on new forms of employment arrangements would be incomplete without some examination of the psychosocial work environment of individuals employed on a seasonal basis. This task is complicated, however, because of the paucity of behavioral research on seasonal employment. Ball (1988) addressed the stereotype that seasonal workers represent the "poorest cousins" of the entire workforce, given the precarious nature of their employment, and the relatively poor benefits they receive. We add to this the lack of control associated with seasonal and migrant work. While there is some support for this notion, Ball (1988) also notes that this only represents part of the picture, with many individuals choosing voluntarily to be employed on a seasonal basis. Seasonal or migrant employment, therefore, would by no means be a homogenous experience. As is the case with many other forms of employment, the individual employee's volition in choosing seasonal employment may have important implications for their subsequent well being.

Psychological Well Being

Much of the literature on seasonal and migrant workers focuses on shifting trends in seasonal and migrant work over time (e.g. Rydzewski, Deming & Rones, 1993), the deleterious behavioral choices on the part of many seasonal and migrant workers (Weatherby, McCoy, Metsch, Beltzer, McCoy & de la Rosa, 1996), and the cultural disadvantages this group may confront (Sharma, 2001). In contrast, there is very little research on their psychological well being. Traditionally, seasonal and/or migrant work have been considered to be among the least desirable forms of employment, marked by poorer working conditions, lower-status jobs, and subsequent and inevitable unemployment. Further, migrant workers in particular may be perceived negatively by locals who see them as 'taking' jobs from local people (Weatherby et al., 1996). Other types of seasonal employment however, such as those in the tourism industry were considered higher-status (Bell, 1988). As with most other forms of alternative employment, workers who enter their employment voluntarily may have relatively more positive psychosocial outcomes than people who enter employment involuntarily.

Physical Well Being and Occupational Safety
The physical health and safety of seasonal and migrant workers has been given some empirical attention. A fairly substantial amount of literature suggests that, as compared to other groups of workers, the behavioral choices and lifestyles of migrant workers are more likely to include a greater propensity for narcotics use (Weatherby et al., 1996), alcohol use (Morales, 1986), and a lack of HIV/AIDS awareness and education among this group (Beltzer, 1995), raising the likelihood of physical and safety problems.

ALTERNATIVE WORK ARRANGEMENTS AND EMPLOYEE WELL BEING: SOME CONCLUDING THOUGHTS

We conclude this chapter by highlighting three concerns that have emerged consistently in our examination of the effects of alternative work arrangements on employee well being. First, in any future research, more complexity is required in the conceptualization and operationalization of alternative work arrangements. As one example, research on the emergence of contingent and alternative work arrangements has suffered from simplistic categorizations that have reinforced outdated stereotypes. The perspective that contingent workers have limited control over how their work is performed, and operate under purely "transactional" contracts (Beard & Edwards, 1995) may in fact be the antitheses of the work experience for many independent contractors who have highly sought-after technical skills. In addition, it is worth pointing to the fact that research on moonlighting has focused more on the people involved in this phenomenon, rather than the work experiences in both jobs. Conceptual understandings will no longer be advanced by simply trying to fit different forms of alternative working arrangements into arbitrary and inherently overlapping categories (e.g. full-time, telecommuter, temporary, self-employed).

Second, from a methodological perspective, it is noteworthy that research on alternative work arrangements and employee well being has relied almost exclusively on correlational data and non-experimental designs. Clearly, any advances in refinement in the conceptualization of alternative work arrangements must now be accompanied by more sophisticated research designs in order to move toward causal inferences.

Last, but by no means least, the research reviewed to date allows two important conclusions. First, the nature of the alternative work arrangement may be substantially less important for subsequent well being than the quality of the employment experience. Second, the nature of the alternative work arrangement is substantially less important for employee well being than the issue of whether employees enter the specific work arrangement by choice or not. These two conclusions have considerable conceptual and managerial implications. Conceptually, an understanding on the nature and consequences of alternative work arrangements may be achieved by diverting primary attention to the psychosocial work experiences; and this represents a viable challenge for future research. From a managerial perspective, organizations might be better served by ensuring that employees benefit from positive work experiences, irrespective of the type of work arrangements in which they find themselves.

REFERENCES

Alder, P. A., & Alder, P. (2001). Off-time labor in resorts: The social construction of commercial time. *The American Behavioral Scientist, 44*, 1096–1114.

Amirault, T. (1997). Characteristics of multiple jobholders, 1995. *Monthly Labor Review, 120*, 9–15.

Aronsson, G. (1999). Contingent workers and health and safety. *Work, Employment and Society, 13*, 439–458.

Aronsson, G., Bejerot, E., & Harenstam, A. (1999). Healthy work: Ideal and reality among public and private employed academics in Sweden. *Public Personnel Management, 28*, 197–215.

Ball, R. M. (1988). Seasonality: A problem for workers in the tourism labour market? *The Services Industry Journal, 8*, 501–513.

Barker, K. (1995). Contingent work: Research issues and the lens of moral exclusion. In: L. E. Tetrick & J. Barling (Eds), *Changing Employment Relations: Behavioral and Social Perspectives* (pp. 31–60). Washington, D.C.: American Psychological Association.

Barling, J. (1990). *Employment, stress and family functioning*. NY: Wiley.

Barling, J. (1999). Changing employment relations: Empirical data, social perspectives and policy options. In: D. B. Knight & A. E. Joseph (Eds), *Restructuring Societies: Insights From the Social Sciences* (pp. 59–82). Ottawa: Carlton University Press.

Barling, J., & Gallagher, D. G. (1996). Part-time employment. In: C. L. Cooper & I.T. Robertson (Eds), *International Review of Industrial and Organizational Psychology* (Vol. 11). NY: Wiley.

Barling, J., Fullagar, C., & Marchl-Dingle, J. (1987). Employment commitment as a moderator of the maternal employment status/child behavior relationship. *Journal of Occupational Behavior, 9*, 113–122.

Barling, J., & Kelloway, E. K. (1998). *Young workers: Varieties of experiences*. Washington, D.C.: American Psychological Association.

Barling, J., Kelloway, E. K., & Iverson, R. D.(in press). High quality work, employee morale and occupational injuries. *Journal of Applied Psychology*.

Barling, J., Rogers, A. G., & Kelloway, E. K. (2001). Behind closed doors: In-home workers' experience of sexual harassment and workplace violence. *Journal of Occupational Health Psychology, 6*, 255–269.

Barling, J., Rogers, K. A., & Kelloway, E. K. (1995). Some effects of teenagers' part-time employment: the quantity and quality of work make the difference. *Journal of Organizational Behavior, 16*, 143–154.

Beard, K. M., & Edwards, J. R. (1995). Employees at risk: Contingent work and the experience of contingent workers. In: C. L. Cooper & D. M. Rousseau (Eds), *Trends in Organizational Behavior* (Vol. 2). Chichester: Wiley.

Bleach, E. A. (1997). Self-employment, stress and strain: A comparison of small business founders and franchisees. *Dissertation Abstracts International: Section B: The Sciences and Engineering, 57*(11-B), 7620.

Bregger, J. E. (1996). Measuring self-employment in the United States. *Monthly Labor Review, 119*, 3–9.

Brewster, C., Mayne, L., & Tregaskis, O. (1997). Flexible working in Europe: A review of the evidence. *Management International Review, 37*, 85–103.

Cappelli, P. (1999). *The new deal at work*. Boston, Massachusetts: Harvard Business School Press.

Carré, F., Ferber, M. A., Golden, L., & Herzenberg, S. L. (Eds) (2000). *Non-standard work*. Champaign, Illinois: Industrial Relations Research Association.

Castillo, D. N. (1998). Occupational safety and health in young people. In: J. Barling & E. K. Kelloway (Eds), *Young workers: Varieties of experience* (pp. 159–200). Washington, D.C.: American Psychological Association.

Castillo, D. N., Davis, L., & Wegman, D. H. (1999). Young workers. *Occupational Medicine: State of the Art Reviews, 14*, 519–536.

Chen, P. Y., Popovich, P. M., & Kogan, M. (1999). Let's talk: Patterns and correlates of social support among temporary employees. *Journal of Occupational Health Psychology, 4*, 55–62.

Chattopadhyay, P., & George, E. (2001). Examining the effects of work externalization through the lens of social identity theory. *Journal of Applied Psychology, 86*, 781–788.

Cohany, S. R. (1996). Workers in alternative employment arrangements. *Monthly Labor Review, 119*, 31–45.

Collinson, D. L. (1999). 'Surviving the rigs': Safety and surveillance on North Sea oil installations. *Organization Studies, 20*, 579–600.

Colquitt, J. A., Conlon, D. E., Wesson, M. J., Porter, C. O. L. H., & Ng, K. Y. (2001). Justice at the millennium: A meta-analytic review of 25 years of organizational justice research. *Journal of Applied Psychology, 86*, 425–445.

Cooke, W. N., & Blumenstock, M. W. (1979). The determinants of occupational injury severity: The case of academic sawmills. *Journal of Safety Research, 11(3)*, 115–120.

Cooper, C. L., & Burke, R. J. (Eds) (2002). *The new world of work: Challenges and opportunities*. Oxford: Blackwell Publishers.

Drucker, P. (2002). They're not employees, they're people. *Harvard Business Review*, (February), 70–77.

Dubinsky, A. J., & Skinner, S. J. (1984). Job status and employee responses: Effects of demographic characteristics. *Psychological Reports, 55*, 323–328.

Duxbury & Higgins (2002). In: C. Cooper & R. Burke (Eds), *The New World of Work: Challenges and Opportunities* (pp. 157–199). Oxford: Blackwell Publishers.

Edwards, L. N., & Field-Hendrey, E. (1996). Home-based workers: Data from the 1990 Census of Population. *Monthly Labor Review, 119*(11), 26–34.

Ellingson, J. E., Gruys, M. L., & Sackett, P. R. (1998). Factors related to the satisfaction and performance of temporary employees. *Journal of Applied Psychology, 83*, 913–921.

Elovainio, M., Kivimäki, M., & Vahtera, J. (2002). Organizational justice: Evidence of a new psychosocial predictor of health. *American Journal of Public Health, 92*, 105–108.

Ettner, S. L., & Grzywacz, J. G. (2001). Workers' perceptions of how jobs affect health: A social ecological perspective. *Journal of Occupational Health Psychology, 6*, 101–113.

Feldman, D. C., Doerpinghaus, H. I., & Turnley, W. H. (1994). Managing temporary workers: A permanent HRM challenge. *Organizational Dynamics, 23*, 49–63.

Feldman, D. C., Doerpinghaus, H. I., & Turnley, W. H. (1995). Employee reactions to temporary jobs. *Journal of Managerial Issues, 7*, 127–141.

Fenwick, R., & Tausig, M. (2001). Scheduling stress: Family and health outcomes of shift work and schedule control. *The American Behavioral Scientist, 44*, 1179–1198.

Fitzgerald, M. A. & Winter, M. (2001). The intrusiveness of home-based work on family. *Journal of Family and Economic Issues, 22*, 75–92.

Frone, M. R. (1998). Predictors of work injuries among employed adolescents. *Journal of Applied Psychology, 83*, 565–576.

Frone, M. R. (1999). Developmental consequences of youth employment. In: J. Barling & E. K. Kelloway (Eds), *Young Workers: Varieties of Experiences* (pp. 89–128). Washington, D.C.: American Psychological Association.

Frone, M. R., & Yardley, J. K. (1996). Workplace family-supportive programmes: Predictors of employed parents' importance ratings. *Journal of Occupational and Organizational Psychology, 69*, 351–366.

Furnham, A., & Hughes, K. (1999). Individual difference correlates of nightwork and shift-work. *Personality and Individual Differences, 2*, 941–959.

Gallagher, D. G. (2002). Contingent work contracts: Practice and theory. In: C. Cooper & R. Burke (Eds), *The New World of Work: Challenges and Opportunities* (pp. 115–136). Oxford: Blackwell Publishers.

Gallagher, D. G., & McLean Parks, J. (2001). I pledge thee my troth . . . contingently: Commitment and the contingent work relationship. *Human Resource Management Review, 11*, 181–208.

Gardner, A. (1995). *The self-employed.* Toronto: Prentice Hall.

Ganster, D. C., Foc, M., & Dwyer, D. (2001). Explaining employee health care costs: A prospective examination of stressful job demands, personal control and physiological reactivity. *Journal of Applied Psychology, 86*, 954–964.

Goodman, P. S., & Garber, S. (1988). Absenteeism and accidents in a dangerous environment: Empirical analysis of underground coal mines. *Journal of Applied Psychology, 73*, 81–86.

Greer, C. R., Youngblood, S. A., & Gray, D. A. (1999). Human resource management outsourcing: The make or buy decision. *Academy of Management Executive, 13*(3), 85–96.

Hill, E. J., Miller, B. C., Weiner, S. P., & Colihan, J. (1998). Influences of the virtual office on aspects of work and work/life balance. *Personnel Psychology, 51*, 667–683.

Hochschild, A. R. (1997). *The time bind: When work becomes home and home becomes work.* New York: Metropolitan Press.

Hock, E., & DeMeis, D. (1990). Depression in mothers of infants: The role of maternal employment. *Developmental Psychology, 26*, 285–291.

Holtom, B. C., Lee, T. W., & Tidd, S. T. (in press). The relationship between work status congruence and work related attitudes and behaviors. *Journal of Applied Psychology.*

Roughton, J. E. (1995). Contractor safety. *Professional Safety,* (January), 31–34.

Hurrell, J. J. (2002). Psychosocial factors and musculoskeletal disorders. In: P. W. Perrewee & D. Ganster (Eds), *Advances in Occupational Stress and Well Being* (Vol. 1). Greenwich, CT: JAI Press.

Jackson, S. E., & Schuler, R. S. (1985). A meta-analysis and conceptual critique of research on role ambiguity and role conflict in work settings. *Organizational Behavior and Human Decision Processes, 36*, 16–78.

Jahoda, M. (1982). *Employment and unemployment: A social psychological analysis*. Cambridge: Cambridge University Press.

Jamal, M. (1999). Job stress and employee well being: A cross-cultural empirical study. *Stress Medicine, 16*, 153–158.

Jamal, M., & Baba, V. V. (1992). How much do we really know about moonlighters? *Public Personnel Management, 21*, 65–73.

Jamal, M., & Baba, V. V. (1997). Shift work, burnout and well being: A study of Canadian nurses. *International Journal of Stress Management, 4*, 197–204.

Jamal, M., Baba, V. V., & Rivière, R. (1998). Job stress and well being of moonlighters: The perspective of deprivation of aspiration revisited. *Stress Medicine, 14*, 195–202.

Jurik, N. C. (1998). Getting away and getting by. *Work and Occupations, 25*, 7–35.

Kahn, R. L., Wolfe, D. M., Quinn, R. P., Snoek, J. D., & Rosenthal, R. A. (1964). *Organizational stress: Studies in role conflict and ambiguity*. NY: Wiley.

Kalleberg, A. L. (2000). Nonstandard employment relations: Part-time, temporary and contract work. *Annual Review of Sociology, 26*, 341–365.

Karasek, R. A., & Theorell, T. (1990). *Healthy work: Stress, productivity and the reconstruction of working life*. NY: Basic Books.

Keil, J. M., Armstrong-Stassen, M., Cameron, S. J., & Horsburgh, M. E. (2000). Part-time nurses: The effect of work status congruency on job attitudes. *Applied Psychology: An International Review, 49*, 227–236.

Krausz, M., Brandwein, T., & Fox, S. (1995). Work attitudes and emotional responses of permanent, voluntary and involuntary temporary-help employees: An exploratory study. *Applied Psychology: An International Review, 44*, 217–232.

Krausz, M., Sagie, A., & Biderman, Y. (2000). Actual and preferred work schedules and scheduling control as determinants of job-related attitudes. *Journal of Vocational Behavior, 56*, 1–11.

Kraut, R. E. (1987). Predicting the use of technology: The case of telework. In: R. E. Kraut (Ed.), *Technology and the Transformation of White-collar Work* (pp. 113–133). NJ: Lawrence Erlbaum.

Lee, T. W., & Johnson, D. R. (1991). The effects of work schedule and employment status on organizational commitment and job satisfaction of full vs. part-time employees. *Journal of Vocational Behavior, 38*, 204–224.

Lewin-Epstein, N., & Yuchtman-Yaar, E. (1991). Health risks of self-employment. *Work and Occupations, 18*, 291–312.

Loughlin, C. A., & Barling, J. (1998). Teenagers' part-time employment and their work-related attitudes and aspirations. *Journal of Organizational Behavior, 19*, 197–207.

Martens, M. F. J., Nijhuis, F. J. N., Van Boxtel, M. P. J., & Knottnerus, J. A. (1999). Flexible work schedules and mental and physical health: A study of a working population with non-traditional working hours. *Journal of Organizational Behavior, 20*, 35–46.

Morales, R. (1986). Drinking patterns among seasonal migrant workers. *Dissertation Abstracts International, 46*(11-A).

Morrow, P. C., McElroy, J. C., & Elliott, S. M. (1994). The effect of preference for work status, schedule and shift on work-related attitudes. *Journal of Vocational Behavior, 45*, 202–222.

Mykletun, R. J., & Mykletun, A. (1999). Comprehensive schoolteachers at risk of early exit from work. *Experimental Aging Research, 25*, 359–365.

Nardone, T. (1995). Part-time employment: Reasons, demographics and trends. *Journal of Labor Research, 16*, 275–292.

Netterstrom, B., & Hansen, A. M. (2000). Outsourcing and stress: Physiological effects on bus drivers. *Stress Medicine, 16*, 149–160.

Nollen, S. D.(1996). Negative aspects of temporary employment. *Journal of Labor Research, 17,* 567–583.

O'Brien, M. E. (1999). Contractor safety: A survey of the semiconductor industry. *Professional Safety,* (February), 32–36.

Olds, J., Schwartz, R. S., Eisen, S. V., & Betcher, R. W. (1993). Part-time employment and marital well being: A hypothesis and pilot study. *Family Therapy, 20,* 1–16.

Personick, M. E., & Windau, J. A. (1995). Self-employed individuals fatally injured at work. *Monthly Labor Review, 118*(8), 24–34.

Pfeffer, J. (1998). *The human equation: Building profits by putting people first.* MA: Harvard Business School Press.

Pfeffer, J. (1999). Six dangerous myths about pay. *Harvard Business Review, 76*(3), 108–119.

Pfeffer, J., & Baron, N. (1988). Taking the work back out: Recent trends in the structures of employment. In: B. M. Staw & L. L. Cummings (Eds), *Research in Organizational Behavior, 10,* 257–303.

Pratt, L., & Barling, J. (1988). Differentiating daily hassles, acute and chronic stressors: A framework and its implications. In: J. R. Hurrell, L. R. Murphy, S. L. Sauter & C. L. Cooper (Eds), *Occupational Stress: Issues and Developments in Research* (pp. 41–53). London: Taylor & Francis.

Rebitzer, J. B. (1995). Job safety and contract workers in the petrochemical industry. *Industrial Relations, 34,* 40–57.

Reilly, P. A. (1998). Balancing flexibility – Meeting the interests of employer and employee. *European Journal of Work and Organizational Psychology, 7,* 7–22.

Rogers, J. K. (1995). Just a temp: Experience and structure of alienation in temporary clerical employment. *Work and Occupations, 22,* 137–166.

Rotchford, N. L., & Roberts, R. H. (1982). Part-time workers as missing persons in organizational research. *Academy of Management Review, 7,* 228–234.

Rydzewski, L. G., Deming, W. G., & Rones, P. L. (1993). Seasonal employment falls over past three decades. *Monthly Labor Review, 118*(7), 3–14.

Sauter, S. L., Murphy, L. R., & Hurrell, J. (1990). Prevention of work-related psychological disorders: A national strategy proposed by the National Institute for Occupational Safety and Health (NIOSH). *American Psychologist, 45,* 1146–1158.

Schaubroeck, J., Jones, J. R., & Xie, J. L. (2001). Individual differences in utilizing control to cope with job demands: Effects on susceptibility to infectious disease. *Journal of Applied Psychology, 86,* 265–287.

Schneider De Villegas, G. (1990). Home work: A case for social protection. *International Labor Review, 129,* 423–439.

Seib, B., & Muller, J. (1999). The effect of different work schedules on the role strain of Australian working mothers: A pilot study. *Journal of Applied Human Behaviour, 1,* 9–15.

Sharma, N. (2001). On being not Canadian: The social organization of migrant workers in Canada. *Canadian Review of Sociology and Anthropology, 38,* 415–439.

Sherer, P. D., & Coakley, L. A. (1999). Questioning and developing your part-time employee practices. *Workforce,* (October), 4–7.

Sinclair, R. R., Martin, J. E., & Michel, R. P. (1999). Full-time and part-time subgroup differences in job attitudes and demographic characteristics. *Journal of Vocational Behavior, 55,* 337–357.

Smith, C. S., Robie, C., Folkard, S., Barton, J., Macdonald, I., Smith, L., Spelten, E., Totterdell, P., & Costa, G. (1999). A process model of shiftwork and health. *Journal of Occupational Health Psychology, 4,* 207–218

Solomon, C. M. (1994). Job sharing: One job, double headache? *Personnel Journal*, (September), 88–95.

Sparks, K., Cooper, C. L., Fried, Y., & Shirom, A. (1997). The effects of hours of work on health: A meta-analytic review. *Journal of Occupational and Organizational Psychology, 70*, 391–408.

Sparrow, P. (1998). The pursuit of multiple and parallel organizational flexibilities: Reconstituting jobs. *European Journal of Work and Organizational Psychology, 7*, 79–95.

Standen, P., Daniels, K., & Lamond, D. (1999). The home as a workplace: Work-family interaction and psychological well being in telework. *Journal of Occupational Health Psychology, 4*, 368–381.

Stanworth, C. (1999). A best case scenario? Non-manual part-time work and job sharing in U.K. local government in the 1990s. *Community, Work and Family, 2*, 295–310.

Steffy, B. D., & Jones, J. W. (1990). Differences between full-time and part-time employees in perceived role strain and work satisfaction. *Journal of Organizational Behavior, 11*, 321–329.

Steptoe, A., Evans, O., & Fieldman, G. (1997). Perceptions of control over work: Psychophysiological responses to self-paced and externally-paced tasks in an adult population sample. *International Journal of Psychophysiology, 25*, 211–220.

Steinberg, L., Fegley, S., & Dornbusch, S. M. (1993). Negative impact of part-time work on adolescent adjustment: Evidence from a longitudinal study. *Developmental Psychology, 29*, 171–180.

Steward, B. (2000). Changing times: The meaning, measurement and use of time in teleworking. *Time and Society, 91*, 57–74.

Stinson, J. F. (1990). Multiple job holding up sharply in the 1980s. *Monthly Labor Review, 113*(7), 3–10.

Sverke, M., Gallagher, D. G., & Hellgren, J. (1999). Alternative work arrangements: Job stress, well being, and work attitudes among employees with different employment contracts. In: K. Isaksson, C. Hogstedt, C. Eriksson & T. Theorell (Eds), *Human Effects of the New Labour Market* (pp. 145–168). NY: Kluwer Acdemic.

Tausig, M. (1999). Work and mental health. In: C. S. Anathensel & J. C. Phelan (Eds), *Handbook of the Sociology of Mental Health* (pp. 255–274). NY: KluwerAcademic/Plenum Publishers.

Terry, D. J., & Jimmieson, N. L. (1999). Work control and employee well being: A decade review. *International Review of Industrial and Organizational Psychology, 14*, 95–148.

Tetrick, L. E., & Barling, J. (Eds) (1995). *Changing employment relations*. Washington, D.C.: American Psychological Association.

Turner, N., Barling, J., & Zacharatos, A. (2002). Positive psychology at work. In: C. R Snyder & S. Lopez (Eds), *The Handbook of Positive Psychology* (p. 715–730). Oxford: Oxford University Press.

Vosko (2000).*Temporary work: The general rise of a precarious employment relationship*. Toronto: University of Toronto Press.

Warr, P. B. (1987). *Work, unemployment and mental health*. London: Oxford Press.

Weatherby, N. L., McCoy, H. V., Metsch, L. R., Bletzer, K. V., McCoy, C. B., & de la Rosa, M. R. (1999). Crack cocaine use in rural migrant populations: Living arrangements and social support. *Substance Use and Misuse, 34*, 685–706.

Zeytinoğlu, I. U. (Ed.) (1999). *Changing work relationships in industrialized economies*. Amsterdam: John Benjamins Publishing.

INTEGRATING MULTILEVEL ANALYSES AND OCCUPATIONAL STRESS THEORY

Paul D. Bliese, Steve M. Jex and
Ronald R. Halverson

ABSTRACT

In this chapter, we integrate occupational stress theory with emerging analytic and theoretical considerations related to multilevel modeling. We begin by differentiating among models at different levels, and identify the inferential errors that can inadvertently arise when applying occupational stress findings to organizations. Second, we discuss the basic framework for using multilevel modeling to study occupational stress processes over time. Finally, we apply the implications of the first two sections to a popular occupational stress model. In so doing, we show how multilevel theory and methodology can be used to enhance our understanding of occupational stress processes. The conclusion of this chapter is that multilevel theory and analytic techniques have much to offer occupational stress researchers from both a theoretical and methodological perspective.

Historical and Current Perspectives on Stress and Health, Volume 2, pages 217–259.
Copyright © 2002 by Elsevier Science Ltd.
All rights of reproduction in any form reserved.
ISBN: 0-7623-0970-9

INTRODUCTION

In this chapter we explore the utility of applying multilevel modeling to occupational stress research. In this exploration, we show that applying multilevel modeling to occupational stress research opens new and exciting theoretical and practical opportunities for both researchers and practitioners. As way of background, interest in multilevel modeling increased substantially in the early 1990s when multilevel modeling procedures became widely available with the introduction of random coefficient modeling programs such as Hierarchical Linear Modeling (HLM) (Bryk & Raudenbush, 1992). Random coefficient modeling represented an important statistical advance because it enhanced researchers' ability to do two things. The first is that it allowed researchers to model context (i.e. group membership) as an explanatory variable in statistical models. Second, random coefficient modeling expanded researchers' ability to model changes in individual processes over time. That is, it provided an innovative way to analyze and conceptualize longitudinal processes.

A key goal in writing this chapter is to integrate occupational stress theory with emerging analytic and methodological considerations related to multilevel modeling. This integration is important because discussions of multilevel modeling often center on either: (a) theoretical considerations related to conducting multilevel analyses; or (b) statistical issues surrounding data analytic techniques. A discussion of theory in the absence of practical statistical advice might raise interesting questions, but would run the risk of failing to spur focused inquiry since it would be unclear how to test the theoretical propositions. In contrast, a discussion of multilevel modeling techniques in the absence of theory "runs the risk of being reduced to a method that examines variation across meaningless groups . . . with meaningless group-level variables and of either not finding much or finding patterns that are difficult to understand" (Diez-Roux, 2000, p. 184).

While multilevel modeling has tremendous potential to be a valuable tool for occupational stress researchers, its use has also brought to the forefront a number of theoretical and practical issues. To a certain extent, research addressing the theoretical and practical issues has lagged behind the statistical advances. Thus, in our review, we emphasize the theoretical relevance of multilevel modeling to two types of occupational stress research – the interactional and transactional frameworks (Cooper, Dewe & O'Driscoll, 2001). The interactional framework is a largely static orientation that focuses on stressor-moderator-strain relationships. In research of this nature, one typically collects information about stressors and strains and looks for potential buffers/moderators of the stressor-strain relationship. Data collected from this framework is generally non-longitudinal and places heavy emphasis on identifying moderators. In contrast, the transactional framework is a process-oriented framework that attempts to understand how individual stress and well being develop. Part of this orientation is an interest in longitudinal processes and part is an understanding of issues surrounding person-environment fit (Cooper et al., 2001). In short, the transactional framework attempts to understand how individual perceptions of stressors evolve in the context of organizational characteristics, and how strains evolve in the context of coping and adaptation.

The chapter is divided into three major sections. The first section introduces levels of analysis issues likely to occur when multilevel techniques are applied to occupational stress research. Much of the first section is directly applicable to research conducted within the interactional framework of occupational stress (Cooper et al., 2001). In the first section, we pay particular attention to types of biases that are present whenever one encounters data with a nested structure. The material in this section is largely drawn from the public health and organizational behavior literatures. The second section discusses the logic behind using random coefficient modeling to study longitudinal processes such as those postulated in transactional models of stress. In the third and final section we apply the material covered in the first two sections to the University of Michigan Institute of Social Research (ISR) model of occupational stress. The purpose of section three is to demonstrate how multilevel modeling principles can be applied to one highly influential occupational stress theory in order to generate new research and application ideas.

1. LEVELS-OF-ANALYSIS ISSUES

In the broad context of behavioral science and public health research, interest in multilevel modeling stems from a theoretical proposition that it is important to consider individuals within their social contexts when attempting to explain outcomes such as performance, behavior, attitudes and health. Clearly, the theoretical notion that individuals are nested in groups, and that groups exert influence on individual behavior is not new and can be traced back at least to the application of general systems theory to behavior in organizations (Katz & Kahn, 1966; Kozlowski & Klein, 2000). What is new, however, is that random coefficient modeling has made it feasible to model influences associated with various levels of nesting. Thus, the last decade has seen an intriguing convergence of general systems theory with emerging practical methodology that allows one to directly test general systems propositions. This convergence, however, has brought to the forefront a considerable number of important levels-of-analysis issues.

This section of the chapter represents our current understanding of levels-of-analysis issues. As noted previously, much of this work will be directly relevant to research conducted within the interactional occupational stress framework. Many of the insights in this section were based on research that began in the early 1990s when two of the present authors observed an intriguing finding when conducting occupational stress research in the U.S. Army (Bliese & Halverson, 1996). Specifically, in an analysis of over 7,000 individuals nested within 100 groups we found a weak link between individual reports of work hours and individual reports of psychological and physical well being ($r = -0.16$). Interestingly, however, when the data were aggregated to the group level and an analysis of group means was conducted, the relationship between average work hours and average well being was quite strong ($r = -0.71$). Our attempt to understand and explain why this occurred (and the unwillingness to simply dismiss it as a form of "aggregation bias") forms the basis of the material in this section.

Our interest in levels of analysis issues has been strongly influenced by both organizational behavior research and public health research. Organizational behavior researchers, of course, are interested in multilevel issues because employees are nested within work groups, departments, organizations, etc., and it is logical to think that group membership impacts employee behavior. In public health research, the levels perspective has emerged because there is considerable interest in moving beyond individual-based germ theories of disease in favor of theories that incorporate both individual and group-based factors (Diez-Roux, 1998, 2000; Susser, 1994a, b; Schwartz, 1994; Schwartz, Susser & Susser, 1999).

In many ways, occupational stress research can be considered a discipline at the nexus of public health and organizational behavior research. That is, occupational stress research shares the goal of enhancing and promoting health and well being (goals similar to those in public health); however it focuses more exclusively on organizational settings than does public health research. Thus, it should come as no surprise that many of the levels-of-analysis issues that are pertinent to public health, and to organizational behavior, are also relevant to occupational stress.

Interestingly, relatively little attention has been paid to levels-of-analysis issues in occupational stress research despite the fact that these issues are fundamentally important to our shared understanding of occupational stress. Multilevel issues are important because they have implications for the types of inferences researchers can draw from various analyses. As one example, consider the comprehensive review of the links between psychosocial job strain and heart disease written by Theorell and Karasek (1996). Thoerell and Karasek address a critical topic area for occupational stress research because the results of this work have implications for how the redesign of jobs might ameliorate cardiovascular disease. In their review, the authors do a commendable job of differentiating between aggregate and non-aggregate studies. The authors of this review inform the reader that these two types of studies are not directly comparable. Furthermore, by separating individual from aggregate analyses Theorell and Karasek demonstrate that they are attentive to multilevel issues. The authors do not, however, provide an explanation of why this level-of-analysis distinction is important (which was appropriate given that they were not writing a levels of analysis review). Nonetheless, there is a strong likelihood that relatively few individuals completely understand the broader implications of the distinction between aggregate and non-aggregate studies. Thus, in this section we examine the literature from organizational behavior and public health to demonstrate the types of issues that arise when undertaking multilevel analyses, and why these issues are relevant to occupational stress researchers.[1]

As a starting point for the discussion of levels-of-analysis issues in occupational stress research it is useful to begin by defining the following three types of analyses: (1) individual-level analyses; (2) group-level analyses; and (3) cross-level analyses. In our discussion of these three types of analyses, several key themes are reiterated. These themes are 'inferential bias', 'emergent processes', and 'top-down processes'. Inferential bias is a common theme in discussions of aggregate analyses and refers to using results from one level of analysis (e.g. individual-level) to make inferences about phenomena that occur at another level of analysis (e.g. group-level; Diez-Roux, 1998). Emergent processes refer to the ways that variables and relationships change as data are aggregated. Emergent processes rely on the notion that the aggregation of variables (either via the creation of group means or other group summary statistics) allows one to create summary variables that are conceptually and empirically distinct from their component variables. Finally, top-down processes refer to ways in which higher-level constructs can impact lower-level relationships. We will show that the three themes of inferential bias, emergent processes and top-down processes play key roles in the application of multilevel theory and analysis to occupational stress research.

In discussing levels issues, we focus primarily on two-level multilevel models. These are models where individuals are imbedded within a primary social group; level-1 refers to individuals within the groups and level-2 refers to proximal social groups. In occupational stress research, the primary proximal social group of interest is likely to be the immediate workgroup. This is because smaller, more proximal groups are likely to exert more of an influence on individual behavior than are larger more distal groups (see Latané, 1981). Depending upon the circumstances, however, the social group of interest could also be a larger entity such as a department, an entire organization, or even a professional group (e.g. physicians).

In many cases, individual behavior in organizations is influenced by multiple levels of nesting. For instance, the immediate work group as well as the department to which an employee belongs may influence individual behavior. We believe, however, that the value of a multilevel perspective in occupational stress research can be illustrated quite well by explicitly considering only two levels – the individual and the group. Nonetheless, readers should keep in mind that it may be important for both theoretical and methodological reasons to test for the influence of multiple levels of nesting. The theoretical points made about two-level models directly generalize to situations with more than two levels, and the methodological aspects associated with estimating models with more than two levels of nesting are clearly illustrated in Snijders and Bosker (1999).

Individual-Level Analyses

Analyses of individual-level relations among variables are the most common form of relationship modeled in organizational behavior and occupational stress research. These types of analysis are also playing an increasingly major role in public health research. The defining characteristic of individual-level analyses is that all variables (e.g. stressors, moderators, and strains) are measured and analyzed at the level of the individual. For example, an individual-level test of Karasek's Demands-Control model (Karasek, 1979) would involve measuring some aspect of individual health such as blood pressure and regressing it on: (a) individual perceptions of work demands; (b) individual perceptions of job decision latitude; and (c) the demand-latitude interaction. Note that an individual-level model does not require the individual to provide *perceptual* ratings on all variables. The example above would be an individual-level model regardless of whether the outcome, health, was a self-report symptom inventory, physician diagnosis, or physiological measure. All that the individual-level model requires is that each variable in the model references or pertains to a specific individual.

In occupational stress research, individual-level analyses are pervasive because the impact of stressors is generally believed to be greatest on individuals (Beehr & Newman, 1978). While individual level studies have contributed significantly to the field of occupational stress, it is nonetheless useful to consider the limitations of the individual-level approach. The main limitation is that they fail to explicitly consider the role of higher-level context on individual-level processes. In organizational behavior, this is recognized as a limitation because there are solid reasons to believe that social systems impact a wide range of individual perceptions and behaviors (e.g. Salancik & Pfeffer, 1978). Thus, organizational researchers potentially hinder their ability to explain individual behavior in organizations when they ignore group context. In fact, one can make a compelling argument that inconsistency in organizational behavior research stems from a failure to adequately explain and model higher-level context (see Rousseau & Fried, 2001).

In public health, the failure to explicitly consider the role of context is also considered a limitation by many (e.g. Diez-Roux, 1998, 2000; Susser, 1994a, 1995b; Schwartz, 1994; Schwartz et al., 1999). Critics of individual-level analyses such as Diez-Roux (1998) decry the "methodological individualism" that has arisen in public health research and have argued that "[i]gnoring relevant group-level variables in a study of individual-level associations may lead to . . . the psychologistic fallacy, that is, assuming that individual-level outcomes can be explained exclusively in terms of individual-level characteristics" (Diez-Roux, 1998, p. 219).

In a similar vein, Schwartz et al. (1999) state that "[t]he interactions among individuals and the interplay between individuals and the environment fall outside the scope and the grasp of most research. Inattention to context leads to a limited and precarious knowledge base for public health action" (p. 17). To illustrate this point, Schwartz et al. (1999) discuss the example of peptic ulcers within the context of two individually focused paradigms – the infectious disease paradigm and the chronic disease paradigm.

In public health, the infectious disease paradigm was dominant during the early part of the 20th century. The key characteristic of this paradigm was that researchers believed that disease was the outcome of a single causal agent. Following WWII, however, pubic health research began to expand into the etiology of chronic diseases – diseases that presumably had no single causal agent. Peptic ulcer research was one of the early diseases examined from the chronic disease paradigm because it apparently had no single causal agent and its expression was thought to arise from a "web of causation" related to the stress of modern life (see also Katz & Kahn, 1978).

Although the study of peptic ulcers was one of the first diseases examined under the chronic disease paradigm, it ironically turns out that peptic ulcers are caused by a single infectious agent (*Heliobacter pylori*). Furthermore, Schwartz et al. (1999) argue that the story of peptic ulcers as an exemplar of the chronic disease paradigm is intriguing because it appears that the etiology of peptic ulcers requires one to consider individuals within the context of broad social changes – one must move beyond both the individual focused infectious disease paradigms and the chronic disease paradigms to understand disease expression. Incorporating both individual and social factors is important because Blaser (1998) has found evidence to suggest that *Heliobacter pylori* infection has been common throughout a large part of human history. Historically, individuals tended to be infected early in life; however, standards of living improved in the broad social and industrial changes following WWII. These standard of living changes thereby resulted in infection later in life. Infection later in life apparently carries more risk, thus the interaction between social trends and individual risk factors explains the rise in peptic ulcers in the post-WWII period (Blaser, 1998). Interestingly, in many developed economies, a large percentage of the population is not infected at all, and so rates have begun to decline. Thus, the story of peptic ulcers is best understood in terms of the interplay among: (a) a single causal agent; (b) individual risk factors such as age; and (c) and societal changes.

Given the limitations of the individually focused chronic health paradigm currently dominating public health, M. Susser and E. Susser and colleagues have suggested that public health research needs to adopt a paradigm that examines how individuals interact with their biological, physical, social and historical environments (Schwartz et al., 1999; Susser & Susser, 1996a, b). M. Susser, E. Susser and colleagues have defined this paradigm "eco-epidemiology" the goal of which is that "individual-level designs and analyses should not be allowed to obscure the context in which its components unfold and act" (Schwartz, et al., 1999, p. 25).

Clearly, the limitations of individually focused studies identified in both organizational behavior and public health are directly applicable to the field of occupational stress. Presumably, many aspects of the occupational stress process are directly or indirectly impacted by social context. For instance, Marmot and Madge (1987), state that "our ability to predict an individual's health status remains limited . . . it has increasingly been stressed that our powers of explanation are due to a failure to take the role of the psychosocial environment properly into account" (p. 3).

Social context is likely to impact all aspects of the occupational stress process from perceptions of stressors to reactions to stressors. For example, the identification and measurement of commonly studied stressors such as role conflict and role ambiguity depend, at least partially, upon social interaction because they require an individual to interpret ambiguous stimuli from the work environment. In other words, the role sending processes require individuals to interpret role-related information that is not always clear (Kahn, Wolf, Quinn, Snoeck & Rosenthal, 1964). In these ambiguous situations, individuals use social interaction as part of the sense-making process (see Festinger, 1954; Salancik & Pfeffer, 1978; Zalesny & Ford, 1990). Thus, interaction among work group members is likely to play a role in helping an individual determine whether an event should or should not be considered a stressor. Social context is also likely to impact how individuals respond to stressors. A social environment that is highly supportive, for example, may mitigate the effects of stressors (Cohen & Wills, 1985). Thus, one might expect individuals within work groups with supportive leadership climates to respond differently to stressors than individuals within work groups with unsupportive leadership climates (see Bliese & Castro, 2000; Bliese, Halverson & Schriesheim, 2002).

In addition to these stated theoretical limitations, there is also an important methodological limitation associated with the reliance on individual-level models. Specifically, occupational stress data is almost always collected from individuals nested within groups, and in many cases individual strains are partially a function of the group to which the individual belongs. For instance, individual reports of well being may be partially influenced by other group members' reports of well being. However, when one collects data from individuals nested within groups, yet ignores group membership in the analyses, one runs the risk of biasing both standard error estimates and statistical inferences drawn from the analysis. The key point here is that if group membership is a known source of variance that is related to individual outcomes, then group membership should be included in the statistical models. For a more detailed discussion of this topic see Bliese (2002a); Bryk and Raudenbush (1992) or Snijders and Bosker (1999).

Individual Inferential Bias.
In concluding the discussion of individual models, it is important to consider inferential biases. Inferential biases occur when one attempts to draw inferences from a specific study to a larger population. It is a tenet of multilevel theory that one runs the risk of introducing inferential bias any time that results from one level of analysis are applied to another level of analysis (Diez-Roux, 1998). This is because there is no mathematical or theoretical reason why an individual-level relationship must mirror a group-level relationship, or vice versa (Thorndike, 1939; Robinson, 1950; Snijders & Bosker, 1999).

Thus, to avoid bias, individual-level results should *only* be applied to individuals. For example, one might conduct an individual-level analysis and find that individual reports of work demands have a moderate positive correlation with individual reports of strain. Obviously, one can infer from this analysis that there is a moderately strong positive relationship between individual reports of work demands and individual reports of strain. One could *not*, however, use these individual-level results to infer the strength of the association between average work demands in a group and the average strain in the group. Doing so would constitute committing an "atomistic fallacy" (Diez-Roux, 1998); that is, a fallacy of using lower-level results to make inferences about variables at higher levels of analysis.

Unintentionally, the atomistic fallacy is commonly committed in occupational stress research. This occurs because researchers typically collect data from individuals, and they use this individual data to explore relationship among stressors, moderators and outcomes. In many cases, researchers may use results from individual analyses to inform decisions about the expected efficacy of group-level interventions. Unfortunately, doing so will lead to poor decisions. For instance, Bliese et al. (2002) explored the ability of leadership to serve as a buffer between task-related stressors and psychological strain (reports of hostility) among a large sample of U.S. Army soldiers deployed to Haiti in 1994. Despite considerable power (over 2000 soldier responses), the individual-level analyses failed to find evidence of moderation.

Based on these individual-level results, it would be tempting to argue that group-based interventions designed to enhance leadership consideration and competence among Army Company leaders would have *little* impact on soldiers' responses to work stressors. Drawing such a conclusion, however, would clearly constitute an atomistic fallacy because one would be using the individual-level results to make inferences about the efficacy of a group-level intervention (Company leadership development training). That this constitutes a fallacy is highlighted by the fact that multilevel analyses of the same data provide strong evidence to support the idea that leadership climate (a group-level variable) provides a strong buffering effect (see Bliese & Halverson, 2002; Gavin & Hofmann, 2002; Markham & Halverson, 2002).

Group-Level Analyses

The defining characteristic of group-level analyses is that all variables are modeled at the group-level. Group-level analyses are often, but not always, conducted using individual-level variables that have been aggregated using group means or other summary statistics. One of the key benefits of group-level analyses is that the aggregation process creates the potential for the identification and modeling of emergent phenomena. We begin by discussing types of group-level variables and then focus on detecting and modeling emergent phenomena.

Susser (1994a) identifies two types of group-level variables. The two types of variables are *integral variables* and *contextual variables*. Integral variables reflect group properties that vary across groups, but do not meaningfully vary within groups. Group size, for instance, is an integral variable because it is completely representative of each group and there is no variability among members within the same group. In contrast, contextual variables are derived from the aggregation of individual group members' responses. Contextual variables are typically calculated using the mean of an individual response (e.g. average work hours), but they can also represent the median or any other group-level summary statistic.

In the organizational behavior literature, Kozlowski and Klein (2000) further divide what Susser (1994a) refers to as contextual variables into *compilation process* and *composition process* variables. A group-level variable created via a compilation process will share little theoretical similarity with its lower-level counterpart. For instance, a compilation process variable could be calculated using the variability (e.g. standard deviation) of age among group members. In this case, the group-level variable is a measure of dispersion (dispersion around age), but the individual-level variable on which the group-level variable is based is simply group members' age. These two constructs at the two different levels clearly measure markedly different phenomena.

In contrast, group-level variables created through composition processes (such as group means) tend to share theoretical meaning with their lower-level counterparts. For example, one expects individuals' work hours to be conceptually related to the average work hours within a group. In composition processes the manner in which lower-level and upper-level variables are used and interpreted requires careful theoretical and methodological consideration (Bliese, 2000; Chan, 1998b; Firebaugh, 1978; Schwartz, 1994).

At one extreme, a group-level composition variable might be isomorphic with its lower level counterpart. For instance, one might expect that individual reports of work hours are conceptually and mathematically identical to average group work hours. One can think of this as a case where the whole (the group average) *is not* more than the sum of its parts. It is generally accepted that if one assumes "isomorphism" then one must also show that group members "agree" about work hours using some form of within-group agreement measure (see Chan, 1998b; Klein, Dansereau & Hall, 1994).

Alternatively, one might reasonably assume that individual work hours differ in meaning from average work hours. That is, one might assume that the whole *is* more than the sum of its parts. In this case, it is important to specify the theoretical basis for the form of the relationship linking the variables across levels. Bliese and colleagues have argued, for instance, that average group work hours measure externally mandated work requirements, since whole groups rarely work long hours for reasons other than work requirements (see Bliese,

2000, 2002a; Bliese & Halverson, 1996). Individuals, in contrast, may work long hours for reasons that may or may not be due to externally mandated work requirements (desire to get ahead, avoid family, etc.). As another example, Gavin and Hofmann (2002) argued that the meaning of individuals' perceptions of task significance differed from group average perceptions of task significance. The former reflects the degree to which *individual respondents* perceive their work as meaningful; the latter reflects the degree to which members of the group collectively perceive that the group has an important mission to accomplish.

The notion of emergent processes reflected in the fact that group means can measure constructs that differ in meaning from their individual-level counterparts is a critical consideration when conducting multilevel analyses. It is a recurrent theme in discussions of multilevel issues in public health, organizational behavior and sociology. Schwartz (1994) writes "[t]he construct referenced on the ecological level [group level] may be the context or social environment in which individuals live, distinct from the attributes of those individuals. Thus, poverty as an individual characteristic and poverty as a neighborhood characteristic may exert different, *independent* effects on health" (p. 820, italics added). Similarly, the sociologist Firebaugh (1978) noted, "an aggregate variable often measures a different construct than its name-sake at the individual level" (p. 560).

In the organizational behavior literature, the most extensive theoretical treatment of emergent processes can be found in Kozlowski and Klein (2000) and Bliese (2000). Kozlowski and Klein state that emergent phenomena "originates in the cognition, affect, behaviors, or other characteristics of individuals, is amplified by their interactions, and manifests as a higher-level, collective phenomena" (p. 55). A key theme in Kozlowski and Klein is that organizational researchers need to fully consider "emergence as a critical multilevel process in organizational behavior" (p. 52). Bliese (2000) has defined emergent processes as "fuzzy composition models" to reflect the fact that aggregation is a composition model, but that the meaning of variables across levels is not isomorphic.

When exploring the notion that a group-mean measures a different construct than its lower-level counterpart, it is important to examine the empirical evidence that supports this proposition. The statistic that provides the most evidence of emergent properties is the reliability of the group mean. If the reliability estimate (commonly referred to as the ICC(2) or Intraclass Correlation Coefficient 2) is at or near zero, then there is little empirical support to suggest that the group-mean is measuring something distinct from the individual-level variable. Details on calculating and interpreting ICC(2) values along with other measures of reliability can be found in Bliese (2000); James (1982) and Shrout and Fleiss (1979).

Emergence in composition processes across levels makes group-level analyses valuable in organizational behavior, public health and occupational stress research. This is because group-mean analyses allow one to detect subtle relationships that might never be identified in individual level analyses. Susser (1994b), for example, provides several interesting examples of how group-based analyses detected relationships that were obscured in individual-level analyses – one of which involves aggressive behavior and enuresis among children exposed to Bangladesh floods in 1988. The point of Susser's example is that aggressive behavior and enuresis did not seem to be related to flood exposure for individual children; however, patterns were detected when one looked at regional summaries. Susser's example suggests that: (a) the extent of devastation in a community is a key driver of aggression and enuresis in children; and (b) average exposure to flooding in a region is a reliable measure for the amount of devastation in a community whereas exposure for an individual child is not a reliable measure of community devastation. In addition, Susser's example suggests that individual differences in children's reactions make it difficult to detect individual-level relationships despite the fact that there are reliable differences in childhood aggression and enuresis across regions. In short, group-level analyses revealed important relationships not evident in individual-level analyses.

Another interesting example from the public health arena involves malaria. Long before the female *Anopheles* mosquito was identified as the necessary causal agent responsible for disease transmission in humans, scientists and laypersons recognized that the disease clustered in specific areas. In the fourth century B.C., Hippocrates (who Desowitz, 1991 identifies as the first epidemiologist) noted that cases of malaria tended to occur near swamps. Hippocrates surmised that a miasma rising from the swamp was throwing body humors out of sync and making people ill. While Hippocrates' miasma theory ultimately turned out to be flawed, his reasoning is still reflected in the term "malaria" which is of Roman origin and refers to "bad" or "evil" air. What is interesting about this example is that a simple group-level analyses examining rates (i.e. group averages) of malaria among groups living: (a) near; or (b) far from swamps would reveal an important relationship that arguably would have been much more difficult to detect by examining individual exposure factors. Keep in mind that in this case it took centuries (1898 to be exact) for Ronald Ross to finally identify the individual-level disease etiology by discovering that the protozoan Plasmodium was transmitted through the salivary glands of the mosquito.

In occupational stress research, group-mean analyses are likely to be particularly important because of the high variability individuals show in perceptions of and reactions to potential work stressors. The variability of individuals' perceptions potentially makes it difficult to estimate the impact of environmental stressors (e.g. workload) on employee health. In contrast, analyses based on group-means may detect relationships that have both statistical and practical significance because the aggregation process creates group-level variables that are sensitive to small, systematic effects that might otherwise go undetected.

For instance, meta-analytic reviews of the relationship between individual work hours and strain indicate that work hours have a very weak, though significant, relationship with employee health. Sparks, Cooper, Fried and Shirom (1997) reported a meta-analytic correlation of 0.15 between work hours and psychological strain, and a correlation of 0.06 for the relationship between work hours and physiological health. Interestingly, however, Bliese and Halverson (1996) and Schmitt, Colligan and Fitzgerald (1980) both found very strong relationships (greater than or equal to 0.60) between average work hours and average levels of strain in occupational groups. Recall that average work hours in a group are likely to reflect externally mandated work requirements, so the group-level results suggest that there is a strong link between average levels of strain in a group and the externally mandated work requirements in the group. These finding have clear implications for the management of employee health within organizations, because they suggest that the group-level or organizational-level management of work hours is important in controlling average levels of strain.

In summary, the key multilevel issue associated with group-level models is one of emergence. Variables created by aggregating individual-level variables need not have the same meaning as the individual level variables on which they are based. There are two important implications associated with emergence across levels. One is that the magnitude of relationships based on individual variables may vary dramatically from the magnitude of relationships based on group-level variables. Second, analyzing group-means and other group-level summary statistics may allow one to detect relationships that are difficult to detect with individual-level analyses.

Group-Level Inferential Biases
In concluding this section, it is important to consider potential inferential biases. The key bias associated with group-level analyses is the ecological fallacy. The ecological fallacy is the inferential fallacy that occurs when one takes results from group-level data (typically group means), and uses these results to draw inferences about individuals. This type of inferential error has been recognized for some time (e.g. Thorndike, 1939; Robinson, 1950); however, researchers

still inadvertently make this inferential error (see Scullen, 1997 for a discussion of this issue).

What makes the ecological fallacy easy to commit is the fact that group-level analyses allow one to make very accurate predictions about the behavior of groups as a whole, while simultaneously providing very little predictive power for specific individuals within the groups. To continue our examples, in practical terms this means that a researcher or practitioner may be able to accurately identify which groups are at risk of: (a) enuresis among children; (b) malaria; and (c) high psychological strain based on: (a) regional average flood exposure; (b) regional proximity to swamps; and (c) average group work hours, respectively. Ironically, however, the group-level information provides very little information about which specific individuals within the groups will exhibit enuresis, malaria or high psychological strain. Consequently, it is important to be cognizant of the fact that only under rather rare circumstances can group-level results be used to make individual inferences. Keep in mind, however, that using group-level data to make group-level inferences is entirely appropriate. Thus, it would be logical to target resources to groups at risk based on group-level analyses even if one could not predict which individuals in the groups would benefit from the targeted resources.

Cross-Level Analyses

Up to this point, we have considered only single level models – models that focus exclusively on either the individual or the group level. In this section, we examine cross-level analyses. In many ways, cross-level analyses can be considered "true" multilevel models because they integrate data from two or more different levels into a single model. Estimating cross-level models requires one to use one of the widely available random coefficient modeling programs briefly mentioned in the conclusion to this paper. While the complete details of these programs are beyond the scope of the present paper, we will attempt to provide a basic explanation of how random coefficient modeling programs can be used to test cross-level models.

Cross-level analyses typically involve examinations of how higher-level variables influence lower-level relationships or outcomes. Thus, cross-level models involve testing what Kozlowski and Klein (2000) refer to as a "top-down process models." In the organizational literature, top-down process models have been used to study a wide range of organizational phenomena including citizenship behavior (Kidwell, Mossholder & Bennett, 1997); collective efficacy (Jex & Bliese, 1999); leadership (Gavin & Hofmann, 2002); leadership consensus (Bliese & Britt, 2001); procedural justice (Mossholder, Bennett &

Martin, 1998); safety (Hofmann & Stetzer, 1998, 1996); satisfaction with health services (Jimmieson & Griffin, 1998) and social support (Bliese & Castro, 2000). In all these cases, the purpose of the research was to explain how group-level variables influenced individual outcomes directly, or moderated relations between individual-level predictors and the individual outcomes.

Kozlowski and Klein (2000) identify three types of top-down process models. These are: (a) cross-level direct-effect models; (b) cross-level moderator models; and (c) cross-level "frog-pond" models. The first two of these are well recognized as top-down process models. By Kozlowski and Klein's admission, the third, frog-pond models, may or may not be considered a top-down process model depending upon one's perspective (see Brass, 2000 for a more in-depth discussion of this issue). Thus, we will discuss each of these variants, but will focus primarily on the first two.

Direct-Effect Models
Direct-effect models examine the direct link between higher-level variables and lower-level outcomes. Direct-effect models are grounded in the theoretical notion that higher-level factors such as group cohesion, group leadership, group collective efficacy and group work demands (among others) have a direct measurable impact on outcomes. The defining characteristic of direct-effect models is that they involve regressing an individual-level outcome (e.g. individual well being) on a group-level predictor.

Direct-effect models use various types of group-level variables as predictors. For instance, one could examine what Susser (1994a) calls integral variables such as group size, or one could create contextual predictors by aggregating individual-level variables through compilation and composition processes. In many cases, direct-effect models take advantage of the emergent properties of data by using group-means of individual-level variables as the group-level predictor.

For instance, one might aggregate individual group members' perceptions of supervisory support to create a "supervisory support climate" measure to see if group supervisory support climate was related to well being. In this example, it would be important to determine whether the group-level measure explained unique variance in well being over-and-above individual perceptions of supervisory support. To do so, one could simultaneously regress individual well being on *both* individual perceptions of supervisory support and the groups' average rating of supervisory support. If the group's average level of supervisory support explained a significant amount of variance with both predictors in the model, it would provide compelling evidence of a direct-effect, top-down process model. Parenthetically, it would also support the proposition that there is differential meaning associated with individual and group-mean ratings of leadership support. That is, it would support the idea that individual perceptions of leadership support differ in meaning from a group-level measure of the same variable.

What we are referring to as cross-level direct-effect models have been labeled "contextual analyses" by sociologists (e.g. Firebaugh, 1978; Lincoln & Zeitz, 1980). In the past, it was common practice to estimate contextual models using Ordinary Least Squares (OLS) techniques such as regression. While it is beyond the scope of this chapter to provide a detailed explanation, readers should be aware of the fact that contextual analyses conducted using regression techniques (e.g. Firebaugh, 1978) *under*estimate standard errors. This biases the tests of the statistical significance of regression coefficients, and increases the likelihood of committing Type 1 errors (concluding the group-level variable is statistically significant when it is not). For this reason, random coefficient modeling is the preferable statistical approach when examining direct-effect top-down processes (see Bliese, 2002a; Bryk & Raudenbush, 1992; Snijders & Bosker, 1999).

In practice, direct-effect models involve regressing the group intercept for the outcome on a group-level predictor (Bryk & Raudenbush, 1992; Kreft & De Leeuw, 1998; Snijders & Bosker, 1999). That is, one is basically modeling the relationships between the group mean on the outcome and the group mean on the predictor. Consequently, cross-level direct-effect models are equivalent to the group-level analyses discussed in the prior section except that: (a) one can control for individual-level covariates; and (b) the group-level analyses in the direct-effect models are weighted so that results from large groups are more influential than results from small groups. The importance of adjusting for group size is that group-level models that give more weight to large groups with more stable intercept estimates are superior to group-level models that weight each group equally regardless of group size. The ability to control for individual-level covariates by simultaneously modeling individual and group effects, however, is probably more important than weighting for group size

The significance of simultaneously modeling direct effects of both individual and group-level constructs was illustrated in the previous supervisory support example. Specifically, the example illustrated that 'supervisory support climate' is important over and above individual perceptions of supervisory support. Nonetheless, it is useful to further consider the utility of this feature in occupational stress by considering how it could be used to integrate two divergent theoretical conceptualizations of stressors.

Broadly defined, theoretical conceptualizations of work stressors can be classified into objective and subjective conceptualizations (see Kasl, 1987 among others). The objective conceptualization proposes that certain aspects of the environment are universally stressful for individuals. In contrast, the subjective conceptualization purports that "a stressor is not a stressor until it is experienced as such" (Kasl, 1987, p. 311). We propose that direct-effect models using both individual responses and group-level responses potentially provide a way of integrating these two views of stressors into a single testable conceptual framework.

Simply put, aggregating group members' perceptions of stressors may blur the distinction between the objective and subjective environments. For example, when one member of a group reports high work overload, it may not be clear whether this represents an accurate assessment of the objective environment (e.g. high task demands in the work place) or some individual trait such as neuroticism. As such, the individual report must be treated as a subjective stressor. In contrast, when the average rating of work overload among group members is high, and there is a high level of agreement among group members, this provides evidence that the objective environment is characterized by high task demands. (One could also argue that a high level of agreement could reflect a shared bias among group members.) Nonetheless, the group-level measure by virtue of being a shared perception can be considered more of an objective rating of the environment than can the individual-level assessment. Thus, these two measures at different levels have the potential to each explain unique variance in strains and may be important for modeling and understanding how both subjective and "objective" conceptualizations of work stressors relate to strain.

Cross-level Moderation
The second version of the top-down process model identified by Kozlowski and Klein (2000) is the cross-level moderator model. The cross-level moderator model uses group-level variables to explain variation in individual-level relations. For example, individuals may react differently to work overload – some individuals may show psychological distress under conditions of work overload, and others may not. Cross-level moderator models allow one to test the hypothesis that group-level variables may, in part, explain some of the variability in individual-level stressor-strain relationships. Cross-level moderator models hold considerable promise for occupational stress research, because they provide a way of determining how the environment in which employees work influences reactions to stressors.

As a brief overview, one tests cross-level moderator models in random coefficient modeling using a two-step procedure. First, one attempts to determine how much variability there is in the stressor-strain slopes among groups. That is, one essentially looks at the relationships between stressors and strains for each group in the sample, and tries to determine whether or not the regression slopes are consistent across groups. For instance, Fig. 1 provides the relationship between work overload and psychological distress for 25 Army Companies (see Jex & Bliese, 1999). Notice that the slopes for most companies are positive (as work overload increases, psychological distress increases), but there is still some variation among companies. In fact, some companies (e.g. the next to last Company in the third row) have negative slopes.

While the slope differences in Fig. 1 may appear to be substantively important, it is possible that the differences simply reflect random variation. Notice, for instance, that negative slopes tend to occur in groups with few respondents. Thus, the first step in testing cross-level moderator models is to determine whether or not the slope variation is greater than would be expected by chance. An analysis of the data in figure 1 suggests that the observed group differences between work overload and distress are entirely due to random fluctuation and should not be considered the result of meaningful group differences.

The second step in testing cross-level moderator models is to find substantive group-level variables that explain significant slope variation. For instance, using the same data set as that in Fig. 1 but looking at different variables, Jex and Bliese (1999) found that the sense of collective efficacy among group members moderated the relationship between work overload an job satisfaction. Specifically, Jex and Bliese found that individuals reacted more negatively (in terms of job satisfaction) to high work overload if they were members of groups with low collective efficacy than if they were members of groups with high collective efficacy. It is this identification of substantive group-level variables that holds considerable promise for explaining differences in how individuals react to stressors.

This short explanation and example are meant only to introduce the key ideas surrounding the estimation of cross-level moderator models. In practice, the estimation of these models requires an integration of theory and empirical evidence and may not exactly conform to this two-step process. For instance, Snijders and Bosker (1999) have argued that one can conduct the second step (looking for group-level variables that moderate individual-level relationships) even if one fails to find evidence of significant slope variability (p. 75). The reason why this is permissible is because the criterion for "significant" slope variation is quite stringent. In practice, one often has slope variation that is not "statistically significant." Thus, the decision to test for cross-level moderation fundamentally rests upon whether one has a strong theoretical basis for expecting group-level moderation. In practice, though, we tend to observe little evidence for cross-level moderation unless there is

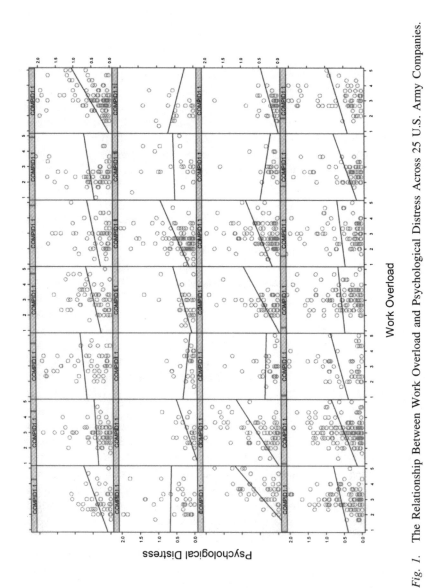

Fig. 1. The Relationship Between Work Overload and Psychological Distress Across 25 U.S. Army Companies.

at least a hint (i.e. *p*-value of < 0.20) suggesting group variation in the stressor-strain slope.

Examples where group-level variables have been found to explain differences in individual stressor-strain reactions can be found in Jex and Bliese (1999); Bliese and Britt (2001) and Bliese and Castro (2000). Bliese and Castro (2000) used a cross-level moderator analysis to show that a proposed individual-level interaction between work demands and role clarity was dependent upon group-level perceptions of supervisory support. Bliese and Britt (2001) showed that the quality of the social environment in groups (measured by the amount of agreement about leadership) impacted individuals' reactions to military work stressors in a deployed environment. In this case, stressor-strain relations were strongest in groups where there was a low level of agreement about the quality of leadership.

Frog-Pond Models
The final top-down process model discussed by Kozlowski and Klein (2000) is the cross-level frog-pond model. The distinguishing characteristic of this model is that it emphasizes the relative position of an individual within his or her group. For instance, a frog-pond model might propose that an individual's perception of work overload is, by itself, of little interest in terms of predicting individual strain. What is important instead is the individuals' rating of work overload *relative* to other group members' ratings. An individual who perceives high work overload relative to others in his or her work group might be expected to report higher strain, compared to an individual who perceives work overload to be low or average relative to his or her peers. An example of a frog-pond model is provided in Van Yperen and Snijders (2000). In this study, the authors found the strongest support for Karasek's (1979) demands-control model when looking at individual job demands and job control relative to other group members. Interestingly, the model was not supported when absolute measures of the variables were used.

Frog-pond models are tested by creating a new individual-level variable from the raw individual variable and the group mean. Specifically, one subtracts the group-mean on the construct of interest from the individual-level value. This is also referred to as "group-mean centering" (see Bryk & Raudenbush, 1992; Snijders & Bosker, 1999). Snijders and Bosker (1999) contend that one should conduct frog-pond analyses only when there are strong theoretical reasons to believe that an individual's relative position within the group is more important than an individual's absolute rating. In occupational stress research, an individual's relative position in a work group may be important in certain situations. For example, if an individual's workload is not particularly high, but it is considerably higher than other members of his or her immediate work group, this may lead to strain due to perceptions of unfairness (Folger & Cropanzano, 1998). At this point, however, we are not aware of any work that has specifically tested occupational stress frog-pond models other than the Van Yperen and Snijders (2000) study mentioned previously.

Section Summary

In this section, we provided a basic introduction to the major issues that surround multilevel analyses with special attention to how these issues are relevant to occupational stress. We argued that occupational stress research has relied primarily on individual-level analyses, and perhaps to a lesser extent, on group-level models; however, we believe that top-down process models (both direct and moderation models) are currently underutilized given their potential. We suspect that part of the reason for the underutilization of top-down process models is that statistical tools for testing these models have only recently become widely available. We have also identified the major fallacies associated with inferences drawn from models at each level, and have attempted to provide a short description of the key methodological issues raised with each type of model.

The points discussed in this section are of importance to the whole field of occupational stress; however, they are particularly relevant to occupational stress research conducted from an interactional stress framework – that is research that tends to examine static rather than dynamic stress relationships. Within this interactional framework, we believe that multilevel modeling provides considerable promise for understanding how social context influences individuals' perceptions of and reactions to stressors. Perhaps the most important facet that multilevel modeling provides is the ability to model contextual factors as moderators. Factors such as leadership climate, collective efficacy, cohesion, and shared social support are only several of a large number of potential contextual factors that might serve as moderators of individual stressor-strain relationships. In the next section, we switch orientation and discuss the application of multilevel modeling to the analysis of change. This application provides the opportunity to explore dynamic stress models from the transactional stress perspective.

2. MODELING CHANGE

As noted by Cooper et al. (2001) and others (e.g. Edwards, 1992), many occupational stress models incorporate the notion of dynamic change and the idea that stressors and reactions to stressors evolve in an interchange between the individual and his/her environment. Cooper et al. (2001) define these models as transactional. In the transactional framework, the stress process is basically seen in the context of establishing and maintaining equilibrium between demands and resources; and a stressor is defined as an imbalance between coping resources and perceived demands.

One of the characteristics of the transactional model that differentiates it from the interactional model is that the transactional model is closely intertwined with the notion of time. That is, it is arguably more important to consider time from a transactional stress framework than from an interactional stress framework. While it may not be immediately apparent, multilevel modeling techniques provide a valuable way to model individual change over time. In this section, we provide a conceptual framework for looking at longitudinal data from a multilevel modeling perspective. This discussion is not intended to be exhaustive; readers interested in statistical detail are directed to Bliese and Ployhart (2002); Chou, Bentler and Pentz (1998); Little, Schnabel and Baumert (2000); Ployhart, Holtz & Bliese (2002); and Willet and Sayer (1994). Readers interested in theoretical detail related to modeling change over time are directed to Chan (1998a); George and Jones (2000) and Mitchell and James (2001). Finally, readers interested in more in-depth discussions of longitudinal occupational stress models are directed to Zapf, Dormann and Frese (1996). This section is designed to provide: (a) a basic understanding of the principles involved in using random coefficient models (multilevel models) to study change; and (b) insights into how this methodology might be applied to occupational stress research.

In discussing cross-level models in the previous section, we introduced the idea that individuals were imbedded within groups. Recall that in cross-level models, group membership potentially exerted two effects that were important in terms of subsequent analyses. First, groups could differ on the key outcome of interest (i.e. there could be intercept differences). Second, the relationship between a predictor and an outcome could significantly vary across groups (i.e. there could be slope differences). That is, some groups might have a strong relationship between a predictor such as work overload and an outcome such as well being, while other groups might have a weak relationship between these two variables. The power of multilevel modeling is its ability to identify group-level variables that might help explain why intercept and slope differences occur among groups.

The basic logic of intercept and slope differences among groups can also be applied to the analysis of change over time. In this extension of the idea, the individual is the grouping factor, and multiple observations on the variable of interest represent the dependent variable. Time is incorporated into these models as the primary level-1 or within-group predictor. So, for instance, a simple longitudinal model from a multilevel modeling framework might involve collecting well being data at three or more time periods from multiple individuals and predicting well being by regressing well being on time.

With data of this nature, the first question one might ask is, "is time related to well being?" That is, does well being increase, decrease, or stay the same when one averages patterns across all the individuals in the sample? Answering this question provides some basic information about the change process for the sample as a whole. While this is a logical start for a longitudinal analysis, the answer may *not* be particularly interesting if one assumes that the stress process is largely unique for each individual (as is typically assumed under the transactional framework). The power of the random coefficient modeling approach, though, is that it allows one to move beyond summary tests of the entire sample and examine individual differences in change patterns over time.

The first individual difference question that one is likely to ask is whether there are intercept differences between among individuals. To use our example, one is likely to be interested in whether there are reliable differences in the mean levels of well being among individuals. Presumably, one would find that some individuals reported higher levels of well being than did other individuals across the repeated measurements. The second individual difference question is whether there are reliable differences among individuals in terms of slopes. In our example, we would be interested in determining whether the relationship between time and well being varied across individuals. For instance, some individuals might have a strong positive slope between time and well being (indicating that their well being was improving over time) while other individuals might have no relationship or a negative relationship between these two variables (indicating that their well being was stable or decreasing over time). As with the cross-level models introduced earlier, a key goal in longitudinal analyses is to identify factors that explain intercept and slope differences. In cross-level multilevel models, one focuses on group-level variables that potentially explain intercept and slope differences, while in longitudinal multilevel models one focuses on individual-level variables (personality, coping styles, etc.) that act as potential explanatory variables.

We believe that transactional occupational stress research can benefit from longitudinal multilevel modeling. For instance, in occupational settings one could identify groups of individuals undergoing organizational change (e.g. first term soldiers on peacekeeping missions, new hires, employees in units undergoing reorganization). Outcomes of interest such as well being could be measured for these individuals over time. One might find that initial levels of well being are strongly related to person-environment (PE) fit indices. That is, individuals with high initial well being might report good PE fit. In examining the slopes, however, one might find that slopes are *un*related to PE fit but that slope differences are related to coping styles (active vs. avoidant), with avoidant coping styles being related to decreases in well being over time.

The hypothetical example provided above may not entirely capture the dynamic nature of the stressor appraisal and coping interaction in the transactional framework; however, it clearly comes closer to reflecting stress processes than do static models. Furthermore, there are interesting variations of the basic longitudinal model presented that allow one to more closely approximate dynamic processes. For instance, the models can be expanded to concurrently look at changes in two variables over time (MacCallum & Kim, 2000). From a transactional framework, one might examine how both stressors and strains change together over time. Imagine a study where PE fit and well being were both measured on multiple occasions. A reasonable expectation would be that changes in fit would be positively associated with changes in well being (when PE fit increases, well being increases). This type of analysis moves even closer to testing models that are congruent with the transactional stress framework. For an interesting example of this type of research conducted in a structural equation modeling rather than a random coefficient modeling design see Garst, Frese and Molenaar (2000). In this research, Garst et al. examined linkages between stressors and strains among former East Germans adapting to broad socioeconomic and employment related changes brought about by reunification.

Other potential variants involve merging both multilevel and longitudinal factors into a single model. One could, for instance, develop three-level models where observations are nested within individuals, and individuals are nested within groups (see Bliese & Ployhart, 2002). Armed with amenable data and a clear theoretical framework one could examine individual changes in strain over time as a function of: (a) coping or other individual characteristics; and (b) group-level characteristics such as a supportive climate. Analytically, these models move one closer to testing the processes identified in transactional models of stress and, indeed, they may have the potential to provide integration of transactional and interactional models.

In summary, in this section we have introduced the basic ideas behind incorporating multilevel modeling into longitudinal investigations of organizational stress. This section only introduces the analytic and theoretical issues involved in longitudinal analyses. Nonetheless, we believe that the rewards associated with conducting such research are likely to be considerable and may play a central role in advancing occupational stress research in the future.

In the next section, we consider how the multilevel issues that we have identified as being important in both static and longitudinal models can be applied to a single theoretical occupational stress model. Specifically, we apply multilevel analysis principles to the ISR model of occupational stress (Katz & Kahn, 1978). The intent of doing so is to illustrate how considering multilevel issues can enrich occupational stress research by suggesting avenues for future research.

3. A MULTILEVEL EXAMINATION OF THE ISR MODEL

Over the years there have been numerous theoretical models designed to explain occupational stress processes, and summaries of many of these exist (e.g. Cooper et al., 2001; Jex, 1998; Jex & Beehr, 1991; Kahn & Byosiere, 1992). Many would agree, however, that the model that came out of the Institute for Social Research at the University of Michigan (e.g. French & Kahn, 1962; Katz & Kahn, 1978) has been a particularly influential model in the occupational stress literature.

The ISR model is neither strictly an interactional nor a transactional framework; rather, it shares similarities with both frameworks. Consequently, our goal is to approach the ISR from both an interactional and a transactional framework and explore how the multilevel issues that we raised in the previous sections of this chapter can be applied to the ISR model presented in Fig. 2. Notice that the model proposes that individuals perceive the objective environment, and from these perceptions, they form a sense of their psychological environment. In the third component of the model, individuals respond to the psychological environment and the responses may or may not lead to adverse mental and physical consequences. Each component in the model is moderated by enduring properties of the individual (e.g. genetic, demographic, and personality), as well as by interpersonal relations. Interpersonal relations reflect the manner in which an individual gets along with his or her co-workers (Katz & Kahn, 1978, p. 584), and is therefore conceptualized as an individual-level construct. Thus, each component of the ISR model is conceptualized and modeled as an individual-level construct.

As Katz and Kahn (1978) note, the model is most informative when considered in terms of the arrows between components. Thus, in applying a multilevel framework to the model, we focus on the specific links between components (e.g. A → B, B → C, C → D). After discussing the links, we conclude by examining component 5 (enduring properties of the individual), and component 6 (interpersonal relations). In our discussion, we interweave multilevel modeling

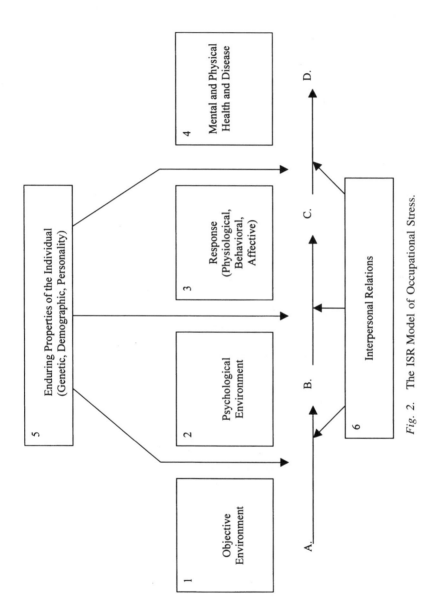

Fig. 2. The ISR Model of Occupational Stress.

propositions with occupational stress processes in terms of both static, interactional processes and dynamic transactional processes.

Linkage 1

The link between the objective environment and the psychological environment is the first focal point in our application of multilevel theory to the ISR model. This is a particularly important link because it (along with the dimension of time) helps differentiate the interactional from the transactional framework (see Cooper et al., 2001).

The interactional framework "focuses on the structural features of the person's interaction with his or her environment" (Cooper et al., p. 12). For instance, a study examining individual ratings of work overload as a stressor centers on individual perceptions of work overload with no particular attention placed on the process by which overload perceptions develop. In essence, one can think of the interactional framework as being concerned with the psychological environment and relatively unconcerned with the objective environment. In contrast, a transactional framework attempts to "encapsulate an understanding of the dynamic stress process itself, not merely the statistical relationship among variables" (Cooper et al., p.11). So, for instance, the objective of a transactional framework might be to facilitate an understanding of how differences between idealized and actual workloads result in perceptions of work overload.

Attaching concrete meaning to individual perceptions of work stressors is complicated because work perceptions represent the confounded influences of between person characteristics and work characteristics (Katz & Kahn, 1978). Clearly, the interactional inclination to define stressors based simply on self-reports of stressors is scientifically unsatisfying; however, we also believe that we can expand upon the current transactional framework by incorporating multilevel theory into our understanding of the links between the objective environment and the psychological environment.

The act of developing a psychological environment is clearly a form of sense-making. Individuals make appraisals about whether or not the objective environment poses a threat, and these appraisals constitute the identification of stressors. The act of sense-making in the appraisal process is undoubtedly an individual-level act (e.g. Louis, 1980) influenced by enduring properties of the individual (Component 5). For instance, individual attributes such as neuroticism and negative affectivity are likely to influence how an individual interprets the objective aspects of his or her work environment (e.g. Bolger & Schilling, 1991; Heinisch & Jex, 1997, 1998).

All too often, however, the sense-making process is conceptualized as an entirely individual-level process. Sense-making is also partly a social phenomenon where individuals look to others to validate their perceptions of the environment. Group-level influences exerted on individual sense-making are likely to be particularly salient in cases involving work stressors because the objective environment cannot be easily confirmed merely by physical evidence (see Festinger, 1954; Salancik & Pfeffer, 1978; Zalesny & Ford, 1990). For instance, Salancik and Pfeffer (1978) write "[t]he social context, through informational social influence processes, can affect beliefs about the nature of jobs and work, about what attitudes are appropriate, and, indeed, about what needs people ought to possess" (p. 233). Therefore, we contend that to completely understand the link between the objective environment and psychological environment, one must account for the potential influences of work group membership – stated another way, individual appraisal processes in occupational settings depend, at least to some degree, on group social contextual factors.

How might multilevel modeling provide information about the role of social context in the processes linking the objective and psychological environments? Consider two cases. In the first case involving an interactional framework one might observe that the slope between work hours and work overload significantly varies among groups. This would imply that high work hours are related to perceptions of work overload in some groups, but not in others. Subsequent analyses might reveal that groups high in collective efficacy provide a buffer to their group members such that high work hours are less likely to result in perceptions of work overload. In this case, collective efficacy is serving as a contextual moderator influencing the link between objective work hours and perceptions of work overload.

In the second case involving a transactional framework, one might observe that the link between idealized hours and actual hours is stronger in some groups than others. A strong correlation implies that members of a group have relatively little discrepancy between idealized and actual work hours (or at least it suggests that members are proportionally equal in their degree of discrepancy). In contrast, a weak correlation suggests varying patterns of discrepancy such that some group members are working an ideal amount while others are not. Subsequent analyses might be undertaken to identify characteristics of groups that enhance P-E fit among group members. For instance, it might be found that members of groups that possess high levels of collective efficacy also perceive high levels of PE fit.

As noted previously, one of the advantages of multilevel modeling is that it allows one to simultaneously examine both individual and group-level moderators. So in our examples, we might simultaneously look at both self-efficacy (a property of the individual) and collective efficacy (a group-level property) as explanatory mechanisms of why individuals differ in whether they view a specific number of work hours as work overload. This allows researchers to conduct in-depth explorations of the links between the objective and psychological environments.

To date, we are unaware of any occupational stress studies that have attempted to simultaneously delineate the role of: (a) social context; and (b) properties of the individual in the link between the objective environment and the psychological environment. We consider this to be an important area for future occupational health research. Given the recent increase in the use of teams in organizations (Offermann & Spiros, 2001), and the trend toward flatter organizational structures (Galbraith, 1995), it is likely that group-level context will have an increasingly important impact on how individuals view their objective environment.

Another way in which multilevel modeling may be informative in the link between the objective environment and the psychological environment rests on the notion that aggregate measures based on statistics of central tendency (such as group means) can measure phenomena not detected by individual-level measures (Bliese, 2000; Kozlowski & Klein, 2000; Susser, 1994a). Recall that aggregating group members' perceptions of stressors in the interactional framework blurs the distinction between the objective and psychological environments. In most research, individual reports of work stressors must be interpreted as reflections of an individual's psychological environment. In contrast, when there is a high level of agreement among group members about work stressors, the aggregate measure provides information about the characteristics of the objective environment. We will consider the implications of having ratings of both the psychological and objective environment when we discuss the link between the psychological environment and the response our discussion of linkage 2. What is important in terms of the first link is that measures at both levels of analysis (the individual and group) have the potential to explain unique variance in other components of the ISR model.

Finally, one could explore the link between the objective environment and the psychological environment from a longitudinal perspective. For instance, over time one might repeatedly collect measures of work hours and perceptions of work overload under conditions of escalating workload (such as in the weeks leading up to revenue reporting periods at quarter ends in business cycles). Analyses could be conducted to determine the relationship between work hours and perceptions of work overload. The models would also allow one to examine individual and group-level characteristics that ameliorated or exacerbated the work hour – work overload relationship (such as coping styles, group cohesion, leadership support or access to coping resources).

In short, we believe that multilevel analytic techniques in combination with a strong theoretical orientation hold considerable promise for more fully understanding the relationship between the objective environment and the psychological environment. Multilevel modeling allows one to build explanatory models that incorporate social processes as pivotal factors in the link between the objective and psychological environment. This, in turn, helps further advance the field's understanding of the ways in which work stressors evolve and may help develop approaches to mitigate the emergence of stressors.

Linkage 2

Consider next the link between component 2 (the psychological environment) and component 3 (the response). In the model, responses can include changes in mood states such as anxiety or reports of well being; changes in physiological responses such as increased mean arterial pressure; or changes in behavior such as increased alcohol consumption or maybe even changes in job performance (Bliese, Thomas & Jex, 2002). Links between various aspects of the psychological environment and responses have received extensive attention using individual-level analyses. So much attention has been devoted to this link, in fact, that certain elements of this link are basically taken for granted. For instance, few occupational stress researchers would be surprised to find that individuals who report high levels of role stressors also report high strain (see reviews by Abramis, 1994; Jackson & Schuler, 1985). The same can be said for other stressors such as a lack of perceived control (Spector, 1986), excessively long work hours (Sparks, et al., 1997), and interpersonal conflict (Spector & Jex, 1998).

From an interactional framework, what makes the second link interesting in terms of occupational stress research and practice are the potential moderators of the link between the psychological environment and the response. To date, research on moderators has focused almost exclusively on enduring properties of the individual. In other words, there have been a number of studies that have examined how component 5 of the ISR model affects the link between perceived work stressors and responses. For instance, researchers have examined the buffering effects of self-esteem (Brockner, 1988; Ganster & Shaubroeck, 1991); self-efficacy (Jex & Bliese, 1999; Jex & Gudanowski, 1992) and hardiness (Maddi, 1990) on the link between the psychological environment (e.g. perceived stressors) and the individuals' psychological responses. In addition, individual differences such as Type A personality have been shown to moderate the relation between stressors and physiological outcomes (Schaubroeck, Ganster & Kemmerer, 1994). In all of these examples, specific enduring properties of the individual serve to either ameliorate or exacerbate individual's responses to their psychological environment.

Relatively absent from the literature, however, are studies that examine the role of social context in the link between the psychological environment and responses. We believe that social context often acts as a top-down, cross-level moderator. That is, social context strengthens or weakens the relationship between an individual's psychological environment and his or her response to that environment. Those studies that have directly examined the influence of social context on this link have been promising. Recall from the previous discussion of cross-level analyses that Jex and Bliese (1999), Bliese and Castro (2000) and Bliese and Britt (2001) found evidence for the importance of social context when examining the link between individuals' reported psychological environment and the individuals' reports of well being. We contend, however, that these studies merely scratch the surface in modeling how contextual effects explain individual differences in reactions to psychological environments, and we consider this to be a fruitful area for future occupational stress research. Note, for instance, that contextual effects have been shown to impact both absenteeism (e.g. Martocchio, 1994), and safety-related behavior (e.g. Hofmann & Stetzer, 1998).

In addition, recall in the discussion of linkage 1, we suggested that aggregating individual measures of the psychological environment was likely to uncover emergent processes that would blur the distinction between the objective environment and the psychological environment. We concluded this discussion by stating that individual ratings of stressors corresponded to ratings of the psychological environment while aggregate ratings potentially corresponded to ratings of the objective environment.

These bottom-up, emergent processes involving the psychological environment have implications for the link between the psychological environment and responses to the environment. Specifically, using cross-level direct effect models, one can simultaneously test the relative influence of stressors that represent both the individuals' psychological environment and the group's objective environment.

For instance, one could estimate the degree to which well being (the response) was related to both individual work overload and group overload, where group overload represented the mean level of individual work overload. It is likely that predictors at both levels would explain unique variance in individual well being. One could interpret this to mean that an individual's subjective perception of work overload (psychological environment) is related to his or her well being.

At the same time, a significant group-level result for average work overload would provide evidence that the level of work overload present in the group as a whole in the "objective" environment was also related to well being. In short, bottom-up process models in conjunction with multilevel modeling theoretically provide a way of specifically accounting for the fact that stressors are likely to have both subjective and objective components.

We propose that the link between the psychological environment and the response could also benefit greatly from multilevel longitudinal analyses. A key element in the transactional framework is the linkage between the psychological environment and the response (Cooper et al., 2001; Edwards, 1992). Dynamic transactional models assume that there is a recursive interplay occurring at this juncture. If, for instance, an individual's response to a perceived threat in the environment is effective, then it will presumably change the psychological environment and homeostasis will be achieved. In contrast, an ineffective response to a perceived threat in the psychological environment may exacerbate the sense of threat.

While it is difficult to fully capture the completely dynamic nature of the link between the perceived environment and the response, one might begin such a study by concurrently assessing perceptions of work overload and potentially relevant avoidant vs. adaptive behaviors. For instance, consider a study focused on sales support personnel in the weeks leading up to revenue reporting periods at quarter ends. In such a study, one might assess work overload perceptions and procrastinating behaviors over time, and one would presumably find relationships between the two slopes such that individuals who increased procrastination behavior also increased perceptions of work overload. The model could be expanded by also including personality attributes such as negative affectivity into the equation.

Linkage 3

Multilevel processes may also play a role in the link between component 3 (response) and component 4 (disease). It is unlikely that everyone who exhibits a specific response to a stressor has the same likelihood of developing disease. Undoubtedly, a great deal of the variability in the link between responses and disease can be explained by enduring properties of the individual. For instance, genetic attributes, demographic characteristics, and personality traits are all likely to play a part in whether or not an individual who uses alcohol consumption as a response to work stressors actually becomes an alcoholic.

While speculative, we contend that contextual factors play a role in this linkage between stress responses and disease. For instance, consider two employees from two different work groups. Both employees are experiencing stressors and respond to their psychological environment by exhibiting increased anxiety; however, one of the employees works in a group where there is a high degree of collegiality and support. In contrast, the other employee works in a group characterized by high internal conflict. These contextual factors may influence whether or not the increased anxiety does or does not lead to poor health. To the best of our knowledge, the effects of contextual factors on the links between responses to the psychological environment and the emergence of disease remains unexplored. There is, however, interesting work in health psychology suggesting that individuals who lack socially supportive environments may have heightened risks of susceptibility to infectious diseases (see Cohen & Williamson, 1991). This suggests that it may be very fruitful to explore how contextual factors moderate links between individual responses to stressors and susceptibility to disease in the work environment.

When one moves beyond studying individuals to study large groups of individuals in a macro perspective, multilevel analyses provide a promising framework for examining the relationship between responses and disease. This is because we believe the high degree of individual variability in the link between responses and disease makes it difficult to reliably detect relationships between these two components of the model. Even the important advancement of including both enduring properties of the individual and contextual effects as moderators may leave much of the variance unexplained. However, emergent bottom-up processes may prove to be beneficial in helping identify links between response and disease because the process of aggregation can serve to magnify weak individual effects. Let us assume that chronic work overload leads to increased mean arterial pressure (Linkage 2). Further assume that increased mean arterial pressure is associated with atherosclerotic vascular disease that, in turn, is associated with heart attack, stroke, kidney failure, etc. Modeling these links for individuals may *not* be fruitful because the high degree of individual variability may make it difficult to detect these effects. In contrast, these links may be clearer in an occupational stress study that examines rates of atherosclerotic vascular related diseases among groups that either are or are not exposed to chronic work stressors (e.g. Theorell & Karasek, 1996). Mathematical simulations have shown that extremely weak individual effects can result in substantial group-level relationships if, in fact, emergent bottom-up factors are present (see Bliese, 1998).

Finally, multilevel longitudinal analyses may help shed light on the link between responses and disease. For instance, by repeatedly measuring individuals reports of well being along with precursors of disease such as mean arterial blood pressure one could presumably learn a great deal about the links between responses and disease. These types of analyses benefit from the increases in power associated with repeatedly measuring individual responses and individual health. While studies of this nature may be difficult and time-consuming to collect they would clearly be valuable. Furthermore, it is likely that data to estimate such models may already exist in medical health databases, thus it may be simply a matter of applying new analytic techniques to pre-existing data.

Enduring Properties of the Individual

On the surface, element 5, "Enduring Properties of the Individual" would not appear to be directly impacted by multilevel properties. On closer examination, however, levels issues may be quite important. For instance, the impact of demographic variables such as age or gender may depend on the social context in which an employee works. For instance, being female may exacerbate the effect of a stressor if an individual is the only female in a group of 10 other employees. On the other hand, a female's reaction to a stressor may be much different when she is one of eight females in a group of 10. These examples correspond to the earlier discussion of "Frog Pond" effects. Research on organizational demography has explored the implications of demographic diversity on group performance (see Milliken & Martins, 1996) and turnover (see Jackson, Brett, Sessa, Cooper, Julin & Peyronin, 1991), but we do not know of any occupational stress studies that have explored the effects of demographic diversity in this fashion. We note, however, the studies that have explored the impact of demography on turnover suggest that individuals have a tendency to leave groups in which they are demographically dissimilar to other group members, suggesting perhaps that such situations are stressful.

Interpersonal Relations

Interpersonal relations can certainly be viewed (as they have been traditionally) as an individual-level variable that impacts one's responses to the environment. An individual who maintains poor interpersonal relations with one or more co-workers, or perceives this to be the case, will probably view the objective environment as negative and will presumably be more likely to develop negative responses and/or develop disease.

On the other hand, the quality of interpersonal relations could also be conceptualized as a group- or even organizational-level variable. Throughout our discussion of the ISR model, we have argued that an individual's perceptions of and reactions to his or her environment may be impacted by the social quality of the interpersonal relations within his or her immediate work group (Bliese & Castro, 2000; Day & Bedian, 1991).

In short, while both approaches have merit, it is clearly important for researchers to specify how they measure and operationalize interpersonal relations. It should be evident that studies that measure and model interpersonal relations as an individual-level attribute are not directly comparable to studies that measure and model interpersonal relations as a group-level attribute. For example, studies that examine social support as a contextual aspect of groups (e.g. Bliese & Castro, 2000) are not necessarily directly comparable to studies that examine social support as an individual-level attribute.

Finally, keep in mind that multilevel modeling allows one to simultaneously examine the moderating effects of interpersonal relations as both individual and contextual factors. For instance, in occupational settings, it is likely that interpersonal relationships involving leaders have at least two (if not more) separate effects. On the one hand, individuals may have an individualized personal relationship with their leader (Graen & Scandura, 1987). On the other hand, leaders may direct behaviors to the group as a whole in the form of establishing a leadership "climate" (Shamir, Zakay, Brienin & Popper, 1998). Traditionally, these views have been presented as competing models, and analytic techniques such as Within-And-Between-Analysis (WABA) have been presented to determine which of these two conceptualizations is best represents the data (Dansereau, Alutto & Yammarino, 1984). In occupational stress research, however, it is theoretically logical to argue that leadership behaviors are important both in terms of individualized relationships and in terms of climatic characteristics. That is, one may find that an individual's interpersonal relationship with his or her leader serves as a buffer between the psychological environment and the response. Simultaneously, one might find that shared perceptions of leadership among group members explains unique variance in the link between psychological environments and responses. Thus, multilevel modeling allows one to expand how one considers and models interpersonal relationships by modeling both individualized and collective social relationships.

SUMMARY AND CONCLUSIONS

Our primary purpose in writing this chapter was to outline the value of incorporating a multilevel perspective into occupational stress research. By so doing we are in no way suggesting that individual-level occupational stress research lacks value. On the contrary, individual-level occupational stress research has produced results that have been both theoretically meaningful and informative for practitioners. Nor are we suggesting that *every* occupational stress study must examine multilevel issues. As with any research design decision, levels of analysis choices made by researchers should be determined primarily by the research question being addressed.

The underlying theme of this chapter is that incorporating a multilevel perspective into occupational stress research will add valuable new insights, and provide organizations with useful guidance as they attempt to create healthy work environments for their employees. We believe that a key benefit associated with incorporating multilevel analyses is that such analyses enhance organizations' ability to reduce stress and stress reactions among their employees. Traditionally, efforts to reduce the impact of job-related stressors have focused on teaching employees a variety of individually-focused strategies to help them cope more effectively (e.g. Beehr, Jex & Ghosh, 2001) and reduce stressors (Hurrell, 1995). Applying a multilevel perspective to the reduction of stressors is useful because there may be cases where a group-level intervention may be far more effective than focusing on individual interventions (Bliese & Halverson, 1996). For example, if workload is an important stressor that is controlled by organizational policies, changing policy to reduce work overload would probably be more effective than teaching individual employees coping techniques.

Throughout this chapter we have discussed many opportunities for advancing organizational stress research by incorporating a multi-level perspective. Our hope is that researchers and practitioners will use these multilevel concepts to help shape how organizations understand what employees perceive to be stressful, how employees respond to and react to stressors and how organizations can reduce stress and debilitating stress reactions among employees. Multilevel analyses that conclusively show links between stressors and outcomes are critical because they provide a basis for encouraging organizations to consider and implement stress reduction policies.

We conclude simply by noting that many of the propositions that we suggested require one to use random coefficient modeling programs. In the early 1990s this might have been a serious limitation as there were very few such analytic programs. Currently, however, random coefficient modeling can be conducted in numerous standalone packages including HLM and the associated software (Bryk, Raudenbush 1992); in open-source languages such as R (Bliese, 2002b; Pinheiro & Bates, 2000), and in major statistical packages such as S-PLUS and SAS (see Bliese, 2002a; Littell, Milliken, Stroup & Wolfinger, 1996; Singer, 1998). Thus, researchers have broad access to random coefficient modeling software. In addition, there are several books that provide excellent introductions to multilevel modeling techniques including Snijders and Bosker (1999) and Kreft and De Leeuw (1998).

NOTE

1. The material in this section is largely drawn from Bliese & Jex (2002), though new material has been added throughout.

REFERENCES

Abramis, D. J. (1994). Work role ambiguity, job satisfaction, and job performance: Meta-analysis and review. *Psychological Reports, 75*, 1411–1433.

Beehr, T. A., & Newman, J. E. (1978). Job stress, employee health, and organizational effectiveness: A facet analysis, model, and literature review. *Personnel Psychology, 31*, 665–699.

Beehr, T. A., Jex, S. M., & Ghosh, P. (2001). The management of occupational stress. In: C. M. Johnson, W. K. Redmon & T. C. Mawhinney (Eds), *Handbook of Organizational Performance: Behavior Analysis and Management* (pp. 225–254). New York: The Haworth Press.

Blaser, M. J. (1998). Helicobacters are indigenous to the human stomach: Duodenal ulceration is due to changes in gastric micorecology in the modern era. *Gut, 43*, 721–727.

Bliese, P. D. (1998). Group size, ICC values, and group-level correlations: A simulation. *Organizational Research Methods, 1*, 355–373.

Bliese, P. D. (2000). Within-group agreement, non-independence, and reliability: Implications for data aggregation and Analysis. In: K. J. Klein & S. W. Kozlowski (Eds), *Multilevel Theory, Research, and Methods in Organizations* (pp. 349–381). San Francisco, CA: Jossey-Bass, Inc.

Bliese, P. D. (2002a). Multilevel random coefficient modeling in organizational research: Examples using SAS and S-PLUS. In: F. Drasgow & N. Schmitt (Eds), *Measuring and Analyzing Behavior in Organizations: Advances in Measurement and Data Analysis* (pp. 401–445). San Francisco, CA: Jossey-Bass, Inc.

Bliese, P. D. (2002b). *Multilevel Modeling in R: A brief introduction to R, the multilevel package, and the NLME package*. Walter Reed Army Institute of Research.

Bliese, P. D., & Britt, T. W. (2001). Social support, group consensus and stressor-strain relationships: Social context matters. *Journal of Organizational Behavior, 22*, 425–436.

Bliese, P. D., & Castro, C. A. (2000). Role clarity, work overload and organizational support: Multilevel evidence of the importance of support. *Work and Stress, 14*, 65–73.

Bliese, P. D., & Halverson, R. R. (1996). Individual and nomothetic models of job stress: An examination of work hours, cohesion, and well being. *Journal of Applied Social Psychology, 26*, 1171–1189.

Bliese, P. D., & Halverson, R. R. (2002). Using random group resampling in multilevel research. *Leadership Quarterly, 13*, 53–68.

Bliese, P. D., Halverson, R. R., & Schriesheim, C. A. (2002). Benchmarking multilevel methods: Comparing HLM, WABA, SEM, and RGR. *Leadership Quarterly, 13*, 3–14.

Bliese, P. D., & Jex, S. M. (2002). Incorporating a multi-level perspective into occupational stress research: Theoretical, methodological, and practical implications. *Journal of Occupational Health Psychology, 7*, 265–276.

Bliese, P. D., & Ployhart, R. E. (2002). Growth modeling using random coefficient models: Model building, testing and illustrations. *Organizational Research Methods, 5,* 362–388.

Bliese, P. D., Thomas, J. L., & Jex, S. M. (2002) Job strain as a mediator between stressors and performance: Evidence from the field. Paper presented at at the 17th Annual Conference of the Society for Industrial and Organizational Psychology, Toronto, CANADA.

Bolger, N., & Schilling, E. A. (1991). Personality and problems of everyday life: The role of neuroticism in exposure and reactivity to daily stressors. *Journal of Personality, 59,* 357–385.

Brass, D. J. (2000). Frogs and frog ponds. In: K. J. Klein & S. W. Kozlowski (Eds), *Multilevel Theory, Research, and Methods in Organizations* (pp. 349–381). San Francisco, CA: Jossey-Bass, Inc.

Brockner, J. (1988). *Self-Esteem at Work.* Lexington, Mass: Heath.

Bryk, A. S., & Raudenbush, S. W. (1992). *Hierarchical linear models.* Newbury Park, CA: Sage.

Chan, D. (1998a). The conceptualization and analysis of change over time: An integrative approach incorporating longitudinal means and covariance structures analysis (LMACS) and multiple indicator latent growth modeling (MLGM). *Organizational Research Methods, 1,* 421–483.

Chan, D. (1998b). Functional relations among constructs in the same content domain at different levels of analysis: A typology of composition models. *Journal of Applied Psychology, 83,* 234–246.

Chou, C., Bentler, P. M., & Pentz, M. A. (1998). Comparisons of two statistical approaches to study growth curves: The multilevel model and the latent curve analysis. *Structural Equation Modeling, 5,* 247–266.

Cohen, S., & Williamson, G. M. (1991). Stress and infectious disease in humans. *Psychological Bulletin, 109,* 5–24.

Cohen, S., & Wills, T. A. (1985). Stress, social support, and the buffering hypothesis. *Psychological Bulletin, 98,* 310–357.

Cooper, C. L., Dewe P. J., & O'Driscoll, M. (2001). *Stress and work in organizations: A review and critique of theory, research and applications.* California: Sage Publications.

Dansereau, F., Alutto, J. A., & Yammarino, F. J. (1984). *Theory testing in organizational behavior: The varient approach.* Englewood Cliffs, NJ: Prentice-Hall.

Day, D. V., & Bedian, A. G. (1991). Predicting job performance across organizations: The interaction of work orientation and psychological climate. *Journal of Management, 17,* 589–600.

Desowitz, R. S. (1991). *The malaria capers: more tales of parasites and people, research and reality.* New York: W. W. Norton & Company.

Diez-Roux, A. V. (1998). Bringing context back into epidemiology: Variables and fallacies in multilevel analyses. *American Journal of Public Health, 88,* 216–222.

Diez-Roux, A. V. (2000). Multilevel analysis in public health research. *Annual Review of Public Health, 21,* 171–192.

Edwards, J. R. (1992). A cybernetic theory of stress, coping, and well being in organizations. *Academy of Management Review, 17,* 238–274.

Festinger, L. (1954). A theory of social comparison processes. *Human Relations, 7,* 117–140.

Firebaugh, G. (1978). A rule for inferring individual-level relationships from aggregate data. *American Sociological Review, 43,* 557–572.

Folger, R., & Cropanzano, R. (1998). *Organizational justice and human resource management.* Beverly Hills, CA: Sage.

French, J. R. P., Jr., & Kahn, R. L. (1962). A programmatic approach to studying the industrial environment and mental health. *Journal of Social Issues, 18,* 1–47.

Galbraith, J. R. (1995). *Designing organizations: An executive briefing on strategy, structure, and process.* San Francisco: Jossey-Bass.

Ganster, D. C., & Schaubroeck, J. (1991). Role stress and worker health: An extension of the plasticity hypothesis of self-esteem. *Journal of Social Behavior and Personality, 6,* 349–360.

Garst, H., Frese, M., & Molenaar, P. C. M. (2000). The temporal factor of change in stressor-strain relationships: A growth curve model on a longitudinal study in East Germany. *Journal of Applied Psychology, 85,* 417–438.

Gavin, M. B., & Hofmann, D. A. (2002). Using Hierarchical Linear Modeling to investigate the moderating influence of leadership climate. *Leadership Quarterly, 13,* 15–33.

George, J. M., & Jones, G. R. (2000). The role of time in theory and theory building. *Journal of Management, 26,* 657–684.

Graen, G. B., & Scandura, T. A. (1987). Toward a psychology of dyadic organizing. In: L. L. Cummings & B. M. Staw, *Research in Organizational Behavior* (Vol. 9). Greenwich, CT: JAI Press.

Heinisch, D. A., & Jex, S. M. (1997). Negative affectivity and gender as moderators of the relationship between work-related stressors and depressed mood at work. *Work & Stress, 11,* 46–57.

Heinisch, D. A., & Jex, S. M. (1998). Measurement of negative affectivity: A comparison of self-reports and observer ratings. *Work & Stress, 12,* 145–160.

Hofmann, D. A., & Stetzer, A. (1996). A cross-level investigation of factors influencing unsafe behaviors and accidents. *Personnel Psychology, 49,* 307–339.

Hofmann, D. A., & Stetzer, A. (1998). The role of safety climate and communication in accident interpretation: Implications for learning from negative events. *Academy of Management Journal, 41,* 644–657.

Hurrell, J. J., Jr. (1995). Commentary: Police work, occupational stress, and coping. *Journal of Organizational Behavior, 16,* 27–28.

Jackson, S. E., Brett, J. F., Sessa, V. I., Cooper, D. M., Julin, J. A., & Peyronin, K. (1991). Some differences make a difference: Individual dissimilarity and group heterogeneity as correlates of recruitment, promotions, and turnover. *Journal of Applied Psychology, 76,* 675–689.

Jackson, S. E., & Schuler, R. S. (1985). A meta-analysis and conceptual critique of research on role ambiguity and role conflict in work settings. *Organizational Behavior and Human Decision Processes, 36,* 16–78.

James, L. R. (1982). Aggregation bias in estimates of perceptual agreement. *Journal of Applied Psychology, 67,* 219–229.

Jex, S. M. (1998). *Stress and job performance: Theory, research, and implications for managerial practice.* Thousand Oaks, CA: Sage.

Jex, S. M., & Beehr, T. A. (1991). Emerging theoretical and methodological issues in the study of job-related stress. In: G. R. Ferris & K. Rowland (Eds), *Research in Personnel and Human Resources Management* (Vol. 9, pp. 311–364). Greenwich, CT: JAI Press.

Jex, S. M., & Bliese, P. D. (1999). Efficacy beliefs as a moderator of the effects of work-related stressors: A multi-level study. *Journal of Applied Psychology, 84,* 349–361.

Jex, S. M., & Gudanowski, D. M. (1992). Efficacy beliefs and work stress: An exploratory study. *Journal of Organizational Behavior, 13,* 509–517.

Jimmieson, N., & Griffin, M. A. (1998). Linking staff and client perceptions of the organization: A field study of client satisfaction with health services. *Journal of Occupational and Organizational Psychology, 71,* 81–96.

Kahn, R. L., & Byosiere, P. (1992). Stress in organizations. In: M. D. Dunnette & L. M. Hough (Eds), *Handbook of Industrial and Organizational Psychology* (2nd ed., Vol. 2, pp. 571–650). Palo Alto, CA: Consulting Psychologists Press.

Kahn, R. L., Wolf, D. M., Quinn, R. P., Snoek, J. D., & Rosenthal, R. A. (1964). *Organizational stress: Studies in role conflict and ambiguity.* New York: Wiley.

Karasek, R. A., Jr. (1979). Job demands, job decision latitude, and mental strain: Implications for job redesign. *Administrative Science Quarterly, 24,* 285–308.

Kasl, S. V. (1987). Methodologies in stress and health: Past difficulties, present dilemmas, future directions. In: S. V. Kasl & C. L. Cooper (Eds), *Stress and Health: Issues in Research Methodology* (pp. 307–318). Chichester: John Wiley & Sons.

Katz, D., & Kahn, R. L. (1966). *The social psychology of organizations.* New York: John Wiley & Sons.

Katz, D., & Kahn, R. L. (1978). *The social psychology of organizations* (2nd ed.). New York: John Wiley & Sons.

Kidwell, R. E., Mossholder, K. M., & Bennett, N. (1997). Cohesiveness and organizational citizenship behavior: A multilevel analysis using groups and individuals. *Journal of Management, 23,* 775–793.

Klein, K. J., Dansereau, F., & Hall, R. J. (1994). Levels issues in theory development, data collection, and analysis. *Academy of Management Review, 19,* 195–229.

Kozlowski, S. W. J., & Klein, K. J. (2000). A multilevel approach to theory and research in organizations: Contextual, temporal, and emergent processes. In: K. J. Klein & S. W. Kozlowski (Eds), *Multilevel Theory, Research, and Methods in Organizations* (pp. 3–90). San Francisco, CA: Jossey-Bass, Inc.

Kreft, I., & De Leeuw, J. (1998). *Introducing multilevel modeling.* London: Sage Publications.

Latané, B. (1981). The psychology of social impact. *American Psychologist, 36,* 343–356.

Lincoln, J. R., & Zeitz, G. (1980). Organizational properties from aggregate data: Separating individual and structural effects. *American Sociological Review, 45,* 391–408.

Littell, R. C., Milliken, G. A., Stroup W. W., & Wolfinger, R. D. (1996). *SAS system for mixed models.* Cary, NC: SAS Institute Inc.

Little, T. D., Schnabel, K. U., & Baumert, J. (2000). *Modeling longitudinal and multilevel data: Practical issues, applied approaches, and specific examples.* Mahwah, NJ: Erlbaum.

Louis, M. R. (1980). Surprise and sense making: What newcomers experience in entering unfamiliar organizational settings. *Administrative Science Quarterly, 25,* 226–251.

MacCallum, R. C., & Kim, C. (2000). Modeling multivariate change. In: T. D. Little, K. U. Schnabel & J. Baumert (Eds), *Modeling Longitudinal and Multilevel Data: Practical Issues, Applied Approaches, and Specific Examples* (pp. 51–68). Mahwah, NJ: Erlbaum.

Maddi, S. R. (1990). Issues and interventions in stress mastery. In: H. S. Friedman (Ed.), *Personality and Disease.* New York: Wiley.

Markham, S. E., & Halverson, R. R. (2002). Within- and between-entity analyses in multilevel research: A leadership example using single level analyses (SLA) and boundary conditions (MRA). *Leadership Quarterly, 13,* 35–52.

Marmot, M. G., & Madge, N. (1987). An epidemiological perspective on stress in health. In: S. V. Kasl & C. L. Cooper (Eds), *Stress and Health: Issues in Research Methodology* (pp. 3–26). Chichester: John Wiley & Sons.

Martocchio, J. J. (1994). The effects of absence culture on individual absence. *Human Relations, 47,* 243–262.

Milliken, F. J., & Martins, L. L. (1996). Searching for common threads: Understanding the multiple effects of diversity in organizational groups. *Academy of Management Review, 21,* 402–433.

Mitchell, T. R., & James, L. R. (2001). Building better theory: Time and the specification of when things happen. *Academy of Management Review, 26,* 530–547.

Mossholder, K. W., Bennett, N., & Martin, C. L. (1998). A multilevel analysis of procedural justice context. *Journal of Organizational Behavior, 19*, 131–141.

Offermann, L. R., & Spiros, R. K. (2001). The science and practice of team development. *Academy of Management Journal, 44*, 376–392.

Pinheiro, J. C., & Bates, D. M. (2000). *Mixed-effects models in S and S-PLUS*. New York: Springer-Verlag.

Ployhart, R. E., Holtz, B. C., & Bliese, P. D. (2002). Longitudinal data analysis: Applications of random coefficient modeling to leadership research. *The Leadership Quarterly, 13*, 455–486.

Robinson, W. S. (1950). Ecological correlations and the behavior of individuals. *American Sociological Review, 15*, 351–357.

Rousseau, D. M., & Fried, Y. (2001). Location, location, location: Contextualizing organizational research. *Journal of Organizational Behavior, 22*, 1–13.

Salancik, G. R., & Pfeffer, J. (1978). A social information processing approach to job attitudes and task design. *Administrative Science Quarterly, 23*, 224–253.

Schaubroeck, J., Ganster, D. C., & Kemmerer, B. E. (1994). Job complexity type "A" behavior, and cardiovascular disease: A prospective study. *Academy of Management Journal, 37*, 436–439.

Schmitt, N., Colligan, M. J., & Fitzgerald, M. (1980). Unexplained physical symptoms in eight organizations: Individual and organizational analyses. *Journal of Occupational Psychology, 53*, 305–317.

Schwartz, S. (1994). The fallacy of the ecological fallacy: The potential misuse of a concept and the consequences. *American Journal of Public Health, 84*, 819–824.

Schwartz, S., Susser, E., & Susser, M. (1999). A future for epidemiology? *Annual Review of Public Health, 20*, 15–33.

Scullen, S. E. (1997). When ratings from one source have been averaged, but ratings from another source have not: Problems and solutions. *Journal of Applied Psychology, 82*, 880–888.

Shamir, B., Zakay, E., Breinin, E., & Popper, M. (1998). Correlates of charismatic leader behavior in military units: Subordinates' attitudes, unit characteristics, and superior appraisals of leader performance. *Academy of Management Journal, 41*, 387–409.

Shrout, P. E., & Fleiss, J. L. (1979). Intraclass correlations: Uses in assessing rater reliability. *Psychological Bulletin, 86*, 420–428.

Singer, J. D. (1998). Using SAS PROC MIXED to fit multilevel models, hierarchical models, and individual growth models. *Journal of Educational and Behavioral Statistics, 24*, 323–355.

Snijders, T. A. B., & Bosker, R. J. (1999). *Multilevel analysis: An introduction to basic and advanced multilevel modeling*. London: Sage Publications.

Sparks, K., Cooper, C., Fried, Y., & Shirom, A. (1997). The effect of hours of work on health: A meta-analytic review. *Journal of Occupational and Organizational Psychology, 70*, 391–408.

Spector, P. E. (1986). Perceived control by employees: A meta-analysis of studies concerning autonomy and participation at work. *Human Relations, 39*, 1005–1016.

Spector, P. E., & Jex, S. M. (1998). Development of four self-report measures of job stressors and strain: Interpersonal Conflict at Work Scale, Organizational Constraints Scale, Quantitative Workload Inventory, and Physical Symptoms Inventory. *Journal of Occupational Health Psychology, 3*, 356–367.

Susser, M. (1994a). The logic in ecological: I. The logic of analysis. *American Journal of Public Health, 85*, 825–829.

Susser, M. (1994b). The logic in ecological: II. The logic of design. *American Journal of Public Health, 85*, 830–835.

Theorell, T., & Karasek, R. A. (1996). Current Issues Relating to Psychosocial Job Strain and Cardiovascular Disease Research. *Journal of Occupational Health Psychology, 1,* 9–26.

Thorndike, E. L. (1939). On the fallacy of imputing the correlations found for groups to the individuals or smaller groups composing them. *American Journal of Psychology, 52,* 122–124.

Van Yperen, N. W., & Snijders, T. A. B. (2000). A multilevel analysis of the demands-control model: Is stress at work determined by factors at the group level or the individual level? *Journal of Occupational Health Psychology, 5,* 182–190.

Willett, J. B., & Sayer, A. G. (1994). Using covariance structural analysis to detect correlates and predictors of individual change over time. *Psychological Bulletin, 116,* 363–381.

Zalesny, M. D., & Ford, J. K. (1990). Extending the social information processing perspective: New links to attitudes, behaviors, and perceptions. *Organizational Behavior and Human Decision Processes, 47,* 205–246.

Zapf, D., Dormann, C., & Frese, M. (1996). Longitudinal studies in organizational stress research: A review of the literature with reference to methodological issues. *Journal of Occupational Health Psychology, 1,* 145–169.

EFFORT-REWARD IMBALANCE AT WORK AND HEALTH

Johannes Siegrist

ABSTRACT

All major contracts in social life, including the work contract, are based on the principle of reciprocity. A fair balance between the costs invested in cooperative activities and the gains received in turn is a prerequisite of a trustful social exchange and individual well being. Conversely, failed reciprocity in terms of high cost and low gain elicits strong negative emotions and associated stress responses. The model of effort-reward imbalance has been developed to identify conditions of failed reciprocity in social contracts, with a particular focus on work, and to predict reduced well being and increased illness susceptibility as a consequence of this exposure. This chapter describes the theoretical foundation of this model and its measurement. Moreover it summarizes empirical evidence on adverse effects on health derived from epidemiological and laboratory investigations. Finally, some policy implications of this new evidence are discussed.

INTRODUCTION

Paid work will probably continue to be important for human health and well being in a major part of adult populations in developed and rapidly developing countries around the world. At the same time the nature of work has changed

Historical and Current Perspectives on Stress and Health, Volume 2, pages 261–291.
ISBN: 0-7623-0970-9

considerably over the past several decades, especially so in economically advanced societies. This is due, in part, to technological progress, in part to a growing number of jobs available in the service sector where many jobs are confined to information processing, controlling and communicating. Moreover, economic constraints produce work pressure, rationalization and cut back in personnel. Over-employment in some segments of the work force is paralleled by under-employment, job instability, or structural unemployment in other segments. These changes go along with changes in the structure of the labor market. More employees are likely to work on temporary contracts, on fixed term or in flexible job arrangements. The workforce is getting older, and an increasing proportion of women are entering the labor market, with an increase of double exposure among women with children or, more general, in dual career families.

In this context it is important to recognize that traditional occupational hazards, such as exposure to toxic substances, heat, cold or noise, though important, are no longer the dominant challenges of health and well being at work. Rather, an unfavorable psychosocial work environment is becoming highly prevalent in modern working life (Cooper, 1998; Dunham, 2001). This situation produces new challenges for the scientific analysis of associations between work and health.

There has been a recognition that the importance of work goes beyond traditional occupational diseases and, indeed, it is likely that work makes a greater contribution to diseases not thought of as 'occupational' in conventional terms. Reduced well being following exposure to an unfavorable psychosocial work environment may result in a high level of absenteeism, in reduced productivity, in an increase of compensation claims and in elevated prevalence of psychosomatic and affective disorders, or even addictive behavior. The direct and indirect costs produced by 'occupational stress' are considerable (Leigh & Schnall, 2000; Levi & Lunde-Jensen, 1996). Thus, efforts towards an interdisciplinary study of occupational health and well being are needed that include psychological and sociological information into the prevailing biomedical and physico-chemical paradigms.

This chapter introduces a distinct approach towards investigating adverse health effects of an unfavorable psychosocial work environment. This approach is 'general' as well as 'analytical'. By general I mean that the theoretical model described below can be applied to a wide variety of different jobs in different countries as it does not focus on situation-specific conditions such as job sector, type of occupation, etc. By 'analytic' I mean that this approach is selective. This is due to the fact that it aims at identifying a few relevant conditions within the complexities of the many different psychosocial work environments.

These relevant conditions are hypothesized to account in a substantial way for the observed associations between work and health.

In other words, a theoretical model is based on risky assumptions, i.e. on assumptions that deviate from predictions derived from what is already known (Popper, 1959). A theoretical model, while being at risk of empirical refutation, has the potential of creating new knowledge. If valid, this new theory-based knowledge can enrich or reshape our understanding and guide those activities that aim at reducing or preventing stress at work.

The Theoretical Model

The model of effort-reward imbalance at work is derived from a more general approach towards analyzing the psychosocial dimension of human health and well being. It assumes that personal self-regulation conducive to health and well being in adult life is largely contingent on successful social exchange as mediated through salient roles (Siegrist, 2000).

The marital and parental roles, the work role and the different civic roles contribute to personal self-regulation through social exchange both in positive and negative ways. For instance, threats to this exchange, lack of reciprocity in this exchange, or exclusion from this exchange have negative consequences as they impair personal self-regulation by weakening a person's sense of self-efficacy, self-esteem, and belonging (or self-integration). These three functions of self-regulation seem to be critical for human well being, and they point to the fragile balance between self and social environment (Kohn & Schooler, 1983; Pearlin, 1989; Siegrist, 2000). Conversely, the experience of successful and rewarding exchange through core social roles may reinforce the self and contribute to beneficial effects on health and well being.

The work role is particularly relevant in this regard as it offers options for all three functions of successful self regulation: the experience of self-efficacy (e.g. a satisfying performance, personal development through work), self esteem (e.g. recognition, adequate payment, promotion prospects), and self-integration (social identity beyond the family, participation in networks) (House, 1981; Kohn & Schooler, 1983). Moreover, having a job is a principal prerequisite for continuous income opportunities which, in turn, determine a wide range of life chances. Alternatively, losing a job and being excluded from the labor market are obvious examples of role termination with deleterious effects on self-regulation, on emotional well being and health (Bartley et al., 1999; Martikainen & Valkonen, 1996).

While termination of the work role by exclusion or loss may define the most visible and stressful experience related to occupational life, other constellations of unfavorable social exchange through the work role are often more prevalent and, perhaps, equally stressful. One such constellation has been identified as the lack of reciprocity between efforts spent and rewards received at work. Again, in view of the centrality of work and occupation in adult life, intense and long lasting effects on disturbed self-regulation, and particularly self-esteem, are expected to occur in this context.

The model of effort-reward imbalance maintains that availability of a work role is associated with recurrent options of contributing and of performing, of being rewarded or esteemed, and of belonging to some significant group (e.g. work colleagues). Yet these potentially beneficial effects are contingent on a basic prerequisite of exchange in social life, that is, reciprocity. Effort at work is spent as part of a socially organized exchange process to which society at large contributes in terms of rewards. Rewards are distributed by three trans-mitter systems as scarce resources: money, esteem and career opportunities. The model of effort-reward imbalance claims that lack of reciprocity between the costs and gains (i.e. high cost/low gain conditions) elicits negative emotions with special propensity to sustained autonomic and neuro-endocrine activation (Siegrist, 1984, 1996).

In structural terms, this imbalance results from the fact that the social exchange between employee and employer is based on an incomplete contract. An incomplete contract does not specify the full range of detailed obligations and benefits (Fehr & Gächter, 2000). In incomplete contracts, assumptions of trust in mutual commitment are made. However, under certain conditions it is likely that incomplete contracts result in high cost/low gain conditions in employees. The risk of non-reciprocity in exchange is particularly high if employees have no alternative choice in the labor market, if their skills are poor or if they subscribe to short term contracts. Less frequently non-reciprocity at work is experienced by workers as a negative life event, as contract violation or failed contract (Foner, 1993).

Employees themselves may also contribute to high cost/low gain conditions at work either intentionally or unintentionally. For instance, they may accept job arrangements that are considered unfair for a certain time for strategic reasons as they tend to improve their chances for career promotion and related rewards at a later stage. This pattern is often observed in early stages of professional careers, among others. Failed success after long lasting investment is particularly harmful to a person's self-regulation.

Finally, there are psychological reasons of a continued mismatch between efforts and rewards at work. People characterized by a motivational pattern of excessive work-related overcommitment and a high need for approval may suffer from inappropriate perceptions of demands and their own coping

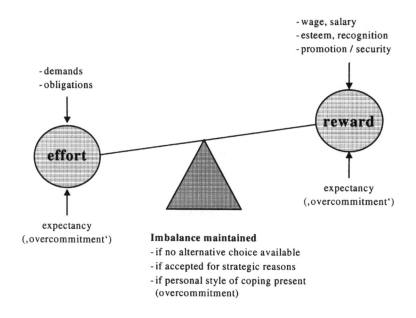

- wage, salary
- esteem, recognition
- promotion / security

- demands
- obligations

reward

effort

expectancy
(,overcommitment')

expectancy
(,overcommitment')

Imbalance maintained
- if no alternative choice available
- if accepted for strategic reasons
- if personal style of coping present
  (overcommitment)

Fig. 1. The Model of Effort-Reward Imbalance at Work.

Source: Modified from J. Siegrist, 1996.

resources more often than their less involved colleagues (Siegrist, 1996, 2001a). Perceptual distortion prevents them from accurately assessing cost-gain relations. As a consequence, they underestimate the demands, and overestimate their own coping resources while not being aware of their own contribution to non-reciprocal exchange.

In summary, the proposed theoretical model is based on the sociological hypothesis that structured social exchange, as mediated through core social roles (the work role), is rooted in contracts of reciprocity of cost and gain. In addition to its significance for social functioning this reciprocal contractual exchange is assumed to produce beneficial effects on individual health and well being. The model specifies the conditions under which contractual reciprocity is not maintained and, thus, may reduce individual health and well being.

These conditions are in part structural (or extrinsic) and in part personal (or intrinsic). Structural conditions of recurrent experience of high effort and low reward at work include lack of alternative choice in the labor market, lack of mobility, low level of skills and confinement to a short-term contract. Personal conditions include strategic choices of the workers and characteristics of individual coping with the demands and rewards at work (overcommitment).

It is important to stress that this model does not represent a black-box approach towards studying work stress that is restricted to the structural level of analysis (such as e.g. the demand-control model (Karasek, 1979; Karasek & Theorell, 1990; see below)), but integrates structural and personal components. However, these two components are distinguished both at the conceptual and methodological level. It is assumed that a combination of both sources of information according to predefined procedures (see below) provides a more accurate estimate of the adverse health effects resulting from non-reciprocity compared to a restriction of information to one of these sources.

The predictions derived from the model of effort-reward imbalance are as follows:

(1) The components of effort and reward each may contribute to reduced health and well being, but the imbalance between high effort and low reward (non-reciprocity) produces adverse effects on health and well being over and above the effects of single components. It is the mismatch between high cost and low gain that matters most (structural component of the model).

(2) A high level of personal commitment ('overcommitment') acts as an intrinsic trigger of non-reciprocal exchange through the work-role (people respond to their work demands with higher motivations and expectations than usual, they assume more responsibilities, they meet more deadlines etc.; personal component of the model).

(3) If structural and personal components act in concert the strongest effects on health and well being are expected to occur.

Several structural and personal conditions can modify the hypothesized effects. For instance, low socioeconomic status (structural) or low autonomy and feelings of helplessness (personal) may enhance these effects whereas a stable, emotionally satisfying social network (structural) or a high degree of self-reliance and self-efficacy (personal) may reduce these effects. Such additional conditions are not specified as part of the model, but their inclusion into a more comprehensive analysis of the links between work and health is crucial in advancing our understanding.

Before describing the measurement of this model it seems mandatory to have a closer look at the pathways that are assumed to link occupational stress with psychobiological responses that ultimately result in somatic disease and reduced well being.

Stress Physiological Basis

A model of occupational stress and health calls for a stress physiological basis which integrates sociological, psychological and biological information. Stress physiology is important as it elucidates the psychobiological pathways resulting in enhanced autonomic nervous system activation, in altered physiological states within bodily systems and, ultimately, in structural lesions of target organs, such as the heart or vessels, the gut, the brain, etc. (McEwen, 1998; Weiner, 1992).

Before discussing stress physiology a clarification of major terms in this field may be useful. 'Stressor' is defined as an environmental demand or threat that taxes or exceeds a person's ability to meet the challenge; 'strain' is defined as the person's response to such a situation in psychological and physiological terms. Psychological responses include negative emotions whereas physiological responses concern the activation of the autonomic nervous system and related neuro-hormonal and immune reactions. Stressors, in particular novel or dangerous ones, are appraised and evaluated by the person, and as long as there is some perception of agency on the part of the exposed person, efforts are mobilized to reverse the threat or to meet the demands. Such efforts are termed 'coping' and they occur at the behavioral, cognitive, affective and motivational level (Lazarus, 1991). When judging strain, the quality and intensity of a stressor as well as the duration of exposure have to be taken into account, in addition to the individual differences in coping and vulnerability to strain reactions. Recent research indicates that only part of human strain reactions are subject to conscious information processing whereas a large amount by-passes awareness (LeDoux, 1996). The term 'stressful experience' is introduced to delineate that part of affective processing that reaches consciousness.

Stressful experience at work is often attributed to adverse working conditions by exposed people themselves. While they usually refer to some common sense notion of stress it is crucial to emphasize that these attributions differ from the explanatory constructs of stressful experience at work that have been identified by science, such as the construct of effort-reward imbalance discussed here.

In current stress physiological research there is evidence of a prominent role of two concepts, 'control' and 'reward'. The construct of control has provided the dominant perspective in health related stress research during the past three or four decades (Skinner, 1996; Spector, 1998; Steptoe & Appels, 1989). The amount of control a person can exert over aversive environmental stimuli is considered a crucial determinant of the psychobiologic stress response. Agency and/or perception of control, striving for control, and threat to or loss of control are associated with marked differences in neurohormonal, autonomic and immune responses, in emotional experience, and in cognitive and behavioral correlates. There is substantial evidence of a mediating role of the hypothalamic-pituitary-adrenocortical stress axis in these processes (Liu & Mori, 1999; Sapolski, 1998; McEwen, 1998).

A second stress-theoretical construct has been proposed, the construct of reward (Olds & Olds, 1969). There is now increasing evidence of a powerful regulatory role for a particular brain system implicated in motivation, rein-forcement and reward in personal and inter-personal well being: the mesolimbic dopamine system which innervates the prefrontal cortex, a brain region involved in cognitive function and anticipatory activity. Reward-sensitive neuronal structures in the orbito-frontal cortex elicit sustained strain reactions following the frustration of reward expectancies or the loss of anticipated gratifications. This mesolimbic system is believed to be involved in the control of basic motivations such as sexual drive and appetite (Blum et al., 1996; Koob & Bloom, 1988). It is also considered a common pathway of processing experi-ences related to addiction.

In an evolutionary perspective of species survival the neuronal networks specified by the constructs of control and reward are of crucial importance. This is due to the fact that they regulate essential activities of self-preservation of individuals, of their procreation and of their maintenance of a basic 'grammar' of social exchange among group members, the grammar of reciprocity and fairness (Cosmides & Tooby, 1992). Hence, recurrent dysregulation of these networks is likely to perturb the organism and to reduce well being.

Control and reward act as bridge concepts, as they connect neuro-biological information with psychosocial information. Either bridge concept is useful as it provides opportunities of linking aspects of the social opportunity structure that are mediated through core social roles with individual self-regulation and well being. With respect to the study of occupational stress the concept of control has served to develop the demand-control model (Karasek, 1979; Karasek & Theorell, 1990). This well-known model posits that jobs character-ized by high quantitative demands and a low level of control (decision latitude, skill discretion) are frequently experienced as stressful by people holding them. The demand-control model has been tested in a large number of investigations, and it is now established as one of the leading general models of occupational stress (for a review see Schnall et al., 2000; Marmot et al., 2002). The model of effort-reward imbalance is rooted in the bridge concept of reward as it identifies distinct conditions of social reward deficiency with impact on the neuronal networks operating in the brain's reward system. This model too has been tested in a variety of work-related investigations (for a review see Schnall et al., 2000; Marmot et al., 2002; and below).

While each bridge concept and each model of occupational stress exhibits unique features there are also communalities and synergies between them. Below I discuss some communalities and differences between the two work stress models, and I explain the promise of combining information from either model. However, before doing this the measurement approach is introduced and the empirical evidence of its role in explaining health and well being is demonstrated.

The Measurement of the Model

The measurement of the model of effort-reward imbalance is largely restricted to self-report data, first, because it combines descriptive and evaluative information on perceived demands (effort) and rewards and, secondly, because it requires information on personal coping characteristics (overcommitment) in addition to information on structural characteristics of the work environment. Moreover, information on more distant working conditions, both in terms of place and time, can hardly be collected by observer assessment or by other techniques of external data collection (e.g. job security, promotion prospects, adequacy of salary in view of training). Thus, assessment of effort-reward imbalance at work relies on indicators that are measured by psychometric scales containing Likert-scaled items. Essentially, three psychometric scales are measured (effort, reward, overcommitment), and the combination of information from these scales according to a pre-defined algorithm provides an opportunity of measuring the underlying latent construct (see below).

In its most economic version the standardized questionnaire contains 23 items, with six items measuring effort, 11 items measuring rewards, and six items measuring the personal coping pattern of overcommitment (short version; the original version of this psychometric scale contains 29 items; Siegrist, 1996). The items of this short version of the questionnaire are displayed in Table 1.

Items measuring effort and reward are answered in two steps. First, subjects agree or disagree on whether or not the item content describes a typical experience of their current or main work situation (dichotomous yes/no response). Subsequently, subjects who agree are asked to evaluate to what extent they usually feel distressed by this typical experience (4 point Likert-scale). Items measuring overcommitment are answered in one step where respondents are asked to indicate to what extent they personally agree or disagree with given statements (4 point Likert-scale).

Items of the effort scale include perceived quantitative and qualitative load, increase of work demands in recent past and perceived physical job demands (six items). The uni-dimensionality of the scale has been confirmed in several

Table 1. Items of the Scales Measuring Effort-reward Imbalance at Work (short version).

Effort scale:
   I have constant time pressure due to a heavy work load.
   I have many interruptions and disturbances in my job.
   I have a lot of responsibility in my job.
   I am often pressured to work overtime
   My job is physically demanding.
   Over the past few years, my job has become more and more demanding.

Reward scale:
   I receive the respect I deserve from my superiors.
   I receive the respect I deserve from my colleagues.
   I experience adequate support in difficult situations.
   I am treated unfairly at work.
   My job promotion prospects are poor.
   I have experienced or I expect to experience an undesirable change in my work situation.
   My job security is poor.
   My current occupational position adequately reflects my education and training.
   Considering all my efforts and achievements, I receive the respect and prestige I deserve at
      work.
   Considering all my efforts and achievements, my work prospects are adequate.
   Considering all my efforts and achievements, my salary/income is adequate.

Overcommitment scale:
   I get easily overwhelmed by time pressures at work.
   As soon as I get up in the morning I start thinking about work problems.
   When I get home, I can easily relax and 'switch off' work.
   People close to me say I sacrifice too much for my job.
   Work rarely lets me go, it is still on my mind when I go to bed.
   If I postpone something that I was supposed to do today I'll have trouble sleeping at night.

Source: www.uni-duesseldorf.de/MedicalSociology

studies, with the exception that the item on physical job demands does not load on the single factor in white collars and in other occupations characterized by absence of a physical load. Internal consistency (Cronbach's alpha) of the scales varies between 0.66 and 0.88.

The 11 items of the reward scale assess perceived adequacy of salary or wage, promotion prospects, job security and esteem experienced by superiors and colleagues. The three dimensions of reward are assumed to load on one latent factor. This assumption is tested by a second – order factor analysis defining a one-dimensional scale. Again a satisfactory model fit was observed in several studies, with acceptable internal consistency (Cronbach's alpha ranging from 0.70 to 0.91) (Niedhammer et al., 2000; Peter et al., 1998; Tsutsumi et al., 2001a).

Two crucial assumptions underlay the model and its measurement. First, as stated above, the imbalance between high effort and low reward defines the critical condition that affects health. In other words, a combination of these two sources of information is expected to explain more variation in health than an estimate of their separate effects. Secondly, according to the theory of affective processing (discussed earlier), only part of the flow of information resulting from the psychosocial environment is subject to conscious computational processing. It is unlikely that the costs and gains at work are subject to people's daily conscious appraisal. Rather, strain reactions and negative emotions elicited by experiences of non-reciprocal exchange at work may bypass conscious awareness, as is the case for a substantial part of affective processing in general. For instance, this is the case in people who for a long time have adapted themselves to an unfavorable work environment. Frequently, these people feel frustrated or distressed without consciously attributing specific work conditions as causes.

In accordance with these two assumptions it was proposed to assess the imbalance between effort and reward by a predefined algorithm based on information obtained from the two respective scales, effort and reward (Niedhammer et al., 2000; Peter et al., 1998; Pikhart et al., 2001). A ratio of the sum score of the effort scale (e) and of the sum score of the reward scale (r) is computed for every respondent according to the formula: $e/(r \times c)$ where c defines a correction factor for different numbers of items in the nominator and denominator. As a result, a value close to zero indicates a favorable condition (relatively low effort, relatively high reward) whereas values beyond 1.0 and close to 2.0 indicate a high amount of effort spent that is not met by the rewards received or expected in turn.

The construction of this ratio serves as an approximate estimate of the costs and gains experienced in everyday working life that are not repeatedly subject to explicit reasoning on trade-off by working people themselves. The ratio thus may capture part of the strain reactions that would be missed if the measurement of imbalance were based exclusively on subjective evaluations (i.e. stressful experience). Moreover, by defining an algorithm we can compare information of effort-reward imbalance between individuals and between groups.

This ratio represents a summary measure of the structural component of the model. As an independent predictor of health outcomes this ratio is either transformed into a binary variable (values ≤ 1.0 versus > 1.0) or is transformed logarithmically into a continuous measure. In this latter case less information is lost, thus offering the opportunity of testing dose-response relations between

effort-reward imbalance and health. Logarithmic transformation of the continuous scale is performed in order to place inverse imbalance of the same
magnitude (e.g. 0.5 and 2.0) in the same distance from 1.0 (where efforts and
rewards are equal).

The overcommitment scale contains six items in its recently developed short
version (Niedhammer et al., 2002). This short version is composed by those
items from the original version containing 29 items that accounted for most of
the larger scale's power in explaining health risks in prospective epidemiologic
studies. Again, the factorial structure of the scale and its internal consistency
was analyzed (Cronbach's alpha ranging from 0.72 to 0.86). In line with
previous analyses a binary variable was computed with scores in the upper
tertile defining a critical level of overcommitment vs. the remaining group with
scores indicating no or moderate overcommitment.

In summary, to test whether the model of effort-reward imbalance predicts
health risks two summary measures enter statistical analysis (usually multivariate
logistic regression analysis): the ratio e/r and the score 'overcommitment'. The
model predicts that each summary measure is associated with an increased health
risk. Evidence on this hypothesis is discussed below. An additional assumption
has been derived from the theoretical model. As stated earlier, the effect of non-
reciprocal exchange at work on health may be particularly strong in people who
score high on overcommitment. Thus, the association of the ratio e/r with health
may be moderated by the level of overcommitment, producing strongest effects in
the group of people who score high on this pattern of coping. Preliminary evidence
of this additional hypothesis is discussed below.

Two critical comments on this measurement approach need to addressed.
First, it has been claimed that self-reported measures of occupational stress
may be influenced by certain personal dispositions such as negative affectivity
(Chen & Spector, 1991). Therefore, it is not clear to what extent the measurement reflects personal traits as opposed to perceived exposure to a stressful
work environment. Moreover, the association with health outcomes may be
biased, especially so if self-reported health measures are used. Therefore, it is
important to explore whether the association of effort-reward imbalance with
health is weakened if a measure of negative affectivity is taken into account
in multivariate statistical analysis. Several studies have included this measure
and have shown that this is not the case to any substantial degree (Bosma et
al., 1998, Stansfeld, 1998, 1999, 2000). In addition, associations of self-
reported work stress measures with objectively assessed health indicators, as
those studied in the majority of investigations reported below, are less likely
to be subject to this type of measurement error. Finally, several attempts were
made to validate self-reported measures of effort-reward imbalance at work by

external assessment or contextual information (Schnall et al., 2000). All these strategies are helpful in an attempt towards strengthening the validity of reported findings.

A second comment concerns the use of a ratio scale instead of single scales of the model. It is hypothesized that the imbalance between high effort and low reward, as reflected in the ratio e/r, produces adverse effects on health over and above the effects of single components. This hypothesis can be tested empirically, e.g. by comparing odds ratios of health indicators produced by single scales to those produced by the ratio e/r. Several investigations were conducted along these lines (Kuper et al., 2002; Peter et al., 1998). In one study it was shown that the odds ratio of poor mental functioning was almost twice as high when using the ratio as compared to the effort scale, and was substantially higher as compared to the reward scale (Kuper et al., 2002). A similar observation was made concerning incident coronary heart disease. A somewhat different strategy of calculating the imbalance between effort and reward was developed in earlier studies, including the first test of the model in the prospective Whitehall II study in Great Britain (see below). In these studies, indicators of effort and of reward were used to create an effort-reward imbalance measure which had three categories: 1 = neither high effort nor low reward; 2 = either high effort or low reward; and 3 = both high efforts and low rewards. This measure was thought to reflect the theoretically postulated cumulative effect of the two components (Bosma et al., 1998). In all respective cases increasing odds ratios were observed from the lowest to the highest category, with a substantial increase between the second and the last category (Bosma et al., 1998; Jonge et al., 2000; Stansfeld et al., 1998, 1999, 2000). Although this issue needs further evaluation current evidence confirms an effect size of health produced by the mismatch between effort and reward that exceeds the effect size of single components.

EMPIRICAL EVIDENCE

This section contains three parts. The first part summarizes results from prospective and cross-sectional epidemiological investigations of an association between occupational stress (in terms of the model of effort-reward imbalance) and cardiovascular risk and disease. Cardiovascular risk and disease, and especially coronary heart disease (CHD), have been chosen as health indicators for three reasons. First, they define a highly prevalent condition in adult life and, thus, make a significant contribution to the burden of disease of total populations (Murray & Lopez, 1996). Secondly, evidence of a pathophysiological role of chronic strain is particularly well substantiated in CHD and its most important risk factors (Stansfeld & Marmot, 2002). Thirdly, CHD has been studied rather extensively in association with models of psychosocial occupational stress (Schnall et al., 2000).

The second part contains information on indicators of health and well being that are less well defined in biomedical terms. Indicators include self-report measures of affective disorders, alcohol dependence, perceived symptoms (e.g. musculoskeletal, psychosomatic), and of self-rated health. As indicated these health complaints define a substantial part of work-related human suffering, and they determine a large amount of the health expenditures attributable to occupational stress.

In the third part, evidence obtained from laboratory studies is discussed as this scientific approach supplements epidemiologic information in a substantial way. So far, few studies only have tested the model in laboratory or experimental designs.

Cardiovascular Risk And Disease

Six studies have reported findings with partial or full confirmation of the model's basic hypotheses about cardiovascular risk and disease. An overview of the major studies is given in Table 2. Three of these studies are prospective: a German study of blue-collar workers, covering some 2,000 person-years (Siegrist et al., 1990), the Whitehall II study of British civil servants where 10,308 men and women were followed in an observational prospective study over a mean 5.3 years (Bosma et al., 1998), and a Swedish cohort study of some 5,720 healthy employed men and women (baseline only) (Peter et al., 1998). Two studies are cross-sectional, one representing a large case-control study of 951 male and female coronary heart disease patients and 1,147 controls (Peter et al., 2002), and one analyzing associations of psychosocial work stress with cardiovascular risk factors in a group of 179 male middle-managers (Siegrist et al., 1997). A follow-up study of 106 coronary patients who underwent coronary angioplasty was conducted to explore the role of effort-reward imbalance in predicting coronary stenosis (Joksimovic et al., 1999).

With regard to incident coronary heart disease during a mean five year observation period, effort-reward imbalance assessed at baseline was associated with a relative risk 2 to 4.5 times higher than in those who were free from chronic work stress. This excess risk could not be explained by established biomedical behavioral risk factors, as these variables were taken into account in multivariate statistical analysis. Given its large sample size and the inclusion of men and women the Whitehall II study is particularly interesting in this respect.

As the original questionnaire measuring effort-reward imbalance was not part of the initial screening, but was included at a later stage, proxy measures were derived for risk estimation. This study of civil servants found that among those men and women who were characterized by an imbalance between cost and gain at work the age and sex adjusted risk of coronary heart disease was more than three times as high compared to the risk of employees who were free from stress at work. After additional adjustment for socio-economic status, negative affectivity and major coronary risk factors, the odds ratio was still 2.15 (confidence intervals: 1.15, 4.01; Bosma et al., 1998; see Table 2). Meanwhile, results on incidence of coronary heart disease over a period of 11 years are available from the same study. A recent analysis revealed that effort-reward imbalance at baseline still predicted disease incidence significantly although less strongly than after five years (Kuper at al., 2002).

Adjusting for major cardiovascular risk factors in multivariate statistical models, such as hypertension, hyperlipidemia or elevated fibrinogen, might result in 'overadjustment' as these risk factors are partly influenced by stress-induced sustained activation of the autonomic nervous system as well. Indeed, several cross-sectional investigations have documented associations of effort-reward imbalance and the prevalence of hypertension, hyperlipidemia or a co-manifestation of these two cardiovascular risk factors (Peter et al., 1998; Marmot et al., 2002). In this context preliminary findings from an investigation conducted in female blue-collar workers in China are of interest given their potential public health significance. Most of these women were married and had to cope with the burden of double roles. Suffering from role conflicts between work and home and suffering from low reward at work were both associated with an elevated prevalence of hypertension, in addition to established risk factors such as overweight and cigarette smoking (Xu et al., 2000).

These findings demonstrate that the explanatory power of the model goes beyond disease manifestation by enabling a more comprehensive definition of people at risk at an earlier stage of disease development. Even in those suffering from manifest coronary heart disease, the model is useful in predicting the further course of disease. For example, one study found a powerful independent effect of overcommitment on the risk of coronary restenosis following successful angioplastic treatment. These findings are supplemented by the observation that components of the model contribute to a characterization of differences between coronary patients and healthy controls.

Further evidence is derived from a Finnish prospective study that did not provide an explicit measure of the model, but documented a significantly elevated risk hazard of cardiovascular mortality (RH: 2.3) among men whose work was defined by a combination of high demands with low income, a finding that the authors interpreted in the framework of the effort-reward imbalance model (Lynch et al., 1997a). In the same study it was also found that progression of carotid atherosclerosis, as established by ultrasound technique, was most advanced in the subgroup of workers exposed to high demands and low economic rewards (Lynch et al., 1997b).

Results also underline the importance of gender or gender role specific interpretations of the work-strain link. In general, models of occupational stress have been designed in a gender (role)-blind manner, as it was assumed that the quality and intensity of stressful experience and of strain reactions do not vary according to gender. However, associations between work strain and disease were more often established in men than in women, especially so with respect to the demand-control model (Schnall et al., 2000). It may well be that a substantial part of stressful experience at work is contingent on the perceived threats associated with one's occupational position, and that men, as a result of socialized gender roles, are generally more vulnerable to these threats than women. For instance, in terms of the social-cognitive theory of gender differentiation (Bussey & Bandura, 1999) women may be better suited to combine different roles or to change roles with more flexibility and, thus, to profit from multiple sources of self-efficacy and self-esteem. Men, on the contrary, more often stick to their occupational role rather exclusively as it provides a major source of their self-reliance.

Broadly speaking, socio-cultural factors influence the appraisal of demands and threats in salient social roles in adult life, and these influences are embedded in gendered practices of coping. Models of work stress might be designed in a way that take these considerations into account.

Interestingly, in one of the studies reported in Table 2, comparing cardiovascular risk in men and women in Sweden, differential effects of the two components of the model of effort-reward imbalance according to gender (role) were observed. In men, the threats of occupational status in terms of low control and low reward were more strongly associated with cardiovascular risk than in women. Conversely in women, inadequate or excessive ways of personal coping with the demands at work (overcommitment) predicted disease risk more strongly than in men (Peter et al., 1998). In a more recent investigation, the case-control study of myocardial infarction patients and healthy controls mentioned, the same pattern was observed again (Peter et al., 2002). It is certainly premature to evaluate the relevance of gender (role) in explaining links between occupational stress and health. Yet, these suggestions point to the promise of developing and interpreting models of work strain with more concern about gender issues.

In conclusion, there is now some support in favor of the stress theoretical assumption that high cost/low gain conditions at work are associated with an

Table 2. Studies of Effort-reward Imbalance and Cardiovascular Risk (overview).

First author (year)	Type of study	Cardiovascular outcome*	High effort/low reward (ERI) and/or over-commitment (OC)	Odds ratio (OR)
• Siegrist 1990	prospective	acute MI, SCD, subclinical CHD	ERI + OC	ranging from 3.4–4.5
• Bosma 1998	prospective	newly reported CHD	ERI + OC†	2.2
• Peter 1998	cross-sectional	prevalence of hypertension	ERI only	♂ 1.6
		prevalence of high LDL cholesterol	OC only	♀ 1.3
• Peter 2002	case-control	acute MI versus healthy control (men)	ERI only	1.7
• Siegrist 1997	cross-sectional	prevalence of high LDL cholesterol	ERI only	3.5
• Joksimovic 1999	semiprospective	coronary restenosis following CHD	OC only	2.8

* Abbreviations:
CHD = coronary heart disease.
LDL = low density lipoprotein cholesterol.
MI = myocardial infarction.
SCD = sudden cardiac death.

†: proxy measure of effort-reward imbalance at work.

increased risk of cardiovascular disease. Results illustrate that a combination of information on perceived structural conditions and on personal coping characteristics has more explanatory power than an approach that is restricted to only one of these two model components.

Other Health Indicators

In the Whitehall II study the model was explored with respect to additional health outcomes. These include new reports of mild to moderate psychiatric disorders, subjective health functioning, and alcohol dependence (Stansfeld et al., 1998, 1999, 2000). In all instances, significant associations were observed. Five further studies, all using the original measures of the model, gave additional evidence (see Table 3).

One investigation was conducted in 190 male and female employees of a small Japanese plant with economic hardship. After adjustment for age, gender, occupational status and job type the ratio of effort and reward was associated with a 3.75 increased risk of depression. Similarly, the odds ratio of overcommitment was 3.10 (Tsutsumi et al., 2001b).

In another study conducted in four post-communist countries in Central and Eastern Europe in a total of 3,941 working subjects the age-sex adjusted odds ratio of the binary measure of effort-reward imbalance for poor self-rated health was 2.65 (Pikhart et al., 2001).

Furthermore, this study provides clear evidence on the assumption that a logarithmically transformed continuous measure of the ratio is superior to the binary measure in statistical terms.

Three additional studies were conducted in the United States and in Germany, respectively. 258 room cleaners in four large hotels in San Francisco reported increased risks of low back pain, upper back pain, severe bodily pain, psychosomatic symptoms and poor self-rated health when exposed to effort-reward imbalance at work (Rugulies & Krause, 2000). Similarly, in a group of 316 male and female employees of a public transport enterprise in Germany scoring high on overcommitment was associated with musculoskeletal pain in the neck, in the hip and in lower extremities (Joksimovic et al., 2002).

Burnout is an important marker of reduced well being and increased illness susceptibility. In a study of burnout in 202 nurses of a German university hospital strong associations of the ratio of effort-reward with emotional exhaustion and depersonalization were observed. Moreover, scores on both scales measuring burn-out were increased in nurses with a high level of overcommitment as indicated by a significant interaction term of the ratio e/r and overcommitment (Bakker et al., 2000; Killmer, 1999). Additional tests of a moderating effect on health of overcommitment were conducted in two large scale studies, a representative cross-section survey of 1,636 employed Dutch men and women exploring associations of occupational stress with different measures of well being (Jonge et al., 2000) and the above mentioned Whitehall II study (Kuper et al., 2002). In this latter study a moderating role of work-related social support was also explored. Interestingly, in the group of civil servants who scored high on the ratio e/r (upper quartile) and who reported a low level of social support at work the risk of fatal or non-fatal acute myocardial infarction was 2.3-fold increased compared to the risk of those who were free from this imbalance.

Table 3. Studies of Effort-reward Imbalance and Other Health Outcomes (overview).

First author (year)	Type of study	Health outcome*	High effort/low reward (ERI) and/or over-commitment (OC)	Odds ratio (OR)
• Stansfeld 1998	prospective	functioning: physical (I), mental (II), social (III)	ERI + OC†	I II III ♂ 1.4 1.7 1.6 ♀ 2.0 2.3 1.8
• Stansfeld 1999	prospective	psychiatric disorder	ERI + OC†	♂ 2.5 ♀ 1.6
• Stansfeld 2000	prospective	alcohol dependence (men)	ERI + OC†	1.9
• Tsutsumi 2001	cross-sectional	depression	ERI OC	3.7 3.1
• Pikhart 2001	cross-sectional	self-rated health	ERI	2.6
• Rugulies 2000	cross-sectional	back pain psychosomatic symptoms, self-rated health	ERI	ranging from 1.9–3.6
• Killmer 1999	cross-sectional	burn-out: exhaustion (I), de-personalization(II)	ERI OC	I II 3.6 2.0 1.8 2.3
• Joksimovic 2002	cross-sectional	musculoskeletal pain	ERI OC	ranging from 1.9–4.3

†: proxy measure of effort-reward imbalance at work

In summary, effort-reward imbalance at work is now considered a significant risk factor for the development of stress-related diseases and ill-health, in particular coronary heart disease, depression, some forms of addiction and poor self-rated health. Current evidence indicates that adverse effects on health are prevalent among men and women in midlife and early old life, and that these effects are not restricted to modern Western societies. The ubiquity and intensity of stressful experience elicited by failed reciprocity points to the evolutionary significance of this norm of social exchange. It will be an important scientific task to explore the pathways leading from conditions of social reward deficiency to stress-related diseases with a particular focus on the brain's reward system (Siegrist, 2000).

Laboratory Studies

Few investigations have explored the model in laboratory study designs. Laboratory research provides an important extension of evidence received from field epidemiologic studies as it contributes to an exploration of psychobiologic pathways that may underlie the association of occupational stress with bodily dysfunction and disease (Steptoe & Marmot, 2002).

In one study, 68 healthy middle-aged men defined according to different levels of effort-reward imbalance at work underwent a mental stress test (a modified version of the Stroop-color-word conflict task). All subjects were middle-managers of a large car producing company in Germany. Heart rate, blood pressure, adrenaline, noradrenaline and cortisol before, during and after the stress experiment were assessed. In the high work strain group (high effort-reward imbalance), significantly lower responsiveness (difference between base line and maximal stress) in heart rate, adrenaline and cortisol was found compared to men with lower levels of work strain (Siegrist et al., 1997b). Trends were similar, but not statistically significant for systolic blood pressure and noradrenaline.

Although surprising at first glance results can be interpreted in the frame of a two-stage model of reactivity. According to this model recurrent high cardiovascular and hormonal responsiveness to challenge (stage 1) in the long run results in attenuated autonomic and neuro-chemical strain reactions mirroring functional adaptation to excessive stimulation (due to chronically high work strain) in peripheral and central nervous system signal transmission (stage 2). At present, however, this hypothesis has not been adequately tested (see also Schaubroeck & Ganster, 1993).

A second study was undertaken in 109 male white-collar employees of a Dutch computer company selected from a larger sample according to high vs. low scoring on the scales of the model (ratio/effort-reward and overcommitment). These men participated in an ambulatory cardiovascular monitoring on three days of the same work week. Blood pressure (BP), heart rate (HR) and a proxy measure of heart rate variability derived from a three-lead ECG (RMSSD: root mean square of successive differences in R-wave to R-wave interbeat intervals were assessed (Vrijkotte et al., 2000)). Figure 2 gives the summary results of this study.

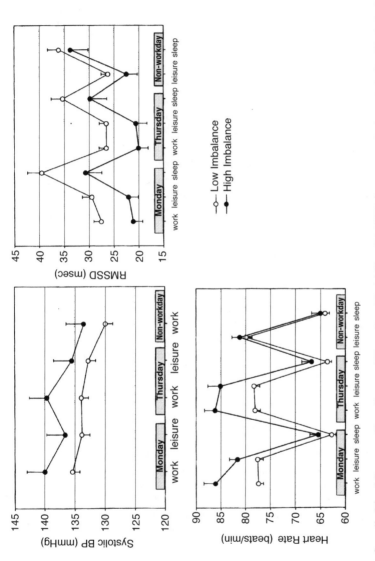

Fig. 2. Systolic Blood Pressure, Heart Rate and Heart Rate Variability (RMSSD) (mean, standard error) during Work, Leisure and Sleep (only heart rate and RMSSD) on Two Work Days and One Non-workday for High and Low Imbalance Group.

Note: BP = Blood Pressure. RMSSD = Root mean square of successive differences.
Source: T. Vrijkotte et al. 2000 (reproduced with permission).

Men classified as having high imbalance had significantly higher work and home systolic BP than men with low or no imbalance. No respective effect was found for diastolic BP. The high work stress group also exhibited significantly higher levels of HR during work, but not during sleep. Finally, data show a trend for the measure of heart rate variability to be lower in the high work strain group during all periods of monitoring (F = 3.7; $p = 0.059$). This latter finding is of special interest as low vagal tone was found to be a risk factor of future hypertension (Sing et al., 1998).

In this study overcommitment was not associated with the three indicators of cardiovascular reactivity, but was found to be highly correlated with indicators of a disturbed metabolic system (changes in insulin, glucose and plasminogen activator inhibitor; see Vrijkotte et al., 1999).

Laboratory evidence of associations of effort-reward imbalance at work with markers of psychobiologic pathways so far is limited. Yet, the few findings available suggest that it is worth exploring these links in further studies that combine the strengths of both the epidemiologic and the laboratory approach.

DISCUSSION

Similarities And Differences Between Models Of Occupational Stress

Despite a growing body of empirical support for the main propositions of the model, relevant challenges are given for further research and policy. Three such challenges are briefly discussed here. The first discussion concerns the similarities and differences between this model and complementary or alternative theoretical formulations of occupational stress, most importantly the demand-control model (or the extended demand-support-model; (Karasek & Theorell, 1990)) mentioned earlier.

There are several similarities between the two models. First, they both represent general models of work stress with a selective analytical focus. Secondly, they are both measured by a standardized self-administered questionnaire where data analysis is conducted according to predefined procedures. However, the demand-control model is open to alternative or supplementary measures (e.g. expert/observer assessment of job characteristics, imputation of job characteristics scores (Schnall et al., 2000)). Finally, not surprisingly, there is a strong conceptual and methodological overlap between the two scales of demand and effort.

Yet, there are clear conceptual and methodological differences as well. First, the demand-control model has been introduced and measured as a concept that is restricted to the structural aspects of the psychosocial work environment whereas the effort-reward imbalance model includes both structural and personal characteristics. Secondly, the demand-control model offers a broader approach as its bi-directional conceptualization includes a stress dimension with relevance to health and a skill dimension with relevance to personal growth and development: active jobs characterized by high demands and a high degree of control and opportunities for skill utilization promote personal growth and feelings of mastery (Karasek & Theorell, 1990). In this regard, the model presented here is more narrowly focused on the biopsychosocial determinants of health and well being.

Third, components of the effort-reward imbalance model (salaries, career opportunities/job security) are linked to more distant macro-economic labor market conditions while the demand-control model's major focus is on work place characteristics. Fourth, in stress theoretical terms, Karasek's approach is rooted in the stress theoretical paradigm of control whereas the effort-reward imbalance model fits better with the stress theoretical paradigm of social reward (see above). Finally, the two different stress theoretical orientations have different implications for policy: whereas the control paradigm points to the structure of power, division of labor and democracy at work, the reward paradigm addresses the issue of distributive justice and fairness.

Apart from these differences the two models offer opportunities for combining information on work strain and health, especially so in view of a close correspondence between the two stress-theoretical paradigms of control and reward. In working life, conditions of low control and low reward often cumulate within specific occupational groups. Therefore, it seems promising to study the combined effects on health produced by both models discussed so far. In fact, preliminary evidence from a large scale study indicates that combined effects of the two models on cardiovascular health are considerably stronger than their separate effects (Peter et al., 2002). Moreover, in the Whitehall II Study (Bosma et al., 1998) it was found that the demand-control model (the control dimension only) and the effort-reward imbalance model were equally strong independent predictors of reports of incident coronary heart disease when appropriate statistical controls were performed. In addition, new reports of anginal complaints were most frequent in the subgroup of civil servants who where simultaneously exposed to low control at work and to high effort-reward imbalance. There is now a growing number of studies available that contain information on both models and, thus, explore their separate and combined effects on health.

Several other general concepts of work stress have been proposed and tested, most notably the person environment fit model (Edwards et al., 1998) and models based on equity theory in social psychology (Walster et al., 1978). While the person environment fit model has brought substantial conceptual and methodological innovations into the field of occupational stress several years ago, it still remains difficult to assess its ability of predicting adverse health effects. As the model is rather complex it seems difficult to deduce and test predictions in an unequivocal way.

Equity theory underlies the dual-level social exchange model (van Dierendonck et al., 1996, 2001). According to this model the cognitive evaluation of an exchange relationship precedes distress. Inequity in exchange is perceived as distressing if the input-outcome association is unfavorable in relation to that of a comparison other. Equity theory predicts a curvilinear relationship between equity and distress: perceiving oneself as deprived as well as perceiving oneself as advantaged evokes distress. Accordingly, receiving too much is considered as detrimental as receiving too little. This proposition clearly differs from the model of effort-reward imbalance where inappropriately low gain only matters for adverse outcomes. This conclusion is in accordance with evidence derived from neuroscience research showing that affective responses are faster and stronger to proximate negative events than to positive ones (Gehring & Willoughby, 2002). Contrary to equity theory the notion of reciprocity is not identical with symmetric exchange in the effort-reward imbalance model. Rather, contracts in occupational life are most often non-symmetric. Reciprocity in this context simply means that the exchange is based on a social norm which is shared by both parties. In fact, the terms of trade between employer and employee have been, and continue to be unbalanced within agreed upon limits.

This difference between reciprocity and equity results in different modeling of their association with strain: in the effort-reward imbalance model a linear dose-response relation is postulated between the amount of imbalance and the intensity of strain reactions. Conversely, equity theory assumes a curvilinear relationship where deviation from symmetry in both directions is associated with strain.

Additional distinctions of the effort-reward imbalance model concern its sociological foundation of structural components of non-reciprocal exchange in the work life and the assumption that this notion can be transferred to other core social roles in adult life (see below). Moreover, an explicit modeling of structural and personal components contributing to strain, as specified in this model, could not be identified in the dual-level social exchange model mentioned.

Apart from conceptual considerations a number of methodological issues need to be discussed in future research. With respect to the measurement of effort-reward imbalance at work they concern additional information on the conceptual or concurrent validity of the scales, a further replication of the factorial structure of the scales using structural equation modeling and more emphasis on justification of the ratio approach chosen to translate the core notion of imbalance into statistical analysis (e.g. as distinct from a multiplicative interaction term in a hierarchical regression model). Moreover, with increasing application of these scales in comparative international studies, item content analysis and exploration of cross-cultural semantic equivalence will define tasks of high priority.

The Work – Non-Work Interface

Having discussed similarities and differences of models of occupational stress a further issue concerns the work – non-work link in stress research. If the general assumption of the theoretical approach presented above holds true we can expect similar adverse effects on health produced by conditions of effort-reward imbalance that are generated in other core social roles (e.g. partnership, family). In fact, an extension of the model beyond work is now being developed.

Despite the fact that there are marked differences between the reciprocity of social exchange at work and outside work that concern the pervasiveness of demands and the nature of social rewards, non-reciprocal exchange is neverthe-less frequently observed in marital and parental roles. In these conditions of an imbalance between one's investments made in advance and unmet, though justified reward expectancies intense feelings of injustice, unfairness and goal frustration are aroused. The same may apply to different civic roles in adult life (e.g. voluntary work, membership in organizations, neighborhood exchange). Preliminary results indicate that non-reciprocity in marital life, between parents and children and in civic life is associated with an increased probability of suffering from depressive symptoms (Knesebeck & Siegrist, 2002).

In future research the interface between work and non-work settings, in particular work and family, needs to be explored more thoroughly. Three terms have been suggested in this context: 'spillover', 'compensation' and 'cumulation'. Cumulation describes the fact that critical components of strain experience, such as lack of control or effort-reward imbalance, generalize across different life domains. Spillover refers to transfer of experience and behavior from one domain to the other, whereas compensation represents efforts to reduce strain in one domain by improving satisfaction in another domain.

Ideally, an adequate assessment of long-term social stressors in adult life and associated strain reactions would require the simultaneous evaluation of salient social roles available to a person, their suitability for compensation of loss or non-reciprocity, and their cumulative burden under deprived conditions. Failed role compensation or role transition is likely to elicit most intense strain reactions (Siegrist, 2001b).

Policy Implications

What are the policy implications of this new information on occupational stress and health? First, it is possible to identify dimensions of work-related strain in a wide range of occupations using standardized, psychometrically validated questionnaires. The questionnaires measuring the effort-reward imbalance model, and similarly the job-content questionnaire measuring the demand-control model (Karasek et al., 1998), are now available in a number of languages internationally. Thus, additional scientific evidence on associations between adverse psychosocial work environments and health indicators in working populations can be obtained. Secondly, apart from scientific interests, it is possible to apply these measures in everyday work. For instance, the amount of work-related strain can be assessed in order to develop and implement intervention measures. Or, it can be used as a frame of reference for quality assurance comparing the performance of different teams, departments, or institutions.

A further application concerns legal procedures and compensation claims regarding the afflictions of work life on health. Here again, quantified, evidence-based information can be useful to support the decision making processes. Yet, it should be mentioned that quantitative evidence on the proportion of a health risk that is attributable to work-related strain is confined to the level of populations, not individuals. Thus, the 'etiological fraction' that is attributable to adverse work conditions can hardly be transferred to the individual case, for instance in the context of justification of a compensation claim (Rockhill et al., 1998).

Probably the most significant policy implication of the information provided above concerns the design and implementation of worksite stress prevention and health promotion programs. Both approaches of effort-reward imbalance and demand-control offer specific suggestions in this respect. Whereas propositions derived from the demand-control model are related to measures of job redesign, job enlargement, job enrichment, skill training and enhanced participation (Karasek, 1992), the current model's focus is on improvements of the exchange between efforts and reward. Examples of such measures include the development of compensatory wage systems, the provision of models of gain sharing and the strengthening of non-monetary gratifications. Moreover, ways of improving promotional opportunities and job security need to be explored. Supplementary measures are interpersonal training and social skills development, in particular leadership behavior. For instance, one recent stress management intervention based on the model was successfully applied in a group of highly stressed inner-city bus drivers. Stress management techniques may also aim at reducing excess levels of overcommitment among employees, thus enabling them to assess cost-gain relations at work more accurately (Aust et al., 1997).

It is evident that the usefulness for policy measures resulting from a 'general' as opposed to a 'situation specific' assessment of occupational stress is limited (Cooper, 1998; Kompier & Kristensen, 2001; Belkic et al., 2000). Yet it is equally true that successfully implemented policy measures derived from general models can have far reaching impact, especially so if they contribute to business priorities in terms of economic success. For instance, an important recent study has indicated that measures such as employment security, selective hiring of new personnel, decentralization of decision making, comparatively high compensation contingent on performance, and extensive training of employees produce economic benefits, apart from their beneficial effects on health and well being (Pfeffer, 1998).

In conclusion, significant progress has been achieved in the scientific study of links between occupational stress, health and well being. While further tasks remain to be solved by researchers the main challenge now consists in reducing the gap between science and policy.

REFERENCES

Aust, B., Peter R., & Siegrist, J. (1997). Stress management in bus drivers. A pilot study based on the model of effort-reward imbalance. *International Journal of Stress Management, 4*, 297–305.

Bakker, A. B., Killmer, C., Siegrist, J., & Schaufeli, W. B. (2000). Effort-reward imbalance and burnout among nurses. *Journal of Advanced Nursing, 31*, 884–891.

Bartley, M., Ferrie, J., & Montgomery, S. M. (1999). Living in a high-unemployment economy: understanding the health consequences. In: M. Marmot & R. Wilkinson (Eds), *Social Determinants of Health* (pp. 81–104). Oxford: Oxford University Press.

Belkic, K., Schnall, P., Savic, C., & Landsbergis, P. (2000). Multiple exposures: a model of total occupational burden. In: P. L. Schnall, K. Belkic, P. Landsbergis & D. Bakker (Eds), *The Workplace and Cardiovascular Disease* (pp. 94–106). Occupational medicine: State of the Art Reviews, 15.

Blum, K., Cull, J. G., Braverman, E. R., & Comings, D. E. (1996). Reward deficiency syndrome: Addictive, impulsive and compulsive disorders – including alcoholism, attention-deficit disorders, drug abuse and food bingeing – may have a common genetic basis. *American Scientist, 84*, 132–145.

Bosma, H., Peter, R., Siegrist, J., & Marmot, M. (1998). Two alternative job stress models and the risk of coronary heart disease. *American Journal of Public Health, 88*, 68–74.

Bussey, K., & Bandura, A. (1999). Social cognitive theory of gender development and differentiation. *Psychological Review, 106*, 676–713.

Chen, P. Y., & Spector, P. K. (1991). Negative affectivity as the underlying cause of correlations between stressors and strains. *Journal of Applied Psychology, 76*, 398–407.

Cooper, C. L. (Ed.) (1998). *Theories of organizational stress.* Oxford: Oxford University Press.

Cosmides, L., & Tooby, J. (1992). Cognitive adaptations for social exchange. In: J. H. Barkow, L. Cosmides & J. Tooby (Eds), *The Adapted Mind: Evolutionary Psychology and the Generation of Culture* (pp. 163–228). New York: Oxford University Press.

Dunham, J.(2001). *Stress in the workplace: Past, present and future.* London: Whurr.

Edwards, J. R., Caplan, R. D., & van Harrison, R. (1998). Person-environment fit. In: C. Cooper (Ed.), *Theories of Organizational Stress* (pp. 28–67). Oxford: Oxford University Press.

Fehr, E., & Gächter, S. (2000). Fairness and retaliation: the economics of reciprocity. *Journal of Economic Perspectives, 14,* 159–181.

Foner, N. (1993). When the contract fails: care for the elderly in non-industrialized countries. In: V. L. Bengstson & W. A. Achenbaum (Eds), *The Changing Contract Across Generations* (pp. 101–117). New York: Aldine.

Gehring, W. J., & Willoughby, A. R. (2002). The medial frontal cortex and the rapid processing of monetary gains and losses. *Science, 295,* 2279–2282.

House, J. (1981). *Work, stress and social support.* Reading MA: Addison-Wesley.

Joksimovic, L., Siegrist, J., Meyer-Hammer, M., Peter, R., Franke, B., Klimek, W., Heintzen, M., & Strauer, B. E. (1999). Overcommitment predicts restenosis after cronary angioplasty in cardiac patients. *International Journal of Behavioral Medicine, 6,* 356–369.

Jonge, J. de, Bosma, H., Peter, R., & Siegrist. J. (2000). Job strain, effort-reward imbalance and employee well being: A large-scale cross-sectional study. *Social Science & Medicine, 50,* 1317–1327.

Joksimovic, L., Starke, D., von dem Knesebeck, O., & Siegrist, J. (2002). Perceived workstress, overcommitment and self-reported musculoskeletal pain: a cross-sectional investigation. *International Journal of Behavioral Medicine, 9,* 122–138.

Karasek, R. (1992). Stress prevention through work reorganization: a summary of 19 international case studies. *Conditions of Work Digest, 11,* 23–41.

Karasek, R. A. (1979). Job demands, job decision latitude, and mental strain: implications for job redesign. *Administration Science Quarterly, 24,* 285–307.

Karasek, R. A., & Theorell, T. (1990). *Healthy work. Stress, productivity, and the reconstruction of working life.* New York: Basic Books.

Karasek, R., Brisson, C., Kawakami, N., Houtman, I., Bongers, P., & Amick, B. (1998). The job content questionnaire (JCQ): an instrument for internationally comparative assessments of psychosocial job characteristics. *Journal of Occupational Health Psychology, 4,* 322–355.

Killmer, C. (1999). *Burnout bei Krankenschwestern.* Münster: LIT-Verlag.

Knesebeck, O. v. d., & Siegrist, J. (2002): Reported non-reciprocity of social exchange and depressive symptoms: extending the model of effort-reward imbalance beyond work. *Journal of Psychosomatic Research* (in press).

Kohn, M., & Schooler, C. (1983). *Work and personality: An inquiry into the impact of social stratification.* Norwood, NJ: Abblex.

Koob, G. F., & Blum, F. E. (1988). Cellular and molecular mechanisms of drug dependence. *Science, 242,* 715–723.

Kompier, M. A. J., & Kristensen, T. S. (2001). Organizational work stress interventions in a theoretical, methodological and practical context. In: J. Dunham (Ed.), *Stress in the Work Place* (pp. 164–190). London: Whurr.

Kuper, H., Singh-Manoux, A., Siegrist, J., & Marmot, M. (2002). When reciprocity fails: effort-reward imbalance in relation to CHD and health functioning within the Whitehall II study. *Occupation and Environmental Medicine* (in press).

Lazarus, R. (1991). *Emotion and adaption.* New York: Oxford University Press.

LeDoux, J. (1996). *The emotional brain.* New York: Simon & Schuster.

Leigh, J. P., & Schnall, P. (2000). Costs of occupational circulatory disease. In: P. Schnall, K. Belkic, P. Landbergis & D. Bakker (Eds), *The Workplace and Cardiovascular Diseases* (pp. 257–268). Occupational Medicine: State of the Art Reviews, 15.

Levi, L., & Lunde Jensen, B. (1996). *A model for assessing the costs of stressors at national level.* Dublin: European Foundation for the Improvement of Living and Working Conditions.

Liu, J., & Mori, A. (1999). Stress, aging, and brain oxidative damage. *Neurochemical Research, 24,* 1479–1497.

Lynch, J., Krause, N., Kaplan, G. A., Tuomilehto, J., & Salonen, J. T. (1997a). Work place conditions, socioeconomic status, and the risk of mortality and acute myocardial infarction: the Kuopio ischemic heart disease risk factor study. *American Journal of Public Health, 87,* 617–622.

Lynch, J., Krause, N., Kaplan, G. A., Salonen, R., & Salonen, J. P. (1997b). Work place demands, economic reward, and progression of carotid atherosclerosis. *Circulation, 96,* 302–307.

Marmot, M., Theorell, T., & Siegrist, J. (2002). Work and coronary heart disease. In: S. A. Standfeld & M. G. Marmot (Eds), *Stress and the Heart* (pp. 50–71). London: BMJ Books.

Martikainen, P., & Valkonen, T. (1996). Excess mortality of unemployed men and women during a period of rapidly increasing unemployment. *Lancet, 348,* 909–912.

McEwen, B. S. (1998). Protective and damaging effects of stress mediators. *New England Journal of Medicine, 338,* 171–179.

Murray, C., & Lopez, A. (1996). *The Global Burden of Disease.* Cambridge: Harvard University Press.

Niedhammer, I., Siegrist, J., Landre, M. F., Goldberg, M., & Leclerc, A. (2000). Etudes de qualities psychométriques de la version francaise du modèle du Deséquilibre Efforts/Récompenses. *Revue d'Epidemiologie et de Sante Publique, 48,* 419–437.

Niedhammer, I., Tek, M. L., Starke, D., & Siegrist, J. (2002). Effort-reward imbalance model and self-reported health: cross-sectional and prospective results of the GAZEL cohort (Paper submitted).

Olds, M. E., & Olds, J. (1969). Effects of lesions in medial forebrain bundle on self-stimulation behavior. *American Journal of Physiology, 21,* 1253–1264.

Pearlin, L. I. (1989). The sociological study of stress. *Journal of Health and Social Behavior, 30,* 241–256.

Peter, R., Alfredson, L., Hammar, N., Siegrist, J., Theorell, T., & Westerholm, P. (1998). High effort, low reward, and cardiovascular risk factors in employed Swedish men and women: baseline results from the WOLF Study. *Journal of Epidemiology and Community Health, 52,* 540–547.

Peter, R., Siegrist, J., Hallqvist. J., Reuterwall, C., Theorell, T., & SHEEP Study Group (2002). Psychosocial work environment and myocardial infarction: improving risk estimation by combining two alternative job stress models in the SHEEP Study. *Journal of Epidemiology and Community Health, 56,* 294–300.

Pfeffer, J. (1998). *Human equation: building profits by putting people first.* Boston: Harvard Business School Press.

Pikhart, H., Bobak, M., Siegrist, J., Pajak, A., Rywik, S., Khyshegyi, J., Gostautas, A., Skodova, Z., & Marmot, M. (2001). Psychosocial work characteristics and self-rated health in four post-communist countries. *Journal of Epidemiology and Community Health, 55,* 624–630.

Popper, K. (1959) *The logic of scientific discovery.* London: Oxford University Press.

Rugulies, R., & Krause, N. (2000). The impact of job stress on musculoskeletal disorders, psycho-somatic symptoms and general health in hotel room cleaners. *International Journal of Behavioral Medicine, 7*(Supplement 1), 16.

Rockhill, B., Newman, B., & Weinberg, C. (1998). Use and misuse of population attributable fractions. *American Journal of Public Health, 88*, 15–19.

Sapolski, R. M. (1998). *Why Zebras don't get Ulcers.* New York: W. H. Freeman.

Schaubroeck, J., & Ganster, D. C. (1993). Chronic demands and responsivity to challenge. *Journal of Applied Psychology, 78*, 73–85.

Schnall, P. L., Belkic, K., Landsbergis, P., & Baker, D. (2000). The workplace and cardiovascular disease. *Occupational Medicine: State of the Art Reviews, 15*, 1–334.

Siegrist, J. (1984). Threat to social status and cardiovascular risk. *Psychotherapy & Psychosomatics, 42*, 90–96.

Siegrist, J. (1996). Adverse health effects of high effort – low reward conditions at work. *Journal of Occupational Health Psychology, 1*, 27–43.

Siegrist, J. (2000). Place, social exchange and health: proposed sociological framework. *Social Science & Medicine, 51*, 1283–1293.

Siegrist, J. (2001a). A theory of occupational stress. In: J. Dunham (Ed.), *Stress in the Workplace, Past, Present and Future* (pp. 53–66). London: Whurr.

Siegrist, J. (2001b). Long-term stress in daily life in a socio-epidemiologic perspective. In: T. Theorell (Ed.), *Everyday Biological Stress Mechanism* (pp. 91–103). Basel: Karger.

Siegrist, J., Klein, D., & Voigt, K. H. (1997). Linking sociological with physiological data: the model of effort-reward imbalance at work. *Acta Physiologica Scandinavia, 161*, 112–116.

Siegrist, J., Peter, R., Cremer, P., & Seidel, D. (1997). Chronic work stress is associated with atherogenic lipids and elevated fibrinogen in middle-aged men. *Journal of Internal Medicine, 242*, 149–156.

Siegrist, J., Peter, R., Junge, A., Cremer, P., & Seidel, D. (1990). Low status control, high effort at work and ischemic heart disease: Prospective evidence from blue-collar men. *Social Science and Medicine, 31*, 1127–1134.

Sing, J. P., Carson, M. G., Tsuij, A., Evans, J. C., O'Donnell, J. C., & Levy, D. (1998). Reduced heart rate variability and new-onset hypertension. *Hypertension, 32*, 293–297.

Skinner, E. A. (1996). A guide to constructs of control. *Journal of Personality and Social Psychology, 71*, 549–570.

Spector, P. E. (1998). A control theory of job stress process. In: C. E. Cooper (Ed.), *Theories of Organizational Stress* (pp. 153–169). Oxford: Oxford University Press.

Stansfeld, S., Bosma, H., Hemingway, H., & Marmot, M. (1998). Psychosocial work characteristics and social support as predictors of SF-36 functioning: the Whitehall II Study. *Psychosomatic Medicine, 60*, 247–255.

Stansfeld, S., Fuhrer, R., Shipley, M. J., & Marmot, M. G. (1999). Work characteristics predict psychiatric disorder: prospective results from the Whitehall II study. *Occupational and Environmental Medicine, 56*, 302–307.

Stansfeld, S., Head, J., & Marmot, M. (2000). *Work-related factors and ill health: The Whitehall II Study.* London: HSE Books.

Stansfeld, S., & Marmot, M. (Eds) (2002). *Stress and the heart. Psychosocial pathways to coronary heart disease.* London: BMJ Books.

Steptoe, A., & Appels, A. (Eds) (1989). *Stress, Personal Control and Health.* Wiley, Chichester.

Steptoe, A., & Marmot, M. (2002). The role of psychobiological pathways in socioeconomic inequalities in cardiovascular disease risk. *European Heart Journal, 23*, 13–25.

Tsutsumi, A., Kayaba, K., Theorell, T., & Siegrist, J. (2001a). Association between job stress and depression among Japanese employees threatened by job loss in comparison between two complementary job stress models. *Scandinavian Journal of Work and Environmental Health, 27*, 146–153.

Tsutsumi, A., Ishitake, T., Peter, R., Siegrist, J., & Matoba, T. (2001b). The Japanese version of the Effort-Reward-Imbalance Questionnaire: a study in dental technicians. *Work & Stress*, *15*, 86–96.

Van Dierendonk, D., Schaufeli, W. B., & Buunk, B. P. (1996). Inequity among human service professionals: measurement and relation to burnout. *Basic and Applied Social Psychology*, *18*, 429–451.

Van Dierendonk, D., Schaufeli, W. B., & Buunk, B. P. (2001). Burnout and inequity among human service professionals: a longitudinal study. *Journal of Occupational Health Psychology*, *6*, 43–52.

Vrijkotte, T. G. M., van Doornen, L. J. P., & de Geus, E. J. C. (1999). Work stress and metabolic and hemostatic risk factors. *Psychosomatic Medicine*, *61*, 796–805.

Vrijkotte, T. G. M., van Dooren, L. J. P., & de Geus, E. J. C. (2000). Effect of work stress on ambulatory blood pressure, heart rate, and heart rate variability. *Hypertension*, *35*, 880–886.

Walster, E., Walster, G. W., & Berscheid, E. (1978). *Equity: Theory and research*. Boston: Allyn & Bacon.

Weiner, H. (1992). *Perturbing the organism: the biology of stressful experiences*. Chicago: University of Chicago Press.

Xu, L. Y., Cao, J. W. U., Lee, L. M., & Critchley, J. A. J. H. (2000). Psychosocial stress and hypertension among working women in Beijing. *International Journal of Behavioral Medicine*, *7*(Supplement 1), 10.

WORKPLACE BULLYING AND STRESS

Helge Hoel, Dieter Zapf and Cary L. Cooper

ABSTRACT

This chapter explores the relationship between workplace bullying and occupational stress. Initially the concept of bullying and its defining features are introduced. Following a brief discussion of bullying and the stress process, an examination of possible stressors as antecedents of bullying is undertaken. Drawing on the empirical evidence available, individual and organizational effects and outcomes of bullying are described. Attention is also paid to the relationship between bullying and the coping process. It is concluded that, despite the fact that evidence is often sparse, a substantial body of research emerged within less than a decade, providing sufficient evidence to suggest that bullying is an important psychosocial hazard in the workplace with very substantial negative implications for individuals and organizations alike. Some methodological concerns are discussed and implications for future research highlighted.

INTRODUCTION

In most developed countries, the 1980s were described as the decade of the 'enterprise culture', with people working longer and harder to achieve individual success and material rewards. We had globalization, privatization, process

Historical and Current Perspectives on Stress and Health, Volume 2, pages 293–333.
Copyright © 2002 by Elsevier Science Ltd.
All rights of reproduction in any form reserved.
ISBN: 0-7623-0970-9

re-engineering, mergers and acquisitions, strategic alliances, joint ventures and the like, transforming workplaces into hot-house, free market environments.

In the short term, this entrepreneurial period improved economic competitiveness in international markets in the countries that embraced it. But as strains began to show, the concept of 'burnout' joined 'junk bonds', 'software packages' and 'e-mail' in the modern business vocabulary (Cooper, Dewe & O'Driscoll, 2001). Nevertheless, work was carried out essentially the same way as before; it was still business as usual in large or growing medium-sized organizations in U.K. Inc, U.K. Plc, Germany GmBH, and so on (Cooper & Jackson, 1997).

During the 1990s, a major restructuring of work, such as was unknown since the Industrial Revolution, was beginning to take place. Organizations throughout the U.K. and the Western world dramatically 'downsized', 'delayered', 'flattened' and 'rightsized'. Whatever euphemism you care to use, the hard reality experienced by many was year-on-year redundancy, constant restructuring and substantial organizational change. Now many organizations are smaller, with fewer people doing more and feeling much less secure. New technology, rather than being our saviour, has added the burden of information overload as well as accelerating the pace of work, as a greater speed of response (e.g. faxes, emails) becomes the standard business expectation.

As we enter the new millennium, many people believe that there are frequently social consequences of this changing nature of work. Some people have noticed a more robust and aggressive management style. The introduction of teamwork, though welcome from a psychological point of view in many respects, has, at the same time, increased mutual dependencies and, thus, the likelihood of conflicts. Moreover, streamlining the organizations has increased the pressure to be productive, but has reduced resources to develop good social relations and deal with negative side-effects such as interpersonal conflicts.

One of the consequences of these supposed changes is workplace bullying. This concept has been labeled differently in the European countries. Some people speak of 'mobbing' (Leymann, 1996; Zapf, Knorz & Kulla, 1996), 'harassment' (Björkqvist, Österman & Hjelt-Bäck, 1994), 'bullying' (Einarsen & Skogstad, 1996; Rayner, 1997; Vartia, 1996) 'victimization' (Einarsen & Raknes, 1997) or 'psychological terror'' (Leymann, 1990). However, they all mean more or less the same, namely the systematic mistreatment of a subordinate, a colleague, or a superior, which, if continued, may cause severe social, psychological and psycho-somatic problems in the person mistreated. Exposure to such treatment has been claimed to be a more crippling and devastating problem for employees than all other kinds of work-related stress put together, and is seen by many researchers and targets alike as an extreme type of social stress at work (Zapf, Knorz et al., 1996).

It is, therefore, natural that the relationship between bullying and stress features prominently in many studies of workplace bullying (e.g. Einarsen & Raknes, 1991; Zapf, Knorz et al., 1996). In part, this reflects the early focus on targets in bullying research, where the impact on the recipient of negative and aggressive behavior has traditionally received more attention than the unethical behavior on the part of perpetrators (Einarsen, Hoel, Zapf & Cooper, in press). In this respect, bullying was considered a subset of social stressors at work, or related to the social relationships within an organizational context. However, the wide variety of approaches in general use (Beehr, 1995; Sutherland & Cooper, 1990) is also reflected in the bullying literature (e.g. Leymann, 1996; Wilkie, 1996). For the purpose of this chapter, stress is understood in line with the transactional model of stress (Lazarus & Folkman, 1984) as the perceived imbalance between the internal and external demands facing an individual, and the perceived ability of the individual to cope.

Since the concept of bullying may be unknown to many readers, the concept and its defining features are discussed in some detail in the first part of the chapter. In the second part we will discuss bullying and its relation to stress. Bullying can both be understood as a response to stressors or stress, and it can be considered as a stressor affecting both the individual's health and the organization by leading to frequent absenteeism and turnover.

Thus, we will start by discussing situational factors which may act as antecedents of bullying as well as increase the vulnerability of targets or recipients of bullying behavior and contribute to their response to such acts. We will thereby follow the taxonomy of Cooper and Marshall (1976) and examine potential stressors relevant to bullying. Second, we will consider bullying as a stressor and discuss its effects on health. Third, we will discuss the organizational outcomes of bullying. Fourth, we will summarize findings on how people cope with bullying. The chapter will be concluded by discussing some implications for future research.

THE CONCEPT OF BULLYING

Bullying relates to persistent exposure to negative and aggressive behaviors of primarily a psychological nature (Einarsen, 1996; Hoel, Rayner & Cooper, 1999; Leymann, 1996). Victims of bullying are subjected to either direct or indirect forms of aggression. Among the direct forms of aggression, accusation in the form of persistent criticism of competence, work effort or results, appears to be central to many cases (Einarsen, Raknes, Matthiesen & Hellesøy, 1994; Thylefors, 1987). Moreover, verbal abuse or humiliating and belittling remarks belong to this category. More indirect types of aggressive behavior used in workplace bullying are gossiping and rumors which undermine the personal as well as the professional standing of the target (O'Moore et al., 1998), and which are "used with the aim or at least the effect of persistently humiliating, intimidating, frightening or punishing the victim" (Einarsen, 2000, p. 8). Finally, social exclusion or social isolation (Schuster, 1996) is used as a subtle and indirect form of aggression. Many of these acts may be relatively common in the workplace in interaction between employees and may not be so serious in isolation (Leymann, 1996), but when frequent and persistently directed towards the same individual they may be considered an extreme source of social stress (Zapf, 1999b) and become capable of causing severe harm and damage (e.g. Mikkelsen, 2001). In other words, bullying is not about single and isolated events where someone is being exposed to others' aggression (Einarsen, 2000). Rather, bullying is a process characterized by a series of negative behaviors systematically directed against a particular person.

The bullying process tends to evolve through a series of distinct phases or stages (Einarsen, 1999; Leymann, 1990, 1996). In line with Leymann (1990), Einarsen (1999) identified four stages of process development and referred to them as *aggressive behaviors, bullying, stigmatization* and *severe trauma*.

In many cases the negative behaviors in the first phase may be characterized as indirect aggression. They may be "subtle, devious and immensely difficult to confront" (Adams, 1992, p. 17) and even difficult to recognize for the persons being targeted (Leymann, 1996). Where bullying evolves out of a dispute or a conflict it may even at times be difficult to tell who may turn out to be the victim (Leymann, 1990). The initial phase, which in some cases can be very brief, tends to be followed by a stage of more direct negative behaviors, often leaving the target humiliated, ridiculed and increasingly isolated (Leymann, 1990). As a result, the targets become stigmatized and find it more and more difficult to defend themselves (Einarsen, 1999).

The frequency and intensity of the exposure also has the function of changing the meaning of the behavior (Leymann, 1996). Thus, the target would tend to feel hounded or at the mercy of someone whose aim is to 'get you' (Einarsen et al., 1999). Not surprisingly, the exposure to such treatment has a significant impact on the target. "The stigmatizing effects of these activities, and their escalating frequency and intensity, make the victims constantly less able to cope with his or her daily tasks and cooperation requirements of the job, thus becoming continually more vulnerable and 'a deserving target'" (Einarsen, 2000a, p. 8). Some researchers, notably Leymann (1990) argue that it is only at this second phase that the negative process has reached the stage of bullying.

Despite the severity of the situation, neither management nor work-colleagues are likely to interfere or take action in support of the victim. On the contrary, if victims complain they frequently experience disbelief and questioning of their own role. Such prejudices against victims often extend beyond management to include work colleagues, trade union representatives, and the medical profession (Leymann, 1996; O'Moore et al., 1998). When management becomes involved victims frequently find themselves being treated as 'a case' and their rights are often ignored or even violated (Leymann, 1990). Note that this does not mean that management and colleagues never successfully intervene in escalating conflict situations. If the interventions are successful, the conflict stops before it would normally be called bullying.

Victims, and their behavior, cannot be seen in isolation from the negative response they often receive and the effects that negative behaviors and the stigmatization process have on them. According to Field (1996), himself a victim of bullying, "the person becomes withdrawn, reluctant to communicate for fear of further criticism. This results in accusations of 'withdrawal', 'sullenness', 'not cooperating or communicating', 'lack of team spirit', etc. Dependence on alcohol, or other substances can then lead to impoverished performance, poor concentration and failing memory, which brings accusations of 'poor performance'" (p. 128). It has also been noted that the erratic and obsessive behavior of many victims may frequently cut them off from support within their own working environment, exacerbating their isolation and the victimization process (Leymann, 1987, 1993).

At this later stage in the process, victims are likely to experience increasingly harsh treatment, with psychological violence sometimes spilling over into physical violence. The situation is frequently marked by helplessness and, for many, lengthy sickness absences may be necessary to cope with the situation (Einarsen, Raknes, Matthiesen & Hellesøy, 1994). When the case enters this stage, victims are also often left with no role in the workplace, or with little or no meaningful work provided. Leymann (1990) refers to this last stage as 'expulsion', where victims are forced out of the workplace, either directly, by means of dismissal or redundancy or, more indirectly, where the victims consider their work situation so impossible that they decide to leave 'voluntarily'. 'They wanted to push me out of the company' was the most frequently reported reason for bullying from the victims' point of view in a study of Zapf (1999b).

Bullying As Opposed To Mobbing

As has been suggested in a previous section, the term 'bullying' has many connotations and may describe a wide variety of situations and experiences. Furthermore, behaviors which today in a British context may fit the term 'bullying' have been given other labels in other countries and in other contexts. In order to avoid confusion some consideration needs to be given to the potential difference between the terms 'bullying' and 'mobbing'.

According to Leymann (1996) the choice of the term 'mobbing' in preference to 'bullying' was a conscious decision. It reflected the fact that the phenomenon in question very often refers to subtle, less direct forms of aggression as opposed to the more physical aggression commonly identified with the term 'bullying', but with the same debilitating and stigmatizing effects. Zapf (1999b) who has adopted Leymann's view with regard to the distinction between the terms argued that 'mobbing' is often concerned with aggression from a group of people, and that this aggression tends to be directed towards one single person. By contrast, Matthiesen et al. (1989) used the term 'mobbing' to refer to aggression from one or more persons against a group as well as against an individual.

Whilst 'bullying' has often been the preferred term in English-speaking countries (e.g. the U.K. and Australia), the term 'mobbing' has recently been introduced as a concept separate from bullying by some researchers in the U.S. (Davenport et al., 1999) and by the International Labour Organization (ILO) (Chappell & Di Martino, 2000). In line with Zapf's (1999b) interpretation of the term, the ILO refers to it as "ganging-up or mobbing a target employee and subjecting that person to psychological harassment" (p. 13). According to this author, 'bullying' is also particularly concerned with aggression from someone in a managerial or supervisory position (e.g. Adams, 1992). However, Einarsen (1996), currently the most prolific contributor in the field, made no distinction between bullying and mobbing, neither with regard to the number of perpetrators or targets involved nor with respect to the organizational status of the perpetrator.

As far as perpetrator status is concerned, Scandinavian research has also shown that the culprit may be found as frequently among colleagues as in management (Einarsen & Skogstad, 1996; Leymann, 1992a). As a result Einarsen and associates have used the terms bullying and mobbing interchangeably. This convention will be observed throughout this chapter and the two terms will be used interchangeably.

Defining Characteristics of Workplace Bullying

Despite a gradual move towards a convergence of definitions of 'bullying', important differences still exist. These definitional discrepancies will be explored below. It is acknowledged that different definitional criteria would apply to a legal context and thus have practical implications for organizations. However, since this contribution is primarily concerned with bullying, stress and the psychological work environment, such issues are considered to lie outside the scope of this article (for a discussion, see Rayner, 1999a).

Based on an analysis of definitions of bullying used in the school context, Hoel, Rayner and Cooper (1999) identified the following common characteristics or parameters which were considered helpful in examining the concept of workplace bullying: frequency and duration of experience; the reaction of the target; the balance of power between the parties and the intent of the perpetrator. In addition, Keashly (1998) in her exploration of the related concept 'emotional abuse', based on a review of the American literature, suggests that the following dimensions or qualities should be included: the nature of the behavior involved; how the behavior is affecting the target and an assessment of the behavior with regard to standard of conduct or a person's rights. In order to arrive at an operational definition, these parameters have been amalgamated, reworded and restructured and each of them will be discussed below.

The Nature of the Behavior Involved

The negative nature of the behavior involved is essential to the concept of bullying and may include "being exposed to persistent insults or offensive remarks, persistent criticism, personal or even physical abuse" (Einarsen, 2000a, p. 7). Based on factor analysis of a random and nationwide sample of approximately 5,300 British employees, Hoel and Cooper (2000) identified four underlying factors: work-related harassment, personal harassment, managerial harassment and intimidation. Whilst *work-related harassment* refers to negative behavior which focuses on the quality and effort of work, *personal harassment* is aimed directly at the person and incorporates behaviors of a humiliating as well as socially excluding nature. *Managerial harassment* typically covers behaviors such as 'someone withholding information which affects your work', 'systematically being given work below your competence' or 'excessive workloads' or 'impossible deadlines'. These acts have that in common that they are identified with, or, the results of, managerial power and control. Finally, *intimidation* refers to acts of an intimidating nature, such as threat of violence, shoving or pushing and shouting or rage. Based on a literature review, Zapf (1999a) found work-related harassment, verbal aggression, 'self-worth-related harassment, social exclusion and spreading rumors to be frequent bullying behaviors, whereas physical aggression was only occasionally reported.

According to Keashly (1998), the way in which the behaviors are perceived by the target should be considered a separate type of bullying (or in her terms 'emotional abuse'). In other words, to fall into the category of bullying or emotional abuse, the behaviors must be perceived as unwanted and unsolicited, and they must be aimed at damaging the person or his or her position in the organization. Whilst there may be an argument suggesting that behaviors or acts such as monitoring or leaving someone with an excessive workload will always be a part of working life, one may argue that such acts turn to bullying when applied on purpose and excessively and when the aim of damaging the person predominates organizational aims such as being productive.

Keashly (1998) also argued that the appropriateness of the behavior needs to be taken into account when considering whether a behavior may be thought of as abusive or not. The main problems with linking bullying to a 'standard of conduct' are the flexibility of such standards and that they are wide open to interpretation. In many cases it is unlikely that employers and employees will draw the line between what is reasonable or acceptable at the same place (Lee, 2000).

The Frequency and Duration of the Experience

Most definitions of workplace bullying include the parameters of persistency or repeated nature of the experience as well as the duration of the experience (e.g. Björkqvist, Österman & Hjelt-Bäck, 1994; Brodsky, 1976; Einarsen, Raknes, Matthiesen & Hellesøy, 1994; Vartia, 1996; Zapf, Knorz et al., 1996). According to Leymann (1996) these are key dimensions of bullying. The prominence of these dimensions in explaining the phenomenon and its effects on the recipient is highlighted by making the point that not all negative behaviors in their own right can be considered to represent bullying; rather they become bullying due to the persistency of the experience. Thus, the emphasis is not on "what is done or how it is done, but on the frequency of what is done" (Leymann, 1996, p. 168).

According to Leymann (1996) it is also this dimension which effectively makes a distinction between what may be considered a conflict and what is 'mobbing' (the term used by Leymann). Einarsen (2000) shared this view in so far as 'repeated and enduring negative acts' are a 'core dimension' of bullying. According to Hoel et al. (1999) the persistency of experience also functions as a separator from the concept of workplace violence which tends to focus on one-off incidents. However, several researchers have emphasized that there will be occasions where bullying may be established by a one-off negative act (Einarsen, 1996; Hoel & Cooper, 2001). For example, in cases of severe aggression the effect may remain for a very long time (Einarsen et al., 1999). Alternatively, there may be incidents of a severe nature where the behavior induces sufficient fear or produces a learnt set of responses in as much that the behavior does not need to be repeated for the effect to remain. In other words, flash-backs or the sheer sight or thought of a previous aggressor may recall memories of the act as powerful as the act itself (Randall, 1997). A violent act or threat of using violence may be examples of such behaviors.

The Effects and the Reactions of Targets

According to Leymann (1996) bullying is a reality when the negative behavior manifests itself in a negative outcome, predominantly of a psychological or psychosomatic nature. The reaction is, therefore, unequivocally tied in with the experience of the negative behavior. This suggests that, where there is no negative effect there is no bullying, highlighting the cognitive nature of the phenomenon. However, it would be wrong to interpret this to mean that if there is no negative reaction (or effect) it cannot be bullying. Whilst Leymann was explicit in including target response as a defining quality of bullying, other researchers, e.g. Björkqvist, Österman & Hjelt-Bäck (1994), implied a negative effect on the target ("Repeated activities, with the aim of bringing mental (but sometimes also physical pain, . . ." p. 173). The presence of bullying behavior may exist independently of how these behaviors are being interpreted and construed. However, the phenomenon of bullying may require a cognitive appraisal of the behaviors which considers the behaviors a threat and where there are insufficient coping resources available to deal successfully with the situation. However, whilst the subjective appraisal may play an important part in the early stages of the bullying process, when the conflict has escalated and bullying dynamic established, the subjective appraisal is likely to be of less importance.

The Intent of the Perpetrator

Considerable disagreement exists with regard to the issue of intent (Hoel et al., 1999). The role of intent in bullying can be linked both to whether the perceived negative action was intended in the first place and to the likely harmful outcome of the behavior. The intent to cause harm on the part of the perpetrator as a key feature of bullying has been suggested by authors who consider aggression theory as an important explanatory concept (e.g. Björkqvist, Österman & Hjelt-Bäck, 1994; Randall, 1997). From this perspective there is no bullying when there is no intention to cause harm. The problem is that it is normally impossible to verify the presence of intent (Hoel et al., 1999). For the same reason intent is excluded from most definitions of sexual harassment (e.g. Fitzgerald & Shullman, 1993).

A further issue to consider in connection with intent is the distinction between instrumental and affective aggression (Hoel & Cooper, 1999). Whilst the bullying behavior may be conscious and intended, there may be no intent to cause severe harm on the part of the perpetrator. There are, indeed, repeated anecdotal reports of perpetrators who were surprised when they were informed about the personal and health problems of the victims (e.g. Leymann, 1993; Zapf, 1999a). As such the bullying behavior may be considered instrumental in order to achieve a certain goal or objective. However, whereas intent may be a controversial feature of bullying definitions, there is little doubt that perception of intent is important as to whether an individual decides to label their experience as bullying or not. In empirical studies on the victims' perspective of bullying, the intent to bully is usually taken for granted when victims say that 'they want to push me out of the firm' or 'a hostile person influenced others' (Zapf, 1999b. p. 76).

The Balance of Power

Another central definitional feature of bullying is the imbalance of power (Einarsen, Raknes, Matthiesen & Hellesøy, 1994; Leymann, 1996; Niedl, 1995; Zapf, Knorz et al., 1996). Power is understood in relative terms, expressed as an imbalance of power between the parties, where the target finds it difficult to defend him or herself against the behavior, as the opportunity for retaliation is ruled out (Einarsen, Raknes, Matthiesen & Hellesøy, 1994; Vartia, 1996). The imbalance of power often mirrors the formal power-structure of the organizational context in which the bullying scenario unfolds. This would be the case when someone is on the receiving end of negative acts from a person in a superior organizational position, and is thus associated with control over rewards and punishment (Aquino, 2000). Alternatively, the source of power may be informal, based on knowledge and experience as well as access to support (Einarsen, 1999; Hoel & Cooper, 2000). In the latter instances, conflicts between individuals of seemingly equal power may gradually escalate, leaving one of the parties increasingly defenseless.

Based on these considerations we will follow Einarsen, Hoel, Zapf and Cooper (in press, p. 23) who suggested the following definition: "Bullying at work means harassing, offending, socially excluding someone or negatively affecting someone's work tasks. In order for the label bullying (or mobbing) to be applied to a particular activity, interaction or process it has to occur repeatedly and regularly (e.g. weekly) and over a period of time (e.g. about six months). Bullying is an escalating process in the course of which the person confronted ends up in an inferior position and becomes the target of systematic negative social acts. A conflict cannot be called bullying if the incident is an isolated event or if two parties of approximately equal 'strength' are in conflict."

BULLYING AND THE STRESS PROCESS

Bullying has frequently been associated with the experience of occupational stress. In recent years, definitions of stress have tended to coalesce around a definition that explains stress as an interactive psychological process or a psychological state between the individual and the situation (Cox, 1993; Di Martino, 1992; Lazarus & Folkman, 1984). According to this model, stress is seen as the perceived imbalance between the combination of internal and external demands facing the individual and the perceived ability to cope with the situation. Essential to this process is the individual's subjective interpretation or appraisal of the situation and the potential threat it may entail, and to what extent the threat is perceived to be within the individual's control. Faced with an external threat, be it from the physical, social or the psychosocial environment, any organism will try to respond by employing its coping resources, developed, for example, from previous experience. This process will be influenced by the nature and the extent of the demands, the character of the individual, the social support available to that individual and the constraints under which the coping process is taking place (Cox, Griffith & Rial-Gonzalez, 2000).

The dynamics of the stress process are emphasized in the model described above. The utilization of coping resources, whether successful or not, will impact on the situation and, therefore, influence any symptoms of stress and the influence from the perception of internal and external demands. Similarly, there exists a dynamic relationship between stress and health, whereby any impairment to health and wellbeing as a result of stress will influence the individual's ability to deal with future stress. Moreover, stress can manifest itself in anxiety and irritability that in turn may influence social relationships at work.

Traditionally relationships and social stressors at work have received little attention in organizational stress research (e.g. Beehr, 1995). Those cases where the issue has been given attention are largely confined to social support as a moderator of stress (Dormann & Zapf, 1999; Zapf, Knorz et al., 1996). It has also been noted that social stressors are difficult to study due to their more subjective nature, often influenced by the interest of observers (Mergner, 1989). The fact that they are closely associated with the situation in which they occur and, thus, cannot be reproduced, further adds to the problem.

STRESS, STRESSORS AND LACK OF RESOURCES AS ANTECEDENTS OF BULLYING

Bullying has frequently been associated with a negative and stressful working environment (Einarsen, Raknes, Matthiesen & Hellesøy, 1994; Leymann, 1996). In order to qualify the following, it should be noted that to date, empirical studies on bullying lack sufficient methodological rigor to allow strict cause-effect statements. To account for the above-mentioned relationship, various work environment factors can be considered to produce or elicit occupational stress, which again may increase the risk of conflict and bullying (Einarsen, Raknes & Matthiesen, 1994). In this respect, Berkowitz (1989) argues that frustration may be mediated to cause aggression by negative affect, brought about by arousal derived from external situations, i.e. stress. By contrast, the 'social interactionist' perspective (Felson, 1992; Neuman & Baron, in press), suggests that situational or external factors may bring about aggression and bullying indirectly by giving rise to behaviors in breach of rules and norms of the group or the larger organization. In this case it could also be argued that bullying can be seen as an intentional response to norm-violating behavior and an instrument for social control (Hoel et al., 1999).

Stress and frustration may also trigger the search for scapegoats as tension and frustration may be relieved by processes of projection (Brodsky, 1976; Thylefors, 1987). Higher levels of stress may, therefore, increase bullying down the line, as managers take their aggression out on their subordinates as well as horizontal bullying, where increased tension among staff is projected onto or taken out on colleagues.

The situation of victims is also likely to give rise to attributional processes and defensive mechanisms which will impinge upon their assessment of their environment (Hoel et al., 1999; Kile, 1990). In such cases a contributory factor may be what Jones and Davies (1965) refer to as the 'fundamental attribution failure', where people tend to explain their own behavior with reference to their environment, whilst personality is what comes to mind when explaining the behavior of others. In the following we will explore the relationship between individual stressors and bullying, thereby utilizing the taxonomy of Cooper and Marshall (1976).

Factors Intrinsic to the Job

Economic globalization has increased competition and in order to survive in the current economic environment, organizations are restructuring and downsizing with the aim of cutting costs, with greater pressures on everyone in work, managers in particular, as a result (Cooper, 1999; Worral & Cooper, 1999).

With leaner organizational structures emerging from delayering processes (Sheehan, 1999), the pressures on individual managers are likely to grow as the span of control increases. According to Sheehan (1999), such structural change processes need to be considered in connection with the greater focus on managerial accountability in general (including responsibility for performance), and the tendency to devolve to line-management many functions previously undertaken by personnel departments.

It is also argued that by introducing market philosophies into areas previously not affected by such pressures, e.g. within the health service and the educational sectors, the relationship between managers and staff has changed, with work intensification and increased managerial discretion and control as a result (Ironside & Seifert, in press; Lee, 2000). Thus, the risk of bullying may increase as managers tend to adopt more autocratic practices to bring about change (Hoel & Salin, in press). Thus, the need for restructuring may encourage more authoritarian management practices with the effect of "lowering of thresholds at which inappropriately coercive managerial behaviors [become] manifest in organizational life" (McCarthy et al., 1995, p. 47).

Although a relationship between structural change processes and bullying is highly plausible, the evidence is still sparse. In a study of the relationship between change and aggression, Baron and Neuman (1998) identified four categories of organizational change: cost-cutting, organizational change, job (in) security and social change. The last category refers to examples of change such as increasing diversity with regard to gender, ethnicity and disability status. In this respect, aggression may be a result of a lack of communication or stereotyping, and, the greater the extent of change, the higher the incidence of aggression. Alternatively, resentment may be another factor accounting for this finding (Quinlan, 1999). Similarly, part-time work is another factor that has also been associated with increased risk of aggression and bullying (Baron & Neuman, 1996; Knorz & Zapf, 1996). Such factors may indirectly act as antecedents of bullying by influencing cost-benefit considerations (Björkqvist, Österman & Lagerspetz, 1994) and, therefore, management behavior, as the risk of retaliation from targets under such conditions is likely to be reduced.

However, according to Pearce (1998) part-time and other precarious forms of work on the margins may in their own right create increasing pressure, upheaval and instability within the work-group, with other employees having to up-date, or cover for their colleagues in their absence. This may also lead to disorganization with increasing role conflict and role ambiguity as a result

(Quinlan, 1999). With the more taxing aspects of work often transferred to permanent, full-time staff, resentment may also develop (Pearce, 1998).

Various studies related bullying to job characteristics. Whilst Appelberg, Romanov, Honlasalo and Koskenvuo (1991) identified time-pressure and a hectic work environment as sources of inter-personal conflict, other studies have in most cases failed to support their findings (Salin, 2001; Vartia, 1996). Nevertheless, it has been argued that the problem of bullying comes to the fore when a high degree of pressure is present in a work environment which offers individuals little control over their own work (Einarsen, Raknes & Matthiesen, 1994). Such an interpretation would be in line with Karasek's 'job-demand-control model of stress' (Karasek, 1979; Karasek & Theorell, 1990) where strain is seen as the likely outcome of a combination of high demands and low decision-latitude.

However, Zapf, Knorz et al. (1996), in a study of German 'mobbing' victims, also contradicted the view that bullying may be related to monotony and a general work-control deficit. Comparing job-complexity and task-control of the mobbing victims with two other samples unconnected to bullying, one of office-workers, the other of metal-workers, the mobbing victims were found to have more variability in their jobs than the office-workers and more work-control than the metal-workers. But victims were found to have less control over time than, for example, the office-workers. Zapf et al. interpreted these findings to the effect that pressure of time may indirectly affect bullying by undermining the opportunity to resolve conflicts. Similar results were found in another study by Zapf and Osterwalder (1998) reported in Zapf (1999a) where the victims report less task and timing control compared to a sample of non-victims, though similar levels of task complexity were reported.

Role in Organization

Looking at the evidence, role-conflict and role-ambiguity are features of the work organization which have been found to be linked to bullying (Einarsen, Matthiesen & Raknes, 1994a). This is particularly so for role-conflict, which describes the extent to which employees perceive contradictory expectations, demands and values in their jobs. In the survey of Norwegian trade union members, not only were victims far more likely to report role-conflict than those reporting not being victimized, but observers of bullying were also more likely to report higher levels of role-conflict. Moreover, significant correlations between bullying and role-conflict were included in all seven sub-samples in Einarsen et al.'s study. In addition, role ambiguity seems to be associated with higher levels of bullying (Einarsen, Raknes & Matthiesen, 1994; Vartia, 1996).

Thus, bullying seems to thrive where employees perceive their job situation and work-objectives as unpredictable and unclear.

Similarly, and based on a large number of interviews with victims, Leymann (1996) concluded that bullying was closely related to poorly organized work-environments where roles and command-structures were unclear.

Moreover increased levels of role conflicts and uncertainty due to partly contradictory goals for bullying victims were also reported by von Holzen-Beusch, Zapf and Schallberger (in press), Zapf, Knorz et al. (1996) and Zapf and Osterwalder (1998). These authors also reported more organizational problems requiring more effort than usual for the victims to complete work tasks. Under such circumstances individuals may be more likely to under-perform, resulting in negative supervisor feedback and response, responses which, if frequently repeated, may be construed as bullying. As far as role-conflict is concerned, the source of such stressors may be linked to the managerial role and, therefore, difficult to challenge. A potential challenge to the managerial prerogative may also in itself lead to a response which may be perceived as bullying (Einarsen, Raknes & Matthiesen, 1994).

Career Development

Career development issues may also be related to bullying. One aspect is job security. With greater job insecurity, whether real or perceived (OECD, 1999), employees may also become less resistant to managerial pressure and more unlikely to challenge unfair and aggressive treatment on the part of managers. Indirect evidence comes from the study of von Holzen Beusch et al. (in press) who found that the fear of losing one's job, and not finding a new one, was the main reason why workers tolerated constant exposure to bullying. With less risk of retaliation individuals in positions of power may also be scrupulous about their behaviour, and more willing to apply bullying strategies to achieve their objectives.

In many studies, supervisors and managers are frequently among the bullies, mostly around 50 to 80% of all cases (Zapf, Einarsen, Hoel & Vartia, in press). However, they are also frequently numbered among the victims. One reason for this may be the compression of career structures resulting from delayering processes, which represent fewer opportunities for advancement thereby increasing the competition between supervisors and managers for promotion to a shrinking pool of jobs (Mullen, 1997; Sheehan, 1999) possibly resulting in increasing interpersonal conflict and bullying. Under such circumstances there would also be less opportunity to seek social support within one's peer-group.

Structure and Climate

With a growing number of people seemingly working in self-directed and autonomous teams, tension and conflict between workers may increase as a result of growing pressure. Various studies found relations between group climate and bullying. In the study by Zapf, Knorz et al. (1996) a higher degree of requirement for cooperation or team-working was reported by victims than various groups of non-victims with whom they were compared. Enforced team-working may, therefore, be considered a possible antecedent of bullying as a fertile ground for conflict development, particularly if linked to inter-team competition for limited rewards. According to Collinson (1988) the introduction of collective bonus systems may reinforce some workers' desire to control their colleagues. In the same way bullying may be considered a way of punishing and getting rid of over- or under-achieving subordinates, or colleagues, who are perceived as threats to or a burden for the group (Kräkel, 1997).

In a longitudinal study of the association between work pressure and group cohesive behaviour, Klein (1996) concluded that where a work-measurement system using quantity of production as a primary criterion for performance evaluation, people tended to increase their effort, which in turn could negatively affect group cohesion as group members perceived others competing.

Low satisfaction with leadership was a second organizational feature found most strongly identified with bullying, in Einarsen, Raknes, Matthiesen and Hellesøy's (1994) Norwegian trade union study. Furthermore, based on survey data, bullying has also been associated with lack of involvement in decision-making processes, work-environments where employees are hesitant to express their views and opinions (Vartia, 1996), communication and cooperation problems, low morale and a negative social climate (Keashly & Jagatic, 2000; Vartia, 1996).

Accordingly, an autocratic leadership and an authoritarian way of settling conflicts or dealing with disagreements have also been found to be associated with bullying (O'Moore et al., 1998, Vartia, 1996). By contrast, people who had neither been bullied, nor had observed bullying taken place, reported that disagreements at their workplace tended to be solved by negotiation (Vartia, 1996). An authoritarian leadership or style of management may also create a climate of fear, where there is no room for criticism and where complaining may be considered futile.

However, abdication of leadership or a so-called laissez-faire style of management may also provide a fertile ground for bullying between peers or colleagues (Einarsen, Raknes & Matthiesen, 1994; Hoel & Cooper, 2000). In addition, managers' ignorance and failure to recognize and intervene in bullying cases may indirectly contribute to bullying by conveying the message that bullying is acceptable. Similarly, dissatisfaction with the amount and quality of guidance, instructions and feedback given has been shown to be associated with higher levels of bullying (Einarsen, Raknes & Matthiesen, 1994).

Among other features of the work environment associated with increased risk of bullying are organizational size and work-sector. As far as organizational size is concerned, bullying has been linked to large and bureaucratic organizations, where the threshold for bullying behavior may be lower due to lesser chance of social condemnation (Einarsen, Raknes & Matthiesen, 1994).

Organizations characterized by an extreme degree of conformity and group pressure seem to be particularly prone to bullying (Hoel & Salin, in press). Consequently, bullying seems to flourish in institutions such as prisons (e.g. Hoel & Cooper, 2000; Vartia & Hyyti, 2002) and the uniformed services, where compliance and discipline are of overriding importance (e.g. Ashforth, 1994). In this respect, a recent study within the Fire Service has demonstrated how the training period functions as a socialization process with respect to harassment and bullying, particularly where large sections of the workforce share the same training experience (Archer, 1999). Thus, Archer explored how bullying may become institutionalized and passed on as a tradition. It is likely that similar processes will take place in non-uniformed services such as training of nurses and doctors. Whilst there is obvious differences between the Fire Service and the health service sector, it is not unlikely that destructive behavior and practices possibly fuelling a blame-culture may be the result of or nurtured by the training process.

Similar discrepancies emerged when comparing groups for other organizational antecedents. Nevertheless, whilst certain features of a work environment may apply to an entire occupation or organization, it is also likely that discrepancies between groups of workers within an occupation will exist. Moreover, different antecedents of bullying of a situational or organizational nature are also unlikely to affect different demographic groups uniformly (Hoel, Cooper & Faragher, 2001).

Home-Work Interface

According to McCarthy, Sheehan and Kearns (1995) 60% of respondents in a study of businesses undergoing restructuring reported an increase in working hours and a greater pressure to take work home. Empirical evidence suggests that more pressure at work would negatively affects one's personal and family live, with marital strains and conflicts as typical outcomes (e.g. Allen, Herst, Bruck & Sutton, 2000; Eckenrode & Gore, 1990; O'Driscoll, 1996). Under such circumstances, one would expect that individuals would be more vulnerable to victimization at work. As family problems may manifest themselves in greater emotional and psychological instability, the chance of becoming targeted in the first place is likely to increase. Moreover, the private situation may affect the appraisal of the conflict situation and the person may be drawn into dynamics which they otherwise would have been able to resist or withstand, thus increasing the risk of an escalating conflict. With family and spouses being a primary source of support in cases of bullying, marital conflict may prevent or interfere with the opportunity of receiving such crucial support, thereby further jeopardizing the position of the target.

Another antecedent of bullying associated with the work-home interface may be associated with role expectations. In a series of case-studies of victims of bullying, Lee (1998) identified men who challenged or departed from stereo-typical gender-roles, as being of particular risk of being bullied at work. Thus, being disinterested in sport and showing an inclination to choose family life and responsibilities over social activities involving ones work colleagues, e.g. going to the pub or drinking after work, could in some environments increase the likelihood of a person becoming a target of aggression from colleagues. Such a view is also supported by Hoel (2002) who reported that male part-time workers experienced more negative behaviors than men in full-time employment. In line with Lee (1998), Hoel (2002) argued that in many cases men's decision to work part-time was associated with responsibility for home and family, which in many work environments would be at odds with the prevailing macho culture. Moreover, from a cost-benefit perspective (Björkqvist, Österman & Lagerspetz, 1994), a reduced status or social standing amongst work colleagues, would also increase the risk of being bullied by a superior, as the risk of retaliation under such circumstances is likely to be reduced with employees less likely to interfere or take action on the part of their victimized colleague. The above discussion supports the view of Keashly and Jagatic (2002, in press), that we need to broaden our scope of investigation to include family and friends of targets.

So far we discussed various ways how bullying may be related to the work environment. Reviewing the literature shows various relations between bullying and antecedents of bullying in the work environment. As we stated initially, strong evidence for cause-effect relations does not yet exist. However, it is unlikely that all evidence so far is due to methodological artifacts, third variable explanations or reversed causation (cf. Zapf, 1999b). Rather, we believe that at least some of the evidence reflect true effects on bullying. In sum, we assume that there are at least four mechanisms underlying the relations between work environment and bullying.

(1) Some conditions (e.g. role conflicts as a result of a bad work organization) increase the base rate for conflicts. The higher the base rate, the higher is the rate of escalating conflicts turning into bullying.

(2) Various work environment factors (work stressors) may reflect the difficult economic situation of an organization putting high pressure on the management and their subordinates alike. In this situation, managers may actively use or passively accept bullying to reach organizational goals.

(3) The difficult economic situation may also increase frustration and aggression in some managers and employees which, in some cases, may turn into bullying.

(4) Finally, certain work environment factors may limit the conflict management potential (e.g. time pressure, lack of control). Conflicts may be allowed to drag on and may turn into bullying.

BULLYING AS A STRESSOR AND INDIVIDUAL HEALTH OUTCOMES

My life is devastated, the effect of the condition denies commitments of any kind, confidence is zero, as is self-esteem. Motivation and will are a much reduced feature of life. I am void of physical, mental, social and emotional stamina. There are frequent periods of utter misery and black moods. The continuing effect of restless sleep, early waking and nightmares create feelings of guilt and anxiety. Preoccupation with and flashbacks of the experience create a deeply negative perspective. I am daily living in fear of a crisis occurring that I simply won't be able to cope with. Panic, dry mouth, aching limbs, tremors and palpitations are frequent (John, 51 year old – Sales Manager).

The relationship between bullying and ill health has been explored in several studies. According to Björkqvist, Österman and Hjelt-Bäck (1994), in nearly all cases victims interviewed by the researchers reported "insomnia, nervous symptoms, melancholy, apathy, lack of concentration, and sociophobia" (p. 181). Other interview-studies have confirmed such findings, emphasizing that the effects may be physical (e.g. sweating, shaking and feeling sick), as well as psychological (e.g. anxiety, panic attacks, anger and loss of confidence) (Adams, 1992; Leymann, 1987). As far as clinical observation of victims of bullying is concerned, it has been revealed that bullying may be associated with social isolation, stigmatization, compulsiveness and despair (Leymann, 1990). However, based on such clinical observation, it has been suggested that by no means all victims react in the same way to their ordeal. Thus, according to Brodsky (1976), whilst some react primarily physically, with aches and pains as typical symptoms, others show symptoms of depression. In other cases other symptoms of a more psychological nature, such as hypersensitivity, nervousness and a feeling of victimization, may be identified. These findings indicate that personality characteristics or traits may act as moderators.

These and similar findings have also been identified by cross-sectional questionnaire studies. For example, in a study of public-sector employees (UNISON, 1997) a total of 75.6% of currently bullied individuals reported that their health was negatively affected by their experience. Of these, 29% reported that they were suffering from stress and 18% from depression.

Based on his national Swedish study, Leymann (1992b) concluded that 'cognitive effects' such as irritability, aggression and problems with memory and concentration, as well as psychosomatic symptoms (e.g. gastric upset, loss of appetite and nausea) were the outcomes which accounted for the greatest difference between bullied and non-bullied subjects. A large-scale Norwegian study of members of six trade unions, found bullying to be most strongly associated with depression, and psychological strain, the latter most often manifesting itself in anxiety and nervous debility (Einarsen & Raknes, 1991). Similar findings emerged from a recent Norwegian study of auxiliary nurses (Einarsen, Matthiesen & Skogsatd). This study also reported that the bullied nurses were more likely to burn themselves out than those who were not bullied.

In a further analysis of the results from Einarsen and Raknes' (1991) study reported above, bullying was found to account for 13% of the variance in psycho-logical ill-health (Einarsen, Raknes, Matthiesen & Hellesøy, 1996). In response to the relatively modest association found between bullying and psychological ill health, Einarsen and associates emphasize that this finding may be explained with reference to the low number of people being bullied (less than 10%), suggesting a stronger relationship between the variables. In this particular study, a significant effect was also found for psychosomatic complaints and musculoskeletal effects, explaining 8% and 6% of the variance respectively.

In a study of employees in an Austrian hospital, Niedl (1996) found that individuals who reported themselves as being bullied had higher scores on depression, psychosomatic complaints, anxiety and irritation than those who were not bullied, at a level which was statistically significant. Similar results were found by Mackensen von Astfeld (2000), Mikkelsen and Einarsen (2001), Zapf (1999a) and Zapf, Knorz et al. (1996). Moreover, among the victim group, women reported higher levels of anxiety as well as psychosomatic complaints than men did. According to Niedl these differences between men and women may be explained with reference to women's greater tendency in general to report more psychological ill health and distress than men (Jick & Mitz, 1985; Sonnentag, 1996). Such findings may reflect a lower threshold with regard to reporting for women than for men. But they may also reflect real differences in psychological and physical health, with certain illnesses possibly affecting women more than men, for example mental health problems and musculoskeletal pain (Grunfeld & Noreik, 1996). By contrast, Vartia and Hyyti (2002) in their study of bullying reported that neither gender nor age acted as a predictor of stress.

In a Finnish study of municipal employees, Vartia (2001) measured perceived stress, referred to as 'general stress' by a single item. To measure psychological stress she used a 14-item validated questionnaire. By means of a factor analysis of these 14 items, a two-factor model emerged, with the two factors labeled 'mental stress reactions' (e.g. feelings of inferiority, helplessness and loneliness) and 'feelings of low self-confidence'. According to Vartia, bullying was identified with a high level of stress. Still, a modest effect of 5% in the variance in general stress, 8% of the variance in mental stress reaction and 5% of the variance in low self-confidence, were explained by bullying.

Vartia divided her sample into three groups, 'bullied', 'observers' and 'non-bullied' and found that 40% of the bullied group were suffering a moderate to very high level of stress. Of the two other groups, 25% of observers and 14% of the non-observers were found to have a similarly high stress level. The fact that bullying may affect observers as well as targets was, according to Vartia, confirmed in a regression analysis which suggested that observing bullying was a significant predictor of 'general stress' as well as of mental stress symptoms.

Quine (1999), in a study of employees in a British health service trust found that people who had experienced bullying within the last 12 months were significantly more likely to report clinical levels of anxiety and depression than those who were not considered bullied. Quine also reported that targets of bullying had higher levels of job-induced stress compared to those who were not bullied. Bullying also appeared to be associated with job-satisfaction, with targets of bullying reporting lower levels of job-satisfaction.

Attempts have also been made to explore the relationship between individual bullying factors (emerging from factor analysis of negative behaviors involved with bullying) and individual outcomes. Thus several studies (e.g. Niedl, 1995; Zapf, Knorz et al., 1996) found that the strongest and most consistent correlation with psychosomatic complaint, irritation, depression and self-esteem emerged for personal harassment ('attacking the private person').

Similar findings emerged from Einarsen and Raknes' (1997) study of industrial workers. In this case the strongest correlation was found between the factor 'personal derogation' and 'psychological health and well-being', followed by the factors 'work-related harassment' and 'social exclusion'. According to the authors a multiple regression analysis revealed that these three factors explained 21% of the variance in psychological health and well being. The authors also speculated whether the time-lag from exposure to the time of measurement, which could be as much as six months, might lead to an under-estimation of the relationship between the variables.

As was the case for health and wellbeing, bullying factors appear to affect job-satisfaction, with significant correlations found for 'personal derogation', 'work-related harassment' and 'social exclusion'. The strongest correlation was found for the first two factors and satisfaction with colleagues.

According to Vartia (2001), the reported symptoms of negative psychological health were associated with neither duration nor frequency of exposure. In explaining her finding, Vartia (2001) points to the argument, previously put forward by Einarsen, Raknes and Matthiesen (1994), that victims represent a small group and that it may be difficult to differentiate between groups of victims as most of them reported relatively high levels of stress.

In line with the previous discussion about the possible influence of demo-graphic factors on outcomes of bullying, Einarsen and Raknes (1997) argued that, not only is it likely that workers and supervisors may make use of different kinds of negative and harassing behavior, but also they may to some extent be affected differently. According to their findings, there is a strong association between the factors 'personal derogation' and 'social exclusion' on the one hand, and 'dissatisfaction with work colleagues', on the other. These strong associations are explained by reference to the presence of a strong shop-floor culture which may often be harsh and unforgiving (Collinson, 1988).

Bullying and Post-Traumatic Stress Disorders PTSD

Post Traumatic Stress Disorder or PTSD, is most commonly identified with the experience of a single traumatic event such as a severe accident. The medical diagnosis PTSD is identified with the following symptoms: a re-experience of the event or frequent flash-backs, a tendency persistently to avoid stimuli associated with the trauma as well as a persistent feeling of irritability sustained for a relatively long period of time (Scott & Stradling, 1994). However, in recent years it has been recognized that similar symptoms to those identified with PTSD may arise from the experience of persistent, work-related extreme stressors such as harassment and victimization. On the basis of their work at a rehabilitation clinic for victims of workplace bullying in Sweden, Leymann and Gustafsson (1996) state that many victims of bullying may be given the diagnosis PTSD, which also may result in a personality or 'character' change. In other words, the individual is no longer the same person as he or she was before the series of traumatic events took place.

It has also been argued that compared with patients who have been diagnosed as suffering from PTSD resulting from involvement in traumatic accidents, victims of bullying showed significantly higher levels of PTSD. This has recently been confirmed in a Norwegian study of long-term sufferers of bullying (Einarsen, Matthiesen & Mikkelsen, 1999). Not only were 76% of the victims studied found to be suffering from the same symptoms as traditional PTSD patients, and above the level indicating psychiatric pathology compared with individuals who had been involved in very serious traumatic events, but the bullying victims were found to have far higher PTSD scores. Furthermore, as many as 45% of the victims, whose experience of bullying went back five years or more, reported symptoms at a level above the threshold value for PTSD. According to the authors, the intensity of the experience appears to affect the level of PTSD. Another recent study carried out in Denmark (Mikkelsen & Einarsen, 2002) supported these findings. In this study, 76% of the victims reported symptoms indicating PTSD, of whom 29% were found to meet all criteria for PTSD whereas 47% failed to meet the A1 criterion of the classification of the DSM-IV-TR (APA, 2000), which means, they did not report serious injuries or threats to their physical integrity. This latter point may actually be a core issue because researchers might doubt that bullying can cause PTSD because life is mostly not supposed to be at risk, thus one of the key criteria for diagnosing PTSD is not met. However, one might at least say that bullying causes symptoms similar to PTSD.

Long-Term Effect on Personality

In order to explain these, by all accounts, extreme effects, we refer to recent Scandinavian work on this issue (Einarsen et al., 1999; Einarsen & Mikkelsen, in press; Mikkelsen & Einarsen, 2002), building on the theories of Janoff-Bullmann (1992) on traumatic life experiences. According to Janoff-Bullmann, an event becomes traumatic when it challenges our most fundamental assumptions about the world: (1) the world as benevolent; (2) the world as meaningful; and (3) the self as worthy. According to this perspective, our views and picture of the world, which for most people appear to be generally positive, have been gradually built up since childhood, with minor adjustment taking place when our experience is somewhat at odds with our basic beliefs about the world. An event becomes traumatic, however, when this well-established picture is fundamentally challenged to the extent that our basic assumptions about the world collapse.

This model has recently been successfully applied to the experience of workplace bullying (Einarsen et al., 1999; Mikkelsen & Einarsen, 2002). From a belief that people generally happen to be positive and well-meaning ('the world as benevolent'), victims of bullying find themselves in a situation where they feel 'hounded' or they have a strong feeling that somebody is trying to 'get them'.

Lack of support from close colleagues or other people may in such situations be hard to bear. Thus, victims would tend to ask themselves: 'why did this happen to me?' ('the world as meaningful'). The assumption of a generally meaningful and just world is now no longer sustainable. This may be particularly hard to understand for the hard-working, apparently successful victim. The victims may now find themselves portrayed in the most humiliating way as incapable and worthless. In such situations it is not surprising that many victims feel that a serious injustice is being committed and that the world is conspiring against them. To the victims it seems unexplainable that someone who has always attempted to do his or her utmost for the best reasons, and frequently appeared to be both successful and popular, now finds him- or herself at the receiving end of persistent negative and aggressive behavior (Einarsen et al., 1999).

For some victims the situation may turn from bad to worse when they experience that those around them do not believe them or their version of events. This experience has been referred to as 'secondary bullying' and bears close resemblance to the experience of many rape victims (Leymann, 1990). Now nothing seems more important to the victim than clearing their name and seeing justice done. In such a situation, victims, out of a need for self-preservation, may go out of their way to portray themselves as hard-working, upstanding employees, at times to an extent which may be at odds with reality (Hoel et al., 1999).

The third assumption ('the self as worthy') implies that as a decent human being one deserves to be treated well. This assumption is closely related to the idea that we have some control over outcomes of our actions and that what we do will normally turn out well. In cases of bullying, neither appears any longer to be true. The central role of work in most people's lives also means that a failure at work turns out to be very threatening to our sense of identity. The result of constantly experiencing that their value as a human being is challenged finally results in loss of self-respect undermining victims' own self-worth. For many victims, the question mark over their own self-worth may be accompanied by suicidal thoughts, threatening their very existence.

The severity of the effects of bullying cannot be exemplified more clearly than in the claims that a considerable number of suicides may have their roots in workplace bullying (Leymann, 1996, based on interviews with priests). No firm evidence exists for such claims, and, furthermore, people very rarely commit suicide for a single reason. However, the fact that up to 40% of targets in a large scale-Norwegian survey (Einarsen, Raknes, Matthiesen & Hellesøy, 1994) stated that they had at times contemplated suicide should emphasize the severity of the effects bullying may have on those involved. No other studies have inquired directly about suicidal thoughts, although several people in the second UNISON study reported such thoughts (UNISON, 2000). It should be emphasized that suicide has not only been linked to targets of bullying, but also to those accused of bullying (O'Moore, 1996).

ORGANIZATIONAL OUTCOMES OF BULLYING AS A STRESSOR

From the previous sections, it is apparent that bullying has various effects on targets, manifesting itself behaviorally as well as in a number of health problems. It would be surprising if such effects had no impact on the organization. However, compared to the effects on individuals, much less evidence has emerged for potential organizational effects.

In a review of the organizational effects of bullying, Hoel, Einarsen and Cooper (in press) argue that the association between bullying and absenteeism has been found to be weak (e.g. Hoel & Cooper, 2000; Price Spratlen, 1995, Vartia, 2001). For example, in a study of U.K. nurses, Quine (2001) reported that 8% had been absent as a result of bullying. However, a study of Finnish hospital workers, undertaken by Kivimäki, Elovaino and Vahtera (2000), deviated somewhat from the general trend in that a review of absence records showed that targets of bullying had 26% higher medically certified sickness, when adjusted for base-line figures one year prior to the study, than those who were not bullied. Similarly, Hoel and Cooper (2000), in a nationwide study of bullying in the U.K. involving approximately 5,300 respondents, calculated that targets of bullying on average had taken seven days more off work than those who had neither been bullied nor witnessed bullying at work. For those who decide to take time off due to bullying, prolonged spells of absence appear to be rather common. Thus, in a U.K. study of police support staff, nearly one in three of those who confirmed that they had been absent due to bullying, reported absence of more than 30 days (UNISON, 2000).

To make sense of the rather weak relationship between bullying and absence, Hoel et al. (in press), refer to the absence model of Steer and Rhodes (1978). In their view absence can be considered the product of a combination of two factors: the opportunity to attend work, and the individual's motivation to go to work. For some individuals absence is a direct response to their health problems resulting from their bullying experience and which is also likely to affect their motivation to attend work. However, as absence may turn out to be a counter-productive strategy, as the bullying may intensify upon return to work, many targets may decide to go to work even if they, strictly speaking, would be better off staying at home. Strict absence control systems, currently in operation in many organizations may in this respect also influence the behavior of targets. A recent finding by Gross and Zapf (2001) also suggests that targets who were successful in coping with their situation were less likely to resort to frequent absence than those who were found to be unsuccessful.

A substantially stronger association has been found between bullying and turnover (e.g. Hoel & Cooper, 2001; Keashly & Jagatic, 2000; Quine, 1999). It may be argued that turnover in many cases, as opposed to absenteeism, can be considered a positive coping strategy, and accords with the advice victims often offer other victims of bullying (Zapf & Gross, 2001). In some instances victims' departure from the organization will be a direct response to their health situation or state of mind (Rayner, Hoel & Cooper, 2002), whilst others may have found themselves expelled or forced out of the organization (Leymann, 1990). There is also evidence that a bullying strategy has been used deliberately to force individuals to 'voluntarily leave the organization' in order to reduce organizational redundancy costs (Lee, 2000).

However, other factors may prevent victims from leaving. One such factor may be lack of mobility or labor-market considerations, which would hit older victims particularly hard. In the study of von Holzen Beusch et al. (in press) on reasons why victims of bullying did not simply leave their job, labor-market considerations and the fear of not finding a new job proved most important. For many it may also be difficult to leave without a positive resolution to their case or at least some acknowledgement of the wrong done to them, which encourages the individual to battle on. Taken together, such factors that prevent victims from leaving would also tend to reduce the strength of association between bullying and turnover (Hoel et al., in press).

Intuitively, being at the receiving end of an ongoing stream of negative behavior is likely to have a negative effect on motivation and commitment. However, the fact that hard evidence is sparse, and that most evidence concerning impaired productivity due to bullying so far has been anecdotal (Bassman, 1992; Field, 1996), may be attributable to difficulties of measurement. In a large-scale Norwegian study, Einarsen, Raknes, Matthiesen and Hellesøy (1994) measured perceptions of productivity in connection with bullying. A total of 27% of respondents agreed with the statement 'bullying reduces our efficiency'. The same question was later incorporated in Hoel and Cooper's (2000) U.K. study, and in this case 33% reinforced the statement. In the same study, the authors were also able to measure current self-rated productivity as compared to normal productivity independently of respondents' experience of negative behavior and bullying by front-loading a productivity measure in the questionnaire. The results showed an average 7% reduction in self-rated productivity among current targets of bullying compared to those who had neither been bullied nor had witnessed bullying.

The above evidence also suggests that bullying may have a negative affect on witnesses or bystanders. The presence of a 'ripple' effect has been explored in several studies (Hoel & Cooper, 2000; Rayner, 1999; Vartia, 2001). According to Rayner (1999), approximately 20% of witnesses of bullying reported that they left their organization due to bullying. Whilst it may be argued that people seldom leave their job for a single reason, this finding has significant implications, bearing in mind that a very substantial number report having witnessed bullying (e.g. Hoel, Cooper et al., 2001; Rayner, 1999). The increasing use of team-working may also be a factor increasing the likelihood of such a ripple effect (Rayner et al., 2002; Zapf, Knorz et al., 1996).

In Hoel and Cooper's (2000) British study, respondents were divided into four groups: 'currently bullied', 'previously bullied', 'witnessed bullying only', and 'neither experienced nor witnessed bullying'. Those currently exposed to bullying were found to have the worst mental and physical health, the highest sickness absenteeism and intention-to-leave rates, the lowest productivity as well as the lowest organizational satisfaction and commitment. The second most affected group were those who were 'bullied in the past', followed by 'witnessed bullying only' and 'neither bullied nor witnessed bullying'. These findings lend support to the idea that bullying may affect third persons to the detriment of the individual as well as the organization.

In addition to absence, turnover and impaired productivity, other potential outcomes of bullying are grievances and internal complaints, litigation, industrial or trade union unrest and actions, and effects on organizational image and public relations (Hoel et al., in press). Taken together, these outcomes may cost organizations dearly. Whilst any estimation of costs is fraught with methodological problems, and often rely on unsound data and evidence, they are likely to cost industry large sums of money. (For a discussion see Hoel, Sparks & Cooper, 2001; Sheehan, McCarthy, Barker & Henderson, 2001).

COPING WITH WORKPLACE BULLYING

Coping with stress is a core issue in psychological stress theories. Stress reactions depend on how well a person copes with a stressful situation. With regard to bullying, there have been a few attempts to study how targets of bullying respond to or cope with their experience. According to Thylefors (1988) three general behavioral patterns may be recognized: hitting back, self-blame and problem-solving. The following featured problem-solving strategies: discussing the problem with the perpetrator, managers or union representatives or collecting evidence. Similarly, according to Keashly, Trott and MacLean (1994) problem-solving in the form of confronting the perpetrator was considered to yield the best outcome. To solve the problem and bring bullying to an end, keeping a diary has frequently been suggested to victims so that they can gather evidence. However, the process of gathering evidence may become an obsession (Rayner et al., 2002), thus in some cases possibly representing a problem in its own right. If noticed by the other party, information gathering may be seen as provoking and may, thus, contribute to the escalation of the bullying conflict.

So far, there are a few empirical studies investigating coping with workplace bullying. In an Austrian study of targets of bullying, in a rehabilitation clinic for victims of bullying, Niedl (1996) tried to establish how individuals responded to their experience. Far from responding with a simple 'fight' or 'flight' response, Niedl found that victims resorted to a number of constructive coping strategies when faced with bullying. Using a model devised by Whitney and Cooper (1989), Niedl reconstructed the responses of victims by mapping the acts of each individual according to four different behavioral strategies: voice, loyalty, neglect and exit. *Voice* referred to individuals' attempts to raise the alarm within the organization or air their grievance, whilst *loyalty* related to ways of actively demonstrating one's commitment. *Neglect* as a strategy pointed to removal or withdrawal of commitment on the part of victims, whilst *exit* suggested that the person decided to leave the organization altogether. In mapping the patterns of actions taken by the victims, it became clear that there was no single common action pathway and that most of the victims had tried a number of strategies before finally resorting to neglect or exit. These findings were replicated by Zapf and Gross (2001). Both studies showed that the victims mostly started with active and constructive strategies and mostly ended with either passive strategies such as withdrawal behavior or leaving the organization which is often a destructive strategy from the point of view of the organization. From the victim's perspective, however, it may be the only solution possible.

The above mentioned studies show a more active and constructive picture of targets' responses to bullying than may previously have been anticipated. One should, however, bear in mind that any attempt to reconstruct reality with hindsight is fraught with difficulties (Groeneweg, 1996). Previous studies of bullying have also pointed out that victims of bullying tend to paint an unrealistically positive picture of themselves and their own actions (e.g. Zapf (1999a). The fact that, in Niedl's (1996) and Zapf and Gross' (2001) studies, all victims without exception initially reported that they had responded with a positive coping strategy, e.g. either 'voice' or 'loyalty', seems to confirm such view. This also lends support to the view which suggests that victims in protecting a faltering self-image may subconsciously try to rewrite the past (Hoel et al., 1999).

Several U.K. questionnaire studies have included questions on the responses targets, and sometimes non-targets, have chosen or would have chosen if they were bullied (e.g. Hoel & Cooper, 2000; UNISON, 1997). In these studies the action most used or approved of was to confront the bully. As far as the target group was concerned, the second highest response group in Rayner's (1997) study was 'do nothing'. Other common responses were turning to your colleagues for support or consulting a doctor. Bearing this in mind, it is interesting to find that, with respect to every single action, the non-bullied group portrayed themselves as far more pro-active than the targets. For example, in the UNISON study 55.1% of the non-bullied group said they would consult a personnel officer and 72% would see their union representative, whilst the figures for the target group were 24% and 26% respectively.

In the study by Hoel and Cooper (2000), the action most frequently taken in response to being bullied was 'discussing the problem with work colleagues' (63.3%) followed by 'discussing the problem with friends and family' (51.5%). A total of 24.4% 'went to the union/staff association' and 12.7% 'went to personnel'. This last figure would increase slightly if the group which reported seeing the welfare department was included. Whilst 15.6% had seen a doctor in response to their experience, only 4.0% visited occupational health. This low figure may in part be explained by the absence of occupational health services in many of the organizations taking part in the study. Nearly a tenth of targets reported having made use of the grievance procedure.

Rayner in her UNISON (1997) study went one step further and looked at the likely outcome of actions taken by targets. The results make for dismal reading with 'nothing' happening in a majority of cases, but with a high number of negative outcomes as a direct response to the action. For example, after putting forward a group complaint, the majority (93%) of those currently bullied reported having been threatened with dismissal. To confront the bully appears to be a risky strategy with up to 43% being 'labeled a trouble maker'. Involving the union representative emerged as the most effective strategy in as much that it is this category which achieved the lowest 'no action' frequency and was perceived as lowest risk as no one who approached their union seems to have been threatened with dismissal.

When considering how targets responded to being bullied, gender appears to have an impact on the action taken. Not surprisingly, women reported discussing their experience with colleagues, family and friends and more frequently than male targets, the largest discrepancy being found for discussing experiences outside work. This is in line with a common perception that women are better or more prepared to discuss their problems with others. Men more frequently respond by 'bottling up' their emotions. This may reflect a macho-type work-environment where admitting to being bullied may represent a sign of weakness.

Admitting to being a target may also carry negative connotations with regard to blame and shame (Einarsen et al., 1999; Hoel et al., 1999). The fact that more female targets had consulted their doctor is in line with such a view and also reflects the fact that women in general are more likely to report health complaints (Zapf, Knorz et al., 1996). It is also possible that avoiding raising the issue with friends and family may be interpreted as a conscious decision, protecting those you care for by preventing them from worrying about you. By discussing the problem it may function as a buffer for further conflict escalation as individuals may have their experience confirmed and validated, thus making them more likely to confront the situation and deal with it before it escalates out of control. Alternatively, input from others may help in adjusting one's own perspective, particularly when this is not in line with reality. However, when organizational status was entered the equation, the differences between men and women tended to tail off towards the top end of the organizational hierarchy (Hoel, Cooper, et al., 2001). It could be argued that female managers might feel more isolated than female workers with less access to someone with whom they could share their ordeal, or less inclined to confide in others, possibly due to competition.

Relatively few targets contacted their union representative and even fewer their personnel/HR department. A lack of trust in their effectiveness may be one reason here (UNISON, 1997), fear of retaliation another. Rayner 's (1997) finding suggesting that the main cause of bullying was that 'bullies can get away with it', seems to support the latter view.

In order to explore whether the time at which the bullying incident took place and the intensity of the experience may have influenced target's chosen courses of action, Hoel and Cooper (2000) divided the targets into three groups: bullied within the last five years, bullied occasionally within the last six months and bullied regularly within the last six months. The results revealed that those bullied recently reported much higher levels of activity for nearly all courses of action than those bullied in the past. However, within the group bullied in the last six months, those bullied on a regular basis were more likely to have been pro-active than those bullied occasionally. Only for the options 'use of the organization's grievance procedure' and 'did nothing' were the differences between the groups not significant. The largest differences between groups were identified with the category 'discussed it with colleagues'. In this case 80.9% of regularly bullied respondents had made use of this particular course of action, followed by 61.9% for those occasionally bullied and 36.0% for respondents bullied within the last five years but not within the last six months.

The fact that those most recently bullied (within the last six months) were found to be far more active in dealing with their problem, or bringing it to the attention of others, may suggest that bullying is increasingly becoming a more widely recognized problem and that there may be a greater trust in the effectiveness of organizational support-systems. An alternative explanation may be that those currently bullied, and the regularly bullied group in particular, may have a stronger personal need to portray themselves as proactive with respect to their own situation in order to protect a faltering self-image, a process which is closely related to the traumatic experience of bullying (Einarsen et al., 1999; Hoel & Cooper, 2000).

In a recent Danish study, Høgh and Dofradottir (2001) conclude that those who were subjected to negative acts which may be construed as bullying (the study measured exposure to a very limited number of negative acts), used problem-solving strategies less frequently than those who were not exposed to the same types of behavior. Moreover, the study confirmed Niedl's (1996) and Zapf and Gross' (2001) finding that targets would tend to use problem-solving strategies in the beginning, but when these fail they would turn to less (positive) responses. Hogh and Dofradottir also make the point that choice of strategy also depends upon the degree to which they believe that the situation may be changed. Feeling trapped without the possibility of escape may lead to feelings of helplessness. Thus avoidance strategies, such as accepting the situation, thinking of something else, or diffusing the situation for example by joking or use of humor, would be used.

Knorz and Zapf (1996) and Zapf and Gross (2001) investigated coping strategies of successful and unsuccessful victims. These victims were differentiated on basis of the item "Have you been able to improve your situation by your behavior?" Those who responded "yes, completely" (9 out of a sample of 149 victims) were defined to be successful, those who responded "no, the situation got even worse" (67 out of 149) were defined as unsuccessful. In line with Rayner (1999), talking with the bullies was the most frequently used strategy. However, it was significantly less often used by successful compared with unsuccessful victims, supporting the view that bullying victims are in an inferior position with little opportunity to actively solve their problem. Also, trying to get support from supervisors, or trade union representatives were often used strategies. However, they all seemed more often to worsen rather than improve the overall situation. Moreover, the successful victims less often used frequent absence from work to cope with bullying. An interpretation of these results is that successful victims tried to avoid escalating and worsening the situation even more and to avoid mistakes in order to not give the bullies additional grounds to bully them.

Overall, most results on coping with workplace bullying support the view that bullying is a no control situation which can be characterized as a series of failing conflict management attempts (cf. Niedl, 1995). Given that harassed individuals repeatedly try to manage their conflict situation rather than doing nothing, it is implicit in the definition of bullying that otherwise successful conflict management strategies such as problem-solving, integrating or compromising have failed in the case of bullying. Otherwise a conflict situation would have been resolved before it became bullying according to the definition presented above.

Further support for this view comes from Aquino (2000), who found that the use of active problem-solving strategies in escalated conflicts actually increased rather than reduced victimization, and from Rayner (1999), who found that open discussion and information-sharing with the bully increased the likelihood of the bully retaliating against the victim. Obviously, problem-solving oriented strategies of conflict management are not very successful if the conflicts are not related to the task anymore (de Dreu, 1997).

To sum up, research has shown that bullying is a no control situation for the victim in which active and constructive coping strategies do not prove useful but often make things even worse. Even seeking help often makes things worse, because the other party can perceive it as provocative. Consequently, it is not surprising that most victims, if making recommendations for other victims, most often suggest leaving the company (Zapf & Gross, 2001). Therefore, any advice to the victims has to be given with utmost care.

CONCLUSIONS AND SOME IMPLICATIONS FOR FUTURE RESEARCH

Within a time-span of less that ten years bullying has become recognized as a serious workplace hazard in Europe and abroad and the issue has rapidly moved upwards the agenda of many organizations. The literature reviewed in this chapter has documented that bullying appears to have a considerable effect on targets, seriously affecting their health and well-being, and for many victims, some of the effects remain for a considerable time after the bullying ceased. In some of the most severe cases targets may even find themselves unable to continue working altogether. The literature review has also revealed a number of issues where evidence is inconclusive, sparse or missing altogether. On the basis of this review it would seem to be important to establish which organizational factors may increase the risk of workplace bullying. Thus, it should be an objective of researchers in the field to continue identifying those work or job-stressors, as well as factors identified with organizational change, which may predict bullying and negative behavior in the workplace.

It should also be acknowledged that research so far has paid little attention to the fact that the problem may be experienced differently by different groups of people (Hoel, Einarsen, Keashly, Zapf & Cooper, in press). Such differences are also likely to affect our understanding of the stress process and its outcomes, thus presenting a further challenge for researchers.

Only a few studies have so far looked at the role of social support in moderating the stressor-strain relationship as far as bullying is concerned (e.g. Einarsen et al., 1996; Quine, 1999). According to Quine (1999) in this respect several roles of social support may be envisaged: Social support may have a direct positive impact on the personal health of victims of bullying. Alternatively, social support may directly influence the experience of bullying or simply reduce the negative effect of bullying on the individual. However, to further clarify the role of social support more research is needed.

The empirical basis of workplace bullying research is still weak. What we have so far are reliable descriptive data on the frequency of bullying, the various classes of bullying behavior, and the devastating health outcomes. However, there is little reliable knowledge about the causes of bullying, cause and effect problems, as well as detail information about the bullying process. This is to a great extent due to the methodological problems that have to be dealt with. Every study on bullying has to deal with the problem that bullying is an infrequent event and that it has a negative image. Thus, very large samples are required to collect a reasonable sample of bullying victims. These large samples often do not allow the administration of all the instruments necessary to cover all the potential antecedents and consequences of bullying, coping with bullying, etc. In-depth studies, by contrast, require a direct approach to victims which is usually done by placing advertisement in newspapers or radio, or by approaching bullying self-help groups. All this makes it almost impossible to collect anything approaching a representative sample.

Most quantitative studies on bullying so far are cross-sectional. Whilst certain methodological problems cannot be avoided in cross-sectional studies, their effects can be reduced. Thus, it appears to be inadequate simply to ask people how they may be affected, as usually victims of bullying will see their health as having been directly affected by their ordeal. For example, in the study by Björkqvist, Österman and Hjelt-Bäck (1994), all victims claimed that their depressive feelings, anxiety and aggression were a direct outcome of their treatment. Similarly, such claims have also been made in U.K. studies (e.g. UNISON, 1997). In order to reduce such problems, particular consideration should be given to questionnaire design and validated instruments applied as far as possible, a fact that has often been overlooked in previous U.K. studies (e.g. Savva & Alexandrou, 1998).

There are, however, some possibilities. Various studies (e.g. Einarsen & Skogstad, 1996; Vartia, 1996, 2001) asked whether people have observed bullying in order to validate the information received from the victims. Clinical interviews of experienced occupational physicians (e.g. Lindemeier, 1996) is another alternative way to validate the victim status.

With regard to stress and coping, various stress researchers have applied diary studies to investigate coping at the interaction level (e.g. Peeters, Buunk & Schaufeli, 1995). This approach may prove useful in investigating differences in conflict management and coping with stress suffered by victims of bullying and non-victims (Gross & Zapf, 2002).

Moreover, with a few exceptions the findings discussed above are the results of cross-sectional studies, which do not allow for robust conclusions with regard to causality (Zapf, Dormann & Frese, 1996). This fact remains, even where findings are supported by evidence from third parties, i.e. observers or witnesses (e.g. Einarsen, Raknes & Matthiesen, 1994; Hoel & Cooper, 2000). Thus, whilst a poor working environment may give rise to bullying directly or indirectly, alternative interpretations may be suggested. For example, anxious or depressed individuals may create tension and elicit negative reactions from colleagues and managers alike (Einarsen, Raknes & Matthiesen, 1994). Moreover, bullying may itself have a negative effect on the work environment, for example by negatively affecting internal communication, thereby giving rise to more stress and further organizational problems (Zapf, 1999b).

Whilst the human costs associated with bullying are immense, the organization is also likely to be affected, due to increased absenteeism and turn-over rates and reduced levels of productivity. Thus, in financial terms there is evidence to suggest that combating bullying makes good business sense. Moreover, the fact that third parties or witnesses of bullying also appear to be affected by their indirect experience further highlights the seriousness of the problem as well as the costs associated with it. Such findings should encourage us to continue our efforts to explore and prevent bullying by developing research and practical interventions.

REFERENCES

Adams, A. (1992). *Bullying at work. How to confront and overcome it*. London: Virago Press.
Allen, T. D., Herst, D. E. L., Bruck, C. S., & Sutton, J. (2000). Consequences associated with work-to-family conflict: A review and agenda for future research. *Journal of Occupational Health Psychology, 5*, 278–308.

Appelberg, K., Romanov, K., Honkasalo, M.-L., & Koskenvuo, M. (1991). Interpersonal conflicts at work and psychosocial characteristics of employees. *Social Science Medicine, 32*, 1051–1056.

Aquino, K. (2000). Structural and individual determinants of workplace victimization: The effects of hierarchical status and conflict management style. *Journal of Management, 26*, 171–193.

Archer, D. (1999) Exploring "bullying" culture in the paramilitary organisation. *International Journal of Manpower, 20*, 94–105.

Ashforth, B. E. (1994). Petty tyranny in organizations. *Human Relations, 47*, 755–778.

Baron, R. A., & Neuman, J. H. (1996). Workplace violence and workplace aggression: Evidence on their relative frequency and potential causes. *Aggressive Behavior, 22*, 161–173.

Bassman, E. (1992). *Abuse in the workplace.* Westport, CT: Quorum Books.

Beehr, T. A. (1995). *Psychological stress in the workplace.* London: Routledge.

Berkowitz, L. (1989). The frustration-aggression hypothesis: An examination and reformulation. *Psychological Bulletin, 106*, 59–73.

Björkqvist, K., Österman, K., & Hjelt-Bäck, M. (1994). Aggression among university employees. *Aggressive Behavior, 20*, 173–184.

Björkqvist, K., Österman, K., & Lagerspetz, K. M. J. (1994). Sex differences in covert aggression among adults. *Aggressive Behaviour, 20*, 27–33.

Brodsky, C. M. (1976). *The harassed worker.* Lexington, Mass.: D. C. Heath and Company.

Chappell, D., & Di Martino, V. (2000). *Violence at Work.* Second Edition. Geneva: International Labour Organisation.

Cooper, C. L. (1999). The changing psychological contract at work. *European Business Journal, 11*, 115–118.

Cooper, C. L., Dewe, P., & O'Driscoll, M. (2001). *Organizational stress: a review and critique of theory, research and applications.* London: Sage Publications.

Cooper, C. L., & Jackson, S. (1997). *Creating Tomorrow's Organization.* New York: John Wiley & Sons.

Cooper, C. L., & Marshall, J. (1976). Occupational sources of stress: A review of the literature relating to coronary heart disease and mental ill health. *Journal of Occupational Psychology, 49*, 11–28.

Cox, T. (1993). *Stress Research and Stress Management: Putting Theory to Work.* HSE Contract Research Report, NO 61. London: HMSO.

Cox, T., Griffith, A., & Rial-Gonzalez, E. (2000). *Research on work-related stress.* Luxembourg: European Agency for Safety and Health at Work.

Collinson, D. L. (1988). "Engineering humour": Masculinity, joking and conflict in shop-floor relations. *Organization Studies, 9*, 181–199.

Davenport, N. Z., Distler Schwartz, R., & Pursell Elliott, G. (1999). *Mobbing: Emotional Abuse in the Workplace.* Ames, Iowa: Civil Society Publishing.

de Dreu, C. K. W. (1997). Productive conflict: The importance of conflict management and conflict issue. In: C. K. W. de Dreu & E. Van de Vliert (Eds), *Using Conflict in Organizations* (pp. 9–22). London: Sage Publications.

Dormann, C., & Zapf, D. (1999). Social support as a moderator between social stressors and depression: Analysis of a 3-wave longitudinal study with structural equations. *Journal of Applied Psychology, 84*, 874–884.

Eckenrode, J., & Gore, S. (Eds) (1990). *Stress between work and family.* New York: Plenum.

Einarsen, S. (1996). *Bullying and harassment at work: epidemiological and psychosocial aspects.* Ph.D. Thesis, University of Bergen: Department of Psychosocial Science.

Einarsen, S. (1999). The nature and causes of bullying. *International Journal of Manpower, 20*, 16–27.
Einarsen, S. (2000). Bullying and harassment at work: Unveiling and organizational taboo. In: M. Sheehan, S. Ramsay & J. Patrick (Eds), *Transcending Boundaries: Integrating People, Processes and Systems* (pp. 7–13). Conference Proceedings, Griffith University, Brisbane, Queensland, Australia.
Einarsen, S., Hoel, H., Zapf, D., & Cooper, C. L. (Eds) (in press). *Bullying and emotional abuse in the workplace. International perspectives in research and practice.* London/New York: Taylor and Francis.
Einarsen, S., Matthiesen, S. B., & Mikkelsen, E. G. (1999). *Tiden leger alle sår: Senvirkninger av mobbing I arbeidslivet.* Institutt for Samfunnspsykologi, University of Bergen.
Einarsen, S., Matthiesen, S. B., & Skogstad, A. (1998). Bullying, burnout and well-being among assistant nurses. *Journal of Occupational Health and Safety – Aust NZ, 14,* 563–568.
Einarsen, S., & Mikkelsen, E. G. (in press). Individual effect of exposure to bullying at work. In: *Bullying and Emotional Abuse in the Workplace. International Perspectives in Research and Practice.* London/New York: Taylor and Francis.
Einarsen, S., & Raknes, B. I. (1991). *Mobbing i arbeidslivet. En undersokelse av forekomst og helsemessige konseqvenser av mobbing pa norske arbeidsplasser.* Forskningssenter for Arbeidsmiljø: Universitetet Bergen, Norway.
Einarsen, S., & Raknes, B. I. (1997). Harassment at work and the victimization of men. *Violence and Victims, 12,* 247–263.
Einarsen, S., Raknes, B. I., & Matthiesen, S. B. (1994). Bullying and harassment at work and their relationships to work environment quality. An exploratory study. *The European Work and Organizational Psychologist, 4,* 381–401.
Einarsen, S. Raknes, B. I., Matthiesen, S. B., & Hellesøy, O. H. (1996). Helsemessige aspekter ved mobbing I arbeidslivet: Modererende effekter av sosial støtte og personlighet. *Nordisk Psykologi, 48,* 116–137.
Einarsen, S., Raknes, B. I., Matthiesen, S. B., & Hellesøy, O. H. (1994). *Mobbing og harde person-konflikter. Helsefarlig samspill pa arbeidsplassen (Bullying and severe interpersonal conflicts. Unhealthy interaction at work).* Soreidgrend: Sigma Forlag.
Einarsen, S., & Skogstad, A. (1996). Prevalence and risk groups of bullying and harrassment at work. *European Journal of Work and Organizational Psychology, 5,* 185–202.
Felson, R. B. (1992). "Kick 'em when they're down": Explanations of the relationships between stress and interpersonal aggression and violence. *Sociological Quarterly, 33,* 1–16.
Field, T. (1996). *Bullying in sight.* Wantage, Oxon, U.K.: Success Unlimited.
Groeneweg, J. (1996). *Controlling the controllable* (3rd ed.). Leiden: DSWO Press.
Gross, C., & Zapf, D. (2002). Social conflicts and bullying in the workplace. First results from a diary study. International Conference on Bullying in the Workplace. Birkbeck College, University of London; 23–24 September 2002.
Grunfeld, B., & Noreik, K. (1996). Syke kvinner og uførepensjonerte menn: noen refleksjoner (Sick women and disabled men: some reflections). *Journal of Norwegian Medical Association, 116,* 988–989.
Hoel, H. (2002). Bullying at work in Great Britain. Unpublished doctoral dissertation, University of Manchester Institute of Science and Technology.
Hoel, H., & Cooper, C. L. (1999). *The role of 'intent' in perceptions of workplace bullying.* Presented at the Ninth European Congress on Work and Organizational Psychology: Innovations for Work, Organization and Well Being. 12–15th May, Espoo-Helsinki, Finland.

Hoel, H., & Cooper, C. L. (2000). Destructive conflict and bullying at work. Unpublished report: University of Manchester, Institute of Science and Technology.

Hoel, H., & Cooper, C. L. (2001). Origins of bullying: Theoretical frameworks for explaining bullying. In: N. Therani (Ed.), *Building a Culture of Respect: Managing Bullying at Work.* London: Taylor and Francis.

Hoel, H., Cooper, C. L., & Faragher, B. (2001). The experience of bullying in Great Britain: The impact of organisational status. *European Journal of Work and Organizational Psychology, 10,* 443–465.

Hoel, H., Einarsen, S., & Cooper, C. L. (in press). Organisational effects of bullying. In: S. Einarsen, H. Hoel, D. Zapf & C. L. Cooper (Eds), *Bullying and Emotional Abuse in the Workplace. International Perspectives in Research and Practice.* London/New York: Taylor and Francis.

Hoel, H., Einarsen, S., Keashly, L., Zapf, D., & Cooper, C. L. (in press). Workplace bullying: the way forward. In: S. Einarsen, H. Hoel, D. Zapf & C. L. Cooper (Eds), *Bullying and Emotional Abuse in the Workplace. International Perspectives in Research and Practice.* London/New York: Taylor and Francis.

Hoel, H., Rayner, C., & Cooper, C. L. (1999). Workplace bullying. In: C. L. Cooper & I. T. Robertson (Eds), *International Review of Industrial and Organizational Psychology* (pp. 195–230). Chichester, U.K.: John Wiley & Sons Ltd.

Hoel, H., & Salin, D. (in press). Organisational antecedents of workplace bullying. In: S. Einarsen, H. Hoel, D. Zapf & C. L. Cooper (Eds), *Bullying and Emotional Abuse in the Workplace. International Perspectives in Research and Practice.* London/New York: Taylor and Francis.

Hoel, H., Sparks, K., & Cooper, C. L. (2001). *The Cost of Violence/Stress at Work and the Benefits of a Violence/Stress-Free Working Environment.* Geneva: International Labour Organisation.

Høgh, A., & Dofradottir, A. (2001). Coping with bullying in the workplace. *European Journal of Work and Organizational Psychology, 10,* 485–495.

Holzen Beusch, E. v., Zapf, D., & Schallberger, U. (in press). Warum Mobbingopfer ihre Arbeitsstelle nicht wechseln [Why the victims of bullying do not change their job]. *Zeitschrift für Personalforschung.*

Ironside, M., & Seifert, R. (in press). Tackling bullying in the workplace: the collective dimension. In: S. Einarsen, H. Hoel, D. Zapf & C. L. Cooper (Eds), *Bullying and Emotional Abuse in the Workplace. International Perspectives in Research and Practice.* London/New York: Taylor and Francis.

Janoff-Bullman, R. (1992). *Shattered assumptions: Towards a new psychology of trauma.* New York: The Free Press.

Jick, T. D., & Mitz, L. F. (1985). Sex difference in work stress. *Academy of Management Review, 10,* 408–420.

Jones, E. E., & Davis, K. E. (1965). From acts to dispositions: The attribution process in person perception. In: I. L. Berkowitz (Ed.), *Advances in Experimental Social Psychology* (Vol. 2). Academic Press, New York.

Karasek, R. A. (1979). Job demands, job decision latitude and mental strain: Implications for job redesign. *Administrative Science Quarterly, 24,* 385–408.

Karasek, R. A., & Theorell, T. (1990). *Healthy work. Stress, productivity, and the reconstruction of working life.* New York: Basic Books.

Keashly, L. (1998). Emotional abuse in the workplace. *Journal of Emotional Abuse, 1,* 85–117.

Keashly, L., & Jagatic, K. (in press). American perspectives on workplace bullying. In: S. Einarsen, H. Hoel, D. Zapf & C. L. Cooper (Eds), *Bullying and Emotional Abuse in the Workplace. International Perspectives in Research and Practice.* London/New York: Taylor and Francis.

Keashly, L., Trott, V., & MacLean, L. M. (1994). Abusive behavior in the workplace: A preliminary investigation. *Violence and Victims*, *9*, 341–357.

Kile, S. M. (1990). *Helsefarleg leiarskap. Ein eksplorerande studie. Rapport til Norges Almenvitskaplege Forskningsråd* (Health endangering leadership. An exploratory study). Universitetet i Bergen: Institutt for Samfunnspsykologi.

Kivimäki, K., Elovainio, M., & Vathera, J. (2000). Workplace bullying and sickness absence in hospital staff. *Occupational and Environmental Medicine*, 57, 656–660.

Klein, S. (1996). A longitudinal study of the impact of work pressures on group cohesive behaviors. *International Journal of Management*, *13*, 68–75.

Knorz, C., & Zapf, D. (1996). Mobbing – eine extreme Form sozialer Stressoren am Arbeitsplatz (Mobbing – an extreme form of social stressors at work). *Zeitschrift für Arbeits- und Organisationspsychologie*, *40*, 12–21.

Kräkel, M. (1997). Rent-seeking in Organisationen – eine ökonomische Analyse sozial schädlichen Verhaltens. *Schmalenbachs Zeitschrift für Betriebswirtschaftliche Forschung*, 49, 535–555.

Lazarus, R. S., & Folkman, S. (1984). *Stress, appraisal and coping*. New York: Springer.

Lee, D. (1998). *The gender dynamics of workplace bullying*. Paper given at the International Harssment Network Annual Conference, May 13–14, Oxford: The Conference Centre.

Lee, D. (2000). An analysis of workplace bullying in the U.K. *Personnel Review*, *29*, 593–612.

Leymann, H. (1987). *Mobbing i arbeidslivet (Bullying in working life)*. Oslo: Friundervisningens Forlag.

Leymann, H. (1990). Mobbing and psychological terror at workplaces. *Violence and Victims*, *5*, 119–126.

Leymann, H. (1992a). *Vuxenmobbning på svenska arbeidsplatser*. Delrapport 1 om frekvenser. (Adult bullying in Swedish workplace: Report 1 about frequencies). Stockholm: Arbetarskyddstyrelsen.

Leymann, H. (1992b). *Psyiatriska problem vid vuxenmobbning*. Delrapport 3 (Psychiatric problems related to associated with adult bullying. Report 3). Stockholm: Arbetarskyddstyrelsen.

Leymann, H. (1993). *Mobbing – Psychoterror am Arbeitsplatz und wie man sich dagegen wehren kann (Mobbing – psychological terror in the workplace and how one can defend oneself)*. Reinbeck: Rowohlt.

Leymann, H. (1996). The content and development of mobbing at work. *European Journal of Work and Organizational Psychology*, *5*, 165–184.

Leymann, H., & Gustafsson, A. (1996). Mobbing and the development of post-traumatic stress disorders. *The European Journal of Work and Organizational Psychology*, *5*, 251–276.

Lindemeier, B. (1996). Mobbing. Krankheitsbild und Intervention des Betriebsarztes (Bullying. Symptoms and intervention of the company physician). *Die Berufsgenossenschaft*, (June), 428–431.

Mackensen von Astfeld, S. (2000). Das Sick-Building-Syndrom unter besonderer Berücksichtigung des Einflusses von Mobbing (The sick building syndrome with special consideration of the effects of mobbing). Hamburg: Verlag Dr. Kovac.

Mattiesen, S. B., Raknes, B. I., & Røkkum, O. (1989). Mobbing på arbeidsplassen. *Tidsskrift for Norsk Psykologiforening (Journal of Norwegian Psychological Association)*, *26*, 761–774.

McCarthy, P., Sheehan M., & Kearns, D. (1995). *Managerial Styles and their Effects on Employee's Health and Well-being in Organizations Undergoing Restructuring*. Brisbane: School of Organizational Behaviour and Human Resource Management, Griffith University.

Mergner, U. (1989). Zur sozialen Konstitution psychischer Belastung durch Arbeit.

Konzeptionelle Uberlegungen und empirische Konkretitionen. *Zeitschrift fur Arbeits- und Organisationspsychologie, 33*, 64–72.

Mikkelsen, E. G. (2001). Mobning I arbeidslivet: Hvorfor og for hvem er den så belastende? *Nordisk Psykologi, 53*, 109–131.

Mikkelsen, G. E., & Einarsen, S. (2001). Bullying in Danish work-life: Prevalence and health correlates. *European Journal of Work and Organizational Psychology, 10*, 393–413.

Mikkelsen, G. E., & Einarsen, S. (2002). Basic assumptions and symptoms of post-traumatic stress among victims of bullying at work. *European Journal of Work and Organizational Psychology, 11*, 87–111.

Mullen, E. (1997). Workplace violence: cause for concern or the construction of a new category of fear. *Journal of Industrial Relations, 39*, 21–31.

Neuman, J. H., & Baron, R. A. (in press). Social antecedents of bullying: A social interactionist perspective. In: S. Einarsen, H. Hoel, D. Zapf & C. L. Cooper (Eds), *Bullying and Emotional Abuse in the Workplace. International Perspectives in Research and Practice.* London/New York: Taylor and Francis.

Niedl, K. (1995). *Mobbing/Bullying am Arbeitsplatz. Eine empirische Analyse zum Phänomen sowie zu personalwirtschaftlich relevanten Effekten von systematischen Feindseligkeiten (Mobbing/bullying at work. An empirical analysis of the phenomenon and of the effects of systematic harassment on human resource management).* München: Hampp.

Niedl, K. (1996). Mobbing and well-being: Economic and personnel development implications. *European Journal of Work and Organizational Psychology, 5*, 239–249.

O'Dricsoll, M. P. (1996). The interface between job and off-job roles: Enchancement and conflict. In: C. L. Cooper & I. T. Robertson (Eds), *International Review of Industrial and Organizational Psychology 1996* (Vol. 11, pp. 279–306). Chichester: Wiley.

OECD (1999). *Implementing the OECD Job Strategy: Assessing Performance and Policy.* Paris: OECD.

O'Moore, M., Seigne, E., McGuire, L., & Smith, M. (1998). Victims of bullying at work in Ireland. *Journal of Occupational Health and Safety: Australia and New Zealand, 14*, 569–574.

Pearce, J. L. (1998). Job insecurity is important, but not for the reasons you might think: the example of contingent workers. In: C. L. Cooper & D. M. Rousseau (Eds), *Trends in Organisational Behavior* (pp. 31–46). London: John Wiley & Sons Ltd.

Peeters, M. C. W., Buunk, B. P., & Schaufeli, W. B. (1995). Social interactions, stressful events and negative affect at work: a micro-analytic approach. *European Journal of Social Psychology, 25*, 391–401.

Price Spratlen, L. (1995). Interpersonal conflict which includes mistreatment in a university work-place. *Violence and Victims, 10*, 285–297.

Quine, L. (1999). Workplace bullying in NHS community trust: Staff questionnaire survey. *British Medical Journal, 3*, 228–232.

Quine, L. (2001). Workplace bullying in nurses. *Journal of Health Psychology, 6*, 73–84.

Quinlan, M. (1999). The implications of labour market restructuring in industrial societies for occupational health and safety. *Economic and Industrial Democracy, 20*, 427–460.

Randall, P. (1997). *Adult Bullying: Perpetrators and Victims.* London: Routeledge.

Rayner, C. (1997). The incidence of workplace bullying. *Journal of Community & Applied Social Psychology, 7*, 199–208.

Rayner, C. (1999). From research to implementation: Finding leverage for prevention. *International Journal of Manpower, 20*, 28–38.

Rayner, C. (1999). *Workplace Bullying.* Ph.D. thesis, University of Manchester Institute of Science and Technology.

Rayner, C., Hoel, H., & Cooper, C. L. (2002). *Workplace bullying. What we know, who is to blame, and what can we do?* London: Taylor and Francis.

Salin, D. (2001). Prevalence and forms of bullying among business professionals: A comparison of two different strategies for measuring bullying. *European Journal of Work and Organizational Psychology, 10,* 425–441.

Savva, C., & Alexandrou, A. (1998). *The impact of bullying in further and higher education.* Paper presented at the 'Bullying at work, 1998 Research Update Conference, Staffordshire University, 1 July, Stafford.

Schuster, B. (1996). Rejection, exclusion, and harassment at work and in schools. *European Psychologist, 1,* 293–317.

Scott, M. J., & Stradling, S. G. (1994). Post-traumatic stress disorder without the trauma. *British Journal of Clinical Psychology, 33,* 71–74.

Sheehan, M. (1999). Workplace bullying: responding with some emotional intelligence. *International Journal of Manpower, 20,* 57–69.

Sheehan, M., McCarthy, P., Barker, M., & Henderson, M. (2001). A model for assessing the impact and costs of workplace bullying. Paper presented at the Standing Conference on organizational Symbolism (SCOS), Trinity College, Dublin, 30 June – 4 July.

Sonnentag, S. (1996). Arbeitsbedingungen und psychisches Befinden bei Frauen und Männern: Eine Metaanalyse (Working conditions and psychological well-being of women and men: a meta-analysis). *Zeitschrift für Arbeits- und Organisationspsychologie, 40,* 118–126.

Steer, S. R., & Rhodes, R. M. (1978). Major influence on employee attendance: A process model. *Journal of Applied Psychology, 63,* 391–407.

Sutherland, V. J., & Cooper, C. L. (1990). *Understanding stress: A Psychological perspective for health professional.* London: Chapman and Hall.

Thylefors, I. (1987). *Syndabockar. Om utstötning och mobbning i arbetslivet* [Scapegoates. On expulsion and bullying in working life]. Stockholm: Natur och Kulture.

UNISON (1997). *UNISON members experience of bullying at work.* London: UNISON.

UNISON (2000). *Police staff bullying report (number 1777).* London: UNISON.

Vartia, M. (1996). The sources of bullying – psychological work environment and organizational climate. *European Journal of Work and Organizational Psychology, 5,* 203–214.

Vartia, M. (2001). Consequences of workplace bullying with respect to well-being of its targets and the observers of bullying. *Scandinavian Journal of Work Environment and Health, 27,* 63–69.

Vartia, M., & Hyyti, J. (2002). Gender differences in workplace bullying among prison officers. *European Journal of Work and Organizational Psychology, 11,* 113–126.

Wilkie, W. (1996). Understanding the behaviour of victimised people. In: P. McCarthy, M. Sheehan & W. Wilkie (Eds), *Bullying: From backyard to boardroom.* Millenium Books, Alexandria, Australia.

Withey, M., & Cooper, W. (1989). Predicting exit, voice, loyalty, and neglect. *Administrative Science Quarterly, 34,* 521–539.

Worrall, L., & Cooper, C. L. (1999). *The Quality of Working Life: 1999 survey of managers' changing experiences.* London: The Institute of Management.

Zapf, D. (1999a). Mobbing in Organisationen. Ein Überblick zum Stand der Forschung (Mobbing in organisations. A state of the art review). *Zeitschrift für Arbeits- & Organisationspsychologie, 43,* 1–25.

Zapf, D. (1999b). Organizational, work group related and personal causes of mobbing/bullying at work. *International Journal of Manpower, 20,* 70–85.

Zapf, D., Dormann, C., & Frese, M. (1996). Longitudinal studies in organizational stress research: A review of the literature with reference to methodological issues. *Journal of Occupational Health Psychology, 1,* 145–169.

Zapf, D., Einarsen, S., Hoel, H., & Vartia, M. (in press). Empirical findings on bullying. In: S. Einarsen, H. Hoel, D. Zapf & C. L. Cooper (Eds), *Bullying and Emotional Abuse in the Workplace. International Perspectives in Research and Practice.* London: Taylor and Francis.

Zapf, D., & Gross, C. (2001). Conflict escalation and coping with workplace bullying: A replication and extension. *European Journal of Work and Organizational Psychology, 10,* 497–522.

Zapf, D., Knorz, C., & Kulla, M. (1996). On the relationship between mobbing factors, and job content, the social work environment and health outcomes. *European Journal of Work and Organizational Psychology, 5,* 215–237.

ABOUT THE AUTHORS

Julian Barling is the Queen's Research Chair in the School of Business, Queen's University. He earned his Ph.D. from the University of the Witwatersrand, South Africa. His research focuses on the different aspects of employee well-being and employee safety, leadership and workplace violence. He is the author/editor of several books, most recently "The psychology of workplace safety" (with Mike Frone). Dr. Barling is the editor of the American Psychological Association's *Journal of Occupational Health Psychology*, and serves on the editorial boards of the *Journal of Applied Psychology, Leadership and Organizational Development Journal,* and *Stress and Health*. He previously served as consulting editor of the *Journal of Organizational Behavior*, and was chair of the American Psychological Association's Task Force on Workplace Violence. In 1997, Dr. Barling received the annual award for "Excellence in Research" from Queen's University; and in 2001, he received the National Post's "Leaders in Business Education" award.

Paul Bliese received his Ph.D. in Organizational Psychology with a minor in Management from Texas Tech University. In 1992, he joined the Walter Reed Army Institute of Research as a member of an interdisciplinary team studying stress and adaptation among Army soldiers. Due to the hierarchical nature of Army data (soldiers imbedded in squads, platoons, companies, battalions, etc.), Dr. Bliese developed an interest in the theoretical and methodological aspects of multilevel data. As an outcome of this interest, he has published methodological and conceptual papers exploring various aspects of multilevel analyses, and has written a multilevel package for the language R. Dr. Bliese has published in *Journal of Applied Psychology, Journal of Applied Social Psychology, Journal of Organizational Behavior, Journal of Management, Organizational Research Methods, Parameters,* and *Work and Stress*. He serves as a member of the editorial board of *Organizational Research Methods* and *Leadership Quarterly.*

Cary L. Cooper is currently BUPA Professor of Organizational Psychology and Health in the Manchester School of Management, and Deputy Vice Chancellor of the University of Manchester Institute of Science and Technology

335

(UMIST). He is the author of over 80 books (on occupational stress, women at work and industrial and organizational psychology), has written over 400 scholarly articles for academic journals, and is a frequent contributor to national newspapers, TV and radio. He is currently Founding Editor of the Journal of Organizational Behavior and Co-Editor of the medical journal Stress & Health (formerly Stress Medicine). He is a Fellow of the British Psychological Society, The Royal Society of Arts, The Royal Society of Medicine, The Royal Society of Health, and an Academician of the Academy for the Social Sciences. Professor Cooper is the President of the British Academy of Management, is a Companion of the (British) Institute of Management and one of the first U.K.-based Fellows of the (American) Academy of Management (having also won the 1998 Distinguished Service Award for his contribution to management science from the Academy of Management). In 2001, Cary was awarded a CBE in the Queen's Birthday Honours List for his contribution to organizational health.

David M. DeJoy is a Professor in the School of Health and Human Performance, Department of Health Promotion and Behavior, at the University of Georgia. Dave has been at the University since 1981, and served as the head of the Department of Health Promotion and Behavior from 1987 to 1997. He conducts research and teaches graduate and undergraduate courses in health behavior, occupational safety, and workplace health promotion. He has served as a consultant and advisor to a variety of governmental and other organizations in the areas of safe work practices, risk communication, behavior change, and workplace health and safety program development.

Daniel G. Gallagher is currently a Professor of Management at James Madison University in Harrisonburg, Virginia. He earned his M. A. and Ph.D. degrees at the Institute of Labor and Industrial Relations at the University of Illinois. His past research has covered a broad spectrum of issues ranging from dispute resolution, organizational and union – commitment and participation, part-time employment, to psychological contracts. Current research and teaching interests include the organizational and individual impact of contingent work contracts, negotiation theory and practice, volunteer workers, and personal and organizational identity. He serves on the editorial boards of a number of journals such as: *Journal of Organizational Behavior*, *Journal of Management*, and *Industrial Relations* (Berkeley). He is a member of the Academy of Management, and serves on the Research Committees of both the Industrial Relations Research Association and the Society for Human Resource Management.

Shannon Griffin-Blake is a Postdoctoral Research Associate and Project Director with the Workplace Health Group at the University of Georgia. Her primary work has focused on evaluating adult health risk behaviors in the area of cardiovascular and chronic diseases and developing behavior modification materials concerning physical activity initiation and maintenance. Shannon has over 12 years of experience in the health promotion and fitness fields having directed, taught, and consulted in a variety of public and private settings, including Proctor and Gamble, SAS, and the North Carolina Public School System.

Ron Halverson is the founder and principal of Halverson Consulting, Inc., a Chicago-based management consultancy that applies multi-level methodology to organizational performance assessment and improvement. Dr. Halverson holds both an MA and a Ph.D. in Industrial and Organizational Psychology from DePaul University, with specialties in research methodology and applied statistics. He has authored numerous publications in journals such as the *Journal of Applied Social Psychology, Journal of Business and Psychology, Journal of Management, Leadership Quarterly, Parameters, Military Medicine* and *Armed Forces and Society*. He has also presented papers to a variety of national professional organizations, two of which won Best Paper awards from the Academy of Management in 1994 and 1996. Ron is the Past-President of the Chicago Industrial and Organizational Psychologists Association.

Helge Hoel is a lecturer in Change Management at the Manchester School of Management, Department of Organizational Psychology, University of Manchester Institute of Science and Technology (UMIST), U.K. His current research interests are in change management, occupational well being and workplace bullying. He is author of the book entitled *Workplace Bullying*.

Michelle Inness is a doctoral candidate in organizational behavior and social psychology at Queen's University, Kingston, Canada. Her primary research interests include occupational health and safety, workplace violence, and social justice. She has previously taught at Saint Mary's University's department of psychology and has worked in applied research in major hospitals in Canada and in New York City. Her concerns for advancing organizational research that bridge academic disciplines, and finding solutions to social problems is demonstrated in her recent research on the social, cognitive, and individual difference factors that impact on workplace aggression, and the motivational factors that contribute to social injustice.

Steve M. Jex is currently an Associate Professor of Psychology at Bowling Green State University. His research has focused primarily on the role of individual differences in work-related stress and has appeared in many journals such as *Journal of Applied Psychology, Journal of Organizational Behavior, Journal of Applied Social Psychology, Journal of Occupational and Organizational Psychology*, and *Work & Stress*. In addition to his research activities, Dr. Jex is the author of two books, *Stress and Job Performance: Theory, Research, and Implications for Managerial Practice* and *Organizational Psychology: A Scientist-Practitioner Approach.*

Lawrence R. Murphy is Research Psychologist in the Division of Applied Science and Technology, National Institute for Occupational Safety and Health (NIOSH) since 1977. He received his M.A. and Ph.D. degrees in Experimental Psychology from DePaul University, Chicago, Illinois, and did postdoctoral training at the Institute for Psychosomatic & Psychiatric Research, Michael Reese Medical Center. He has conducted research in the area of job stress and health for over 20 years, and published numerous journal articles and book chapters in the area of job stress and stress management. His edited books include *Issues in Occupational Stress Research* (1988), *Stress Management in Work Settings* (1989), *Organizational Risk Factors for Job Stress* (1995), *Job Stress Interventions* (1995) and *Healthy and Productive Work: An International Perspective* (2002). His current research involves identifying characteristics of healthy work organizations and examining the health and safety consequences of organizational downsizing and restructuring.

Kyoung-Ok Park is a doctoral candidate in the Department of Health Promotion and Behavior at the University of Georgia. Kyoung-Ok's research interests are social support, psychological well being, and worksite health promotion. Her dissertation is about the comprehensive effects of social support at work on depression and organizational productivity. Kyoung-Ok has worked for the Healthy Work Organization project since 1998. She worked for a worksite-based stress project and a community-based health project as a co-director in Korea. She also participated in two stress projects for hospital workers and for high school students in China.

Johannes Siegrist is a Professor of Medical Sociology and Director of the School of Public Health at the Medical Faculty, University of Duesseldorf, Germany. Born in 1943 in Switzerland he received his Ph.D. in Sociology from the University of Freiburg i.Br. Subsequently he became Professor at the

University of Marburg and Visiting Professor at the Institute of Advanced Studies in Vienna, Austria and at the Johns Hopkins University, Baltimore/USA. In 1994, he held the Belle van Zuylen Chair at the University of Utrecht, Netherlands. His major research field is social determinants of health in midlife and early old age, with a special focus on stressful psychosocial work environment. He is currently Scientific Director of a European Science Foundation program on social variations in health expectancy in Europe. Honors include membership of Academia Europaea.

Lois E. Tetrick received her doctorate in Industrial and Organizational Psychology from Georgia Institute of Technology in 1983. Upon completion of her doctoral studies, she joined the faculty of the Department of Psychology at Wayne State University and remained there until 1995 when she moved to the Department of Psychology at the University of Houston. Professor Tetrick is an Associate Editor of the *Journal of Occupational Health Psychology*, has served as associate editor of the *Journal of Applied Psychology* and is on the editorial boards of *Journal of Organizational Behavior* and *Advanced Topics in Organizational Behavior*. Dr. Tetrick's research has focused primarily on individuals' perceptions of the employment relationship and their reactions to these perceptions, occupational health and safety, occupational stress, and organizational commitment. Dr. Tetrick is a fellow of the American Psychological Association, the Society for Industrial and Organizational Psychology, and the American Psychological Society. She is currently the chair of the Human Resources Division of the Academy of Management and has just been elected as APA Council representing Division 14 Industrial and Organizational Psychology.

Robert J. Vandenberg is a Professor in the Terry College of Business, Department of Management at the University of Georgia, and is also currently the coordinator of the organizational behavior program. In addition to his research in these areas, he teaches undergraduate, MBA and doctorate-level students in the areas of organizational change and interventions, organization development, organizational behavior and leadership. Bob is currently an associate editor for *Organizational Research Methods*, and is past division chair (2000–2001) of the Research Methods Division of the Academy of Management. His research has appeared in such journals as *Organizational Behavior and Human Decision Processes, Journal of Applied Psychology, Organizational Research Methods*, and *Journal of Management* – journals on whose editorial boards Bob has also served.

Mina Westman is a Senior Lecturer and Researcher, at Tel Aviv University's Leon Recanati Graduate School of Business Administration. She received her Ph.D. in Organizational Behavior from the Faculty of Management, Tel Aviv University. Her primary research interests include determinants and consequences of job stress, crossover of stress and strain between partners, effects of vacation on the individual, the family and the organization, and travel stress. She has authored empirical and conceptual articles that have appeared in such journals as *Journal of Applied Psychology*, *Human Relations*, *Journal of Occupational Health Psychology*, *Journal of Organizational Behavior*, *Applied Psychology: An International Journal*, and *Journal of Vocational Behavior*. She was co-editor of a special issue on work and family in *Journal of Occupational Health Psychology*. In addition she has also contributed to several book chapters and presented numerous scholarly papers at international conferences. She is on the editorial board of the *Journal of Organizational Behavior*.

Mark Wilson is an Associate professor and coordinator of Graduate Programs for the Department of Health Promotion and Behavior at the University of Georgia. He has been conducting research, teaching and consulting in the workplace health promotion arena for over 16 years. Mark has consulted with organizations such as Georgia-Pacific, Home Depot, New England Telephone, AT&T, and Centers for Disease Control and Prevention on projects ranging from the evaluation of a cholesterol reduction program to a comprehensive evaluation of a worksite health promotion program.

Deiter Zapf is Professor of Organizational Psychology in the Department of Psychology at the Johann Wolfgang Goethe-University, Frankfurt am Main, Germany. He has earned degrees in both Psychology and Theology. His research interests are in occupational stress, emotion and emotional labor, job satisfaction and workplace bullying.